Using Picture Story Books to Teach Literary Devices

Recommended Books for Children and Young Adults

Volume 4

SUSAN HALL

Using Picture Books to Teach

LIBRARIES
UNLIMITED
A Member of the Greenwood Publishing Group
Westport, Connecticut • London

Library of Congress Cataloging-in-Publication Data

Hall, Susan, 1943 July 11-
    Using picture story books to teach literary devices : recommended books for children and
young adults / Susan Hall.
        p. cm. — (Using picture books to teach)
    Includes bibliographical references and indexes.
    ISBN 978-1-59158-493-3 (vol. 4 : alk. paper)
    1. Children—Books and reading. 2. Figures of speech—Bibliography. 3. Picture books for
children—Bibliography. 4. Style, Literary—Study and teaching. 5. Children's stories—Study
and teaching. I. Title
    Z1037.H23 2008
    016.0883'9—dc20

British Library Cataloguing in Publication Data is available.

ISBN: 978-1-59158-493-3

First published in 2008

Libraries Unlimited, 88 Post Road West, Westport, CT 06881
A Member of the Greenwood Publishing Group, Inc.
www.lu.com

Printed in the United States of America

∞™

The paper used in this book complies with the
Permanent Paper Standard issued by the National
Information Standards Organization (Z39.48–1984).

10 9 8 7 6 5 4 3 2

CONTENTS

❖❖❖❖❖❖❖❖❖❖❖

INTRODUCTION

❖❖❖❖❖❖❖❖❖❖❖

Strong, stunningly memorable writing can occur in the spare text of a picture story book. Language in picture story books demonstrates the same literary devices that are widely observed in general print or non-print literature—in whatever format people choose to express themselves.

Tony Johnston's *Angel City* (Penguin, 2006) is a book about an old black man, who finds in a Los Angeles dumpster a thrown-away Latino baby he names Juan. Despite demanding energy and stamina required for the task, Old Joseph promises God he will raise the infant—even when he goes sleepless and, looking skyward, grumbles, "Promise still holds."

The old man and child live together with nothing much except profound love. Out of the creativity of a skilled writer, even in the venue of a picture book, the literary device of imagery can be striking: "While the old man fits pipes and snakes out drains, Juan swashes toilets with a long-armed brush, for fun. Creates small indoor rains."

Existing at the edge of poverty, the tiny family in this story ekes out financially by raising sweet corn on an abandoned lot they share with a junked Volkswagen Beetle. When the boy's best friend is shot by a stray bullet from a passing car, the old father can think of nothing to say to comfort his son as the boy sits forlorn in the car hulk. Old Joseph crawls inside it too "and cradles him. They need no words, just the hymn of the corn."

As in previous Volumes 1–3 of *Using Picture Story Books to Teach Literary Devices*, each book chosen for inclusion in this edition has literary merit. Only those exhibiting a well-developed plot, superior text, examples of literary devices, and quality artwork were considered. Books with slight or non-existent plots were rejected, whether or not they may have demonstrated literary devices.

Schools and libraries have budget dollars for quality, not quantity, of materials. This edition, which focuses on picture story books published primarily since 2000, continues the tradition of selecting a few books of better value that clearly demonstrate the presence of commonly used literary devices.

Also, as in previous volumes, this reference/index fourth volume of *Using Picture Story Books to Teach Literary Devices* is designed to help language arts educators assist students of all ages to recognize how, for example, satire, simile, symbol, or serendipity might operate in a "simple" thirty-two-page picture story book.

Once understanding has been achieved at this level of literature, students can better recognize such literary devices in grade-level literature and, more importantly, may choose to implement these general literary devices in their own compositions whether in blogging, twittering, or even non-electronic writing!

Consider parallelism, the useful device of deliberate side-by-side repetition of phrases or sentences to draw a reader's or listener's attention to something the writer wishes to emphasize. This particular literary device is a favorite of speech writers to help politicians make their point: "I will not seek and I will not accept," said Lyndon B. Johnson, when he told the American public of his intention not to run for another term as president.

Speech writers frequently employ parallelism, but so do writers of any kind of literature, including picture story books. The lyrical Jane Yolen particularly uses it to good effect.

Raising Yoder's Barn (Little, Brown and Company, c1998) is about an Amish child's role in the all-important community barn-building process. Yolen uses parallelism as a good device to illustrate how evident is the tension of the moment. "The neighbors heard the [fire] alarm and came: some in wagons, some on horseback, most on foot."

And, when the anxious boy is afraid the grownups will forget him in the parceling out of jobs, the literary use of parallelism serves to illustrate his frustration. "I waited to be told, waited for Papa's call. Waited while the first of the frames was ready to be hauled into place."

VOLUME 4—LITERARY DEVICES

Students who are knowledgeable about literary devices have a richer, more enjoyable reading experience than students who never see the sly fun in a pun or the cunning in connotation.

Similarly, students who understand the power of deliberately choosing specific literary devices in their own writing are simply better wordsmiths than those who don't realize the potential of parallelism, the meaning in metaphor, the abruptness of antithesis, the lilt in alliteration, the spoof in satire, or the feasibility of forty-three of the commonest literary devices found in general literature.

Close examination of the text of current picture story books has resulted in a slightly revised list of literary devices chosen for this Volume 4. A few new ones have been included; a few from previous editions have been excluded.

Volume 4—New Literary Devices Included: Aptronym, Archetype, Colloquialism, Counterpoint, Solecism, Surprise/Twist-in-the-Tail, and Wit/ Humor.

Aptronym, the naming of characters to fit their personality or lifestyle, has, over the years, been demonstrated to good effect by many fiction authors;

Charles Dickens comes to mind. However, its use is ubiquitous, especially in humorous writing, as the name "Poulette" illustrates in a story (to be discussed) about ballet-dancing young chickens.

In Teresa Bateman's *A Plump and Perky Turkey* (Marshall Cavendish, c2001), greedy townspeople intend to lure an unsuspecting turkey into becoming the centerpiece for their Thanksgiving meal. The city's wily leader is "Ebenezer." His henchman is named "Jacob."

In John Frank's *The Toughest Cowboy, or How the Wild West Was Tamed* (Simon & Schuster, c2004), a bunch of uncouth cowboys are appropriately named "Grizz Brickbottom" and his sidekicks "Chuck Wagon," the cook; "Lariat," the fastest rope thrower; "Bald Mountain," the biggest broncobuster; and their dog, "Foofy," a miniature poodle who loves catching tossed pie plates but does not seem to get the hang of guarding livestock.

Tammi Sauer's *Cowboy Camp* (Sterling, c2005) is another story featuring the apparently popular theme of cowboy life in recent picture story book fiction. In a reverse of stereotype and aptronym, this story stars a wanna-be cowboy with the unlikely cowboy name of "Avery." This central character wishes he had a more suitable cowboy-sounding name, like the other kids—"Hank" or "Dan" or "Jimmy Jean." Avery immediately fears he may not measure up to cowboy standards. He doesn't like beans and can't ride or rope. Ironically, his un-cowboy ways save the camp from destruction by bad guy "Black Bart." After talking to Avery, Black Bart goes away, convinced there can't be a cowboy camp around there after all. Nobody like Avery would be learning cowboy ways. Must have been given the wrong directions to the camp.

Archetype, another literary device appearing for the first time in the fourth edition, is suggestive of exaggeration of character traits. Archetype and stereotype and satire often combine to create a sense of the ludicrous, as they do in Peter Reynolds' satire of today's workaholic lifestyle, *So Few of Me* (Candlewick Press, c2006).

In this story, the obsessive archetype, Leo, finds that one of him is not enough to get all his work done. Another Leo would be the answer. Now, two are just as busy as one. In fact, even ten clones, "each one busier than the next," are not enough. Exhausted, he slips away to nap. The other nine angrily demand to know what he was doing. When he replies that he was "dreaming," they retort that dreaming is not on his list to do! Eventually, Leo concludes that perhaps if "I did less—but did my BEST," then one Leo would be enough.

Colloquialism, though not necessarily implying poor grammatical construction, is also not quite standard English. It does serve to lend authenticity to dialogue and setting and is being acknowledged in this edition for the first time.

From Mary Jane Auch comes the gritty *Hen Lake* (Holiday House, c1995). "Wow!" clucked Gertrude. "Get a load of those tail feathers!"

With a nod to puns and aptronym, "Percival" Peacock tries to discourage the efforts of budding ballet choreographer "Poulette." "Dancing chickens," he screeches. "What a hoot!" The hens become discouraged during their practices and snap at each other. "Oh, go lay an egg," squawks Zelda.

Eventually, their efforts do prevail, and they bring down the house in their opening performance. Seeing how despondent the envious Percival is, Poulette generously invites him to join them in their final scene. "I'll perk up his feathers," she promises, thereby proving she not only is a successful dancing chicken but also exemplifies better character than her detractor.

Counterpoint is close contrast that illustrates the varied interactions between one thing and another, as between conversations, settings, or actions. This device is being included for the first time in the fourth edition.

Elise Broach's *Cousin John Is Coming!* (Penguin, c2006) illustrates counterpoint. Mother, unaware of the angst she is causing, babbles on about things the two boys can do together when Cousin John visits. Meanwhile, Ben and his cat are in a state of near panic as they visualize what this bully will really cause to happen in comparison to Mother's innocuous suggestions.

Mother suggests: "You and Cousin John can play the games you always play, like ... magicians."

Ben visualizes a scene in which Cousin John is sawing through boxes where Ben and his cat are trapped.

Counterpoint also operates in Amy Young's *Belinda and the Glass Slipper* (Viking, c2006), another ballet story featuring the familiar plot of the "Cinderella" fairy tale and two determined ballerinas. Belinda's gentle classic professionalism is contrasted sharply against Lola's rough, underhanded, manipulating tactics.

After Belinda has been awarded the prize role of Cinderella, Lola still won't relinquish the contest. Belinda "did a gorgeous pas-de-deux." Lola "swooped in to claim her dance with the prince." Lola tries to crush Belinda's foot. Belinda pirouettes out of reach. Lola springs after her. Belinda protects herself with a well-executed battement. When it's time to try on the glass slipper, "just before it was Belinda's turn, Lola pushed her out of the way."

Of course the audience loves this unusual version of the story. Belinda is honored at the after-show party; Lola leaves in disgrace—but apparently not in defeat. She goes on to discover her own personal success as a hockey player, an activity that better suits her personality, anyway.

Solecism, a definite deviation from conventional grammar, is used like colloquialism to achieve an air of authenticity in the dialogue of era or setting. This device has also been added to the fourth edition.

Vaunda Nelson's *Almost to Freedom* (Lerner, c2003) is an Underground Railroad story of slaves escaping to freedom. It is narrated from the point-of-view of a rag doll that belongs to a slave child. Solecism naturally advances the story: "I don't have no hair. I used to think about havin' me some hair, but now it don't bother me none."

Surprise/Twist-in-the-Tail is common in many forms of literature. It is, of course, the unexpected turn a story may take at its resolution or, perhaps, within its plot, prior to denouement. Indeed, surprise endings are the stock-in-trade of most fictional books of mystery. Surprise is fun and so obvious, readers can hardly be unaware of its effect.

This device has been acknowledged in Volume 4, particularly when it occurs in deliciously shocking effect as it does in Pep Montserrat's *Ms. Rubinstein's Beauty* (Sterling, c2006). "Nobody notices Ms. Rubinstein's beauty—her pretty hands, the special grace of her small feet, her wonderful nose, very beautiful eyes, because all that people see—is the bushy beard of Ms. Rubinstein."

Ms. Rubinstein notices that Mr. Pavlov sits elegantly and has a refined way of holding his walking stick. Nobody sees the love growing between these two circus performers. "No, they only have eyes for Ms. Rubinstein's bushy beard—and the extraordinary trunk of Mr. Pavlov, the Elephant Man."

Wit/Humor has finally been acknowledged in Volume 4. Its artful effect can seem shocking, amusing, ludicrous, comical, whimsical, clever, spontaneous, and always delightful. Not to acknowledge that it seems monumentally neglectful of an author's talents to make us smile.

Nancy Wood's wonderfully unique *Mr. and Mrs. God in the Creation Kitchen* (Candlewick Press, c2006) is a very humorous tour-de-force version of the creation of the universe. Said Mr. God to Mrs. God about the boiling hot earth, "You made it. You cool it off." So, Mrs. God "whipped together some clouds and poured them over the glowing ball. At last it began to turn blue."

Mr. God made some animals "you'd notice." He wanted "something big. Something with a terrible noise. He looked through all the boxes in the pantry to find just the right ingredients. Growls and roars. Sharp teeth. Huge feet." When he showed Mrs. God the dinosaur, she wasn't impressed. "They're hideous. What were you thinking?"

Eventually the pair work on a final creature. "What are they?" asks Mrs. God. "Who knows?" replies Mr. God. They decide, "We'll just have to wait and see," as Man and Woman join hands and look up at the sky together.

Volume 4—Literary Devices Excluded: Anachronism, Analogy, Caricature, Cliché, Parallel Story.

Anachronism and **Cliché**, unlike solecism, often come off as seeming to be writing mistakes. Authors don't often deliberately choose to use either one. These two devices are, therefore, not common and are excluded in the fourth edition.

Analogy has been discontinued in favor of today's more common use of metaphor and symbol. Quick comparisons are more often served through metaphor or simile. More lengthy comparison is effectively developed through symbolism.

The consistently good storyteller Eve Bunting manages to nicely implement both metaphor and symbol in her *Pop's Bridge* (Harcourt, c2006), a story about the building of San Francisco's Golden Gate Bridge. The bridge is metaphorically described as "a harp for the angels to play. Wind strums its music through the stretch of the cables."

In this story, two boys of differing ethnicity work together on a jigsaw puzzle while their respective fathers work together on the bridge. As both projects, the bridge and the puzzle, are nearing completion, the story's young narrator has learned that everyone's contribution in a task is equally important. He asks each father to fit into the puzzle the final two halves of the last piece, symbolizing completion of a joint goal. "I just watch as the two pieces fit in, so perfectly, so smoothly. 'Team effort,' my pop says."

Caricature has been dropped, too. It is somewhat similar to the more common archetype or stereotype. But within caricature is an inherent concept of distorted exaggeration that promotes a sharper, somewhat cruel imitation. This nuance of meaning differentiates caricature from other satirical literary devices, making it necessarily less commonly employed in general writing, better reserved for edgy literature and art.

Parallel Story, in which two distinct stories are going on at the same time in the framework of one textual body, also seems less commonly employed than the simpler use of counterpoint, a device more generally used to show most examples of contrasting side-by-side interaction. In Volume 4, counterpoint has been used in lieu of parallel story.

VOLUME 4—ARRANGEMENT
Main Body Entries

Volume 4 has changed the layout of the book's main body. The reader may now see under one entry all that a particular book offers. Each picture story book, arranged alphabetically by author name, has an annotated bibliographical citation, a list of curriculum tie-ins, a notation of art style, and the examples of all literary devices operating in the book.

In some entries, italics have been added within quotations to highlight a particular literary device.

Indexes

To enhance usage, Volume 4 does continue the tradition of supplying cross-referencing indexes: Author, Title, Literary Devices, Curriculum Tie-In, Art Style, and All-Ages.

The alphabetical *author index* and the alphabetical *title index* each include the book's bibliographic information and a listing of all the literary devices found in the book. These indexes help the user see by author or by title all the devices a book illustrates.

An alphabetical *literary devices index* contains a definition for each of the forty-three devices. Under each device are the books demonstrating that device arranged alphabetically by author name and bibliographic information, followed by a listing of other devices also operating in the same book. This index helps the user find books that illustrate specific devices.

A glance at the **curriculum tie-in index** shows that picture story books cover a great many of life's topics. This index is arranged alphabetically by broad educational disciplines such as history or social science. Specific picture story books explore subjects that fall under general school courses. The curriculum tie-in index is useful to help educators expand on textual course material.

For example, under History, a particular picture story book explores the internment of Japanese Americans during World War II. Under Social Science, certain picture story books delve into topics like "bullying" or "international peace relations" or "time management."

The **art style index** includes brief definitions of the main art styles observed in picture story book art. Books are alphabetically arranged by author name under the art style they demonstrate. The primary use for this particular index is for teachers interested in helping students to identify common picture art styles.

The **all-ages index** continues the practice of noting some books for their special appeal to a broader age range, even including students in high school. Excellent language and maturity of subject matter is no respecter of genre. And, beautiful art should be shared wherever it occurs. Besides appealing to educators trying to reach more sophisticated students, this index might also be helpful for those seeking the most-bang-for-the-buck purchases.

BOOK ENTRIES

❖❖❖❖❖❖❖❖❖❖❖

*Adler, David A. *The Babe and I.* Illus. by Terry Widdener. New York: (Gulliver Books) Harcourt Brace & Co., c1999.

While helping his family make ends meet during the Great Depression by selling newspapers, a boy meets Babe Ruth.

Curriculum Tie-in: Athletics (Baseball), History (Great Depression), Social Science (Family Relationships—Parent/Child), Social Science (Friendship)

Art Style: Blocky, acrylic painted *Expressionism*

DEVICES

Ambiguity

The concept of being a team has different meanings to the characters struggling with the Great Depression in this story. The bottom line is that they depend on each other for financial survival.

As the best team in baseball in 1932, the Yankees are newsworthy because of the Babe's performances. Because the team is good, more people attend the games, earning more money for the players. And, the Babe's stardom enables the boy to sell more papers, thereby helping his family financially.

The boy considers he is in partnership with the Babe: "He and I were a team, too."

And, because the boy and his father were both into street corner sales: "I knew Dad and I were also a team. We were both working to get our family through hard times."

---

*Asterisks are used throughout to indicate all-ages books.

Antithesis

Not understanding the extent of his family's poor financial situation, the boy is disappointed and irritated with his birthday gift.

"For my birthday I was hoping my parents would give me a bicycle. They gave me a dime."

Foreshadow

"We were lucky. My father had a job." However, the boy's family "never seemed to have much money." The boy attributes having so little to the fact that "where we lived in the Bronx, New York, everyone was poor." Yet, the father left each morning carrying a briefcase to go to his job. Why should a family with a briefcase-carrying main provider still be as poor as families without employment?

Inference

Father and son silently acknowledge the true nature of their respective jobs. Each is selling at a street corner. The boy sells newspapers; the father sells apples out of his briefcase.

"Were you ever on Webster Avenue?" asks the father. "Once," replies the boy. "'I didn't tell Mom.' He squeezed my hand. Tears were rolling down his cheeks." The father knows the boy saw him peddling apples.

The Babe buys a paper from the boy and tells him to keep the change, which he and his friend use to buys tickets to the game. Proudly the boy tells the man sitting next to him that Babe Ruth "paid for my tickets. He gave me five dollars so I could see the game." Clearly the man doesn't believe this unlikely declaration. "The man smiled."

Irony

Before the boy understands the true condition of his family's finances, he embarrassingly tries to get rid of his paltry birthday dime by buying a couple of apples from an out-of-work street vendor. When he rounds the corner, he sees his own father similarly selling apples. "I looked up and there was Dad, selling apples like the others. I realized how he had earned my birthday dime and was sorry I had spent it. I wished so much someone would buy an apple from him. But no one did." The boy in his innocent ignorance had used the very dime his father had earned selling apples to buy apples from another street vendor.

Paradox

Even though it was his birthday gift, the boy was "glad to be rid of the dime" because "it reminded me of the present I didn't get." With the dime gone, so was the birthday disappointment.

During these hard times, some people deliberately chose criminal behavior just to get arrested and thereby improve their circumstances by being housed in a warm jail and getting meals there. "On Monday the front-page story was about a nineteen-year-old boy who had robbed a telegraph office because he wanted to be arrested. He knew he would get something to eat in jail."

Tone

The pathos of the Great Depression is sensitively illustrated in text and picture:

Though the father does not notice, the boy unexpectedly discovers his father selling apples from a street corner. "There were tears in my eyes as I watched people walk past my father." Later, at home, the boy hears his father say, "I was really busy at the office today. I'm tired." The boy wanted to tell him he didn't have to pretend he still had a job, "but I couldn't."

In mutual desperation, the boy and a neighbor come to an arrangement that benefits them both. He needs something to carry large batches of newspapers. His neighbor has a baby carriage she doesn't use every afternoon. She agrees to loan it to him in a business deal. "With my carriage you'll make extra money, so I should make some, too," she tells him. The rental agreement is ten cents each afternoon.

The boy learns something of his father's fierce pride in an exchange they had when the father brings home a bottle of milk and a bag of apples after a day at work.

The father tells his family, "I bought the apples from an unemployed man I passed on my way home." With new understanding that his own father has become an apple-selling street vendor, the boy replies, "That man is not unemployed. Selling apples is a job." But, the father is not ready to acknowledge such lowly activity is real work. "No it's not. It's just what you do while you wait and hope for something better." His father looks so upset the boy "realized how important it was for him to keep his secret."

*****

Allen, Jonathan. *I'm Not Cute!* New York: Hyperion Books for Children, c2005.

> Baby Owl gets very upset when all the other animals think he is cute, but Mama knows just what to say.
>
> > **Curriculum Tie-in:** Social Science (Character Development—Self-Esteem)
> >
> > **Art Style:** Observant wit and understanding of the human psyche in appealing pastel *Expressionism* in *Cartoons*

DEVICES

Antithesis

"I'm not cute! And I'm not small. I am a huge and scary hunting machine with big soft and silent wings."

"I'm not cute! And I'm not fluffy. I am a huge sleek hunting machine with great big see-in-the-dark eyes."

Counterpoint

"You're so cute, Baby Owl," say Rabbit and Fox and Squirrel.

"'I'm not cute!' he stubbornly, loudly, and increasingly hysterically insists."

Foreshadow

Baby Owl decides to explore the world. "Nobody will bother ME," he thinks. In his own mind he is tough. But, how will the animals in the forest perceive him?

Motif

"I'm not cute!" No matter how much Baby Owl rages and shouts, everyone who meets him thinks he is.

Paradox

When the forest animals call him cute, it infuriates Baby Owl. When Mama calls him cute, he accepts it from her and agrees with her assessment because she also agrees with his own assessment of himself. "You're so cute, Baby Owl," she whispers. "For a huge, scary, sleek, sharp-eyed hunting machine, that is."

*****

Amico, Tom and James Proimos. *Raisin and Grape.* Illus. by Andy Snair. New York: (Dial Books for Young Readers) Penguin Young Readers Group, c2006.

> A young grape and his grandfather, a wrinkly raisin, enjoy spending time together telling jokes and going to the park.
>
> **Curriculum Tie-in:** Social Science (Family Relationships—Grandparents/Grandchildren)
>
> **Art Style:** Bold color marker and felt pen *Expressionism* in *Cartoons*

DEVICES

Antithesis

On the way to the park Grape says of his grandfather, Raisin: "He walks slow. I'm fast."

Raisin reminds Grape "to stop and smell the flowers. I would forget that without him."

Connotation

"Come on down, *squirt*." Little Grape is, of course, in his youthful prime, full of juice—and an ample quantity of mischief.

Hyperbole

Grape talks about growing up: "I'll probably be a king or something."

Grape comments on Raisin's wrinkles: "Grandpa must have a kazillion."

Grape says Raisin likes to tell stories: "Grandpa has a kajillion stories."

Inference

Grandpa Raisin tells his grandson Grape, "You couldn't pay me to be a grape again." Despite the wrinkles, there must be compensations to age.

To impress upon Grape the need to obey, Grandpa Raisin tells him how grape juice is made: "They just let some grapes cross the street without holding their grandpa's hand."

Again, to keep Grape's youthful enthusiasm in check at the park, Grandpa is a "good yeller. I come back to him."

Grape tries to be attentive to Grandpa's long stories: he "listens short. But, I like the parts I do listen to."

Grape thinks the two make a great team. When a pesky prune keeps Grandpa talking too long, Grape pulls Grandpa away, saying, "It's time for your nap." On the way home, Grandpa thankfully whispers to him, "You've saved me again."

There is real affection between these two: Grandpa says, "When I was a grape, I was just like you." Grape replies, "When I'm a raisin, I want to be just like you."

Pun

The two think they make a great team because "we're from the same vine, after all!"

As they sit together on a teeter-totter, Grandpa Raisin teaches Grape "about life's ups and downs."

Plump with youthful life, Grape is called down from a tree by his nervous Grandpa, "Come on down, squirt."

Tone

The author emphasizes the difference between the headlong energy of youth and the cautious approach of maturity:

While Grandpa admonishes him to stop and smell the roses, in a typical kid joke, Grape replies, "I stop to smell my armpits. Fresh and clean."

Grape admires his grandfather's wrinkles: "Awesome!" He is impressed that his grandfather has been "allowed to cross the big street for more years than I can count."

Grape and Raisin respect and love each other: Raisin tells Grape he was just like Grape when he was young. Grape returns the compliment, saying, "'When I'm a raisin, I want to be just like you.' Then we hug."

Understatement

Grape finds it advantageous to obey his grandfather Raisin promptly: At the city park, Grape runs ahead of Grandpa. "But Grandpa's a good yeller. So I come back to him."

Grape's attention span is not up to Grandpa's stories: "Grandpa tells long stories. . . . I can only listen short."

They hug "sometimes too tight." Grape's juice gets squeezed out!

Wit/Humor

When Grandpa reminds Grape to stop and smell the flowers, he sniggers, "I stop to smell my armpits."

*****

Arnosky, Jim. *Grandfather Buffalo.* New York: G. P. Putnam's Sons, c2006.
When Grandfather Buffalo, the oldest bull of the herd, trails behind the group, he finds he is joined by a newborn calf and proves, despite advanced age, he is an important member of the herd.
Curriculum Tie-in: Science (Bison), Social Science (Elderly), Social Science (Family Relationships—Grandparents/Grandchildren)
Art Style: Natural lush watercolors in full-page *Realism*

DEVICES

Atmosphere

The narration begins with life-affirming dignity: "Grandfather Buffalo was old and slow, but he was still strong."

Because he is slow, he is in a unique position to help save the life of the newest member of the herd, who would have perished in a dust storm if the old bull had not been a gentle guide for the young calf, who also moves slowly.

The narration ends in life-affirming dignity: "Grandfather Buffalo was old and slow, but he was still a part of the herd."

Foreshadow

"Grandfather Buffalo slowly stood, shook the dust off his sides, and followed. Each time, he was left a little farther behind." Could a crisis situation happen to a lone animal separated from the safety of the herd?

Inference

"When some cowboys came looking for their cattle, Grandfather Buffalo snorted at them and pawed the ground until they rode away." The old one functions as the lone protector of the "young cow carrying the heavy weight of her unborn calf."

After the calf's birth, the old buffalo becomes the calf's protector. In a dust storm, "the calf lost sight of his mother" and "accidentally ran into Grandfather Buffalo." The old one "grunted, and kept grunting as he walked. The calf followed the sound through the blinding dust" until they reached the herd.

The calf recognizes the old bull as a safe friend. When Grandfather Buffalo goes off by himself and awakens after a solitary nap, he notices "something pressing against his ribs. It was the calf napping by his side."

Motif

"Grandfather Buffalo was old and slow, but . . ." Though he consistently falls behind the herd, he still demonstrates he is a worthy member with a role to play in the overall well-being of the group.

Theme

There is a role and a place for all members of a society. Even slow Grandfather Buffalo proves to be a vital member of the herd when he finds himself the sole protector of a cow, who is also traveling far behind the others with her newborn calf. The cow welcomes Grandfather Buffalo's ministrations, "nudging the calf along."

*****

Asher, Sandy. *Too Many Frogs!* Illus. by Keith Graves. New York: (Philomel Books) Penguin Young Readers Group, c2005.

Rabbit's comfortable nightly routine is disturbed by exuberant Froggy, who, without being invited, settles in comfortably for a snack and a story.

Curriculum Tie-in: Social Science (Character Development—Empathy), Social Science (Character Development—Kindness), Social Science (Friendship)

Art Style: Bright full-page acrylic paint, inks, and colored pencil in boisterous, humorous *Expressionism*

DEVICES

Allusion

As the illustrations show, among the books on Rabbit's fireplace mantel are *War and Peas, Lord of the Radish, Paul Bunnyon,* and *Hucklebunny Finn.*

Aphorism

"Sharing an activity with friends heightens its pleasure."
"Change is good."

Internal Rhyme

"So Froggy hopped—and popped—and whipped—and flipped—and mixed—and fixed . . ."
Froggy "fluffed—and puffed—mooshed—and smooshed . . ."
There were "billows of pillows."

Irony

"It was a simple way of life—no fuss, no clutter. And Rabbit liked it." That was Rabbit's life before Froggy. Along with Froggy came fuss and clutter. Now, "it was a different way of life. And Rabbit liked it." What Rabbit thought he preferred became just the opposite.

Parallelism

"He cooked for himself. He tidied up after himself."
". . . no fuss, no clutter."
"Rabbit blinked once. He blinked twice."
"I never invited you in. I never invited you to fix a snack. I never invited you to get all comfy-cozy. I never invited your family to join me."

Theme

Mutual respect and the shared love of an activity can bridge personality differences. Rabbit and Froggy have in common only the joy of reading aloud. It proves sufficient to bring them together in happy companionship.

Tone

Genuine feelings are acknowledged and respected. The result is an attitude adjustment.

High-spirited but clueless, Froggy is finally told bluntly that he is intruding and has not been invited into Rabbit's home. Suddenly, Froggy is quite abashed. "This will never do. Thanks for your kindness. Never meant to be rude." Froggy brings his whole family to apologize. "Brought you a T-shirt." It says "Frog Family Reunion." They all are sitting at the front door "waiting patiently to say they were sorry."

Rabbit acknowledges Froggy's efforts to make amends. And, in a similar spirit, Rabbit capitalizes on the Frog Family's love of stories. After their apology, Rabbit replies, "I was about to read a story. Would you like to join me?"

*****

Ashman, Linda. *Desmond and the Naughtybugs.* Illus. by Anik McGrory. New York: (Dutton Children's Books) Penguin Young Readers Group, c2006.

Desmond is a well-behaved boy most of the time, unless he's being attacked by the Peskies, Sloggies, Squirmies, Whineys, or Snarlies and cannot seem to be good.

Curriculum Tie-in: Character Development—Honorable/ Dishonorable Behavior.

Art Style: Oil pastels show the chaotic world of the Naughtybugs in *Cartoon and Expressionism.*

DEVICES

Foreshadow

"But when the Naughtybugs showed up, it was hard to be good. VERY hard."

After a bad week of Naughtybugs, Desmond promises to be good from now on. "And he was mostly. At least until the busload of Grumblies drove over from Henry's house and slipped through the back door."

"The Whineys, who thrive on rainy days, began gathering in the playroom. Finding Desmond looking mournfully out of the window, they proposed another form of entertainment."

Inference

Desmond "tried to be good all the time ... and most of the time he was." But, sometimes the Naughtybugs lured him into bad behavior. "And you just never knew when they might show up."

Irony

It was a rainy day, and Desmond is bored in the playroom. "It was no use. There wasn't a single thing to do." Desmond wasn't in the mood for a rescue with his fire truck, couldn't think of anything to paint except black clouds, flipped through his favorite bug book, "but even the spider page didn't hold his interest." So he whines at his mother, "I'm thirrrrsty" and demands "aaaaple juice nowwwww," forgetting even to say the magic word first. Desmond finds himself sitting in his time-out chair, "with no toys, and no apple juice, suddenly remembering all sorts of fun things that he could be doing in the playroom."

Parallelism

The family is weary of a long week of Naughtybug incidents. Tempers flare during bath time:
"Stop that, you Lather-Nose!" yells Desmond.
"Stop that, you Foamy-Face!" yells his mother.
"Stop that, you Bubble-Heads!" yells his father.
"The Snarlies grabbed Desmond's hand forcing him to throw his ducky in the water."
"The Snarlies grabbed Father's hand, forcing him to throw the rubber whale in the water."
"The Snarlies grabbed Mother's hand, forcing her to smack a chickie in the water."

*****

Atwood, Margaret. *Up in the Tree.* Toronto, Ontario: Greenwood Books/ House of Anansi Press, c1978, 2006.
>Two children love their life up in a tree until their ladder is taken away, stranding them and making them anxious before they are beneficiaries of helpful kindness that provides them an opportunity to make themselves independent from this hazard.
>>**Curriculum Tie-in:** Social Science (Character Development—Kindness), Social Science (Character Development—Self-Reliance)
>>**Art Style:** Whimsical illustrations, reminiscent of Dr. Seuss, in two-color pen-and-ink painted *Cartoons.*

DEVICES

Antithesis

"It's fun in the sun
and a pain in the rain, ..."

Hyperbole

"We've run out of tea, we'll have to eat leaves ..."
"How will we get down, ... are we stuck here forever ..."

Internal Rhyme

"We swing in the Spring and we crawl in the Fall ..."
"And we dance on the branches ..."
"Don't fall off, don't wriggle or cough ..."
"Down, down to the ground ..."
"Oh moan! Oh groan! There's no telephone!"
"Now, we're down on the ground, safe and sound."
"... with table and chairs we work hard making stairs, ..."

Irony

The children like their "old tree, our home in the tree," until the ladder is gone. Then they fear being "stuck here forever in this horrible tree."

"Now we're down on the ground, safe and sound, safe and sound, and we want to climb back to our home in the tree."

Motif

"Way up in a tree" is the phrase that begins a narration of each of the activities that describes the children's life in their tree home.

Parallelism

"Don't fall off, don't wriggle or cough,"
"There's nowhere to go! There's no one to talk to ... there's no more hot water ..."
"We've run out of pancakes, we've run out of tea, ..."
"Oh my! Oh me!"

*****

Auch, Mary Jane. *Hen Lake.* New York: Holiday House, c1995.
> Tired of the bragging of Percival the peacock, Poulette convinces the other hens in the barnyard that they can outperform the boastful bird in a ballet she creates.
>> **Curriculum Tie-in:** Fine Arts (Ballet), Social Science (Character Development—Self-Esteem)
>> **Art Style:** Lush, bright, primary color, humorous oil pastel in *Expressionism* in *Cartoon* illustrations make the dancers stand out larger than life in their grand costumes and naked emotions.

DEVICES

Allusion

"We'll call the ballet ... Hen Lake! You can be the Hen Maidens, and I'll be the Hen Queen." Poulette convinces the barnyard hens to join her in "a corps de ballet" as she creates a new ballet for the talent contest. And, in true theatrical tradition, before the successful performance, she tells her fellow dancers to "break a drumstick."

Aphorism

When Poulette Hen's fellow dance team members express doubt concerning their abilities, she tells them, "If you believe in yourselves, you can do anything."

Aptronym

"Poulette" is a play on the word *pullet,* the term used for a young female chicken who has not yet matured enough to lay an egg. This French-sounding spelling enhances her inclination toward the fine arts.

Archetype

The peacock, among all birds, is typically depicted as arrogant and suffering from a superiority complex. True to form, Percival the peacock lords it over them in his relationship with the barnyard chickens, birds he considers beneath him. In all things, he claims to be able to do better than the lowly hens. If he cared to scratch for bugs, he could do better than they. If he should want to sing, he would have a magnificent voice. If he should care to dance, he would show how much more graceful he is than the hens.

Colloquialism

"Wow!" clucks Gertrude. "Get a load of those tail feathers!" But, the fellow with the fine plumage says, "I don't do bugs," when the hens ask him to join them in catching some.

He is most skeptical of the concept of dancing chickens. "What a hoot!"

Practicing is strenuous for the ill-equipped hens. Tempers are short. They snap at each other. "Oh, go lay an egg," squawks Zelda.

Connotation

The self-centered, spoiled peacock, never actually willing to exert himself, is "Percival," a name that conjures images of somewhat sissy affectations.

Inference

The hens' humble, homemade dance costumes are critiqued unkindly by the superior-acting peacock, who recognizes what Poulette has substituted for sequins. Percival Peacock detects the telltale odor of the cheap imitation and sneers, "Interesting costumes." Smirking, he remarks, "Do I smell fish?"

Motif

The "ordinary" is contrasted with the "superior."

"We were perfectly happy being ordinary hens," the nervous dancers complain to the patient Poulette as she cajoles them into bettering their efforts.

Percival Peacock pronounces his new farm home "rather ordinary, compared to my last home." He pronounces himself the superior dancer: "You call *that* dancing? I'm much more graceful than you are." He is the superior singer: "I have a magnificent voice." He is the superior bug catcher: "I could catch more bugs than everyone else, if I wanted to."

Theme

Poulette's inspiring encouragement enables her dance team of common hens to realize their own amazing potential while finally recognizing that the showy, bragging peacock is not really "any more special than we are." Poulette clarifies this truth, that "under all those fancy feathers, a peacock is just a long-necked chicken." This is a believe-in-your-dreams positive message.

*****

Bang, Molly. *In My Heart*. New York: Little, Brown and Company, c2006.
    A mother describes how her child is always in her heart no matter where she is or what she's doing.
        Curriculum Tie-in: Art (Expressive Painting), Social Science (Family Relationships—Parent/Child)
        Art Style: Engaging *Expressionism* in *Cartoons* with overtones of *Surrealism*

DEVICES

Inference

The illustrations answer Mother's question: "Guess who's always in that great big heart of *yours*?" It shows a prominent picture of his parents, smaller pictures of Grandma, his teacher, his cat, and his school friends, all sized according to a child's sense of importance.

Motif

"Inside my heart" is how the loving relationship between the mother and her child is expressed: Though the mother and child are apart during the day, all that is necessary for each to feel happy is to look "inside my heart." The mother assures her child "You're in my heart." There is plenty of room for him. She can't go anyplace without him. No matter where the child is, no matter what the mother is doing, he is "Still here in my heart."

Tone

In this multi-ethnic household, there is loving acceptance of all members.

And when "I come back home . . . aaaaaa." No words can express the mother's delight in being back with her child. There is camaraderie in the shared household tasks and loving interaction.

"And when you're finally fast asleep, then do you know what? You are *still* inside my heart. How do you *do* that, always being in my heart?"

*****

*Bateman, Teresa. *Keeper of Soles*. Illus. by Diego Herrera (Yayo). New York: Holiday House, c2006.

A shoemaker repeatedly outwits a black-robed figure who knocks on his door, demanding his soul.

Curriculum Tie-in: History (Middle Ages—Death)

Art Style: Acrylic *Surrealism* in *Cartoon* images associated with the Grim Reaper and the cobbler's trade

DEVICES

Ambiguity

"Death was unpleasant enough without adding to the misery." The cobbler notes that "Death" appears to be suffering from ill-fitting shoes, which could make him testy enough to cause the cobbler undue hardship in this business of facing imminent mortality. There is death, and then there are unpleasant extenuating circumstances plus death.

"I have come for your soul, and I will not be denied this time," says the Grim Reaper. "And, what do you think I've been giving you all these many years? I've given you sole after sole," Colin replies. Death laughs at this truth. "I'll wait until the soles you have given me have worn out. Then I'll come for the soul I should have taken in the first place."

Aphorism

When people speculated that there must be magic in Colin's cobbling, he just laughed. "A well-made shoe does what it's supposed to do." All that is asked of anything or anyone is to simply do that.

Death is willing to wait. "All men must come with me eventually." This truth cannot be denied or avoided.

Black Humor

Colin works carefully on Death's new boots: "He wanted them to be perfect because, after all, you don't want Death showing up on your doorstep with pinched toes or a blister."

"Do you prefer brown leather or black? Yes, of course, black. Something that will blend in nicely with the robe."

The idea of stalling his impending departure by making Death a pair of shoes crosses Colin's mind: " 'Have you ever noticed,' he said casually, 'that your feet hurt after work?' "

After having made a couple of pairs, and stalling for time, the ever resourceful Colin has another suggestion. "Perhaps Death might want something a little sportier." He says, "Boots are fine for bad weather, but you must cover a lot of ground. A good walking shoe with a solid tread and arch supports would be perfect."

Colloquialism

Colin was "the best shoemaker in the *kingdom*."
There was "magic in Colin's *cobbling*."
Some shoes "sold for mere *coppers*."
The dark-robed figure "pulled a *parchment* from a long dark sleeve."
He "grabbed a piece of charcoal and sketched around Death's feet."
He suggested "fancy *court shoes* for special occasions."

Such language suggests a past time when commerce was comprised of cottage industries and the Grim Reaper was as real and near as one's neighbor.

Connotation

The cobbler's shoes were sold for *mere coppers*. They were affordable to all and worth much more than they were being charged.

A cold wind *slithered* in. Death, sneaky and somewhat dishonorable, comes in uninvited.

Imagery

"... a knock came at his door—a slow, thudding sound—and a cold wind slithered in."

" 'I'm Death,' he declared in a voice that spoke of graveyards and dark, starless nights."

"... shoes for dancers that were as light as air, walking shoes that promised nary a blister, baby shoes that made children wish to walk, and ladies' shoes that made any woman who wore them beautiful."

Inference

"... the profit Colin made on rich people's shoes was offset by the profit he lost on the shoes he made for the less fortunate. Those he sold for mere coppers, though the workmanship was just as fine as the others ..."

When asked by Death if he was Colin the cobbler, "Colin was tempted to say that he wasn't, but, being a truthful man, he nodded his head."

"Colin looked at the work left undone on his bench, and he thought of the feet that would go cold and bare, ... "

Though nimble-witted enough to suggest a pair of sandals, winter boots, soft slippers, and sportier walking wear to put off dying, the cobbler is also kind-hearted and conscientious in his craftsmanship.

Irony

Death will come to collect Colin when the soles of the shoes the cobbler has made for him wear out. But, because the cobbler makes such fine, sturdy shoes, it "would be years before Death would stand on his doorstep again."

Paradox

"Colin grew older, and Death visited him often enough that they became friends, if such can be said of Death."

Parallelism

"... they were good shoes, solid shoes, well made shoes."
"Death was out the door again, boots on his feet and sandals in his hand."

Pun

Keeper of Soles, the book's title, is a pun for both characters in this story. Colin keeps his village in well-soled shoes. The Grim Reaper keeps a list of the souls he collects when their time on earth has ended.

Understatement

When Colin suggests making sandals for Death, who has never worn anything on his feet, Death is startled and notes, "Most people, when facing that solemn journey to the other side, did not comment on feet."

Colin makes a case for creating solid shoes for Death: "You go all over the world. Doubtless there are places where it's quite cold."

After the boots are finished, Colin pursues the theme of appropriate foot wear. "Boots are fine for bad weather, but you must cover a lot of ground."

In between visits, Colin prepares each pair of shoes for Death. Customers notice them and want to buy these finished products. Colin refuses each offer. "Sorry, those are for a special client."

*****

Bateman, Teresa. *A Plump and Perky Turkey.* Illus. by Jeff Shelly. New York: Marshall Cavendish, c2001.

> The townspeople of Squawk Valley try to trick a turkey into being their Thanksgiving dinner, but are frustrated in their efforts when the turkey tricks them instead.
>
> **Curriculum Tie-in:** Social Science (Greed)
>
> **Art Style:** Vivid full-page watercolor and gouache *Expressionism* in *Cartoons*

DEVICES

Alliteration

"plump and perky through the pines"
"plump and proud"
"We'll fill our fair with folks and fun ..."
"downhearted and depressed"

Allusion

The greedy townspeople have self-centered concerns like those of the characters in Charles Dickens' nineteenth-century tale, *A Christmas Carol.* There is *Ebenezer* Beezer, the wily city leader, and his fellow citizen *Jacob* Green.

Ambiguity

"We could hold an arts-and-crafts fair, ... a fair with one grand turkey prize—that all of us could win!" The townspeople are thinking they will get a turkey for their Thanksgiving dinner; the turkey thinks he will not be their prize.

Aptronym

With their minds fixed on obtaining a Thanksgiving turkey, the villagers live in the aptly named "Squawk Valley."

Irony

After their best-turkey artwork-sculpture contest goes awry, "folks learned a lesson that stuck firm with them forever. A plump and perky turkey can be pretty doggone clever." They had expected to trick Pete the turkey into becoming their Thanksgiving meal; instead, he has tricked them and even taken their oatmeal artwork for his own dinner when he escapes.

Parallelism

"There were turkeys made of spuds,
There were turkeys made of rope."

"There were turkeys made of paper,
There were turkeys made of soap."

"He was cocky, he was clever."

Poetic Justice

The turkey meant for their Thanksgiving meal was tricked into coming to Squawk Valley to pose for a best look-alike turkey art exhibit. But, he escapes and, besides, took with him a modeling fee—"The oatmeal bird was gone." The townspeople had to settle for a Thanksgiving meal featuring shredded wheat.

Surprise/Twist-in-the-Tail

The villagers create some fine turkey works of art, but when it's time to grab the model as their prize, they can no longer distinguish the real bird from all the sculpted turkeys. "For a clever bird like Pete, it was perfect camou-flage.... Pete judged each piece of artwork as the hungry crowd all cheered. He stopped to take a closer look, and then he disappeared!"

Theme

Dishonorable intentions will not lead to good results. Because Squawk Valley residents meant to trick a turkey into being their meal, they ended up eating shredded wheat instead.

Understatement

After their failed ruse to entrap Pete and left with nothing but artwork made of rope, paper, soap, and such, the chagrined townspeople note "The only turkeys left in town appeared too hard to chew."

*****

Bernstein, Dan. *The Tortoise and the Hare Race Again.* Illus. by Andrew Glass. New York: Holiday House, c2006.

> Tired of being a celebrity, the Tortoise challenges the Hare to race again, this time with the intention of losing.
>
> > **Curriculum Tie-in:** Literature (Aesop's Fables), Social Science (Problem Solving—Ingenuity)
> >
> > **Art Style:** Colored pencil and watercolor *Expressionism* conveys high jinks, personality, and ambience.

DEVICES

Alliteration

The alarm-clock necklace sounded "bells, buzzers, bongs, beeps, chirps, chimes, and cuckoos."

Allusion

Rabbit-kind had nothing nice thing to say to the one among them who lost a race with a turtle—not *Pete R. Rabbit*; *Hare E. Plodder*; *Warren Rabbit*; *Rabbit Foote,* the luckiest rabbit; *Stu Rabbit,* who got boiling mad; *Jack Rabbit,* who ran circles around him; *White Rabbit,* who dashed down the nearest hole; and *General Rabbit E. Lee,* who marched his floppy rabbiteers in the opposite direction.

Tortoise and Hare agree that if Tortoise won the rematch race, Hare would buy him some cool sunglasses because he "thought sunglasses would allow him to hide. He had heard this worked in Hollywood."

The Tortoise just wanted a normal life, "working at the *shell* station, shining turtles' backs."

Ambiguity

Tortoise makes sure the hare wins the race by donning a powered rabbit suit across the finish line, making certain a "rabbit" will definitely win the race.

And, although Hare does not actually remember winning the race (since he was napping when the winner crossed the finish line), he receives so many congratulations, he becomes convinced. Hare comments, " 'You know what won this race? Speed, baby. That wasn't just a hare they saw out there. That was a machine!' The hare never found out how right he was."

Foreshadow

Tortoise is determined not to emerge winner in this rematch race. To what lengths will he go to make sure Hare wins? "The tortoise plodded to the starting line wearing a small yellow backpack."

After an hour of running, Hare can't even see the poky Tortoise. "Maybe I'll rest my eyes," he thinks to himself. Is history about to repeat itself—especially since he has placed along the race course a "big brass bed with fluffy pillows" for his anticipated snooze?

Paradox

Tortoise soon discovers that "winning the Great Race wasn't that great." He hated being in the spotlight, preferring a normal life of sleeping long hours and slurping juicy worms. As the winner, he is determined to undo this "mistake" so he can live his accustomed life of anonymity.

Parody

Hare and Tortoise engage in a race again, but this time both of them seek the same outcome—victory for the hare. It's not going to be easy though. Hare still makes the same foolish mistake of stopping to nap when he's ahead. This time, however, Tortoise is prepared with careful subterfuge and mechanical assistance. Come what may, a "rabbit" is going the cross the finish line first. All is well that ends well. The reputation as winner is restored to the hare. Tortoise is happy and content retiring from a racing career.

Pun

It was another *bad-hare* day for the rabbit, who endured ridicule from everyone in the village.

Tortoise won the Great Race: By a *hair*.

Tortoise wrote a book: *My* Hare-Racing *Experience.*

Hare expects to be a hero, the *toast* of all the rabbits. Teenaged turtles chant, "Rabbits on toast! Rabbits on toast!"

The big brass bed with fluffy pillows was, naturally, the rabbit's own "*hare-brained* idea."

Just as Tortoise had feared, he "spotted a *hare ball*" curled up and snoozing under a tree.

". . . winning the Great Race wasn't that great."

*****

Borden, Louise. *Across the Blue Pacific: A World War II Story.* Illus. by Robert Andrew Parker. Boston: Houghton Mifflin, c2006.

A woman reminisces about her neighbor's son, who was the object of a letter-writing campaign by some fourth graders when he went away to war in 1943.

Curriculum Tie-in: History (World War II, 1939–1945, U.S. Navy), Social Science (Grief)

Art Style: Ethereal pen-and-ink watercolor *Impressionism*

DEVICES

Aphorism

"In wartime small victories become big things to celebrate...."
"Sometimes it's best to be by yourself when you're missing someone."

Atmosphere

The solemnity of waiting casts a pall over youthful routines and common experiences. There is intense relief when word of the war's end reaches every community.

"... on rainy November days, I was glad to be indoors. Somehow Mrs. Lindsay's classroom made our world feel cozy and safe."

"We pulled on our coats without even buttoning them and hurried next door. It was so quiet and still outside, such a hushed world of snow."

"Missing. It seemed like such a little word for such a big thing."

"The next few days dragged by, one at a time, and they weren't filled with holiday joy. Just dark gray mornings when everybody woke up, hoping."

"On August 14, 1945, the war was over, over, over!"

Connotation

Missing—such a little word for such a big thing, the narrator discovers. Their emotions hinge on the outcome of this label.

Flashback

"The U.S. serviceman that I knew was Lieutenant Ted Walker, my next-door neighbor on Orchard Road.... Ted Walker was a navy man. While he was away at college in Maryland, my brother, Sam, and I were still learning how to tie our own shoes." But, as the story opens, the narrator is entering fourth grade and Ted is in a submarine. It's 1943 and America is in World War II.

Flash-Forward

"The war years on Orchard Road and Mrs. Lindsay's map of the blue Pacific are now far behind me. Sam and I are all grown up with families and streets of our own."

Foreshadow

Much military action for Americans occurred in the Pacific because it was enemy territory. What will this mean to Ted's future?

When the war started, Ted is assigned from duty in the South Atlantic to "another ocean—this time, the Pacific."

"… when Sam and I looked out across the side yard, things didn't seem quite right at Mrs. Walker's house … there were too many cars in her driveway for such a snowy day."

"A telegram had come from the United States Navy … the kind of message that had not yet come to a house on our street."

Imagery

"Just one submarine and one crew living together, close as a family, in a steamy narrow space full of engines and pipes and gauges and dials … with that periscope coming up to take an important look, turning, turning again, always watching for other ships … maybe a whole convoy … or just one boat."

"Diving … diving … bow pointed down, feet braced against the steep dive."

"A thousand leaves rattled into the corners of the playground."

"… so quiet and still outside, such a hushed world of snow."

"… our lives became steadier. The winter days blurred into a muddy spring."

Inference

"I wanted to go out and shout against the cold sky: Where are you, Ted? Where are you? But I didn't want Ted's mother, Mrs. Walker, to hear."

Ted had taught the narrator how to spit polish shoes. "Those shiny black shoes were only a small part of the many important stories. But they belonged to me."

When the narrator remarks that it's sometimes best to be by yourself when you're missing someone, her brother "Sam pulled his cap down low over his eyes and nodded."

As a proud legacy of her acquaintance with her sailor neighbor, she remembers him saying to her brother, "You bet, Crenshaw," and then giving him a thumbs up when her brother declares the snowman they built together is "a lieutenant like you." Later, when the war is over, the girl replies, "You bet," and gives a thumbs up when her former teacher asks her, "Ready for fifth grade, Crenshaw?"

Motif

The unknown fate of a beloved neighbor is fraught with "maybes": "Maybe the crew had gotten off the *Albacore* safely and were on an island." Maybe they had been captured but were still alive.

The "story" of war is universal: "Around the world, soldiers and sailors in all the countries returned to their families and their neighborhoods…. I think about how, all over the world, the stories are passed down in different ways and in different voices from family to family."

Paradox

The narrator's fourth-grade teacher was "strict in a soft kind of way." (She expected excellent work from her students but wasn't harsh.)

"It was so quiet and still outside, such a hushed world of snow. And yet it seemed to me as if my heart were beating as loud as a drum."

Parallelism

"No letters. No word from home."

You had to be smart to "to outfox the enemy ships, to be as quiet as you could be, to catch those enemy ships by surprise."

"Every story we told about Ted Walker became a story we never wanted to forget. Every story seemed important enough to keep."

"Missing. It seemed like such a little word for such a big thing."

"Peace. Another small word for such a big thing."

"There she was, ready to greet her new fourth graders, ready to teach them important things."

Simile

"... keeping your torpedoes ready, then firing them, like fast underwater arrows ..."

"... one crew living together, close as a family ..."

Theme

The vast and common loss in the war experience affects all neighborhoods in all countries similarly.

*****

Bowen, Anne. *The Great Math Tattle Battle.* Illus. by Jaime Zollars. Morton Grove, IL: Albert Whitman, c2006.

> Harley Harrison, the biggest tattletale and best math student in second grade, meets his match in both areas when Emma Jean Smith joins him in Mr. Hall's class.

> **Curriculum Tie-in:** Mathematics (Adding and Subtracting), Social Science (Character Development—Self-Esteem), Social Science (Tale-Bearing), Social Science (Team Cooperation)

> **Art Style:** Acrylic, *Naive, Expressionism,* and *Cartoons* humorously complement typical youthful tattling in a misguided attempt to impress authority figures

DEVICES

Connotation

To both of these students, math is a *piece of cake*, easy, something they enjoy.

Paradox

These good math students finally discover that by cooperating they could be even better. Though they work fast separately, together they are able to catch each other's mistakes in a pairs timed contest. They divide up the remaining problems so they are able to finish within the time allotted. "It didn't take a math whiz to notice everyone else was almost finished."

Parallelism

Harley could figure out 45 plus 39 "faster than you could spell 'Mississippi.'"

At first, the two eschew joining forces and decide to separately add and subtract "faster than you could spell 'Alabama.'"

When they finally figure out they could finish faster as a team, they are "faster than you could spell 'Massachusetts.'"

"No wonder no one wants to be your math partner."

"No wonder no one wants to help you with your art project."

"No wonder you eat lunch all by yourself."

"He couldn't believe his ears" when Emma Jean points out some math errors Harley has made.

"He couldn't believe his eyes" when Emma Jean reports him for wasting too much time getting a drink of water.

Poetic Justice

New student Emma Jean shows the class tattletale how it feels to be on the receiving end of bad reports to the teacher. Harley finds himself written up for "wasting everyone's time at the water fountain" and for "excessive pencil sharpening."

Harley also learns how it feels to be caught making errors in his best subject and experiences the audacity of being told how lucky he is that she has helped him "with those problems or they would be all wrong."

Theme

Being best at something alone is not as pleasurable as being best together.

*****

Bradley, Kimberly Brubaker. *Ballerino Nate.* Illus. by R. W. Alley. New York: (Dial Books for Young Readers) Penguin Young Readers Group, c2006.

> After seeing a ballet performance, Nate decides he wants to learn ballet, but he has doubts when his brother, Ben, tells him that only girls can be ballerinas.
>
> > **Curriculum Tie-in:** Fine Arts (Ballet), Social Science (Character Development—Perseverance), Social Science (Family Relationships—Siblings)
> >
> > **Art Style:** Pen-and-ink, watercolor, and colored pencil *Cartoons*

DEVICES

Ambiguity

Nate misunderstands when a male dancer answers his question by replying that he's not a ballerina:

"... men can't be ballerinas." Nate "looked at the ground. He felt like crying, 'I know,' he said."

Then the man "lifted Nate's chin as well as his spirits. Ballerino is the word for men."

Archetype

Nate's older brother, Ben, is a kill-joy, constantly trying to deflate Nate's aspirations to become a ballet dancer. He takes malicious pleasure in making his brother doubt the veracity of his dreams.

He tells Nate that ballerinas all have to wear "pink shoes and a dress." He slyly adds that even in Little League, everyone, girls included, must wear the same uniform.

When Nate walks into his first ballet class, Ben points out, "They're *all* girls." On the way home, Ben needles Nate, "Was I right?" and Nate can only nod his head miserably. His class was, indeed, all girls. Ben is right again.

Inference

Though Nate's parents are supportive of his ballet interests, his brother, Ben, undermines his confidence. Since Little League girls must wear the same uniform that Little League boys wear, "Nate hid his head in his arms" at the implication of what he will have to wear as a ballet dancer.

After putting up with hearing Ben's put-downs, Mom wants to curtail Ben's damage. "Please go wait for me in the lobby," she says. He's definitely not helping Nate's initiation process into his first day of ballet class.

Motif

"Boys can't be ballerinas" is the refrain Nate's brother Ben loves to say to discourage him from pursuing his ballet dancing interests.

Parallelism

"Nate loved the ballet. He loved the fluttery costumes that the dancers wore. He loved the way the dancers jumped and leaped and spun. He loved the way their movements looked like music. Nate loved the ballet teacher. He loved the ballet class."

"All summer Nate danced. He danced on the smooth cold tile in the kitchen. He danced in the long tickly grass on the lawn. He danced on the rough hot driveway."

Stereotype/Reverse Stereotype

Ben tries to undermine Nate's determination to become a ballet dancer, because "boys can't be ballerinas." Ballerinas must all wear the same uniform, like Little League ball players. Nate will have to wear pink shoes and a dress. Everyone in Nate's first ballet class is girls. So, it looks like Ben is right. Boys can't be ballerinas.

*****

Broach, Elise. *Cousin John Is Coming!* Illus. by Nate Lilly. New York: (Dial Books for Young Readers) Penguin Young Readers Group, c2006.

> Upon learning that the cousin he dislikes is coming for a visit, a boy imagines horrible things that could happen to him at the hands of this unwelcome visitor until a sudden inspiration gives him reason to believe things might turn out fun after all.
>
> **Curriculum Tie-in:** Social Science (Bullying), Social Science (Character Development—Self-Reliance), Social Science (Family Relationships—Cousins)
>
> **Art Style:** Mischievously sly comic-book-style *Cartoon*

DEVICES

Ambiguity

Mother's comments on the coming visit contrast sharply to Ben and his cat's interpretation of her words.

"You two are so good at entertaining yourselves!" (Ben visualizes Cousin John spinning the merry-go-round so fast he and the cat are thrown off.)

"We can go to ... even the aquarium." (Ben imagines Cousin John dangling him and the cat on a hook at the end of a fishing pole over a pool with a hungry alligator ready to snap its jaws on them.)

Ben abruptly changes his mind about the visit and even makes a "Welcome" sign when he learns his cousin has developed a recent allergy to cats. Mother misunderstands Ben's sudden motive to be an inviting host. "Oh Ben, isn't that nice! I knew you'd be excited."

Archetype

A classic bully, Cousin John misuses Ben in games, frightens him for his own amusement, endangers his safety, and always takes the best snacks and the best seat to watch TV. Ben doesn't relish playing pirate with him, going out for ice cream together, to the beach, or to the playground. "The best part," says Mother, is "there's a good chance that Cousin John can stay all week!" Ben and the cat sneak to the door with packed bags.

Counterpoint

Mother's story of Cousin John's proposed visit is upbeat and hopeful. Ben and his cat are gloomy and fearful. Mother doesn't know the relationship between the visitor and hosts is that of bully and victims.

"It's just wonderful the way you two get along." (Ben and the cat recall Cousin John dangling them out an upper floor window.)

"Oh, I forgot to tell you! Cousin John is going to bring a pirate set that he got for his birthday. I know he'll share it with you." (Ben and the cat imagine being forced, at the prod of a sword, to walk the plank out over a box of sharp tacks in a briar patch with two porcupines in it.)

"We'll go out for ice cream." (Ben and the cat imagine Cousin John taking away their cones and smashing the ice cream-side down on top of their heads.)

"But no playing in the basement this time, Ben. Remember how that door sometimes sticks." (Ben and the cat gleefully recall barring shut the door with Cousin John behind it and chain locking it and bolting it.)

"But you'll have to remember not to take him up in the tree house. He didn't like that for some reason." (Ben and the cat recall cutting the rope ladder just as Cousin John is on his way up to get at them.)

Inference

Before Mother mentions how Cousin John has developed a new allergy to cats, Ben and his cat are sneaking to the door with packed bags—so terror stricken are they by this impending visit.

Mother then says something that changes their mind about leaving. "His face swells up like a balloon, his eyes water, and he can't stop sneezing. So we'll have to be careful to keep the kitty away from him."

Suddenly, possibilities for this visit take a new turn, and Ben and the cat are looking forward to welcoming Cousin John. As they anticipate the course of events, they hope that the visit will be brief and be the last one they will ever have to endure. Ben envisions throwing his cat into Cousin John's arms.

The cat envisions wrapping itself around Cousin John's head, hugging him, and swiping his tail across Cousin John's plate of food and climbing inside his pillow.

Irony

In the past, a visit from Cousin John has always made Ben and the cat miserable. Now they have the ammunition to make him miserable when Mother mentions the "terrible allergy" Cousin John has suddenly developed to cats ever since he "got badly scratched by a cat a few months ago."

"I mean it Ben. If we're not careful to keep the kitty away from Cousin John, . . . he probably won't be able to stay with us. Do you understand?"

Instead of dreading a visit from this bullying cousin, Ben and his cat are positively gleeful.

Paradox

Ben and his cat do not like Cousin John. They don't want to be around him. Yet, they are looking forward to his visit—ever since Mother explained that Cousin John has developed a new allergy to cats. They are planning an enthusiastic "welcome" for him. This visit is likely to change their relationship with Cousin John forever.

*****

Bunge, Daniela. *The Scarves.* Trans. by Kahryn Bishop. New York: Penguin Young Readers Group, c2006.

> Grandpa and Grandma separate, but their granddaughter believes they still love each other and sets in action a plan to bring them back together.
>
> **Curriculum Tie-in:** Social Science (Character Development— Empathy), Social Science (Family Relationships—Grandparents/ Grandchildren)
>
> **Art Style:** Colored pencil, full-page *Naive*, delightful detail

DEVICES

Archetype

Without taking sides, the granddaughter serves as consummate match-maker, complete with unsigned notes to each grandparent and a secretly planned rendezvous for their reunion.

She listens to their grievances. She asks pertinent questions. "Don't you like Grandma anymore?" "It's not that simple," Grandpa responds. "We're just so different." She asks Grandma the same question and gets the same response.

She observes how sad each is (hiding tears) without the other. She watches the effect when they reminisce about old photos of themselves together. She notes that each especially has fond memories of ice skating together when they were young.

She takes secret action. She knits them identical scarves of their favorite colors. She secretly delivers to their apartments these gifts and identical unsigned letters setting up a meeting at the ice skating lake.

In secrecy, she watches "a couple dancing on the ice. It was Grandpa and Grandma with their scarves flapping in the wind."

Finally, she sits back and "just smiles" at the fruits of her labor when Grandma later tells her the two "will be going on a trip soon" and she will have to look after the cat while they go to the mountains and to the beach together.

Counterpoint

The granddaughter visits first one and then the other grandparent, noticing how each visit illustrates that though the two are now living separately and at first they happily decorate their apartments to please themselves, and eat what they want to eat, and do what they want to do, there is loneliness. Grandpa looks at old pictures of them together.

At Grandma's house she is also looking at old pictures.

Grandma likes the beach. Grandpa, who does not like the beach, buys beach equipment for a vacation he might take.

Grandpa likes soccer. Though she does not even understand the game, Grandma is, for the first time, watching it on television.

Foreshadow

The granddaughter intends to reunite her grandparents, who seem unhappy being separated. "Grandma and Grandpa still loved each other, that was clear." She knits a scarf for each one using red and blue yarn, their favorite colors. She sends them the scarves along with a note secretly inviting them on a date. The identical letters say, "Sunday afternoon 2:30 at Little Lake. Bring your ice skates."

Inference

As Grandpa shares a photo of himself with Grandma, the granddaughter notices "his eyes twinkling as he stared at one of the pictures."

The granddaughter notices that when Grandma looks at a photo of herself and Grandpa with rosy cheeks, "suddenly Grandma had red cheeks too."

On one of her visits to Grandma's apartment, the granddaughter finds her watching Grandpa's favorite television program. "Since when did Grandma like soccer?"

It is Grandma who longs to go to the beach. It is Grandpa who tells his granddaughter on one of her visits to his apartment that though he can't swim, "I might go to the beach for a vacation."

The granddaughter's matchmaking appears to have been successful. When next she goes to Grandpa's apartment, Grandma is there, eating chocolate pudding he has made for her.

Irony

After the separation, Grandma, who complained that Grandpa didn't leave her enough chocolate pudding, "could eat all she wanted now, but she didn't seem to have any appetite.... Grandma didn't eat one bite."

After the separation, Grandpa, who had complained that Grandma would wake him too early in the morning, "can sleep till noon. Without Grandma it was boring. He looked lonesome and lost sitting there among his houseplants."

Grandpa couldn't swim and never wanted to go to the beach as Grandma wished. But, "at his apartment he proudly showed me his new bathing suit" and says he "might go to the beach for a vacation."

Grandma didn't like winter mountain vacations, but she fondly remembers meeting Grandpa, the "best skater" on the lake, 30 years ago.

Symbol

The granddaughter knits two identical scarves made with her grandparents' favorite two colors. The scarves serve to blend together their differences and knit back their separated lives by reminding the grandparents how they really feel about each other. The fun they once again share on the lake ice skating together with their scarves flapping in the wind cements a recommitment to each other.

*****

Bunting, Eve. *Butterfly House.* Illus. by Greg Shed. New York: Scholastic Press, c1999.

With the help of her grandfather, a little girl makes a house for a larva and watches it develop before setting it free. Every spring after that, butterflies come to visit her.

Curriculum Tie-in: Science (Butterflies—Metamorphosis), Social Science (Family Relationships—Grandparents/Grandchildren)

Art Style: Dreamy *Impressionism* in genteel gouache on canvas

DEVICES

Atmosphere

An ethereal mood of lovingly shared mutual interests is expressed both through text and art. "I saw a small black creature like a tiny worm and saved it from a greedy jay, who wanted it for lunch." Grandfather and granddaughter work together to create temporary living quarters for the creature. Later they move the chrysalis from a glass jar to a box home. The girl had made "a painted garden in a box, so she'd see beauty as she hung in that half sleep ... inside the chrysalis that kept her hidden from the world."

Connotation

The narrator enjoys being in her garden and having the butterflies *kiss* her with a *painted* wing. The colorful creatures touch her as they fly past.

Flash-Forward

"So many years have passed. I am as old as Grandpa was that spring when I was young. I live in the house that was his."

Imagery

"... green with tops of trees that seemed to sway in soundless air."
"A place of flowers and space and waiting stillness...."
"... came out, drooped, limp and slack, with crumpled wings."
"... watched her falter as she felt the first warm touch of sun, saw trees, felt breezes brush across her wings...."
"When I walk they flutter by to kiss me with a painted wing."

Internal Rhyme

"A human face so big and scary, strange and starey...."
"... cone flowers, purple-blue, and marigolds, lantana, bright as flame, and thistle, too."
"... so her wings could dry once she became a butterfly."
"... all spotted, orange, black, and brown as if someone had shaken paints and let the drops fall down."
"... too far back to say, was saved from being eaten by a jay."

Paradox

The young girl thinks how remarkable it is that both she and her grandfather, when he was at her age now, had both been interested in raising a butterfly. She is moved to say, "We would have been best friends if I'd been there back then." Her grandfather replies, "It worked out anyhow. We're best friends now." They didn't have to be children together for an enduring friendship.

Point-of-View

The girl imagines what it will be like for the emerging butterfly when it comes out of its chrysalis in its box home. "What would she see? A human face so big and scary, strange and starey?"

Later, as a grown woman, she imagines why butterflies are thick in her garden. She believes their ancestor told them the story of "how she was once saved from being eaten by a jay" and how "this young girl made a house for her." So, thereafter, "we visit her each spring to give her back the love she gave to us so long ago."

Simile

"I saw a small creature like a tiny worm . . ."
". . . lantana, bright as flame, . . ."
"I made a curve of rainbow like a hug . . ."
"They float and drift like blossoms."
"Sometimes they cling as though I am a flower myself."
"They fill your air like autumn leaves. . . ."

*****

Bunting, Eve. *One Green Apple.* Illus. by Ted Lewin. New York: (Clarion Books) Houghton Mifflin, c2006.

While on a school field trip to an orchard to make cider, a young immigrant named Farah gains self-confidence when the green apple she picks perfectly complements the other students' red apples.

Curriculum Tie-in: Agriculture (Food Production—Apples), Social Science (Character Development—Self-Confidence), Social Science (Friendship), Social Science (Immigrants)

Art Style: Sun-drenched watercolors in *Impressionism*

DEVICES

Antithesis

"The students know each other, but they don't know me and I don't know them."

"Some are friendly. But some look at me coldly and smile cruel smiles."

"It's not that I am stupid. It is just that I am lost in this new place."

"Laughs sound the same as at home.... It is the words that are strange."
It is my first outside-myself word. There will be more."

Inference

"I hear my country mentioned, not fondly." Farah realizes as an immigrant she faces hostility and suspicion because of having lived in a Muslim country.

Symbol

Farah selects "a tree, shorter than the others, that does not seem to belong. It is small and alone, like me. A few hard green apples hang from its branches. I twist one off." As the children leave the orchard, Farah has come to think, "I will blend with the others the way my apple blended with the cider."

Theme

People the world over are more similar then different in life's basic require-ments. Young Muslim immigrant Farah comes to realize there are comforting similarities between this new land and her old home.

When the dogs at the apple farm crunch apples, "their crunches sound like Haddis's," her own dog's.

"Laughs sound the same as at home. Just the same. So do sneezes and belches and lots of things."

*****

Bunting, Eve. *Pop's Bridge.* Illus. by C. F. Payne. New York: Harcourt, c2006.
> Robert and his friend Charlie are proud of their fathers, who are working on the construction of San Francisco's Golden Gate Bridge.
> **Curriculum Tie-in:** Architecture (Bridge Engineering), History (Golden Gate Bridge, San Francisco, California), Social Science (Character Development—Empathy), Social Science (Ethnic Relations), Social Science (Friendship)
> **Art Style:** Mixed media *Realism* with *Expressionism*

DEVICES

Antithesis

"... there's less talking and joking now among the men. There's a remembering."
"... this wasn't just a job to my pop. He loves the bridge."

Aphorism

"Equal work, equal danger...." The narrator learns no one laborer is more important than another, no one job is more important than any other.

Foreshadow

Before the young narrator's attitude is changed, he can only see the bridge project in personal terms: "My Pop is building the Golden Gate Bridge." His mother reminds him: "There's a crew of more than a thousand men working on that bridge, Robert. Including Charlie's dad." Though the boy says he knows, he "just shrugs." "To me, it's Pop's bridge."

Robert's father is a sky-walker. Charlie's dad is a painter. Not even Robert's father can impress on his son that it takes everyone equally to build the bridge. "If it weren't for the painters starting their job before the bridge is finished, it would rust away." The boy is still dismissive: "I think he's just saying that to be nice. The sky-walkers have the most important job of all." Robert has some awareness growth ahead.

Inference

After the scaffolding failure, the young narrator finally realizes all the bridge builders are vital to the project. "One of those men in the water could have been Pop. Or Charlie's dad. I finally understand, and I feel ashamed."

Metaphor

As the Golden Gate Bridge nears completion, Robert's father sees it as "a harp for the angels to play." The boy notes how "the wind strums its music through the stretch of the cables."

Simile

"... the men cling to the girders like caterpillars on a branch."
The boy's father describes the Golden Gate Bridge "like a giant harp."
The painters swing "in a bosun's chair, like a knot on a rope."

Symbol

It took all the workers equally to make the Golden Gate Bridge a reality. And, while construction has been underway, together the two boys have been building a jigsaw puzzle of the building project, symbolizing their shared goal with the workers. Robert cuts the final puzzle piece in half. "I put a half piece in Mr. Shu's hand and the other in my Pop's. 'Finish it,' I say. 'It's your bridge. It belongs to both of you.'" The boy watches as "the two pieces fit in, so perfectly, so smoothly. 'Team effort,' my Pop says."

Theme

A large goal requires the contribution of all. Each person is equal in value to further the mutual goal.

"We raise our glasses of sarsaparilla to celebrate the laborers and riveters, the carpenters and the painters and the sky-walkers. All the men who worked together to build the most beautiful bridge in the world."

*****

Bynum, Janie. *Nutmeg and Barley: A Budding Friendship.* Cambridge, MA: Candlewick Press, c2006.

Neighbors Nutmeg the squirrel and Barley the mouse believe that they have nothing in common until an emergency forces them to discover surprising things about each other.

Curriculum Tie-in: Social Science (Character Development—Kindness), Social Science (Friendship)

Art Style: Watercolor, pencil, and pastel in charmingly appealing *Expressionism*

DEVICES

Ambiguity

When Nutmeg comes to call on Barley to thank him for the flowers he brought her, she hears a squeaky groan drifting from his window but misunderstands his reply to her question.

She: "Do you need anything?"

He: "Would love some tea!"

Through the whistling wind, Nutmeg thought he said, "Should leave me be!"

Antithesis

"Nutmeg loved bright sunshine and loud thunderstorms to her favorite tune."

"Barley loved cool shade and gentle breezes."

"Every afternoon Barley tended his garden while Nutmeg soaked up the sunshine."

"Every afternoon Nutmeg called to her neighbor, 'Come on up for a visit. The view is delicious!'"

"As usual, Barley just shook his head and went back to weeding, stopping only for a cup of tea—which he sipped alone."

Foreshadow

These two neighbors unknowingly have in common a love of music. Perhaps this will eventually bring them together? Nutmeg "loved to dance to her favorite forest tune." Barley "loved to relax with a little music" at the end of his day.

Parallelism

"Nutmeg opened a book and tried to read. But she couldn't sit still."

"She made her favorite snack—pecan biscuits with tickleberry tea. But she wasn't hungry."

"She built a fire in the old wood stove and brewed some tea for her sick little neighbor."

"She read her favorite books to Barley."

"She sat up with him all night, making sure he was comfortable."

Theme

It's not necessary to have everything in common to be friends. Friendship means putting aside misunderstandings in an emergency.

Here are two "who have a couple of things in common—a love for lively music and their heartfelt friendship."

*****

Chen, Chih-Yuan. *The Featherless Chicken*. Alhambra, CA: Heryin Books, c2006.

    Scorned at first by others, a featherless chicken finds a way to fit in before discovering that his new friends may not be as beautiful as they appear to be.

        Curriculum Tie-in: Social Science (Character Development—Self-Esteem), Social Science (Individuality)

        Art Style: Amusing *Expressionism* in *Folk Cartoons*

DEVICES

Alliteration

"All five chickens squished and squawked. . . ."

"With a whoosh and a whack, the boat flipped."

". . . all the chickens joined him, chortling and cackling . . ."

Archetype

The four feathered birds are snobs. When a lonely featherless bird asks to go boating with them, they reply, " 'Oh no. We don't play with chickens without feathers.' Then they tipped their beaks up high and stepped into their boat."

Connotation

Having fallen in a mud puddle, the now sticky featherless chicken soon becomes covered in leaves and other *random* things that are blown around in the storm. These unlikely adornments are not things generally associated with a chicken's appearance—a spoon, a tin can, and such.

Inference

The dunk in the lake when their boat tips over proves to be a great equalizer. Water has washed over them all. "Everyone stared in horror at each other's bare bodies. They shook their heads in disbelief." Then the featherless chicken suddenly begins to laugh. "And one by one, all the chickens joined him." Obviously each one has been hiding its own featherless condition with equally fake disguises. Now that they are all exposed, there is no reason to act superior.

Internal Rhyme

"One day, the egg jiggled and cracked and wigged and snapped, . . ."

Irony

The featherless chicken accidentally becomes covered with leaves, a tin can hat, and "other random things" when he falls into a mud puddle and these decorations are blown on to him by the wind. His new accidental adornment has suddenly made him appealing to the other chickens. But after overturning in the boat with them, all this new apparel sloughs off in the water. He's bare again. However, the others lose their own finery in the same upset. Now their true status is identical to that of the featherless chicken. No one is superior. They have each resorted to trickery in order to be beautiful. Now, all can only laugh with the featherless chicken at their former, foolish snobbery.

Satire

Seeking after the beautiful people and its attendant ephemeral popularity and celebrity status is playfully shown for the hollow reality it is. The featherless chicken has only to fall into a mud puddle to end up as lovely as those he aspires to join. His decorations are the subject of great admiration. "And that

hat is simply the tops." But, a spill into the lake is all it takes to once again reduce everyone, admired and admiring alike, to their common beginnings.

Serendipity

It appears that a featherless chicken, rejected by his peers, is fortunate to have stumbled into a sticky mud hole on a windy day. He is quickly plastered with random debris. "The four chickens in the boat noticed the featherless chicken's new look." They are impressed. "I've never seen such a gorgeous chicken!" In an instant he has gone from humiliating rejection to celebrity status all because of an accidental fall.

Simile

". . . like an artist, the wind decorated the chicken's muddy body. . . ."
"The leaves fluttered like feathers."

Theme

Seeking acceptance by those who primarily value only outward appearances leads to disappointing and unrewarding ends. But, accepting folks as they are results in satisfying relationships.

Tone

In a mockingly playful manner, the author uses a freak accident with a humble mud puddle and a strong wind to highlight the overrated concept of popularity and beauty. "He looked down at himself. He was beautiful!" The featherless chicken is covered in paper, leaves, "and other random things" that "fluttered like feathers." Now he is suddenly noticed by the other chickens and is invited to join them in a boat ride on the lake. Soon all the wings flapping in the close space "was too much for the featherless chicken's sensitive nose. He let loose an explosive sneeze." The boat overturns, and when "the lake finally grew still, things started to appear. One of them was the featherless chicken, spluttering for breath." Other things floating on the surface turn out to be the result of the collective vanity of all the other chickens, now equally featherless.

Wit/Humor

A featherless chicken, sad at the rebuff he receives from his feathered peers, finds his fortunes improved thanks to an incident involving a mud puddle and a strong wind. A soup can lands on his head, also a dinner fork. The other chickens suddenly find him "gorgeous." "And that hat is simply the tops!"

*****

*Coombs, Kate. *The Secret-Keeper.* Illus. by Heather M. Solomon. New York: (Atheneum Books for Young Readers) Simon & Schuster, c2006.

> The people of Maldinga and the surrounding area bring their deep, dark secrets to Kalli, who keeps them all safe until they become too much for her to bear.
>
> > **Curriculum Tie-in:** Literature (Fairy Tales), Social Science (Character Development—Kindness), Social Science (Neighbor Relationships)
> >
> > **Art Style:** Watercolor, oil, and collage, *Expressionism, Folk* period paintings

DEVICES

Ambiguity

As all the villagers try to revive a frail, secret-laden Kalli by telling her a plethora of good secrets, one of them, the baker, tells the secret-keeper, "I run my business fairly." A farmer calls out, "That's no secret!" Kalli and the baker, however, know it is! "Kalli nods, spring leaves lifting from her hand into the cool air." What the farmer doesn't know is that the baker has made a previous visit to Kalli, at which time the baker shared, "I sell loaves weighing less than full measure." The baker's life has turned around; Kalli's life is on the mend, too.

Connotation

Before falling ill, Kalli had normally enjoyed the quiet time of winter with its *blue shadows*. There were secrets waiting out there that in due time the villagers would be sharing with her come springtime. But, during the respite of cold winter, no heart-breaking secrets came. Soon enough, when the snow was *still thin* and spring nearly arrived, people would inevitably *trudge* to her home again to leave their worrisome secrets.

Foreshadow

The villagers are in despair thinking they are losing their secret-keeper. Then, a child suddenly divulges: "I haven't told anyone yet. I'm going to be a painter when I grow up." The news shocks his mother, "but his father shushed her, and when Kalli opened her thin hands, a butterfly with blue wings flew past the villagers into the matching sky. Kalli smiled." This "good" secret is beginning to have a restorative effect on the village's secret-keeper, so weighed down with the town's secret miseries.

Imagery

"Kalli bought a green bowl with a goblin face and a pitcher the color of a lake in autumn."

"The red and yellow leaves fell, catching in Kalli's hair ..."

"When the snow was still thin and sun sometimes shone, the villagers bundled up and trudged out to the little cottage to murmur their secrets in clouds of breath."

"When the snow grew deep and the wind bayed through the village, they huddled beside their fires, hoarding their secrets till spring."

"The secret-keep had always liked winter with its blue shadows."

"... butterflies pinwheel in the spring air ... children pick violets and the sunrise-colored roses that grow all around Kalli's cottage."

"... innkeeper's face turned poppy-red ..."

"An ancient man creaked up with his wrinkled wife by his side."

"A purple dragonfly rode the breeze."

Inference

Every day villagers "straggled through the woods to the clearing where Kalli's cottage stood." They come to the secret-keeper "one by one, never in twos or threes." Clearly this somber, portentous opening implies there are heavy burdens that are too hard to share with close personal friends or family.

The job of the secret-keeper is also a hard and heavy burden. "The villagers, folk from neighboring towns, and even a few strangers from farther away came to the clearing in search of the secret-keeper. Then they went away, a little lighter of heart." What toll is the keeping of these secrets having on the secret-keeper?

Only the potter's son never tells her a secret. She buys "two plates painted with spring flowers" from him and finds herself returning to his shop. "The other villagers smile politely," but "edged away whenever they saw her in the square." What can life be like for someone who holds other people's most difficult secrets?

Irony

Kalli, the secret-keeper, safeguards everyone's most burdensome secrets. Now it is their turn to help unburden her.

When she falls ill under the unrelenting, crushing responsibility of their sorrows, "for the first time they come to her home in groups of two and three, whispering worriedly." Thinking to relieve her despondency, they decide at long last to share their good secrets with her. The result is a quick recovery. Thereafter, "one morning every spring the villagers gather in the clearing to give her their happiest secrets."

Metaphor

The "secret-keeper" serves as the community's collective conscience. After telling her their troubled concern, they "went away a little lighter of heart" because acknowledging their burden in this "confession" eases them of the woe they had been carrying alone.

Motif

In all seasons, the secrets are delivered to the secret-keeper. People come "when the sun was high and hot." People come "when the snow was still thin and the sun sometimes shone."

Only when "the snow grew deep" did they stay home, "huddled beside their fires, hoarding their secrets till spring."

As soon as "the snow melted at last ... the village folk began to tramp through the mud to knock at Kalli's door."

Serendipity

When life force ebbs low in Kalli, the secret-keeper, the villagers revive her with good secrets. Then the one person who has never shared a secret finally comes forward at last with the best secret of all. "He looked into Kalli's eyes and whispered, 'I love the secret-keeper.'"

Simile

"The secrets are so heavy. Dim and dark and sad, like a child lost in the snow."

"Bright and fair secrets, like a spring morning."

"... a rainbow fluttered out the window like bouquet of flowers."

Symbol

As villagers confide their distressing secret sorrows, Kalli, the secret-keeper, catches the words in her hand. When she opens her hand, each secret has turned into a physical representation of the nature of the secret, which she then dutifully "keeps" in "one of the hundreds of tiny drawers that lined the walls of her cottage." The baker's secret of "selling loaves weighing less than full measure" becomes "a small gray rock, like a stale bread crumb." After good secrets are also shared, these become "a purple dragonfly" or a "robin's egg" that she releases. The potter's secret that he loves the secret-keeper becomes a "sunrise-colored rose" in her hand, symbolizing her newfound happiness.

Tone

One by one each somber tale is told; each sensitive secret is received respectfully. "And so it went—day in, day out.... By and by, all of the villagers had come to talk to Kalli, some more than once."

In the cold they came to "murmur their secrets in clouds of breath."

"Days passed, and the snow melted at last. Still Kalli lay in her bed counting secrets growing pale and sad." Kalli "couldn't imagine anyone without a secret."

A sense of unbearable responsibility is contrasted at last with the uplifting joy of hearing happy secrets. She catches each and releases it in a burst of spring—"a butterfly with blue wings flew past the villagers into the matching sky." "A rainbow fluttered out the window." "Kalli's hand freed a meadowlark." "A green frog hopped through the morning grass." They "filled the morning with laughter and springtime."

*****

Crummel, Susan Stevens. *Ten Gallon Bart.* Illus. by Dorothy Donohue. Tarrytown, NY: Marshall Cavendish, c2006.

> On the day he is supposed to retire as sheriff of Dog City, Ten Gallon Bart learns that Billy the Kid is on his way to devour the town.
>
> **Curriculum Tie-in:** Fine Arts (Western Movies), Social Science (Character Development—Responsibility)
>
> **Art Style:** Energetic, layered, textured paper collage *Expressionism*

DEVICES

Allusion

". . . when Miss Kitty got stuck in a tree, it was Bart to the rescue."

"When Buffalo Gal got her hoof tangled in a fence, it was Bart to the rescue!" (Later that night she responded with a thank-you dance!)

"Billy the Kid" is the "roughest, toughest, gruffest goat in the country."

Sheriff Bart is assisted by his two deputies, "Wild Bill Hiccup" and "Wyatt Burp."

Billy the Kid enters town and immediately begins chomping, but out of nowhere comes Miss Kitty, screeching "like a cat on a hot tin roof."

When it's time for a showdown with Billy the Kid, the outlaw notices Sheriff Bart is the only one confronting him. "Looks like you're the Lone Sheriff to me."

Archetype

Sheriff Bart is "brave, courageous, and bold." When Miss Kitty got stuck in a tree and Buffalo Gal got her hoof tangled in a fence, "it was Bart to the rescue." He'd done his job well. "Dog City was the most peaceful town in the West." And, when Ten Gallon Bart must face the bad guy, it's without town support, even from his own deputies. He sighs, "A dog's gotta do what a dog's gotta do." He's been on the job ten years—"that's seventy in dog years."

Billy the Kid is the "roughest, toughest, gruffest goat in the country." When he steps off the train, he yells, "I'm baa-aa-aa-aa-d!!" He sneers at Bart, "Looks like you're the Lone Sheriff to me." "I see this place is going to the dogs." And, when he chomps the sheriff's hat, he snickers, "Now he's Nine Gallon Bart."

Colloquialism

"felt a heap better"
"mighty brave of you"
"would a hightailed it outta here"
"howl at the moon"
"hogwash"

Connotation

Billy the Kid was dreaded because everywhere he went; he *ravaged* the towns. He ate his way through them.

Inference

Sheriff Bart is displeased with his pig deputies. If they don't come out of the chicken coop, where they're hiding, and get back to work, he warns them, "I'll be fixin' bacon for breakfast."

Sheriff Bart has been butted unconscious by Billy the Kid. When the sheriff comes round, he can't believe his eyes. "Feathers, fur, hair, mohair—flying everywhere." The townspeople have come to his defense and are beating up on the chomping invader.

Internal Rhyme

"He wanted to sleep until noon, howl at the moon . . ."
The mean Billy the Kid would eat anything and everything in his way—
"soap and rope, saddles and paddles, socks and clocks."

Motif

The townspeople assure their old sheriff he "won't be alone." They all promise, "We'll be there. We'll do our part. We're behind you, Sheriff Bart!" When their intentions are put to the test, Sheriff Bart is standing alone to face Billy the Kid.

Parody

Just as in a *Gunsmoke* television western, the noble sheriff must fight off the bad guy alone. But, his reward is respect from the town citizens. Sheriff

Bart slams down his water bowl on the counter of Miss Kitty's place, telling her, "I'm thirsty." His bowl is filled fast.

Miss Kitty admires Sheriff Bart. "Mighty brave of you to stay on the job, Sheriff. I Mean, with Billy the Kid comin' and all. Most dogs would a hightailed it outta here." Sheriff Bart sighs, "A dog's gotta do what a dog's gotta do."

Poetic Justice

Billy the Kid eats his way through western towns. He even chomped Sheriff Bart's ten gallon hat and his star, the symbol of his authority. However, Sheriff Bart rallies and jumps on Billy the Kid's back. The goat starts bucking and coughing. Out flies everything he ate, including his meanness. The town hosts a big celebration and Billy the Kid has to do all the dishes!

Pun

"I see this place is *going to the dogs,*" snarls Billy the Kid . . ."

"*You gotta bone to pick?*" asks Sheriff Bart.

"Billy the kid grabs the sheriff's had and chomps it. 'Now, he's *Nine Gallon Bart!*'"

Miss Kitty lands on Billy the Kid and claws out, "*You old goat!*"

For her bravery during the crisis, Miss Kitty is elected the new sheriff. "*You're no scaredy-cat,*" Bart tells her. "*You're the cat's meow!*"

Before he becomes civilized, he's "*b-a-a-a-a-d*" Billy the Kid; after his defeat, he's "*glaa-aa-aa-aa-d*" to help!

To help rid the town of the goat menace, Sheriff Bart has a couple of *hefty porkers* as deputies. These pigs hide in the chicken coop pretending to be roosters. "*Hogwash!* A couple of *chickens* is more like it," pronounces the sheriff.

Solecism

"hightailed it outta here"

"gotta do"

"fixin' breakfast"

Stereotype/Reverse Stereotype

Like any retiree, Ten Gallon Bart, long-time sheriff of Dog City, receives a going-away present for his many years of faithful service—a fishing pole for the R&R time ahead.

Typically, Sheriff Bart is "brave, courageous, and bold." When confronted with duty, he steps to the plate—"'A dog's gotta do what a dog's gotta do.' He'd done his job and done it well. Dog City was the most peaceful town in the West."

In typical bronco-busting style, Sheriff Bart jumps on the back of Billy the Kid, riding the "meanness right out of him."

Despite assurances of support, the townspeople run at the critical moment, leaving their sheriff to face the menace alone. Finally, seeing their brave leader down, they are bestirred to rally and come to his defense. The sheriff can't believe his eyes. "Feathers, fur, hair, mohair—flying everywhere." Billy the Kid is being trounced.

Tone

Ten Gallon Bart had been sheriff of Dog City ten years—"That's seventy in dog years."

Billy the Kid would sweep through towns eating everything. "You name it, he ate it."

To replace the retiring sheriff, Miss Kitty was elected—"paws, hooves, and wings down."

After coughing out all the stuff he ate in the towns he ravaged, Billy the Kid "felt a heap better."

Wit/Humor

Sheriff Bart needs the help of his two deputies, *a couple of hefty porkers.*
"Feathers, fur, hair, mohair—flying everywhere."

As a sign of the town's respect for their law enforcement officer, when Sheriff Bart "*slams his bowl*" on the counter of Miss Kitty's place and declares he's thirsty, she fills it with water fast.

Ten Gallon Bart has been sheriff of Dog City ten years—"*That's seventy in dog years.*"

"*Why, Miss Kitty was elected—paws, hooves, and wings down.*"

After coughing out all the stuff he ate, the goat "*felt a heap better.*" Bart had ridden that "*meanness right out of him.*"

*****

*Cullen, Lynn. *Moi & Marie Antoinette.* Illus. by Amy Young. New York: Bloomsbury Publishing, c2006.

Sébastien relates the life of Marie Antoinette as she goes from being a teenager devoted to him, her pug dog, to becoming the queen of France and mother to two children.

Curriculum Tie-in: History (Marie Antoinette, Queen, 1755–1793, France), Social Science (Character Development—Empathy), Social Science (Character Development—Self-Esteem)

Art Style: *Expressionistic* gouache *Naive* period paintings

DEVICES

Archetype

In a futile attempt to seek happiness, the young queen heir-apparent, Antoinette, mistakes endless indulgence with peace and satisfaction. "A swarm of tiresome ladies woke her each day, dressed her as if she were a doll ... decked out in more layers than a royal wedding cake." She "tried smothering herself in jewels, and when that did not suit, she teased and tugged and tortured her hair into a towering pouf. Her hair was so high that whenever she dashed off to one of her dazzling parties, she had to kneel on the floor of the carriage."

Atmosphere

Self-absorbed, wry humor marks the dog's narration of his life with beloved Antoinette.

"I was besting Antoinette at tug-of-war with some freshly stolen underpants, . . ."

"We both knew that neither thunder nor the dark was the least bit foolish. We were scared to pieces of them."

The dog learns from Antoinette's mother that the King of France wishes the girl to marry his grandson, who will eventually be king himself. "This news was not as exciting as tender morsels of chicken, but I would have to make do."

"As I grew from a darling pup into a handsome dog, Antoinette was told to stop skipping and taught to glide like a queen."

Counterpoint

Antoinette and her dog are best buddies. Then, one day the Empress calls her, asks her a series of questions, and life forever changes. Many years later, now queen herself, Antoinette asks her own daughter, young Therese, those same questions as reported by faithful Sébastien. The questions remain disturbingly familiar to those the Empress asked of the young princess those many years ago before she was swept off to France. Her daughter's responses, according to the beloved family pet, seem to be the same as were Antoinette's.

" 'Therese, for a child of six, you look small. Have you been eating your fish?' I knew that, like me, she hated anything that had once swum."

" 'Do you allow yourself to be properly washed and combed each day?' Like me, she was naturally stunning and had little need for grooming."

" 'Are you afraid of thunder, or the dark, or any such foolish thing?' Even if Therese had not been squeezing me tight, I could have scarcely breathed. I had heard these words before."

" 'Do you wish for true happiness child?' If only I could squirm loose and warn her: no, no, a thousand times NO!" The child declares, "I have

Sébastien." And, that is enough for her. There will be no traveling to a foreign land for this child.

Foreshadow

As narrated by the pet dog: "Antoinette looked up from her cards. She seemed surprised to see me. Was that a smile I spied before she turned to her daughter?" She soon launches into the same questions that her own mother had asked her before she was wheeled off to France, never to come home again. But, will these questions of young Therese lead to the same fate that befell the mother, or does the smile that Sébastien detects indicate Antoinette is merely in a teasing frame of mind? Perhaps this time there will be a difference in the outcome?

Hyperbole

"Off to France she went, accompanied by one hundred ladies, two hundred servants, three hundred horses. . . ."

"Time passed—enough for a thousand glittering nights to swirl by . . ."

"Not a thousand sweet treats nor a million soft pillows could bring the joy that spilled from my grateful heart."

Inference

". . . perhaps when I am queen and not merely a princess, I shall be happier." The glitter of a royal lifestyle is not making the young Antoinette wish she had come to France.

"Now that I am queen, . . . I may do things my own way. Then I shall be happy." The passage of time has not changed her initial feelings about this foreign land.

Eventually, dog and queen do find happiness together, but not until the queen's child intervenes. Young Therese declares she is happy right where she is. "I have Sébastien." The dog licks "Therese's dear cheek" in appreciation. But, then, realizing the mother will not separate them as he feared, and realizing the mother is the source of their mutual newfound happiness, "I gave Antoinette my paw."

Motif

It is Antoinette, of history, who is remembered. But, it is her faithful Sébastien who enlightens us about her life—and his role in it.

"Off to France she went, accompanied by [an entourage] . . . and *moi*."

Just before entering her new adopted country, Antoinette's things are taken away, but, "she'd hardly made it in into France before she was slipped the only reminder of her past . . . *moi*."

As she marries the young heir to the French throne, "few knew that under her diamond-covered skirt there quaked a certain fine creature . . . *moi*."

"I was prepared to nip his lace-covered ankles—until I noticed his face. He was more terrified than . . . *moi*!"

The dog feels neglected at the new palace. "Play with *moi*! I barked. Play with *moi*! *Moi*! *Moi*!"

"Just when I thought it could be no worse, Antoinette gave birth to a baby. Why would she do such a thing? She had *moi*!"

The first baby grows. Another baby comes. Little Therese, the first child, complains to the dog. "'Mama had another baby today. A boy. Now she will never have time for me.' Humpf, I sniffed. The child thought she had troubles. What about *moi*?"

Finally, there is resolution. "As we three gathered close, I knew someone who had found at last the truest of happiness: *moi*."

Parallelism

"Antoinette held me close. Like me, she hated the taste of anything that had once swum."

"Antoinette hugged me closer. Like me, she was naturally stunning and felt little need to be groomed."

Point-of-View

"You would think life would be perfect for two adorable creatures such as Antoinette and myself."

When Antoinette's mother asked her if she wished for true happiness, Sébastien opines, "If the empress was offering soft pillows or tender morsels of chicken, of course we wanted them. I licked Antoinette's face in encouragement."

Before entering France and her new life, Antoinette was stripped of her possessions. "Naked as a newborn pup, she stepped into clothes befitting a French queen."

"She put up such a fuss, she'd hardly made it into France before she was slipped the only reminder of her past, *moi*."

Serendipity

During a moment of mutual despair, Sébastien and young Therese bemoan their abandonment together. A clap of thunder frightens them both. "The child latched onto my lovely self. . . . The child shuddered, then buried her face in my fur."

Therese reveals something else in common with the dog. "I hate fish!"

She proves herself adept at the same games her mother used to play with him. Sébastien gave her an acorn. "Her mother would have known just what to do with it, but would this child? Good heavens, the child could throw!" At last, Sébastien finds happiness again.

Simile

"... naked as a new-born pup."

"... shaking like a royal rattle, he placed a ring on Antoinette's finger."

"She soon had my Antoinette decked out in more layers than a royal wedding cake."

"I retreated to the park, as forgotten as yesterday's bone."

Surprise/Twist-in-the-Tail

It would seem that poor little Therese might end up going to a foreign land and living just as unhappily as had little Antoinette before her. Sébastien is witness to the same questions of Therese that had once preceded Antoinette's being sent away to a new life. But, there is a twist in the tale. When her mother asks little Therese if she wishes for true happiness, the child declares, "I have Sébastien. I *am* happy." The mother smiles. No one will be sent away. Sébastien is overjoyed. He has his beloved Antoinette and now her daughter, Therese, too.

Wit/Humor

"As I grew from a darling pup into a handsome dog, Antoinette ... had to quit playing with dolls and start playing the harp. I myself was already perfect."

"For weeks, we trundled down muddy roads lined with cheering townspeople. I thought my tail would uncurl from boredom."

When the dog and girl first see the palace that will be their new home, "Antoinette is sure she will be happy there.... Until I tasted the chicken, I would reserve my judgment."

"But, being married to the future king was not all juicy snacks and squishy pillows."

Said Sébastien, "I was left to gnaw on chair legs and water the statues." and "I made great sport on the palace lawn with the king's best wig."

*****

da Costa, Deborah. *Snow in Jerusalem.* Illus. by Cornelius Van Wright & Ying-Hwa Hu. Morton Grove, IL: Albert Whitman, c2001.
    Although they live in different quarters of Jerusalem, a Jewish boy and a Muslim boy are surprised to discover they have been caring for the same stray cat.

Curriculum Tie-in: Geography (Jerusalem Living Quarters—Muslim, Christian, Jewish, Armenian), History (Jerusalem—Jews, Muslims), Social Science (Character Development—Empathy), Social Science (Friendship), Social Science (International Peace Relations)

Art Style: Watercolor and pencil *Impressionism*

DEVICES

Connotation

When the two boys meet, they are mutually jealous of each other's relationship with the white cat. They are tensely uncertain how to relate to each other. Silence *crackled* in the air between them.

Counterpoint

When the Jewish boy's mother sees him feeding a stray white cat, she remarks, "Avi, my love, are you feeding that cat again? We'll never get rid of it now!"

Avi believes the cat is a miracle, "a gift from Hashem, the Holy One." Each time the creature pads away, he wonders where she goes. "Next time I will follow you!"

When the Muslim boy's mother sees him feeding this same stray white cat, she says, "Hamudi, my darling, are you feeding that cat again? It will never leave us now!"

Hamudi knows the cat is a miracle, "a gift from Allah!" Each time it pads off, he wonders where it's going. "Next time I will follow you!"

When the cat does not return, "Avi worried." "Hamudi worried."

Imagery

"The silver mezuzah in the doorframe above him sparkled in the sunlight."

The cat "ducked into shaded, cobbled alleyways and pranced through sunlit courtyards fragrant with the sweet smell of rosemary."

". . . narrow streets were filled with shiny brass pots, colorful plates, and tapestries the color of fire."

"Snowflakes floated gently through the air, swirling and twirling on their way to earth."

". . . rubbed the fuzzy velvet tummy of one kitten."

". . . many other cats, skinny cats with wild, hopeless eyes . . . all had bony ribs and patchy fur."

The cat "sat in the feathery whiteness. She sniffed at the crisp, cold air."

Simile

"... fear like a dark cloud, began to follow them...."
"... faint sound like the muffled whine of the wind."
"... big eyes as clear and blue as the sea."

Symbol

The Jewish boy Avi and the Muslim boy Hamudi represent their respective national ethnic differences by quarreling over the same white cat. One boy from the Jewish Quarter and another from the Muslim Quarter chase a cat through the streets of the Christian Quarter and eventually find the animal in the Armenian Quarter. But, their mutual need to care for this vulnerable animal brings them together in a cooperative effort. This mother cat shows them the way by affectionately rubbing against both boys.
"She does not want us to fight."
"She wants peace."
"Then we will share."
Together the two head back to their homes in the Old City of Jerusalem, "the place some call the Center of the Universe."

Theme

Cooperation leads to mutual benefits.

*****

Danziger, Paula. *Barfburger Baby, I Was Here First.* Illus. by G. Brian Karas. New York: (Penguin Young Readers Group) G. P. Putnam's Sons, c2004.
Five-year-old Jonathan is not pleased when neighbors and relatives come to visit and admire his new baby brother.
Curriculum Tie-in: Social Science (Character Development— Empathy), Social Science (Character Development—Self-Esteem), Social Science (Family Relationships—Cousins), Social Science (Family Relationships—Siblings), Social Science (Jealousy)
Art Style: Gouache and acrylic pencil *Cartoons*

DEVICES

Inference

Jonathan isn't sure he's convinced that his relationship with the baby is headed for improvement based on his Aunt Patty's comments and what he observes.

She says, "Remember when the twins were born ... how unhappy Charlie was when they came home? Look at them now. They get along so much better." The twins and Charlie are making faces at each other.

Aunt Annie isn't helping Jonathan's mood when she whispers to him, "You'll always be my Jonathan Pookie Bear." He crashes his new toy truck.

Jonathan is learning to respond to family comments with self-confidence and self-respect. He told his family that from now on he's "just Jonathan," not Jonathan Pookie Bear. That remark earns sarcasm from his cousin Charlie, who mocks him: "Hey Jonathan! Just Jonathan." But, Jonathan doesn't react to the taunt: "I just run my truck over his foot."

Irony

Developing a bit of empathy for baby Daniel because of what he's had to endure with his own nickname, he turns over to the baby his Winnie Pookie Bear, along with the Pookie Bear moniker. And, he promises that if they get along, he'll even teach him how to say GRRRRR like he does when Daniel, too, is feeling frustrated.

Jonathan earns cousin Charlie's newfound respect when he builds a Lego town that even the older boy admires. The two become closer to equals as they build together. Charlie tells Jonathan that now he's a big brother, too, they could start a Big Brother Club.

Motif

Whenever Jonathan doesn't like what older people say, he makes a special "Grrrr ... Grrrr" to show his feelings. "Double Grrrrr" when big cousin Charlie and the twins giggle and tease him: "Jonathan Pookie Bear has no hair ... and he's bare!"

When Jonathan's self-confidence improves enough to share Winnie Pookie Bear with the baby, he's even willing to teach him the useful "Grrrrr" coping strategy.

To build up his own self-esteem, Jonathan does so at the expense of the vulnerable baby, denigrating his importance with insulting, belittling nicknames like "Barfburger" Baby when he spits up and "Gasburger," "Spaceblobburger," "Giggleburger," "Poopburger," "Sneezeburger," "Snotburger," and "Yuckburger."

✻✻✻✻✻

Edwards, Pamela Duncan. *The Mixed-Up Rooster.* Illus. by Megan Lloyd. New York: HarperCollins Children's Books, c2006.

Ned the rooster is fired from his job because he cannot wake up in the morning, but he restores his reputation after discovering his usefulness as a night-watch bird.

Curriculum Tie-in: Social Science (Character Development—Courage), Social Science (Character Development—Respect), Social Science (Individuality)
Art Style: Humorous *Expressionism* in *Cartoons*

DEVICES

Foreshadow

Because he's hiding his eyes during a game of hide-and-seek, Ned, the rooster, doesn't notice "one of the rabbits had raised its white bobtail, signaling danger." When he looks, it is dark and silent and his playmates have all run away. Ned is left to face the henhouse threat alone.

Parallelism

"He played tag with the bats.
He danced ring-around-the-rosy with the rabbits.
He sang with the tree frogs."

Pun

Ned couldn't wake up promptly in the morning, and so he failed to get the day going for the henhouse crowd. "Then Ned became a real *night bird* [night owl]."

Daisy Mae, the hen, "gave him a sharp peck" to wake up rooster Ned. He falls back asleep; she pecks him again. Tired of prodding him to do his morning duty, she fires him. Ned replies, "Okay then. I've had enough of this *henpecking*. I'm off!" He adds, "It's not worth getting your *feathers ruffled*."

Serendipity

Because Ned happens to be awake at night when the rest of the henhouse residents are asleep, he is in a position to notice the black snake slithering toward the open henhouse door toward the eggs. Ned raises the alarm, while the other birds are asleep, including the new rooster, who was hired only for wake-up duty. After averting disaster, Ned has gained new respect. Daisy Mae says, "I've got a much better job for Ned." He is quickly hired as head of night security.

Stereotype/Reverse Stereotype

Though a rooster, Ned is not an early riser. The hens get a late start each day on their egg production because Ned doesn't get them started at break of day. Ned is fired for his "laziness." He prefers to stay up late at night and sleep during the day. But, he proves to have a use after all. Thanks to being awake at night, he was able to sound the alarm when danger threatened the sleeping birds. So, he becomes the henhouse night guard, a job much better suited to his unique biorhythm.

Theme

There is value in the contributions made, also, by individualists, who are different from the norm. Daisy Mae recognizes and rewards a rooster unable to wake up at the right time, because he can safeguard the henhouse during the other hours of the day.

Wit/Humor

Humorous interaction among the henhouse crowd makes for lively, entertaining dialogue. Disgruntled hen Daisy Mae gives rooster Ned a sharp peck. "Take that you lazy rooster. What happened to heralding the dawn? Cock-a-doodle-doo and all that stuff?" He snores. She's had it. "You're fired. You're ruining my egg business."

*****

Eversole, Robyn. *The Gift Stone.* Illus. by Allen Garns. New York: Alfred A. Knopf, c1998.

Jean, who lives underground in an Australian opal-mining town, finds a precious stone that makes it possible to realize her dream of once again living in a house with a pointed roof and windows.

Curriculum Tie-in: Geography (Australia—Opal Mining), Science (Opal Gemstone), Social Science (Character Development—Generosity)

Art Style: Oil pastel *Realism* in earth hues replicate an environment of dust and rock.

DEVICES

Antithesis

"Aunt Grace says it is my opal," but "Dad says it isn't."
"I think I'll sell the opal.... But, then I decide I won't."

Aphorism

"The opal was a lovely present," Grandma says, "but having you here will be an even better present for me." Loved ones trump material possessions.

Atmosphere

A sense of monotones overlaid with dust permeates the restless girl's perception of the home where she lives. Describing her community, the narrator says, "The walls are rock, streaked rust-orange and white, the doorways are rock, the floors, everything is cool, hard rock."

The longing for a regular house is evident. "We used to live in a house with a pointed roof and windows, and grass outside, down in South Australia."

Connotation

The arid gray landscape has lost its bright colors, which seem to all be "*trapped* inside the beautiful opal" and nowhere else in the girl's environment. Instead of the colors of lush greenery and flowers that ought to have been present, the only place color can be found is inside the stone.

Inference

The narrator finds something of great value:. "I see something gleam down there, just where the baseboard would be if this were a real house."

Aunt Grace's housekeeping diligence is at issue: "I can tell she thinks it means bad housekeeping to have an opal in your wall and not know it." But, Uncle Peter saves face: "I'd bet your Aunt Grace has scrubbed away a good bit of wall to get at that opal." The narrator thinks: "That makes Aunt Grace feel better."

For a moment, ownership of the opal is uncertain. Jean's father declares, "We can't accept such a present." Uncle Peter says, "Don't be ridiculous! Jean found it. It's hers!" Jean notes: "I'm glad Dad decides not to be ridiculous."

Irony

Jean would like nothing better than to leave the mining community and live above ground in a real house. After she finds the opal, at first she thinks she will sell it and spend the money. Then, she decides to keep it in a matchbox until the day the family takes a trip to Adelaide, where her grandparents live.

When her grandmother sees the opal that Jean gives her, her mouth opens "like something blooming." Later, Jean remarks that "living here is like living in an opal." Her grandmother "gets this thoughtful look and nods, and tucks the opal into her purse and doesn't look at it anymore." Jean hears later that night "her and Dad up late talking."

The next day, the narrator says, "the opal has turned into schoolbooks and clothes and a spare bed." Jean will be staying with her grandparents in a real house, after all. The opal she could have spent on herself, instead of giving it away, has, in fact, been spent on her.

Metaphor

The narrator likes finding bits of opals because "when you stare into one, you see colors—colors you don't see anywhere else in Coober Pedy. It's like all the bright green and purple and red that we ought to have out here got trapped inside rock." Except for the deeply iridescent colors visible in the opal gemstone, there is nothing colorful where she lives. The opal represents the only source of color she sees.

Motif

Because it is largely lacking in her environment, the narrator is fixated on color, referencing ordinary things and experiences in her life through colorful images. Her grandmother's mouth opens "like something blooming" when she first sees the opal Jean gives her.

She associates color with houses that have windows and grass yards. Looking out her grandparents' window, she sees "Grandma's roses and the trees outside, all greener than anything in Coober Pedy."

When at last Jean is living in a "real house," she even lifts bugs up that come "burrowing up from their homes underground. I let them come onto my hand . . . so they can see everything, too."

Parallelism

". . . my dad in the proper mine . . ."
". . . me in the rock piles . . ."

Simile

Looking deeper and deeper into an opal is "a little like looking out a window."

". . . her mouth opens like something blooming."

Living in town "is like living inside an opal."

Symbol

The narrator equates her grandparents' town to "living inside an opal—the biggest, brightest opal there ever was." The town is as colorful as an opal with "houses that have yards and pointed roofs and flower gardens."

*****

Fleming, Candace. *Muncha! Muncha! Muncha!* Illus. by G. Brian Karas. New York: Atheneum Books for Young Readers, c2002.

> After planting the garden he has dreamed of for years, Mr. McGreely tries to find a way to keep some persistent bunnies from eating all his vegetables.

Curriculum Tie-in: Agriculture (Food Production—Gardens), Social Science (Character Development—Perseverance)
Art Style: Humorous gouache and acrylic with pencil *Cartoons*

DEVICES

Allusion

Similar to another tale, Mr. *McGreely*, like Mr. *Mcgregor*, has no luck thwarting vegetable-loving, garden-robbing rabbits.

Aptronym

Increasingly frustrated by persistent rabbits, who continue to raid his garden despite his countermeasures, Mr. McGreely labels them ever more harshly: bunnies, puff-tails, twitch-whiskers, flop-ears.

Irony

Mr. McGreely is diligent about foiling the persistent bunnies. He spends much time and energy erecting barriers against their entrance and ends up unwittingly carrying them inside his garden, after all. They hide in his harvesting basket and have a free ride right to the vegetables.

Motif

The rabbits get into the garden, and soon Mr. McGreely hears them: "Muncha! Muncha! Muncha!" He is driven to ever more desperate measures to keep them out. But, each time, they find a way in: "Muncha! Muncha! Muncha!" Finally, the big block wall seems to have thwarted them at last. But, when Mr. McGreely reaches into his harvesting basket for a snack: "Muncha! Muncha! Muncha!" The rabbits have been carried into the garden inside the basket and are enjoying the vegetables he puts in it.

Onomatopoeia

This is a cumulative tale of relentless assaults by three rabbits determined to get at garden vegetables, regardless of the barriers erected against them. Once inside, it's: "Muncha! Muncha! Muncha!"
First, over a small wire fence: "Tippy-tippy-tippy, pat!"
Next, over a taller fence: "Spring-hurdle, Dash! Dash! Dash!"
Then, under a tall wooden wall: "Dig-scrabble! Scratch! Scratch! Scratch!"
Then, through a deep wet trench: "Dive-paddle. Splash! Splash! Splash!"
Finally, a huge block barrier: "Tippy-tippy-tippy-STOP!"

Parallelism

"Gnawed sprouts . . ."
"Nibbled leaves . . ."
"Chewed stems . . ."
"Chomped blossoms . . ."

Surprise/Twist-in-The-Tail

The huge block barrier wall Mr. McGreely has erected has finally stopped the bunnies. They hop away. But, not for long. The next day they discover a different way to access the garden vegetables. Mr. McGreely carries his basket into the garden and fills it with vegetables. He reaches in under the towel "for something yummy." He's startled to hear "Muncha! Muncha! Muncha!" The bunnies have enjoyed a free ride to the free goodies at last.

*****

*Frank, John. *The Toughest Cowboy, or How the Wild West Was Tamed.* Illus. by Zachary Pullen. New York: Simon & Schuster Books for Young Readers, c2004.

>   Uncouth cowboys are inspired by a miniature French poodle to improve their circumstance.
>
>   **Curriculum Tie-in:** History (Wild West, United States), Literature (Tall Tale), Social Science (Character Development—Self-Improvement)
>   **Art Style:** Character-oriented oil-painted *Expressionism*

DEVICES

Allusion

After tossing pie plates to Foofy, the poodle, Grizz opens his own business in town manufacturing flying plates. "He branded his first name and last initial on the bottom of each one—Grizz B—and before long folks were lining up all across the frontier to buy his product."

Ambiguity

"Cowboy Grizz points out the flaws in his fellow cowboys," such as using your fingers to "pick your noses." Cowboy Lariat thinks Grizz is only addressing him. "Didn't know I had more'n one nose."

After retiring from cow herding, sometimes Grizz "still liked to drive cattle across the open range." The illustration shows Grizz driving in an open motorcar with a long-horned cow (goggles over its eyes) riding along with him in the seat with Foofy, the poodle.

Aptronym

Grizz *Brickbottom* was the toughest cowboy ever. He has a buddy named *Chuck Wagon*, the cowboys' cook. Cowboy *Lariat* threw the fastest rope in the Wild West. Cowboy *Bald Mountain* is the biggest bronco-buster this side of the Rockies. The camp dog is *Foofy*, the miniature poodle.

Atmosphere

Grizz is disgusted with his fellow cowboys for their unappetizing personal habits. He watches the "other cowboys wiping their mouths on their sleeves and digging at their teeth with their fingernails."

Then life for the cowboys changes because of Foofy, the miniature poodle, who is given regular baths. "They became so fond of the smell of soap that they even move to town, just so they can take regular warm baths themselves."

Colloquialism

The cowboys are shocked to see Foofy the miniature poodle catch a hurled tin plate before it hits the ground. "Well, I'll be dipped in horse droppings," says Grizz. "Before you could say 'Don't squat with your spurs on,' the cowboys were jostling to toss the tin plate for Foofy."

"... Grizz must have rubbed against a lucky horseshoe ..."

"All you buckaroos've got the same bad habits. And it's high time we hitched up with someone who don't."

Foreshadow

Foofy may not be a proper kind of cowboy dog. After an afternoon of lesson, "Grizz came back dragging his heels, Foofy padding behind." He pronounces the dog "ain't of a mind to herd cattle." But, he predicts, "it's nothin to fret over, though. After supper I'm gonna teach her to chase mountain lions." Then "a mouse popped out of a hole in the ground and scurried past Foofy." She lets out a whimper and "ran and hid behind Bald Mountain."

Hyperbole

The toughest cowboy on the open range could drink "a quart of Tabasco sauce a day, flossed his teeth with barbed wire, and kept a rattlesnake in his bedroll to cool his feet at night." He "could grind a branding iron into a belt buckle—with the stubble on his chin." He ate a hearty supper of "fried boots and lizard gizzards." He used a "spur to scrape the gnats out of his nostrils." He leaned "against a cactus" to relax.

"The campfire crackled and a spark leaped into the air. Lariat grabbed a rope, tied the end into a tiny noose, swung the rope over the flames—and lassoed the spark before it could hit the ground."

"Bald Mountain heaved the plate so far that it looked as if it might knock the evening star right out of the sky."

Inference

Though declaring they won't cater to a dog of such trivial worth, after learning Foofy the poodle loves to chase and bring back tin plates, Chuck Wagon wants to "cook her the finest supper that's ever been made." Bald Mountain booms, she won't be going to bed "before I've brushed her hair!" And Lariat wants "that hair shinin' like silk when I tie my ribbons in it." The dog seems to have changed their hard stance against her.

Irony

Grizz is determined to get a camp dog to chase off bobcats and mountain lions. Instead, he brings in Foofy, who is frightened of a mouse, and who so thoroughly changes the cowboy lifestyle that they move to town, where mountain lions and bobcats aren't a problem anyway.

Parallelism

Cowboy Grizz realizes something is missing in his life: "Someone with silky hair. Someone with a lovely smell. Someone who would give him lots of sweet kisses."

Before the cowboys discover Foofy's special pie-plate catching talent, they can't be bothered with her needs. That dog can comb "her own dang hair" and tie "her own dang ribbons" and fix "her own dang meals." Even Foofy's owner is disappointed with her. Grizz calls her to task. "A dang cow ain't gonna hurt you!"

Then the cowboys see for themselves Foofy's special skill: "Bald Mountain dropped his jaw. Lariat dropped his rope. Chuck Wagon dropped his finger from his nose."

Pun

Chuck Wagon picks his nose when he makes dinner so he can "smell when the food was done cookin'." Grizz tells him he would "druther you stick to pickin' your guitar."

Grizz says his new dog can ride up front with him. Chuck Wagon isn't sure it's a good idea to have a "horse with a dog on it." Grizz says that will be a good name for the dog. "I'll call 'im Dog-On-It."

Cook Chuck Wagon is surprised at the kind of dog Grizz has selected for the camp dog. He shows his dismay by stomping his boot on the ground.

"Doggone it." Cowboy Lariat notes how smart the dog is: "He's already learnin' his name."

"You can't teach an old cowpoke new tricks. But a dog—that's another story."

Simile

Grizz was feeling "ornery as a bull with a blow-fly in his ear."

Bald Mountain is "tall as a house."

The cowboys watch the new dog disapprovingly, arms crossed, "sour as unripe prickly pears."

The plate "spun across the sky, level as a silver dollar on a poker table." And, "quick as a jackrabbit, Foofy took off after the plate."

"By sundown they were having more fun than a Young'un-of-a-Wrangler at his first rodeo."

"... a good song would be like a breath of fresh air."

Solecism

"ain't of a mind to herd cattle"

"ain't gonna hurt you"

"gonna teach her to chase mountain lions"

"hitched up with someone who don't"

"shinin' like silk"

"got no upbringing"

Stereotype/Reverse Stereotype

Grizz is "the toughest cowboy ever to drive a herd of cattle across the range."

Foofy, the camp dog expected to herd cattle and keep them safe from mountain lions, is a miniature poodle.

"After a long day on the dusty trail," Grizz enjoys listening "to Chuck Wagon's lonesome song."

Grizz complains that his companions are typical cowboys: "You got no upbringing. You ain't had a bath in six months, you never heard of a napkin, and you use your fingers to clean your teeth and pick your noses."

Tone

Cowboy manners are best suited to isolated camp life. Chuck Wagon objects to Grizz's characterization of their having worse manners than a dog: "If I didn't pick my nose while fixin' supper, I couldn't smell when the food was done cookin'."

Bald Mountain without his hat on "didn't have much of a roof on top. 'I don't know how to use a hairbrush!'"

Understatement

The cowboys watch Grizz try to teach Foofy how to chase off mountain lions. When a mouse runs past her, she hides behind one of the cowboys. "Better be a pretty small mountain lion," suggests another cowboy.

Wit/Humor

Grizz realizes something is missing in his lonely cowboy camp life. He needs someone who smelled good, who had silky hair, and who could give him sweet kisses. "He needed . . . a dog!"

The cowboys take umbrage when Grizz declares a dog acts better than they do, what with their nose-picking habits. Chuck Wagon rounds on him: "Now, that ain't fair, Grizz. A dog ain't got any fingers to pick his nose with."

Old cowboys can't change their ways, but a "dog'll be behavin' just the way you want 'im to—herdin' cattle, chasin' off bobcats and mountain lions, takin' regular baths."

*****

*Franklin, Kristine L. *The Gift*. Illus. by Barbara Lavallee. San Francisco: Chronicle Books, c1999.

>A young boy goes fishing with a woman the town considers a witch and not only learns to catch and give away his first salmon, but is blessed by experiencing a pod of whales, along with a lesson in character development.
>
>**Curriculum Tie-in:** Environmental Studies (Fishing), Social Science (Character Development—Empathy), Social Science (Character Development—Generosity)
>
>**Art Style:** Vibrant *Naive Folk* watercolors in glowing sea hues of blue, green, and red

DEVICES

Ambiguity

As Fish Woman and Jimmy Joe set out in their boat, he asks, "What are we after?" She mysteriously returns the question to him, "What are you after?" Taking her literally, he names some common fish his mother can use to make stews. She tells him she "knows something better than stew fish." Again, he thinks literally and suggests a higher grade of fish—salmon. She says she knows something even better than salmon but only grins as they go off to pursue his catch. To the boy, the day will be a simple fishing expedition; to the old woman, the day will become a learning and growth experience for the boy.

Connotation

The boy notes that the sharp smell of gasoline mixed with the salty smell of the ocean comprises what he terms a *fishing* smell. These are the odors he associates with that activity.

Foreshadow

When the trip begins, Fish Woman tells the boy, "I know something better than stew fish ... even better than salmon." Together they will hunt the salmon, but in the background something else awaits the boy, both bigger physically and psychologically.

Jimmy Joe is confident he can handle his fishing gear by himself, but Fish Woman knows differently. "If you hook a salmon, let me know. You'll need help."

The struggle with the fish was over. "It was something to be proud of. But something was wrong." Why wasn't he happier?

Imagery

"Once it had been white. Now it was the soft color of a rain cloud."

"The water made a thick, salty plop as Jimmy Joe's bait and weights disappeared into the bay."

"The water was flat and slick and gray."

"... Jimmy Joe saw nine glossy black backs and sharp dorsal fins ..."

"The Wolves of the Sea don't waste their time on skinny boys and tough old women."

"With one monstrous gulp, it grabbed the fish and dove out of sight. The little boat danced and jumped in its wake."

"The sharp smell of the gasoline mixed with the salty sea. It was a good smell, a fishing smell."

Inference

Jimmy Joe's mother helps him get into clothes suitable for his fishing trip. When he asks her whether Fish Woman knows "everything about the sea," his mother only nods. When he tries to pursue his curiosity about Fish Woman by asking if she is really a sea witch, his mother only smiles and tells him, "Catch a few dozen."

The huge whales come close to the small fishing boat. "Jimmy Joe looked at Fish Woman. Then he looked at the salmon." They agree without words what to do with the fish he caught. He has found a better purpose for taking the salmon's life.

Jimmy Joe earns Fish Woman's respect when he tells her that the sighting of whales is "better than cod or sole or sea perch.... It's better than catching salmon." She grins "so hard her eyes disappeared."

Irony

After finally landing the big salmon in the boat, "Jimmy Joe tried to feel happy. He imagined the surprise on his mother's face when he brought home such a huge fish. But looking at the beautiful, dead fish made Jimmy Joe feel cold inside." What should have been a moment of pride and triumph was tainted with sadness and regret for having been responsible for ending the life force of another creature.

Onomatopoeia

"Pffffest—Haah!" went the sound of air through the whale's blow hole.

Simile

"... tall trees stand guard like soldiers along the shoreline."
"... then Fish Woman heaved the little boat into deep water and hopped aboard as nimbly as a squirrel."
"Jimmy Joe's heart flipped and flopped like the big fish."
"Its skin glittered silver and gold, like a pirate's treasure."
"Pffffest—Haah! went the sound, exhaled through blowholes the size of his fist."
"'What do they want?' asked Jimmy Joe in a voice that quivered like a jellyfish."

Surprise/Twist-in-the-Tail

When the huge whales surround the small fishing boat, Jimmy Joe hears his fishing companion, Fish Woman, "Whisper a single word: 'Welcome.'"

Symbol

Fish Woman represents an awakening to maturity for the child. The "gift" she presents to him is not the chance to bring back his first big sea catch. It is the chance to give away his first big catch and to recognize the value of this offering. Fish Woman will take him out to learn how to land a large fish, but in the process, the boy will learn something more important. He will begin to see his role in life and how best to use his skills. She is a self-appointed fisher of character development in the children of her community.

Fish Woman, who knows her time invested with the boy is not wasted, says to him, "I'm glad you think so, Eyes-Like-Blackberries" when he finds the sighting of the magnificent whales better than "catching salmon."

The two "looked at the salmon. . . . Together they slipped the big fish into the sea." Jimmy Joe has learned a better purpose for taking the salmon's life. It will meet the needs of the great whales.

He has passed an unspoken test of character she had set up for him. The "bigger" thing she sought for him on this fishing expedition—the thing that would be even better than catching his first salmon—turns out to be his realization of the proper ecological relationship humans have with their environment.

Theme

A mysterious Fish Woman has her eye on a child to whom she simply suggests, "Let's go for a boat ride." During the outing the boy not only learns how to land a huge salmon but, more importantly, gains the gift of understanding when to give it away.

*****

Garland, Sherry. *My Father's Boat*. Illus. by Ted Rand. New York: Scholastic Press, c1998.

A Vietnamese American boy spends a day with his father on his shrimp boat, listening as the father describes how his own father fishes on the South China Sea.

Curriculum Tie-in: Career Education (Fisherman), Geography (Vietnam), History (Vietnam War, 1967–1974), Social Science (Family Relationships—Parent/Child)

Art Style: Breathtaking acrylic, watercolor, and chalk seascapes and intimate portraits in *Impressionism*

DEVICES

Antithesis

"... he could not leave the land he loves, and I could not stay."

"Once he was young and strong.... His hair must be gray by now and his eyes growing dim."

Aphorism

"A father never forgets his children, no matter how far away they are or how long they are gone."

"The heart doesn't count the years."

Connotation

The day's work begins early while the sun *still sleeps*. Boats go out before sunrise.

Counterpoint

Lyrical text tenderly explores and contrasts three generations of fishermen, separated by time and sea:

"His rubber boots make squishy noises on the deck. And so do mine as I walk behind him."

"His face is brown and cracked from squinting out the rays.... He gives me the baseball cap from his head to shade my eyes...."

"My father sings songs he learned in Vietnam, and he teaches me the words."

"Your grandfather is a fisherman, too.... He taught me all that I am teaching you."

"I wonder if my grandfather said those same words to my father when he was a boy like me. I wonder if I will say the same thing to my own son one day."

Imagery

"The last stars are fading through heaven's dusty veil and the laughing seagulls are once more on the wing...."

"Early one morning, while the sun still sleeps, ..."

"The whispering wind and slapping waves and soft chug-chug of the engine are the only sounds around us."

"His face is brown and cracked from squinting out the rays of ten thousand suns rising and sinking over the ocean."

Metaphor

"The swirling fog is scary, but my father says it is only dragon's breath ..."

Parallelism

"I wonder if my grandfather's hands are strong and callused, too."

"I wonder if he thinks of us while he sips his steaming tea ..."

"More than the mountains and rivers, more than the waving fields of rice."

"I will show you his beautiful boat, ... I will show him how well you have learned the lessons of a fisherman."

Simile

"... my eyelids are as heavy as curtains of lead."

"Rows of shrimp boats stand out like black skeletons against the sky, ..."

"... men's voices float, deep and hoarse, as if they haven't drunk their morning coffee yet."

"... the mist tingles my face like cool, wet fingers."

Theme

There is connection between the generations despite separation by time and distance. This connection is the lifelong love of working on the water as a fisherman.

*****

Gerstein, Mordicai. *Carolinda Clatter!* New Milford, CT: (Roaring Brook Press) Holtzbrinck, c2005.

> The excessively quiet town of Pupickton and the sleeping lovesick giant upon which it was built are both awakened by the joyful noise of a little girl's songs.
>
> > **Curriculum Tie-in:** Literature (Fairy Tales), Music (Lullabies)
> > **Art Style:** Gloriously spirited pen and gouache *Expressionism* in *Cartoons*

DEVICES

Allusion

In deference to the heavenly orb that is the moon, the earthly giant tries to seduce the moon by singing of their future children—the "pretty planets" they will have and "maybe even a comet or two."

Antithesis

The child's uncaring exuberance is contrasted to the townspeople's fearful silence:

"Carolinda just banged on pots and pans for good measure."

"The people of Pupickton hid under their beds and lived in fear."

Aptronym

The town is quiet until *Carolinda Clatter* is born. Such a name bodes ill for a town devoted to silence. Not only will she be noisy (Clatter), she promises to be musical (Carol-linda).

Counterpoint

The giant sang, "Come dance and marry me."

"But the moon shone coldly and silently and said nothing."

"He begged and pleaded with her."

"But the moon sailed across the sky, waxing and waning . . . and ignored him."

Flash-Forward

"Carolinda grew up, and she and all her children … were famous for their singing. Now visitors come from all over the world to hear the music of the people of Pupickton."

Foreshadow

The townspeople and animals tried to be quiet so as not to disturb the sleeping giant upon which they lived.

"Then, one night, Carolinda Clatter was born." "She was born noisy."

Life for the timid, quiet residents, who live on the chest of the giant, will never be the same.

Hyperbole

"For five thousand years the giant sang and danced for her."

"The giant lay down, looked up at her, and for ten thousand years he raged and wailed, he moaned and wept."

"Over a hundred years, grass grew all over him."

"After ten thousand years, his eyes became two ponds."

"His tears became two waterfalls."

"His beard and the hair on his head became forests."

"After a hundred thousand years, people came."

Internal Rhyme

The giant awakens: "The rumble became a *grumble* … and the grumble became a *tumble* of words."

Irony

Carolinda fearfully goes to the giant to apologize for being noisy all her life and causing him to awaken. But, far from being offended and angry with noise, as the village people had wrongly believed through the generations, he is pleased. They have been unnecessarily quiet. He asks, "Is it you who sings the beautiful songs and makes the beautiful music?" He tells her he hasn't heard music for thousands of years. "It makes me happy!"

Metaphor

The preparation of earth for the habitation of humans is explained in this fairy tale through the changes to the giant's body over the millennia. The "raging" and "wailing" and "weeping" makes the earth's atmosphere supportive for the development of life through creation of air and water. Time passes and grass grows over the giant, his eyes become ponds, his weeping develops water-falls. His beard and hair become forests. Then, "after a hundred thousand years, people came."

Motif

The town residents perceive the outline of a giant human in the landscape terrain upon which their community it located. "Shhhhhhhh! You'll wake the giant." This mantra rules their lives because, according to legend, if ever he awakens, his rage and grief would destroy the town.

Parallelism

"No one laughed. No one wept. No one sang. No one even sneezed."

"The animals were quiet too—no moos or barks. No twitters or chirps."

"Hearing Carolinda, birds began to chirp. Cows began to moo. Dogs barked and howled. Cats yowled."

The giant's words were "so slow and loud and old and rusty."

"Then there were giggles. Then there was laughter and shouting, cheering and applause. Then Carolinda taught them all to sing."

The giant asks, "Would you sing me a song? A sweet, happy song? A soft, soothing song?"

Wit/Humor

The giant fell in love with the moon because "there was no one else large enough for him to love."

He sings to the moon about the kind of future they will share: "We'll have a lovely family of little giants and pretty planets—maybe even a comet or two."

The only sounds in Pupickton "were whispers and the purring of cats."

Carolinda responds to the giant when he praises her beautiful music: "It's just noise. But it's what I love to do."

*****

Goode, Diane. *The Most Perfect Spot*. New York: HarperCollins Children's Books, c2006.

Jack tries to have a perfect picnic with his mother, but things do not turn out as they expected.

Curriculum Tie-in: Social Science (Family Relationships—Parent/Child)

Art Style: Energetic pen-and-ink watercolor *Cartoons*

DEVICES

Foreshadow

The reader easily observes why no place in the park is going to be suitable for the boy's planned picnic. Spot, the family dog, is the machination behind the day's bad luck. In a final coup d'état, as the boy and his mother rush home in the rain, "they did not look back!" If they had, they would have seen Spot and another dog tugging to tear apart Mama's "very best hat," the final indignity to a day of mishaps spearheaded by Spot.

Irony

Spot, the family dog, not only ruins the day's picnic, he is apparently rewarded for his efforts. With rain slashing against the windowpane, and the picnic moved back to the apartment on the living room floor, there sits Spot sharing picnic food—even sitting on Mama's lap.

Motif

"It seemed like the most perfect spot. But … suddenly … who knows why," something mysteriously, if predictably, always interferes with the day's planned picnic. A flock of ducks ruins the boat ride; horses gallop by and kick mud on them; the carousel unexpectedly turns too fast at dizzying speed; a pack of dogs rush past the picnic blanket just as it starts to rain.

Pun

After a day of exhausting incidents at the city park, Jack and his mother are relieved to race back to their apartment, where home is really "the best picnic spot. Just Mama and Jack … and a dog they named Spot, the most perfect Spot!" The dog, of course, has not been at all perfect. Every mysterious incident at the park had Spot behind the scenes—spooking the ducks that causes their rowboat to upset, leading a pack of dogs with Mama's hat, causing the carousel ride to speed up, and generally spoiling every relaxing event the boy has planned for the perfect picnic.

*****

Henke, Kevin. *Kitten's First Full Moon.* New York: (Greenwillow Books) HarperCollins, c2004.

> When Kitten mistakes the full moon for a bowl of milk, she ends up tired, wet, and hungry trying to reach it.
>> **Curriculum Tie-in:** Science (Cats), Social Science (Character Development—Courage), Social Science (Character Development—Perseverance)
>> **Art Style:** Black pencil and gouache *Cartoons*

DEVICES

Irony

Kitten exhausts herself all night trying to achieve an impossible goal. No matter how hard she works, she can't reach the bowl of milk in the sky. Only when she gives up and finally goes home in defeat does she realize her heart's desire. Without even trying, she finds a bowl of milk waiting for her.

Motif

Kitten tries and inevitably fails to get the bowl of milk in the sky:
"Poor Kitten!"
Each time the plucky and admirably tenacious, if misguided, kitten makes a fresh try for the illusive bowl of milk, the author notes:
"Still, there was the bowl of milk, just waiting."

Tone

Despite her doomed goal, the author reveals a sympathetic attitude toward Kitten's undaunted determination. He doesn't leave her bereft. Wet, tired, and sad, she returns home to find a "great big bowl of milk" on her porch step, just waiting for her.

*****

High, Linda Oatman. *Barn Savers.* Illus. by Ted Lewin. Honesdale, PA: Boyds Mills Press, c1999.
> A young boy helps his father recycle a nineteenth-century barn.
> > **Curriculum Tie-in:** Environmental Studies (Barn Recycling), History (Barns, United States), Social Science (Family Relationships—Parent/Child)
> > **Art Style:** Play of light through full-page watercolor *Realism* and *Impressionism*

DEVICES

Atmosphere

A quiet chilly morning previews a satisfying day of companionable labor in the peaceful country setting.
"... walk through weeds and across a frosty field stubby with cornstalks ..."
"... sniffing the barn smell of old hay and horses."
Everything is saved, "even the old pig trough."

"I look at the weather vane and think of how the horse once galloped across the high roof of the barn, twisting this way and that with the winds of long ago."

Connotation

The old barns that the boy and his father salvage contain windows *wrinkled* and *wavy*. This aged glass is evidence of an appearance associated with antique glass-making methods.

Imagery

"old boards, splintered with cracks"
"wrinkled, wavy window"
"voice raspy with dust"
"frosty field, stubby with cornstalks"

Metaphor

"The moon is a sliver of ice ..."
"... Papa's truck, slick from the melting moon, ..."

Parallelism

"... people building barns,
    people building houses,
    people building houses to look like barns,
    people fixing up barns for houses."
"... barns high and barns low, barns old and barns new, more barns for the barn savers to save."

Simile

The sun rolls before us *like a wagon wheel.*
Red paint on the barn boards peel *like a sunburn.*
Dust floats in the air *like chicken feed.*
The sun sinks low in the sky *like a sleepy, red-faced farmer.*
Darkness falls soft and silent *like chicken feathers.*

*****

James, Simon. *The Wild Woods.* Cambridge, MA: Candlewick Press, c1993.
    Jess, who would like to take it home, follows a squirrel through the wild woods, while Granddad follows Jess, cautioning her along the way about the difficulties of keeping a squirrel as a pet.

Curriculum Tie-in: Environmental Studies (Exploring Nature), Science (Squirrels), Social Science (Family Relationships—Grandparents/Grandchildren)
Art Style: Pen-and-ink in sun-dappled watercolor *Cartoons*

DEVICES

Inference

Granddad assumes he has finally met his burden of proof in his granddaughter's perception. A wild animal will not make a good pet. Jess does conclude that she can't keep a squirrel because "he belongs in the wild." Granddad is so relieved he is willing to bring her back to the woods tomorrow. However, she hasn't quite given up the notion of taking a woodland creature home. She says, "One of those ducks might need taking care of."

Motif

Hoping to eventually get through to his exuberant granddaughter, Granddad says again and again, "You can't keep a squirrel," citing all the usual adult reasons: they're too wild, and what would you feed him, and where would he sleep?

Point-of-View

Through means of expressive illustrations, a frisky squirrel, an agile child, and a long-suffering grandfather each separately experience the tranquil beauties of a forest and the joys (and hardships) of a pleasant summer day of following an animal in its natural habitat.

Wit/Humor

Not to be deterred by practical considerations, Jess replies to Granddad's question, "What are you going to feed him?" with the wry observation, "He likes our sandwiches." Together they watch the creature help himself to their lunch bags.

*****

Jeffers, Oliver. *Lost and Found*. New York: (Philomel) Penguin Young Readers Group, c2005.
While trying his best to help a penguin get back home, which has shown up at his door, a boy journeys all the way to the South Pole, only to realize that the penguin was never lost.
Curriculum Tie-in: Science (Penguins), Social Science (Friendship)
Art Style: Deceptively simple watercolor *Cartoons*

DEVICES

Antithesis

"He asked some birds if they knew where the penguin came from. They ignored him. Some birds are like that."

"The boy asked his duck. The duck floated away. He didn't know either."

Foreshadow

"It felt strange for the boy to be on his own. There was no point telling stories now because there was no one to listen." Slowly, the boy is realizing, now that the penguin is no longer with him in his boat, that he was becoming a friend and is being missed.

"Quickly he turned the boat around and rowed back to the South Pole as fast as he could." But, while he has determined to go back to collect his penguin friend, the penguin has, meanwhile, determined to paddle out to sea to catch up with the disappearing boy in the rowboat. Each has, however, gone on opposite sides of an iceberg and are, therefore, destined to miss seeing each other.

Inference

The boy thinks he's merely returning a creature to its homeland. But, together on their journey, "there was lots of time for stories, and the penguin listened to every one, so the boy would always tell another." The two seem to be good company for each other.

The boy looks back at the penguin after delivering him to the South Pole: "The penguin was still there. But it looked sadder than ever." Being back home doesn't seem to have pleased the penguin after all.

Irony

When they finally arrive at the South Pole, "the boy was delighted but the penguin said nothing. Suddenly it looked sad again as the boy helped it out of the boat." Being brought "home" again ought to have made the penguin pleased, but it seems to have had the opposite effect.

After the boy realizes the penguin was never really lost, just lonely, he quickly rows right back to the South Pole to collect him.

The penguin, meanwhile, has cast off in his own little boat trying to catch up with the boy, who is now far out to sea.

Just when the two recognize they belong together, each has set out on opposite sides of the iceberg and they are in danger of missing the opportunity to reunite.

*****

Jenkins, Emily. *That New Animal.* Illus. by Pierce Pratt. New York: (Frances Foster Books) Farrar, Straus and Giroux, c2005.

> The lives of two dogs change after a new animal, a baby, comes to their house.
>
> **Curriculum Tie-in:** Social Science (Family Relationships—Pets), Social Science (Jealousy)
>
> **Art Style:** *Expressionism* in elongated, humorous acrylic *Cartoons*

DEVICES

Black Humor

The dogs' jealousy leads them to consider eating the new animal. They decide, "We'd get in trouble." They consider just biting it, no—just a little bit—no. Maybe they could bury the new animal under the tree, with the dog bones—or sleep in the new animal's cradle, on top of it.

Instead, they take out their frustration chewing up three dolls, two board-books, and six little outfits. And, one of the dogs, Marshmallow, pees on the carpet in several different places.

Paradox

Though the two dogs don't want the new animal in their household, it is, nevertheless, their animal. They won't let Grandpa near it. They are showing possessiveness. "It's not his new animal to go picking up whenever he feels like it. It's our animal ... to hate as much as we want to." They develop a protective bond with the baby. Eventually, the "new animal" smell has become familiar. "It isn't that new animal, anymore. It is just that animal. Their animal. To hate as much as they want to. And to like, just a little bit."

Parallelism

"No one has thrown a stick in a long time. No one has tossed a ball."

Point-of-View

When the dog Marshmallow whines, he's told to pipe down. When the dog Fudge-Fudge barks, she is sent to the corner. When the new animal (the baby) cries, it is cuddled and kissed.

The dogs are puzzled when the people fail to throw a stick or toss a ball. What can be so fascinating about the new animal? It doesn't know "dog" or "sit" or "breakfast" or "bone."

People don't care that the "new animal is using Fudge-Fudge's spot on the couch." People are just sitting there not noticing "that Marshmallow is showing his tummy, all ready to be scratched."

*****

Johnson, Angela. *Wind Flyers.* Illus. by Loren Long. New York: Simon & Schuster Books for Young Readers, c2007.

> A boy's love of flight takes him on a journey from the dusty dirt roads of Alabama to the war-torn skies of Europe and into the history of America.
>
> **Curriculum Tie-in:** History (Tuskegee Airmen, United States), History (World War II, 1939–1945, U.S. Army Air Force—Black Pilots), Social Science (Racism)
>
> **Art Style:** Bold, ethereal *Expressionism* in pastel paintings

DEVICES

Connotation

After the war, returning pilots had few venues to use their beloved skill of flying. Many turned to civilian crop dusting as their only means to *catch* the clouds in an airplane. They could still get that special feeling they enjoyed when flying in an open cockpit plane up among the clouds.

Imagery

Great Uncle talks about flying: "It's what heaven must be. With clouds, like soft blankets, saying, 'Come on it, get warm. Stay awhile and be a wind flyer too.'"

The story narrator describes his great uncle's attitude about flying: "And when his plane left the red Alabama dirt and flew in the air, he hoped he would never come down."

"Uncle crop dusted some, right after the war. That's the only way he could still fly, the only way he could still catch the clouds and feel the wind."

"He holds my hand, and we watch new wind flyers jet through the clouds."

Great Uncle describes the black flyers of long ago: "Young and brave. Brave and young, all."

Inference

" 'Air Force didn't want us at first. Only four squadrons like us.' He says, touching his mahogany face." The black pilots faced racism in World War II.

Motif

An airman's mantra—"wind flyer"—is reserved for those who made their mark as black World War II pilots:

> "... a wind flyer
> a smooth wind flyer
> a Tuskegee wind flyer."

"... flying into the wind,
against the wind,
beyond the wind,
the magical wind."

Paradox

"Some of us didn't come back, but we never lost a plane we protected." Though individual pilots and their fighter planes perished, the slower flying bomber planes the Tuskegee pilots were escorting all arrived safely.

Parallelism

"a wind flyer.
A smoother wind flyer.
A Tuskegee wind flyer ..."

"With his arms flapping, he jumped off a chicken coop when he was five." "Then he jumped off a barn into soft hay when he was seven."
"He knew what it was like to go into the wind, against the wind, beyond the wind."
"... the only way he could still fly, the only way he could still catch the clouds ..."

*****

Johnson, Lindan Lee. *Dream Jar.* Illus. by Serena Curmi. New York: Houghton Mifflin, c2005.
When a young girl has nightmares, her sister helps her by sharing the secret of the dream jar.
Curriculum Tie-in: Social Science (Character Development—Self-Reliance), Social Science (Family Relationships—Siblings), Social Science (Problem Solving—Ingenuity), Social Science (Psychology—Dreams)
Art Style: *Expressionism* in dreamlike nighttime atmosphere using pencil and acrylic *Cartoons*

DEVICES

Allusion

Taking her sister's advice, the story's narrator imagines scary dream monsters as funny horselike creatures friendly enough to let her ride on them in the sea waves. "Hi-Ho, Sea Biscuit!" she shouts.

Antithesis

As the narrator describes her bedroom, she states, "My bed is on the left. Her bed is on the right."

There is a pleasant bedtime routine that includes her mother reading with the girls, tucking them in, giving them a snuggle, turning down the light, and kissing them good night before they go to sleep. "This is the way bedtime is supposed to be. Some nights it is not."

Her sister tells her that her bad dreams are the result of an active imagination. "My sister says I can save myself. I think she's the one with the imagination."

Foreshadow

After she relates to her sister every scary detail of her nightmare, her sister "lowers her voice and mysteriously tells her, 'I think it's time to tell you the secret.'" Will she say something to stop the bad dreams?

Thankfully, her sister is always present to save her at night from her bad dreams, "Until—without even a teensy warning—something terribly horrible happens." Her sister is invited to a sleepover. She will not be there if a bad dream occurs!

Before leaving on her sleepover, the narrator's sister tells her something that promises to help if bad dreams occur: "'Tonight, you'll find the answer to your dreams. Look for it when the lights go off.' She smiles her most mysterious smile."

The narrator is disappointed to find the "help" her sister devises is only a plain, blue paper–wrapped jar. But, her mother hints, "Things are not always what they appear to be."

Inference

When the light is dimmed in her room, the stars on the blue paper around the jar glow. A note left for her from her sister says, "This is the Dream Jar I made for you—just like the one Mom made for me!" Her mother is smiling. "She must be remembering." Maybe the jar will help her, after all, if it once helped her sister with bad dreams.

She opens a Dreamy Dream paper from the Dream Jar. "I smile and close my eyes." The narrator feels confident that she can stop the next bad dream all by herself.

Motif

Dreams are the overriding presence in this girl's life—especially bad ones. "Where is it? Where's the answer to my dreams?" she wails when her sister is about to abandon her for a sleepover away from their shared bedroom. Her sister makes a Dream Jar for her to use when she needs to derail a nightmare. When she is able to finally turn scary dreams into "fabulously fun dreamy dreams," she has control, at last, of her nightmares.

Parallelism

"I stare at the plain jar on the night stand. I frown at the plain jar on the nightstand."

"Let's make a list of things that make us laugh or feel good. Things we like to spend a long time thinking about."

"You can change the story of your dreams if you practice.... you can make it into a good one."

Symbol

"And when morning comes, the sun shines on me in my bed on the left of our sky-blue room at the top of the stairs." The sight of morning sunshine shining on the narrator's bed is a sign that all is well after the terrors of the nightmare episodes. She has learned to rely on herself without her sister's presence. She used to describe mornings with the sunshine on her bed when her sister was there with her, having helped her through bad dreams. And, now, this is how she can describe mornings even without her sister having been there to help her.

Understatement

The narrator says her mother tells her the bad dreams she has are "just a stage I'm growing through." She says, "I think I'd rather skip it."

*****

*Johnston, Tony. *Angel City*. Illus. by Carole Byard. New York: (Philomel) Penguin Young Readers Group, c2006.

An old black man finds a baby abandoned in a dumpster and raises him in a rough Los Angeles neighborhood to know both African American and Mexican American ways.

Curriculum Tie-in: Geography (Los Angeles), Social Science (Ethnic Relations), Social Science (Family Relationships—Parent/Child), Social Science (Grief)

Art Style: Acrylic soulful *Impressionism*

DEVICES

Allusion

"While the old man heats Spaghettio's, Juan uses his crayons on the wall. Pop-Pop sighs. 'Perhaps that's how Siqueiros began.'" (David Siqueiros was a famous Mexican muralist.)

Ambiguity

"Angels done flown this coop.... Where's the love?" The city with the name of Los Angeles does not seem to fit the reality of conditions where the old man is trying to safely raise a child.

"There's a tree outside, hunched over from bucking the wind. Every day he sees that tree and thinks, 'I do my best, but I can't keep Juan from the wind.'" He prays, "Lord, maybe you can."

Antithesis

Juan's friend Chucho always husks the corn while Juan sells it in their little business venture. After Chucho is shot, Juan is willing to change the job arrangement if only his friend can live. "When you get well, you can count the money. I'll husk the corn."

"Juan closes his eyes and for a moment he sees Chucho. Then Chucho's gone. Pop-Pop's there."

Atmosphere

"Old man Joseph plods along, alone. Past the homeless ... buildings that tilt ... a wall pocked with bullet holes."

"Bundling it in his jacket, close to him, he takes the baby home."

"He is my gift from God ... I am to care for him."

Colloquialism

Pop-Pop can't abide "no gommin' and piddlin' around."

"Grow, you sons-of-turtles!"

"Grab a gob, son!" as the piñata breaks open.

"Angels done flown this coop...."

Connotation

Grieving together over the boy's dead friend, father and son sit in the Volkswagen hulk with just the *hymn* of the corn for comfort. This balm from a gardening sound references religion's eternal coping mechanism for times when logic fails.

Counterpoint

Old Joseph wants the boy raised to know both his biological and his adopted heritage. When the boy begins school, his lunch box contains both "a tamale and sugared grits."

"Sometimes people watch them and wonder about the old man slow as summer with the Mexican child who moves like a chapulin, a grasshopper."

"In Georgia, where Pop-Pop was raised, there are cornfields that whish and whisper. There are fields of corn, too, in Mexico, where Juan's people come from."

"Juan knows that in his deep heart he'll always be lonely for his friend. Pop-Pop knows that too."

Foreshadow

"The old man chants [a get-well chant] a lot. Seems to help small hurts. But every day he worries about other wounds. From knives, from guns." The old man's neighborhood is a dangerous place to raise a child. Will tragedy interrupt their loving relationship?

Imagery

"Dawn grays Los Angeles like a great pigeon wing."

"Slowly, he learns old mysteries—of diapering and burping and spitting up, the feel of a baby full of sleep."

"He's so excited, he grasshoppers his way through the market aisles ..."

"After that, in summer, they sit in the sun—growing up together—in Angel City, selling corn."

Inference

Old Joseph's love for his foundling is pervasive despite the trials of parenting. He considers the baby a gift from God and promises to care for him. When he goes sleepless, he looks skyward and grumbles, "Promise still holds."

"While the old man fits pipes and snakes out drains, Juan swashes toilets with a long-armed brush, for fun. Creates small indoor rains."

Old Joseph hears of a mural. "When they go there, he leans close so Juan, piggyback, can get a good look. 'Though he's only three,' he tells everyone, 'my Juan needs to know great art.'"

"Time to time, Pop-Pop scours the trash for cans to turn in, to buy little extras for his son."

When his friend is killed, Juan's mood and the weather are a match. "All his tears fall down. And it rains. And it rains."

Metaphor

Old Joseph finds "a baby, perfect and new. Swaddled in dawn."

"... buildings that tilt their old chins toward the sun ..."

"They sit outside and flurr the air. Two big bugs."

"... there are cornfields that whish and whisper.... Juan needs to know the song of corn."

"A storm comes from nowhere, stinging the streets with bullet-rain. Beside the newborn corn, Chucho is struck by a bullet from a phantom car."

Where they live in Los Angeles, "next door there's a vacant lot, jeweled with bits of broken bottles, ..."

"At the hospital, Juan stares at Chucho's window, its square eyes glassy and blind."

"Full of candy, the piñata waits ... with wild broom-swipes, Juan spills its sweet rain."

"They need no words, just the hymn of the corn."

Motif

"Angel City. Where's the angels? Where's the love?" The old man, bitter about life in the barrio, vows to raise an abandoned infant he finds in a dumpster. And he keeps his promise as, day to day and year after year, he discovers where the love really is.

Paradox

The two boys meet for the first time: "Once, while they work, a boy sneaks inside the car and pretends—drives, shouting, 'Move over, you son-of-turtle!' Juan loves this noisy driver. At once they are friends forever."

One of the boys is shot to death. The father mourning with his grieving son over the loss of his son's best friend, sits with him in the hulk of a wrecked car. "The old man crawls in and cradles him ... a man and a boy in a field green with life. In Angel City, here is love."

Parallelism

"Past the homeless sleeping like small lost boats,
Past buildings that tilt their old chins toward the sun,
Past a wall pocked with bullet holes"

Old Man Joseph makes sure his son learns "Georgia things. Georgia tunes, Georgia vittles, Georgia flutter fans."

"Sometimes he hugs Juan for no known reason.
Sometimes Juan does the same."

"... know what it is to turn the soil. What it is to sweat in the sun. What it is to pray for rain. They know what Georgia farmers and Mexican farmers have always known."

Simile

"... homeless sleeping like small lost boats"
"... a whimper frail as life"
"Like a large strange bird, the old man clucks to it."
"The days go quickly, gulped down like milk."
"His voice sings like a fine-skinned drum."
"Juan is already four and sprouting up like a flower."
When given a box of crayons, "Juan squeals with delight, then snaps them in two, like beans."
"... black man slow as summer ..."
"... a car hull like a huge charred beetle."
"Juan loves Chucho because he's wild as wind. Restless as corn."
"... a star with steamers like tassels of corn."
"News moves through the building like a cat thin as a squint."

Symbol

As a backdrop to daily life in their transplanted city, "in summer, they sit in the sun—growing up together—in Angel City, selling corn" from the crop they grow on a vacant lot. This common thread—the corn patch that the old man grows with his son and later the son grows with his best friend—serves as a bridge between the boy's dual ethnic heritages, the adopted African American Georgia cornfields where his Pop-Pop came from and the Mexican cornfields where his biological parents came from. The cornfield later becomes the balm for life's greatest loss.

The old man feels it's important that Juan learns the "whish and whisper, the song of corn." They grow it and sell it. It is in the corn patch that Juan first meets Chucho sitting in an old car hulk that resides in the cornfield. They instantly become best friends. The two boys sell corn together.

And, eventually, it is the soothing "hymn of the corn" that helps to heal the boy's broken heart when his best friend is killed.

Theme

Families can be chosen as well as be biological. Love will transform a bleak environment into one that flourishes.

Tone

This moving tribute to the warmth and strength of family, no matter the form, is demonstrated by the old father's determination to provide as best as possible for his precious child. He finds "a baby, perfect and new" and "bundling it in his jacket, close to him, he takes the baby home." "He is my gift from God ... [and] I am to care for him." The old man scours the trash for cans to turn in "to buy little extras for his son." He lets the boy scribble on the wall, because maybe "that's how Siqueiros began" his career as a muralist. "Sometimes he hugs Juan for no known reason. Sometimes Juan does the same." He provides a piñata for the boy's birthday even though the boy is still mourning his best friend, but, nevertheless, urges him to "Grab a gob, son!" "Juan knows that in his deep heart he'll always be lonely for his friend. Pop-Pop knows that too."

Wit/Humor

"He draws it with stubs of crayons, every color but green. At age four he ate that one."

"Once, while they work, a boy sneaks inside the car and pretend-drives, shouting, 'Move over, you son-of-a-turtle!' Juan loves this noisy driver."

*****

Johnston, Tony. *The Barn Owls.* Illus. by Deborah Kogan Ray. Watertown, MA: Charlesbridge, c2000.

For at least one hundred years, generations of barn owls have slept, hunted, called, raised their young, and glided silently above the wheat fields around an old barn.

Curriculum Tie-in: History (Barns, United States), Science (Owls)
Art Style: Close-up full-page watercolor *Realism*

DEVICES

Antithesis

"Sometimes nothing answers.
Sometimes something does."

Atmosphere

"The barn has stood in the wheat field one hundred years at least."
"... an owl awakes to a shadow—or nothing at all—..."
"... an owl goes floating away ... to where wheat and sky are one."
"Owls have hunted in this place; mice have hidden in this wheat one hundred years at least."
"Eggs have hatched in the loft of the barn one by one white and warm."

Imagery

"Owls have ... dozed in the scent of wheat."
Owls "hunt for mice while moons swell and shrink."

"Where owls hunted, spiders spun to hold the barn to earth."
"Old owls watching, new owls born in the redwood barn in the whisper of wheat . . ."

Metaphor

"Sometimes by day an owl awakes . . . and leaves the barn through a *bale* of light . . ." (A bright yellow compressed bale of straw is compared to the bright sunny daylight coming through the glassless square barn window.)
". . . bees hummed their hymn of wheat."

Motif

"One hundred years at least"—this is the refrain running through this timeless story of an animal's life in its environment:
"The barn has stood in the wheat field one hundred years at least."
"Owls have hunted in this place; mice have hidden in this wheat one hundred years at least."
They "hunt for mice as they always have. One hundred years at least."

Parallelism

"Sometimes by day an owl awakes to a shadow . . ."
"Sometimes by day an owl goes floating away, away . . ."

". . . one by one stars come out and blink.
One by one owls wake up and blink."

"Where owls hunted, spiders spun . . .
Where owls hunted, long snakes sunned . . ."

". . . to grow up and sleep and wake and blink and hunt . . ."

Simile

". . . long snakes sunned and split their skins like chaff . . ."

Tone

The awesome seasonal cycle and sameness of an animal's quiet routine, irrespective of man's existence, enthralls the author's poetic sense. "The barn has stood . . . owls have slept."

*****

Karon, Jan. *Violet Comes to Stay*. Story by Melanie Cecka. Illus. by Emily Arnold McCully. New York: (Viking) Penguin Young Readers Group, c2006.

Violet, a little white cat, tries out several homes before she finds just the right one.

Curriculum Tie-in: Religion (Trust and Faith), Social Science (Character Development—Honorable/Dishonorable Behavior), Social Science (Family Relationships—Parent/Child)

Art Style: Enchanting pen-and-ink watercolor *Cartoons*

DEVICES

Alliteration

Violet is taught the rules by her mother concerning mousing: "Prowl silently. Plan your leap carefully. Pounce boldly."

Aphorism

"God has a plan for each of us." This comforting wisdom from her mother helps soothe Violet when she is brought back to the kitchen of her birth each time another new-home trial fails.

Connotation

"Heat *ribboned* out from the oven doors" during the baking of fresh bread in the kitchen where Violet is born. It wafts out in forcefully undulating waves that fill the room with a yeasty, spicy odor.

Foreshadow

Violet's mother knows each of the people who come to select her kittens. They all required a mouser, which is not Violet's strong point. But, she is unfamiliar with the bookseller, who fancies Violet. She tells Violet, "I don't know this one, but have faith." This person does not speak of needing a mouse-catcher. Perhaps she will be a much better match for Violet.

Imagery

"Heat ribboned out from the oven doors, and the air was filled with the scent of fresh bread and spices."

"Long tables held trays bright with petunias, geraniums, and pansies, while nearby butterfly bushes gave off a heavenly scent."

"Around her neck were strings of colorful beads that shimmered in the sunlight."

"It was small and gray, with twinkling eyes and a pink nose that quivered with fear."

Inference

Several shopkeepers need a kitten to catch mice. Violet is mismatched with them.

"The man lifted Violet from the crate and peered into her bright green eyes. 'I suppose a little mouse catcher is better than none at all.'" Will this person love Violet for herself or just the task he has in mind for her?

Violet tries to be helpful. She helps the gardener straighten wobbly rows of clay pots on the workbench; he places her on the floor. She tries to help the baker knead bread dough; she is shooed off the countertop. It is clear these living arrangements are not suitable for Violet.

Then, the bookseller sees Violet. "Aren't you a lovely one!" She strokes Violet's back. She promises "to take extra good care of her." Nothing is said about mouse-catching. But, what will happen to Violet when she "assists" by pulling the receipt tape from the register? Not to worry—the bookseller says, "What would I do without such a helpful cat?"

Irony

The gardener and the baker reject Violet because she fails to be a successful mouse-catcher. At the bookstore, where mouse-catching was not mentioned, she actually does catch one. She believes she should "finish off the mouse; after all, it was her job." She "lifted her paw—and let the mouse go." Now surely again she will be rejected and taken back to the kitchen where she was born. Instead, she hears the bookseller praise her for not killing the mouse. "I'm so glad you let that little mouse go.... Mice are nuisances. But they're God's creatures, too. We'll find other ways of keeping them out." The task Violet was born to do and fails to do well, isn't important to her mistress.

Motif

The gardener and the baker don't appreciate Violet's efforts to be helpful in their business enterprises. She is there only to catch mice for them. When she tries to do other things, "Not now, Violet. I've got my job to do, and you've got yours." Each time Violet fails to meet the mousing criteria, her presence is no longer welcomed. "Oh no! I'm afraid this won't do. I need a cat to catch mice, not turn my shop upside down."

Violet hears this again and again. But, she doesn't like her job—until she finds a home where she is appreciated for not being a mouser.

Onomatopoeia

As Violet tries mouse-catching, "Crash! went the seed rack."

"Rat-tat-tat!" went the rakes that Violet accidentally knocks down.

"Smash! Smash! Crash!" went the wobbly clay pots that fell off the counter when Violet tries to arrange them neatly.

"Bam! Bam!" went a stack of baking sheets. Violet is responsible.

Point-of-View

Violet watches her brother pounce on Cook's shoe and hold fast. She asks her sister, "What game is that?" Daisy tells her it's not a game. "He's learning to catch a mouse." Violet wants to know, "Why would he want to catch a mouse?" Violet's mother replies that "mice are the enemy.... It's our job to kill them." But, later when she does accidentally manage to pounce on a mouse successfully, she "was amazed to see a tail beneath her paw." When she sees the mouse connected to the tail she thinks, "*This* tiny thing was the enemy?"

Violet's mother tries to prepare her for her new home. "See the dirt under his nails? He runs the nursery." Violet wonders, "What was a nursery? How would she be able to keep her white fur clean in a dirty place?"

Simile

"The baker tucked Violet under her arm *like a little loaf of white bread ...*"
"Violet's downy fur turned *as white as fresh milk.*"
"Violet crept forward *as quietly as a moonbeam through a window.*"
"Violet tensed herself *like an arrow about to be shot from a bow.*"

Theme

Have trust and faith that God will provide a plan that is just right for each individual.

*****

Kasza, Keiko. *Grandpa Toad's Secrets.* New York: G. P. Putnam's Sons, c1995.
> Grandpa Toad teaches his grandson the secrets of survival, but Little Toad is the one who saves the day when a huge monster attacks them.
> > **Curriculum Tie-in:** Literature (Folktale, Modern), Social Science (Character Development—Self-Reliance), Social Science (Family Relationships—Grandparents/Grandchildren)
> > **Art Style:** Watercolor and pen *Expressionism* in *Cartoons*

DEVICES

Irony

Grandpa teaches Little Toad three things to stay safe. Soon, this wisdom is put to test. Grandpa saves Little Toad two times until they meet "a humongous monster." It was Little Toad who "quickly decided what to do." Because of his brave and smart actions, "the monster ran away as fast as he could," which proved Grandpa's third and final secret to staying safe: "In case of emergency, be sure to have a friend you can count on."

Each time Little Toad was saved, he was always grateful for Grandpa's cleverness, saying, "You were smart. You were wonderful." When Little Toad showed his own cleverness, it was Grandpa who said, "You were brave. You were smart. You were wonderful."

Motif

During the walk in the woods, there were many hungry enemies after the toads. Each time they met a new one, "Little Toad screamed and ran away to hide." "But was Grandpa scared? Not a bit." Luckily, on the one day when Grandpa was afraid, Little Toad remembered Grandpa's secrets: "Be brave and be smart!"

Oxymoron

A "humongous monster" has grabbed poor Grandpa and trapped him in a sandwich. As the monster is about to take a bite of the Grandpa-Sandwich, Little Toad manages to frighten the monster with a bit of trickery. Though Little Toad is tiny and vulnerable in the monster's clutches, the creature shouts, "Help! Help! These mean toads are poisoning me!"

Serendipity

Just as Little Toad's grandfather is about to be eaten in the monster's sandwich, Little Toad "saw some wild berries and quickly decided what to do." The monster did not notice Little Toad throwing them at him, creating suspicious looking red splotches. Little Toad helps him believe they are poisonous, which frightens the monster into dropping Grandpa and running away.

Stereotype/Reverse Stereotype

Elders protect children. In this reversal of the ways of life, the child protects the elder. Grandpa shares three secrets to help Little Toad stay safe from predators. Little Toad is grateful.

Little Toad then shows how well he has listened to Grandpa's wisdom. It is he who thinks quickly and saves them both from the biggest monster of all. Grandpa is grateful.

Surprise/Twist-in-the-Tail

As they escape one predator after another, Grandpa has been teaching survival secrets to an admiring Little Toad. Each time they face a threat, Little

Toad runs away in fear. "But, was Grandpa scared? Not a bit." Grandpa saves Little Toad's life each time with trickery—until Grandpa is captured and about to be eaten in a monster's sandwich. This time Little Toad does not run. It is he who pulls a trick on the monster and sends it running. He saves Grandpa's life.

Tone

The loving relationship between Little Toad and Grandpa has room for mutual respect. Each time Grandpa saves them from danger, Little Toad is impressed. "You were wonderful." When Little Toad saves Grandpa, Grandpa returns the compliment: "You were wonderful." "Grandpa and Little Toad hugged each other."

Wit/Humor

Though poor Grandpa is about to be eaten in the monster's sandwich, Little Toad bravely follows through on his trickery (in Brer Rabbit fashion) with the red berries he throws at the monster. He shouts loudly, "Let that poor monster go! Grandpa, it's not very nice of you to go around poisoning monsters. Your poison is already creeping up his legs. Soon he'll have spots all over his behind. And then he'll die. Shame on you, Grandpa!" The ruse fools the monster. "Help! Help! These mean toads are poisoning me!"

*****

Kessler, Christina. *The Best Beekeeper of Lalibela: A Tale from Africa.* Illus. by Leonard Jenkins. New York: Holiday House, c2006.

> In the Ethiopian mountain village of Lalibela, famous for its churches and honey, a young girl determines to find a way to be a beekeeper despite being told it is only something men can do.
>
> > **Curriculum Tie-in:** Agriculture (Bee Culture), Geography (Africa), Social Science (Character Development—Perseverance), Social Science (Feminism)
> >
> > **Art Style:** Bright full-page acrylic *Expressionism*

DEVICES

Antithesis

"So far to go, she thought, looking up.
So far to fall, she thought, looking down,"

"'Very clever,' said the Priest,
and very simple too!"

Aphorism

"All great endeavors require great effort." Almaz cannot accomplish her desire to become the best beekeeper in her village by using the same methods the male beekeepers employ. They climb trees to the hives that hang far out on limbs. She lacks the ability to climb and the strength to reach out to the heavy hives. If she is to be successful at bee culture, she will have to utilize different means and does so through trial and error.

Atmosphere

"Where purple shadows fill the valleys and heavy mists hug the hillsides," a determined girl is pursuing a serious endeavor in a land that is well suited for it, if one studies the art and is prepared to buck tradition.

Foreshadow

Almaz is methodical about her study of the honey sellers' wares and her plan to be one of them. As she moves from stall to stall, tasting at each one, she says "to no one but herself, 'It's all very good, but one day mine will be the best.'"

Pun

After finally conquering problems safeguarding her beehives, and after winning hard-earned praise from the male beekeepers, Almaz drips some of her honey into her mouth. "Life is sweet," she pronounces.

Serendipity

Almaz needs a means of keeping ants out of her beehive. Her attempts to deter them using a moat of water just turn the ground to a muddy mess. "Then one morning her brother gave her the answer.... He passed by pulling his favorite toy. Bumping along the ground behind him on a string was an old tomato can filled with water." This gave her the idea of putting her hive on a table with its legs in tomato cans filled with water so the ants couldn't reach the sweet contents of the hive.

Simile

"... honey dripped down her finger like a string of golden diamonds...."
"Just like a worker bee, Almaz was busy for eleven days."

Stereotype/Reverse Stereotype

Almaz tells the male beekeepers she wants to make the "best honey in all of Lalibela." They laugh at her. The oldest man says, "That's men's work, little girl. Go find your mother and learn to cook and clean and gather firewood. You have a lot of work of your own, so forget about bees."

A beekeeper must be able to climb a tree to bring down a hive. She tries but becomes fearful. "The men laughed as she scooted down.... 'If you can't climb trees, then you can't keep bees. So go and learn the work of women.'"

*****

Krensky, Stephen. *How Santa Lost His Job.* Illus. by S. D. Schindler. New York: (Aladdin) Simon & Schuster, c2001.

Frustrated by Santa's slowness at Christmastime, Muckle, the elf, creates a mechanical replacement called the Deliverator and proposes a series of contests to prove that it can do Santa's job better than he can.

Curriculum Tie-in: Science (Inventions), Social Science (Holidays), Social Science (Problem Solving—Ingenuity), Social Science (Values)

Art Style: Bright, predominantly red, watercolor and ink *Cartoons*

DEVICES

Foreshadow

The elves believe their machine will do all the tasks Santa does but will "do them sooner, faster, and better." Santa says mysteriously, "There's more to my job than meets the eye." The machine does perform well, but Clara, the mail lady, warns, "'Santa isn't just about meeting a schedule. He cares about getting things right.' But, nobody would listen."

Inference

When the elves learn how the human element could contribute a necessary component to the success of the annual operation, Santa is happily reinstated to his position. But, as happy as he had been, "he was even happier in the years to come." Illustrations show Santa marrying Clara, the mail lady.

Irony

Test results are conclusive. The Deliverator machine can race down a chimney like Santa and finish putting out the toys first (because it doesn't care about cookies and milk). But, the elves discover it can't handle program changes. Santa, though slower, can take an extra gift at the last minute. He can change the route for weather conditions. The faster, more efficient machine fails during actual conditions.

Paradox

After experimenting to improve the toy delivery system with disastrous results, the elves realize that reinstatement of poky Santa, despite delays and hectic mix-ups, actually results in a "perfectly normal" mission. Though the Deliverator can scan a toy request at lightning speed, Santa can satisfy a request more precisely. He looks behind the request: "Oh I don't think he'd really like this" and "She didn't play with the one she got last year."

Satire

Santa's weaknesses are enumerated. He gets "hopelessly behind." He takes time-consuming bubble baths. He wears boots and "one of his boots usually gave him trouble." He must trim his beard. He "wastes time and energy." The elves complain about "always a last-minute rush." But, what can they do? "After all, Santa was only human."

Understatement

The efficient machine fails to handle unexpected travel plan adjustments. Illustrations show it spiraling to a crash on Christmas Eve. The elves go to Santa: "We need you Santa. We need you, now."

*****

*Lamm, C. Drew. *Gauchada*. Illus. by Fabian Negrin. New York: Alfred A. Knopf, c2002.

> A necklace is lovingly passed from one person to another, traveling much farther than the Argentine gaucho who made it will ever go.
>
> **Curriculum Tie-in:** Geography (Argentina), Social Science (Character Development—Kindness), Social Science (Love)
>
> **Art Style:** Gouache and pastel full-page *Folk*

DEVICES

Antithesis

"You would buy this necklace if you could.... This moon will be given."

Atmosphere

A sense of peaceful quiet, great open areas, and great distance pervades the story:

"... a mother listening to leaves of a lone ombu tree as they touch in the breeze."

"The moon and the stone travel farther than the gaucho will ever roam."
". . . an open space where cows stamp the land and champ the pampas, . . ."

Connotation

A writer *spins* with pencils and *whims* in an activity that suggests a process of capturing imagination and setting it down permanently.

Flashback

Coming full circle, the story that begins with a gaucho carving a gift necklace and giving it to a loved one ends with a recipient telling of where, in an "open space . . . a gaucho, an Argentine man, sits carving."

Imagery

"He works with hands, dirt-lined and leathery,"
"There's music in his hands and he sings as he carves."
". . . grandmother sharp and alive behind old eyes."
". . . a girl who smiles when she dreams feels the cool of the moon in her palm."
"The moon rises and falls as a writer spins with pencils and whims."
". . . a baby who's shimmering new, . . ."

Internal Rhyme

". . . where cows stamp the land and champ the pampas . . ."
". . . a baby who's shimmering new, . . . a friend who has always been true . . ."
". . . as a writer spins with pencils and whims . . ."
". . . the stone travels farther than the gaucho will ever roam."
". . . knows to whom the gift of the moon bone goes."
". . . sharp and alive behind old eyes . . ."
". . . before thunder's roar of the rain that will pour . . ."
". . . the gaucho who chose the bone . . . and placed the stone . . ."
". . . slides off its silver chain like rain . . ."

Irony

A thing of great enduring beauty, admired widely by many recipients, and passed on to persons all over the world, was created by the dirty, leathery hands of a simple, unknown gaucho who never left the cattle he herded in a place no one remarks upon.

The young gaucho who dances "a thousand zambas" chooses among all possible recipients for his art treasure—a grandmother.

Metaphor

In this flat open land of great distances, the moon represents the passage of the seasons and years as well as the passage of its namesake necklace from loving owners to grateful recipients. A girl "smiles when she dreams, feeling the cool of the moon in her palm." "You would buy this necklace if you could," but "this moon will be given." All the owners must decide "where the gift of the moon will go."

Motif

The moon is the inspiration for the carved moon-shaped bone necklace, created in a place of open, barren spaces, where the artist knows the passage of time only through the passage of the moon in its cycles. The single beautiful object in the environment becomes the model for the single beautiful object he carves.

Parallelism

"... he chooses silver. Silver to frame the moon. Silver to shine on the edge of the bone."

"Perhaps after the rains have again greened the pampas,
perhaps after the cows stampede through the quebradas,
perhaps after he has danced a thousand zambas, ..."

"As he knows before thunder's roar of the rain ...
as he knows before the cow lies down ...
just as he knew this chip of bone would be moon ..."

"As she knows before winter ...
as she knows before the downbeat her heart will lead,
just as she knows before words the story she'll weave, ..."

Surprise/Twist-in-the-Tail

Each owner of the necklace knows "where the gift of the moon will go." The grandmother to the young mother, to her daughter:

"Perhaps to a baby who's shimmering new,
perhaps to a friend who has always been true—perhaps to you."

Theme

Love is meant to be given. The gaucho, who made the art object "with hands, dirt-lined and leathery," sings as he carves and chooses precious "silver to frame the moon ... to shine on the edge of the bone ... and smoothed the silver and placed the stone" and will finally "know where the necklace will go." It travels from hand to hand, from heart to heart.

*****

Lasky, Kathryn. *Pirate Bob.* Illus. by David Clark. Watertown, MA: Charlesbridge, c2006.

> The life of a pirate, named Bob, is marked by the uneasy relationships he has with his fellow pirates as he contributes his role to their nefarious career by cutting steering cables and crippling the ships he and his shipmates will loot.
>
> > **Curriculum Tie-in:** History (Pirates), Social Science (Character Development—Honorable/Dishonorable Behavior), Social Science (Character Development—Trustworthiness), Social Science (Friendship), Social Science (Greed)
> >
> > **Art Style:** Grotesque ink and watercolor *Expressionism* in *Cartoons*

DEVICES

Antihero

"... having a best friend on a pirate ship can be complicated. Nobody trusts anybody."

"... he wonders how much yellower Yellow Jack will get before he dies. And if he does die, it would be a shame for all that loot to lie buried forever."

"We'll blow you to kingdom come if you don't let us board."

"He has one thought, one purpose: to cut the steering cables. And, to cut anything, anyone, between him and the steering cables...."

"... you might be hunted down, captured, and hanged—for after all, pirates are outlaws."

Antithesis

The relationship between pirate shipmates is delicate. "'Your face is brighter than that moon, Jack.' Bob laughs. Jack snarls."

Archetype

"The Captain's voice never waivers. The Captain never seems frightened. His voice is still cool and steady and clear."

"Pirate Bob is an expert in wrecking wheels and rudders."

"They carry daggers, pistols, and hand grenades made by filling old bottles with gunpowder."

"Their hearts beat faster. Their eyes begin to glint with dreams of gold...."

"The cannon will not work. Bob knows this because Yellow Jack is an expert at plugging the torch holes of cannons."

"Each pirate has his job. The point is to get the cargo."

"All the treasure stolen from the ship will be divided among the pirates. The Captain and his First Mate will get the most. The longer someone has been a pirate, the more he can expect."

Atmosphere

Surprisingly, states of sad introspection and grim duty rather than hearty, jovial fun seem to be the actual experience of pirating. "He has one thought, one purpose: to cut the steering cables. And to cut anything, anyone, between him and the steering cables ... you might be hunted down, captured, and hanged—for after all, pirates are outlaws."

Black Humor

"... he wonders how much yellower Yellow Jack will get before he dies. And if he does die, it would be a shame for all that loot to lie buried forever, if Yellow Jack should die of scurvy."

"We'll blow you to kingdom come if you don't let us board."

Bob is thinking of retiring. He'll find friends who don't know he was a pirate. They'll like "plain old Bob with a scar on my nose and a ring in my ear.... I'll be happy ... I think."

Colloquialism

"Crack on sail! Loose the mainsail! Loose the topsail! Sheet home!"
"Ship ahoy!"
"Avast! Heave to, ..."

Connotation

Pirates are always on the lookout for sailing ships *heavy* with gold or silver. Those are the ones that make the dangerous risk and work of stealing the goods worthwhile because there will be enough for all.

Hyperbole

Bob decides he'll remain a pirate long enough to raid just one more ship. "One more Spanish galleon ... a few pounds of pearls, three or four of silver, twenty of gold, maybe a few emeralds."

Imagery

"The men had just stormed over the rail—flashing their cutlasses, their pistols spitting fire—when Bob ran right into the point of a cutlass."

"The favorite time of a pirate's day begins at night—a cloudy night with a full moon, and on the sea a slow ship sailing heavy with gold or silver."

Inference

"The crew is happy with all the loot. Bob thinks he should feel happier. He has lots of loot now, but not as much as Yellow Jack." Bob thinks the reason for his vague dissatisfaction is tied to matching or surpassing the loot his friend has.

Just one more raid. "Then, Bob tells himself, I'll be happy . . . I think."

Motif

Pirate friendship is always tinged with suspicion. Pirates want to be liked but live a lifestyle that makes everyone believe this cannot really be possible.

"Yellow Jack likes Bob but thinks Bob might like him only for his loot and might want to find out where the map is."

"Bob genuinely likes Yellow Jack." But, what will happen to the loot "if Yellow Jack should die of scurvy?"

Bob thinks after one more ship he'll leave pirating and find friends who will like him, "not because they think I have buried treasure but because of who I am."

Parallelism

"This is a pirate's nose. It has a scar . . ."
"This is a pirate's ear. It has a small hole with a gold earring . . ."

"Right now Bob is waiting and so are his mates . . ."
"They are waiting for the perfect night . . ."

"The parakeet's name is Elaine. No one knows why that is her name, but it is."
"No one knows why the *Blackbird* is the Captain's ship, but it is."

"He likes his jokes. He likes his stories. He even likes Yellow Jack's singing."

"He is fast. He is exact."

Theme

Gold won't bring happiness or true friendship. There is always one more ship to plunder before it's enough. Bob has a plan, if that final ship should ever become a final ship. He will bury his treasure and "go out and look for friends—real friends who will like me not because they think I have buried treasure but because of who I am."

*****

Lee-Tai, Amy. *A Place Where Sunflowers Grow.* Illus. by Felicia Hoshino. San Francisco: Children's Book Press, c2006.

While interned with her family at Topaz Relocation Center during World War II, Mari gradually adjusts as she enrolls in an art class, makes a friend, plants sunflowers, and waits for them to grow.

Curriculum Tie-in: History (Japanese Americans—Internment, 1942–1945), Social Science (Character Development—Kindness), Social Science (Family Relationships—Parent/Child), Social Science (Friendship)

Art Style: Full-page watercolor and ink *Folk Cartoons* in shades of browns and yellows in accordance with the dry, harsh landscape of Utah

DEVICES

Aphorism

When Mari questions her father about why the family is in a camp and whether she will ever see her old friends again, he turns to Japanese philosophy: "Spring comes after winter, and flowers bloom again. Peace comes after war."

Atmosphere

"Mari and Papa walked the windy, dusty mile from their home on Block 29 to Topaz Art School on Block 7. They passed beneath watchtowers where military police pointed guns at anyone they feared might escape."

"The mountains, the vast sky, and the blazing sun made Mari feel as small as a sunflower seed."

The first drawing Mari made was hung on the bare wall above her bed in the tarpaper barrack shack where they lived. "It added a little cheer to their dark, one-room home, even when it was time to close the door."

One day while Mari was walking home with her new friend, "suddenly a wall of dirt, twigs, and sagebrush roots rushed toward them, stinging their skin."

Connotation

The place where the interned Japanese Americans must live is made inhospitable with *blazing* sun and, during windstorms, a *wall* of dirt, twigs, and sagebrush. The sun is hot; the air is dirty.

Inference

Despite living where she "can't think of anything that makes me happy at Topaz," Mari does begin to slowly respond to loving encouragement.

Her teacher is kind. "Mari-Chan, I noticed that you didn't draw anything in our last class. Some other students also had a hard time." She assures Mari she isn't the only one: "It happens quite often."

Her artist-papa admits he, too, sometimes can't think of something to draw, "but I don't give up."

Mama also helps. "Mari-Chan, are you worried about today's class? ... Remember Papa's advice. You will be able to draw, just like your sunflowers will be able to grow."

A classmate takes interest in her first drawing. "Your backyard looks like a lot of fun." Mari is able to respond, "Maybe you can visit when we all go home."

Motif

Drawing is therapy, a link between Mari's old life and life in the camp. Drawing becomes the means for Mari to open up and engage with others in the harsh environment where she suddenly finds herself living.

Before her teacher suggests she draw "something that made you happy before you came here," she could "barely talk or laugh anymore." When Papa asks her if she wants to talk about it, she can't, "though she actually had many questions." Once she creates her first drawing of her backyard at home, the questions flow. "It was as if, with every drawing she created, Mari found another question to ask, and the courage to ask it."

Finally, she is able to volunteer to share one of her drawings with the class. Mari finds an interested classmate. "In that moment, her old life, and whatever her new life would be like after the war, didn't feel so far away."

Symbol

Mari wonders if anything can bloom at Topaz. The progress of the sunflower seeds symbolizes Mari's own slow budding growth despite inhospitable conditions.

"Will these flowers grow as tall and beautiful as the ones in our old backyard?" Her mother replies, "It will take time, patience, and care," because "flowers don't grow easily in the desert."

Neither do little children thrive in a bleak world devoid of nourishing culture and familiar friends. Mama says, "You will be able to draw, just like your sunflowers will be able to grow."

Eventually, Mari is able to share a first drawing with her class. It includes herself, her new friend, and her sunflowers. "The sunflowers towered above their heads so high they couldn't even reach them on their tiptoes!"

As Mari and her new friend walk home together, Mari says, "I've watered my sunflower seeds every day for three months now. I wonder if my sunflowers are ever going to grow here." At sight of a tiny seedling, finally, she thinks "whatever her new life would be like after the war didn't feel so far away."

Theme

Kindness, patience, and loving care will help both a flower and a child to thrive.

*****

McClintock, Barbara. *Adele & Simon.* New York: (Frances Foster Books) Farrar, Straus and Giroux, c2006.

When Adele walks her little brother, Simon, home from school, he loses one more personal possession at every stop they make.

Curriculum Tie-in: History (Early Twentieth-Century Paris), Social Science (Character Development—Responsibility), Social Science (Family Relationships—Siblings)

Art Style: Pen-and-ink detailed period *Cartoon* drawings filled with soft watercolors

DEVICES

Aptronym

The grocer is "Madame Biscuit."
The school art teacher is "Madame Quill."
The pastry sweet shop waiter is "Monsieur Bonbon."

Foreshadow

As the story opens, when Adele picks up her little brother, Simon, at school, he has his "hat and gloves and scarf and sweater, his coat and knapsack and books and crayons, and a drawing of a cat he'd made that morning." Seeing him ready to embark, she says, tellingly of his character, "Simon, please try not to lose anything today." His response is, "I'll try." Perhaps, thinks the reader, these two have a difficult history of getting home intact.

Inference

Long-suffering, exasperated Adele is familiar with her brother's careless habits with his belongings.

She sets out his afterschool snack on a park bench. He is up a tree. "Come down this minute!" she scolds.

He loses his scarf in the natural history museum. "Simon, how can you lose things like this?"

As they walk, he notices a missing glove. "Oh Simon, not again!"

Now, the other glove is also gone. "Simon! We are spending the whole day looking for your things!"

His hat disappears while they watch a parade. "What is Mama going to say?"

His crayons cannot be found during their stop at the art museum. "Simon hugged Adele before she could scold him."

As he continues losing things, "Adele sighed. "It's getting late. Let's go." Everything he started out with at school is gone now. She heads home defeated—again, by her little brother's air-headed forgetfulness.

Parallelism

"At last they were home, and Adele was tired.
Tired of Simon losing things.
Tired of looking for the things Simon lost.
Tired of looking for Simon."

Tomorrow would be another day, bringing Simon home. He asks,
"Is tomorrow a school day?"
"Yes," said Adele.
"And will you pick me up to bring me home again?"
"Yes," Adele sighed.

Wit/Humor

The children arrive home. "Simon," said Mama, "where are your hat and gloves and scarf and sweater, your coat and knapsack and books and crayons?"

"And the drawing of a cat he made at school," adds the rueful older sister.

*****

McElligott, Matthew. *Backbeard and the Birthday Suit*. New York: Walker & Company, c2006.

> Backbeard is so smelly, hairy, and ornery that parrots won't stay with him; it's time for change, if he can still retain the respect of his fellow pirates.
> **Curriculum Tie-in:** History (Pirates), Social Science (Character Development—Etiquette), Social Science (Character Development—Respect), Social Science (Character Development—Tolerance)
> **Art Style:** Pencil and fabric collage *Cartoons* humorously follow the pirate's sartorial renovation

DEVICES

Allusion

The messy, stinky pirate Backbeard sounds very much like Blackbeard. His ship is the *Five O'Clock Shadow*, appropriately named for a hairy, un-groomed

pirate. When parrots quit his employ, he secures a more suitable mascot—
a pig.

Ambiguity

All decked out in his garish new finery of brightly patterned green pants,
pink coat, red shoes, monocle, and straw boater, and with a pig riding on his
shoulder, he "noticed people staring at him." He thinks, "The poor landlubbers. They're jealous of my suit."

Antihero

After his birthday party, Backbeard's "clothes were in tatters. His shirt was
stained with punch ... and his underwear was full of frosting." He looks in his
mirror and tells his parrot, "Even for a pirate ... I'm a mess."

Outfitted in his new clothes, he replies to the salesman, who asks for "seven
pieces of eight, please": "Blimey! I don't pay for things—I'm a pirate!"

Antithesis

Backbeard's crew isn't sure what to make of their captain in his new
clothes:
"You sound like the Captain."
"You look like a goofball."

Aphorism

Will other pirates still respect Backbeard in his new suit? His crew point
out he's still himself. He's still stupid. He still stinks. "A fancy suit and a pig
don't change that."

Aptronym

Backbeard's fellow pirates are named Sweaty McGhee and Mad Garlic Jack
and Scarlet Doubloon.

Archetype

Backbeard is "stupid. He stinks." He's the "toughest, loudest, most unsanitary pirate ever."

He and his mates celebrate his birthday: "They drank punch and scratched
and spit. They hit each other with bottles and sang pirate songs. Then they
had cake and opened presents. Afterward, Backbeard threw them all overboard. 'What a great party.'"

But, he notices that "even for a pirate, ... I'm a mess" and goes on a shopping trip. In the clothing store, the salesman asks, "What happened to your

pirate suit?" Backbeard rudely answers, "I had a birthday party. Is that a problem?"

Atmosphere

Raucous, slapstick low humor marks this version of the typical pirate's life. The captain is the "toughest, loudest, most unsanitary pirate ever." His crew points out that he's "stupid" and "he stinks." After a birthday party, his "pants had a hole the size of his bottom." There is a good deal of name-calling: "Bottom-feeder," "Jellyfish," Stinkbottom," "Drivelswigger." Backbeard is so bad he can't keep a parrot. "Most quit after the first few days." After a crew member throws an egg at him and tells him not to come back when he goes ashore on a shopping trip, Backbeard fondly thinks, "I love these guys."

Colloquialism

"Listen up, you jellyfish," he hollered.
"Stay out of trouble or you'll walk the plank."
"Shiver me timbers!"
"Blimey!"
"Arrgh, . . ."
"poor landlubbers"
". . . lower the gangplank"
"barnacled scallywags"
". . . wrinkle my suit and you'll swab the deck for a year!"
"Hornswaggle"
"What say we go down there and batten his hatch?"

Hyperbole

"His pants had a hole the size of his bottom." He was "so hairy, it was sometimes tough to tell if there was a pirate underneath." He was so bad it was "hard for him to keep a parrot. Most quit after the first few days."

Irony

Backbeard and his mates are rough, bad-mannered louts. When he tells the crew he's going into town for a while, they shout, "Don't come back!" Someone threw an egg at Backbeard's hat. As he leaves, he thinks, "I love these guys."

To most people, Backbeard's combination of clothing choices are awful. But, he meets one person at least, a little girl, who is in perfect agreement with his choices because she, too, is wearing exactly the same striking color schemes of patterned pink over patterned green with boater hat, red shoes, and pink top coat.

Point-of-View

When Backbeard sees the little girl staring at him, he fears he will be seen as a sissy in his new outfit. He takes umbrage.

"Are you staring at me?" he demands.

"Yes sir," she says. "You have pretty clothes."

"Thank you!" Backbeard laughs, relieved. "So do you." (Naturally, he would think so.)

Even the pig on the pirate's shoulder matches the stuffed pig toy being carried by the child. These two definitely share the same sartorial point-of-view even if no one else does.

Solecism

"What say we go down there"

"a pig don't change that"

Wit/Humor

Backbeard worries that his new outfit will ruin his image, but his crew assures him that he is still stupid, still stinks, and not even his fancy suit and a pig will change that.

After a fine birthday party of fighting, breaking bottles, spilling food, and speaking rudely to each other, the captain throws them overboard, the perfect ending to a perfect party.

"You stinkbottom!"

"Drivelswigger!"

"Bottom-feeder!"

*****

Manushkin, Fran. *The Shivers in the Fridge*. Illus. by Paul O. Zelinsky. New York: (Dutton Children's Books) Penguin Young Readers Group, c2006.

    One by one, the members of the Shivers family disappear from the inside of their chilly refrigerator home.

        Curriculum Tie-in: Literature (Fantasy—Mystery)

        Art Style: Pastel and watercolor *Expressionism* in *Cartoons*

DEVICES

Inference

The reader begins to understand the nature of the family's environment with the help of illustrations, when Grandpa Shivers warns, "'Watch Out! My old bones feel an earthquake coming! Everybody—hide!' Sure enough, the whole world began to shake, and a great blazing light shone forth. A monster appeared! Its long, long claws reached out." The earthquake is the opening refrigerator door letting in kitchen light as a lady's hand reaches inside for food.

Papa Shivers sets out to discover a warmer world and must negotiate past various foods. "He squeezed past Orange Hills, tiptoed around Egg Valley, and—oops! He tripped on Buttery Cliff."

Mama Shivers is drawn to a bowl of warm-looking gelatin when it is set on a shelf. "Mama found something new: a clear Emerald Lake." She jumps into it. "'It *is* warm. I'm so comfy. I could stay here forever.'" The gelatin soon firms up. "Mama got stuck in—tight!"

Grandma Shivers finds herself the perfect hiding place—Spooky Jungle. "She wedged herself in nice and tight," which the reader observes from the art to be a stalk of celery.

When it's Sonny's turn to negotiate the contents of the refrigerator, "Sonny scooted up Purple Boulders. 'The monsters are always snatching these,' he said." Illustrations show him on top of grapes.

At last the family is happily reunited. Papa pronounces, "We keep this whole world running." Illustrations show the refrigerator magnet family holding up important family notes and reminders.

Motif

The operative word for this family is "shiver." "Shiver my Bones! It's COLD," roars Grandpa.

Grandma has no use for bedtime stories. She tells Sonny, "Shush now, and shiver yourself to sleep."

Finally, restored to their magnet positions on the fridge door, the family "stood tall and proud, and they never ever shivered again!"

Parallelism

Each night Sonny begs, "Mama, tell me a story." Mama tries through chattering teeth until Grandma pokes Mama with her pointy elbow, scolding her for filling the boy's head with nonsense and tall tales.

"Once upon a time there was a warm and cozy family." The next morning Papa ponders, "Maybe Mama's right, and there is a warmer place to live. I'll search the world until I find it."

The next morning there was an "earthquake," a "great light," and, "when it was over, Eggy Valley, Buttery Cliff—and Papa! were gone."

"Once upon a time there was a family who stood tall and proud." The next morning Grandpa declares, "Maybe Mama's right, and there is a place we can stand tall. I'm going to find it—and Papa too!"

Soon came the "earthquake" and the "great light," and "when it was over, Onion circles, Mt. Ketchup—and Grandpa!—were gone."

"Once upon a time there was a family who were brave and strong." In the morning, Mama sets out to find them.

After the "earthquake" and "bright light," "Emerald Lake, Jolly Whip—and Mama!—were gone."

It is Grandma's turn. She doesn't believe in Once-Upon-A-Time. But, she will search for the family members. A monster reaches in. "Mt. Mayo, Spooky Jungle—and Grandma!—were gone."

Now that Sonny is all alone, he tells himself a bedtime story. "Once upon a time there was a brave, strong, and happy family." Soon, when the fridge opens, Sonny is swept up and will be joining his family as he stands bravely on top of the grapes.

Point-of-View

The Shivers family feels an "earthquake" every time the fridge door opens. "Monsters" snatch items, such as "Cheesy Square," from their environment. "Phoomph," the earthquake is over and the family is plunged back into darkness again. Each time the earthquake happens, "Everybody—hide!" the family warns one another, afraid they will be snatched with one of the other things selected.

Grandma predicts, "Cold we are and cold we'll always be." But, Papa isn't so sure. He thinks there could be a warmer place to live. "I'll search the world until I find it."

Grandpa sneezes and wheezes past "Horseradish Ridge." When the earthquake strikes, "Mt. Ketchup trembled and teetered and the furious light blazed, and a monster reached out."

"Standing tall, Sonny Shivers faced that monster—and the monster smiled!" Suddenly, Sonny finds himself flying through the air out into the light and is happily joined with his family on the outside of the fridge. They have so much to read, this family of magnets holding up household notes.

Pun

In this cold world of food storage where this family finds itself, Grandma tries to deter Grandpa from leaving. "Stop!" She gives him a *sour* look and warns him, "Don't get into a *pickle*!"

With *tear-filled eyes* he treks through *Onion Circles*.

As Mama tries to tell Sonny a bedtime story, Grandma scolds, "*Baloney*! Stop talking such *applesauce*!"

When Sonny is finally all alone after his family disappears, he hugs his *Honey Bear* for comfort. But all he gets is *sticky*.

"Sonny slept so well, he woke up with a *cool* look in his eye and a mind as *sharp as mustard*."

"No more *cold feet* for me!" he declares.

"Oh what a *warm* reunion they had!" Freed at last from inside the fridge, they assume new positions on the outside of it.

Understatement

Papa sighs, "Sometimes I think this is a strange place to live." Mama assures him, "Now, now, no place is perfect."

Wit/Humor

As he reads labels on the food, "Sonny, don't read in the dark," warns Mama. "You'll ruin your eyes."

With only Sonny and Grandma left in the cold box at night, Sonny begs her to tell him a story. "I don't know any," she replies. "Shush now, and shiver yourself to sleep."

Restored at last to their rightful positions on the fridge door holding up notes and calendars, Sonny marvels, "There's so much to read."

*****

Michelson, Richard. *Across the Alley.* Illus. by E. B. Lewis. New York: (Penguin Young Readers Group) G. P. Putnam's Sons, c2006.

Jewish Abe's grandfather wants him to be a violinist while African American Willie's father plans for him to be a great baseball pitcher, but it turns out that the two boys are more talented when they switch activities.

Curriculum Tie-in: Athletics (Baseball), Career Education (Baseball Player), Career Education (Violin Musician), Music (Violin), Social Science (Ethnic Relations), Social Science (Friendship), Social Science (Prejudice)

Art Style: Haunting *Impressionism*

DEVICES

Aphorism

"Ignorance comes in as many colors as talent."

Counterpoint

Willie shows Abe how to hold a baseball: "He knew just where I should stretch my fingers across the stitches.... Willie showed me how to throw a real big-league slider."

Abe teaches Willie how to hold the violin:. "I tell him where to rest his chin on the chin rest and how much rosin to slide across the hairs of the bow."

Willie is expected to be the next Satchel Paige on the mound.

Abe is expected to be the next Jascha Heifetz as he prepares for his recital at the temple.

"My daddy was a starter in the Negro leagues," Willie tells Abe.

"Grandpa was a great violinist in the old country," Abe tells Willie.

"There was a war and the Nazis broke all of his fingers and worked him like a slave," Jewish Abe tells Willie.

"My great-granddaddy was a slave too," Black Willie tells Abe.

"All weekend I stay in my room practicing."

"Willie tells his daddy he's sick so he can stay in his room, too."

"I take a break to practice my own wind-up, so I pass my violin out the window to Willie," says Abe. "My arm's spinning like the Coney Island Ferris Wheel and his bow's kicking up so much breeze, there's not a single fly left to swat in the city."

Grandpa accepts that the Negro child is the true violinist. " 'You'll be the next Jascha Heifetz.' ... And then he shows Willie the correct position of his bow."

"Let people stare," Willie's daddy says as he steps ahead of Grandpa into the temple." Willie's father accepts that he is a violinist, not a baseball player.

Willie's first notes are screechy, but he closes his eyes "and you can tell by his face" he's going to play well. "I tell Willie he sounded great, but he's already rushing me toward the door."

"In half an hour Willie's daddy is leading us to the sandlot and I'm penciled in to do the pitching." Abe's first pitch "flies over the batter's head" but "out of the corner of one eye" he sees Grandpa, Willie, and Willie's daddy. "They're all cheering." His "next pitch slides straight over home plate."

Inference

"During the day we don't play together, but at night, when nobody's watching, Willie and I are best friends." The black and the Jew find enjoyment in one another's company, though their neighborhood wouldn't approve.

Finally, they flaunt their friendship. "It's Tuesday afternoon and we're walking side by side, like best friends, and everybody's watching."

"Let people stare."

The future violinist is more mindful of baseball than music. "Down the street, those other boys are always batting and having fun." Abe is intrigued with baseball. Abe "sees a grounder run full steam through Willie's legs.... Then a pop-up drops out of Willie's glove." Maybe Willie won't be following his father's career.

The future baseball pitcher seems more interested in the violin. "After Grandpa gives me my lesson, I go to my room to practice. Willie leans out his window and asks if he can play." When Abe's grandfather hears some good playing, he doesn't know it came from Willie. "My palms turn sweaty like I've been caught throwing a spitball. I want to tell him it was Willie, but I can't think of anything to say."

Irony

The Jewish boy, who is supposed to be more cerebral, thinks about baseball all the time and throws a great pitch. The Negro boy, who is supposed to become a great athlete, is awkward playing ball but a talented natural violinist.

Abe prefers to "practice his wind-up." Willie prefers "kicking up" a fast bow.

Metaphor

"Willie's first notes sound like the radio when I'm searching for the signal that announces the Dodger games. But, then Willie closes his eyes, and you can tell by his face that he's found the right station."

Point-of-View

Abe, the Jewish boy, tells this story. "Every night, after Grandpa turns out the light, I count to twenty before I tiptoe out of bed and tug open my shade." Across the alley, I know Willie's doing the same.

Abe tells Willie the Nazis broke all his grandfather's fingers "and worked him like a slave." Willie is quiet and Abe thinks, "I wonder if I said something wrong. Maybe he doesn't know about the Nazis."

Finally, Willie says, "My great-granddaddy was a slave too. I never knew any white folks that were."

Simile

". . . a grounder run full steam . . . like a rat racing for the sewer."

"His fingers fly up and down the fingerboard like the pavement's too hot to set your bare feet on the ground."

"My palm turn sweaty like I've been caught throwing a spitball."

". . . my arms spinning like the Coney Island Ferris wheel."

". . . my stomach feels like it's stuck riding the roller coaster."

Stereotype/Reverse Stereotype

"God gave you a brain. . . . Let those Negro kids play ball," the Jewish grandfather tells his grandson Abe. "Grandpa says Jewish kids shouldn't waste time with baseball. He thinks I should spend every minute practicing the violin."

"When Willie and his daddy sit down [in temple for the recital], most people get up and slide across the aisle."

Eventually, the elders realize where the young ones' talents really lie. Grandpa "shows Willie the correct position of his bow." Willie's daddy "is leading us to the sandlot and I'm penciled in to do the pitching," says Abe.

Theme

Friendship should not be dictated by race. The boys are comfortable going publically against neighborhood tradition: "We're walking side by side, like best friends, and everybody's watching."

Careers ought not to be imposed upon individuals from others but should develop from natural talents. Grandpa "shows Willie the correct position of his bow." Willie's father has "penciled in [Abe] to do the pitching" at the sandlot game.

*****

***Montserrat, Pep.** *Ms. Rubinstein's Beauty.* New York: Sterling, c2006.

When Mr. Pavlov and Ms. Rubinstein look beyond each other's strange characteristics, they discover beauty and grace that no one else has ever noticed.

Curriculum Tie-in: Career Education (Circus Performer), Social Science (Individuality), Social Science (Love)

Art Style: *Naive* solid-colored illustrations, in shades from cream to orange and browns

DEVICES

Antithesis

"Today is the circus's day off. Today there is no show."

"But their eyes don't see their eyes anymore, just their hearts."

"Nobody sees their smiles. [For] ... they only have eyes for Ms. Rubinstein's bushy beard ... and the extraordinary trunk of Mr. Pavlov."

Atmosphere

Two circus troupes have come to town—one with a bearded lady and the other with an elephant man. Spare and tight prose, with strategic pauses, combines with stunningly unexpected twists:

"Finally, he looks directly into her eyes ... as she meets his."

"And Ms. Rubinstein and Mr. Pavlov know that this must be ... falling in love."

"Nobody sees the love growing between them. No, they only have eyes for Ms. Rubinstein's bushy beard ... and the extraordinary trunk of Mr. Pavlov, the Elephant Man of Circus Guston ... also visiting the city."

Connotation

The bearded lady and the elephant man don't see each other's eyes any-more, just their *hearts*. They see beyond their physical faces into their person-alities. They like what they alone notice about each other. They are finding that they love each other.

Counterpoint

"Ms. Rubinstein's nose is wonderful.
But, nobody pays attention to her wonderful nose."

"Ms. Rubinstein's pretty hands move harmoniously and delicately.
But, nobody notices the delicate harmony of her pretty hands when they move. . . ."

"Everyone in the park at that moment sees only Ms. Rubinstein's bushy beard. No one notices her nice gesture . . . except Mr. Pavlov, who now sits next to Ms. Rubinstein."

Ms. Rubinstein is "the Bearded Lady of Circus Balius, now visiting the city."
Mr. Pavlov is "the Elephant Man of Circus Guston . . . also visiting the city."

Inference

These two circus performers, rejected by most of society, are able to see beyond the single odd feature each has in order to appreciate each other's other admirable traits.

"Mr. Pavlov secretly notices Ms. Rubinstein's small graceful feet. And out of the corner of her eye, she sees him sitting and crossing his legs in a very ele-gant manner."

He "admires the delicate harmony of her hands," while she, "without his noticing, observes his refined way of holding his walking stick."

Motif

"Nobody notices . . ." Except the two special people who see values in each other with their hearts as well as with their eyes, managing to notice, espe-cially, the pleasing characteristics.

Parallelism

"Ms. Rubinstein is a beautiful woman.
But nobody knows it."
"Ms. Rubinstein has very beautiful eyes.
But nobody sees them."

"Nobody sees their smiles.
Nobody sees the love growing between them."
"No, nobody notices these things...."
"No, they only have eyes for ..."

Surprise/Twist-in-the-Tail

Nobody notices Ms. Rubinstein's beauty—her pretty hands, the special grace of her small feet, her wonderful nose, or her very beautiful eyes "because all that people see ... is the bushy beard of Ms. Rubinstein."

"Everyone in the park at that moment sees only Ms. Rubinstein's bushy beard. No one notices her nice gesture. No one except the pigeons and Mr. Pavlov, who now sits next to Ms. Rubinstein."

"No, they only have eyes for Ms. Rubinstein's bushy beard ... and the extraordinary trunk of Mr. Pavlov, the Elephant Man."

Theme

When love sees beauty, it looks beyond physical imperfections.

*****

Nelson, Vaunda Micheaux. *Almost to Freedom.* Illus. by Colin Bootman. Minneapolis, MN: (Carolrhoda) Lerner, c2003.
>A young girl's dramatic escape from slavery by means of the Underground Railroad is told from the perspective of her beloved rag doll.
>**Curriculum Tie-in:** History (Slavery), History (Underground Railroad)
>**Art Style:** In keeping with the somber topic of escaping slavery during the dark of night are dark full-page *Expressionism* in acrylic paintings

DEVICES

Allusion

"Come sundown, we sit 'round and listen to stories about little critters foolin' big ones," alludes to Uncle Remus tales.

Atmosphere

"It's dead quiet 'cept for the sound of the boatman pushin,' pushin,' pushin' his oars. My face soaks up little splashes of water as we glide along."

"Miz Rachel squeezes the boatman's hand. Lindy's papa leads us through the night woods."

"Miz Rachel spreads two blankets on the dirt floor, ..."

"Miz Rachel serves up supper. Nobody talks. Too tired. Too scared. They sop up the last of their stew with bread."

"Then I'm fallin', fallin' till I hit the dirt floor.... The silver-haired woman is closin' up the floor.... The boards shut out the light."

"I want Lindy. But I know she ain't comin' back, can't. The loneliness swallows me up."

"I see light from a lantern and a woman wrappin' up a little girl in a blanket. The child's shiverin', more scared, I think, than cold. Her eyes look tired and tearful."

Colloquialism

"Bein' Lindy's doll baby is a right important job."

"... the long days seem a mite easier ..."

"... about slaves outsmartin' massas."

"Some say you can buy Freedom, but it's so dear we never hearda anybody ever could."

"But Miz Rachel don't pay no mind."

"Much obliged, ma'am, ..."

"Lindy whispers she needs to make water."

"... carries the lantern and privy bucket up the ladder."

"After a spell, I'm thinkin' maybe slave catchers is watchin' this house."

"Mighty fine stitchin'."

Foreshadow

"Lindy ties me 'round her waist with a rope," says the rag doll. "The knot's kinda loose."

The family's father is sold trying "to get to Freedom." Then, Miz Rachel "sits up at night lookin' at the sky." She sings, "Steal away, steal away home. I ain't got long to stay here."

Hyperbole

"Maybe the hidin' place ain't safe. Maybe I'll lay right here for the rest of my days."

Imagery

"We run and hide, run and hide, 'til we come to a house with a lantern glowin' soft in the window. We crouch behind the barn."

"I smiles inside, rememberin' the cracklin of the straw mattress when Lindy'd roll over me in her sleep."

"I's tied to Lindy, but when the whippin' starts, I slip out and fall. My face is on the ground but I hear the overseer's blacksnake whip. I hear Lindy screamin'.'"

Inference

"The overseer holler, 'Git up, there!' like he's talkin' to a couple of horses. He's ridin' over carryin' his whip."

"'Night, Sally,' she whispers. 'We almost to Freedom.' If I coulda, I'da smiled, too."

Accidentally left behind in the cellar hiding hole, the dolly passes time "listenin' to Miz Mouse make herself a nest and raise her young'uns. I's sorry when they finally go."

"If I coulda made tears, them blankets woulda been wet clean through."

Parallelism

"I give a lot of time to prayin'...."
And I give a lot of time to grievin'.'"

When the dolly belongs to Lindy: "She hug me so hard I think my insides'll bust out my seams."

Later a new owner finds the dolly: "Willa hugs me so hard I think my insides'll bust out my seams."

Lindy says: "Your name be Sally. We gonna be best friends."
Willa says: "Your name Belinda. We gonna be best friends."

At the beginning of the dolly's story: "Bein' Lindy's doll baby is a right important job."

At the end of the story: "I's mighty glad to be Willa's doll baby. It's a right important job."

Personification

The story's narrator is the child's dolly: "I see light from a lantern and a woman wrappin' up a little girl in a blanket. The child's shiverin', more scared, I think, than cold. Her eyes look tired and tearful."

Poetic Justice

"Lindy ties me 'round her waist. I guess sleep still has her 'cause the knot ain't tight." The dolly is left behind in the basement. "I want Lindy. But I know she ain't comin' back. Can't. The loneliness swallows me up."

Much later another child hides in the same basement. "She blows the dust off my face and holds me closer." The new girl, Willa, says, "Your name Belinda." The dolly thinks that sounds like Lindy and, therefore, likes her new name. "I's mighty glad to be Willa's dolly baby."

Point-of-View

"I started out no more'n a bunch of rags on a Virginia plantation. Lindy's mama was my maker."

". . . there's whisperin', an Lindy's gettin' her clothes on. The sun ain't awake yet, but field workers is always up 'fore dawn, so I don't think much of it."

". . . we sneak out behind our shack and run into the night. I know I ain't runnin', but I feels like I am. Feels like I'm flyin'."

"'Lindy! Wait!' But she can't hear me, 'cause I ain't got no voice."

"I give a lot of time to thinkin' about Lindy and her folks, where they was, and if they ever got to Freedom like they was wantin'."

Simile

"Branches slap us along the way like they scoldin', warnin' us to go back."

"The night is dark as inside a possum."

"Lindy's papa calls out—'Whoo! Whoo!'—like a hooty owl."

"Lindy lays me on the pillow. It's the softest thing. Like a cloud from heaven."

Solecism

"I don't have no hair."

". . . but now it don't bother me none."

"Miz Rachel done a fine job . . ."

"I ain't sure."

"I wish the silver-haired woman would come. But she don't."

Understatement

"'Mama say we be with Papa soon.' Soon don't come real soon."

*****

Palatini, Margie. *Bad Boys Get Cookie!* Illus. by Henry Cole. New York: HarperCollins Children's Books, c2006.

> Wolves Willy and Wally try to satisfy a sweet-tooth craving by dressing up as private eyes and chasing down a runaway cookie.
>
> > **Curriculum Tie-in:** Literature (Fairy Tales), Social Science (Character Development—Honorable/Dishonorable Behavior), Social Science (Greed)
> >
> > **Art Style:** Rollicking *Cartoons*

DEVICES

Allusion

The baker describes the runaway cookie, reminiscent of a certain Gingerbread Man: "He's about this high. Thin. Lightly browned. Full of sugar and spice. Dark raisin eyes. Round currant mouth. He's wearing a white-icing jacket with gumdrop buttons. Oh dear, he's just hot out of the oven."

Says the runaway: "Na-na-ni-na-na! Lookee! Lookee! You can't get me. I'm one smart cookie!"

To try to lure the cookie, two wolves disguise themselves in a manner suggestive of another fairy-tale duo:

"Woe is me.... Oh, brother Hansel.... Yah, sister Gretel.... That is one smart cookie.... Maybe he will help us get back to our mama and papa.... 'Could you spare a few crumbs so we can find our way out of the forest?'"

When the wolves fail to get their cookie quarry, they come to an enticingly decorated house in the woods. "Yoo-hoo! Kiddies. Why don't you help yourselves to something to eat at my house?" When they enter, the old woman is bent over her open oven door, pulling out a pan. The innocent wolf "children" are standing by with forks and knives at ready, assuming a meal is coming—and not knowing what the old woman might be planning to serve.

Foreshadow

"Cookie tossed them each a gumdrop button and waved good-bye as he floated away on a log," thinking he has escaped. The "log" quickly emerges with malevolent eyes and a hint of sharp teeth.

Inference

Will the two investigators return the missing cookie to the baker, who hires their services? "Wally grinned at Willy. Willy grinned at Wally. They both licked their lips."

One plan to snare the illusive cookie involves a hollow log with a pool of honey at one end. "One slip. One slide. One cookie!"

At the gingerbread house, the wolves in disguise are invited to help themselves to something to eat. But what (or who) is for dinner? "I've got the oven warming right now," invites the old woman, who opens the oven door and pulls out a pan.

Motif

These two unscrupulous fellows stop at nothing to satisfy their craving for sweets. The cookie is equally determined not to allow them that pleasure:

"Brain ditto!" What one thinks up, the other simultaneously thinks.

"Bad. Really, really bad." They try various tactics to get the cookie. "Lookee! Lookee! You can't get me. I'm one smart cookie!"

Parallelism

"Please toss me another caramel, dear pal," said Willy to Wally.
"I believe I could go for a couple of bonbons myself," said Wally to Willy.
"A piece of chocolate cake? A slice of pecan pie? A bit of brownie?"
"Willy's ears perked. Wally's eyes twinkled."
"Wally grinned at Willy. Willy grinned at Wally."
"Oh my, they were clever!
Oh my, they were cunning!"
"They watched. They inched. Further. Farther."

Poetic Justice

The cookie braggart thinks he has escaped the bungling wolves only to end up on the back of an alligator he mistakes for a log in the river. He flings off his gumdrop buttons to his pursuers in a final disdainful salute. But, sharp teeth on the "log" are opening up for the "one smart cookie."

Pun

The wolf detectives assure the baker they can handle the investigation of the missing cookie. "Don't worry. Detective Wallace and I will *sniff* him out." Willis and Wallace "always get their *cookie*."

As they spot the cookie running toward the hill, the baker shook his head in puzzlement. "Oh dear. I'm afraid I added too much *spice*."

The detectives note: "That is one smart cookie. And he looks so *sweet* too."

They have a plan to catch the runaway cookie. "It's a *honey*," they declare as they pour "a sticky squirt" in a puddle outside a hollow log.

When they see the cookie on the alligator's snout, they decide the "little *crumb* isn't as smart as he thinks he is."

The wolves have worked up "quite an appetite trying to get that one little *cookie*."

Tone

"Those bad boys, Willy and Wally Wolf, had two big bad sweet tooths.... But mere candy was not enough to top two big bad sweet tooths of two big bad wolves. Oh heavens no!"

As the cookie leads the wolf detectives on the chase, those bad boys "blew through a couple of fields of head-high corn."

"Yes, those bad boys needed a plan! An idea! A trap! ... a trick!"

Understatement

The boys creep out to the end of a tree limb to drop a net over the passing cookie. The limb breaks under their combined weight. They find themselves tangled together on the ground. "'Oh dear,' said Willy, seeing stars. 'Do you think perhaps we went out a bit too far?'"

Inside the hollow log the two wolves wait in darkness for the cookie to become entrapped in the puddle of honey. They hear a slip, feel a bump, take a whiff. "I'm afraid, dear chum, that is not the aroma of sugar and spice" as they discover a skunk in the honey puddle.

As the cookie dances on the back of a log, not realizing it is really an alligator, the wolves observe, "I believe that little crumb is not as smart as he thinks he is."

Wit/Humor

The baker says of the runaway cookie, "I thought he was such a good cookie. I don't know what's gotten into him. I gave him the best of everything. Butter. Cream. Sugar."

As the wolves watch from shore, the cookie disappears on the back of a green log that has eyes and sharp teeth. "I believe that little crumb is not as smart as he thinks he is."

*****

Pearson, Tracey Campbell. *Bob.* New York: Farrar, Straus and Giroux, c2002.

> While looking for someone to teach him how to crow, a rooster learns to sound like many different animals and finds that his new skills come in handy.
>
> **Curriculum Tie-in:** Literature (Folk Tale, Modern), Social Science (Character Development—Perseverance), Social Science (Character Development—Self-Reliance), Social Science (Individuality)
> **Art Style:** Bright, full-page pastel and watercolor *Cartoons*

DEVICES

Ambiguity

Bob is searching to discover the correct sound a rooster makes. An owl calls "Whoo? Whoo?" Not wishing to be rude, the rooster responds, "Bob, Bob." Again, the stranger repeats "Whoo" and Bob repeats his name. "And so it went all night long, over and over again."

The fox, terrified and amazed by all the animals that are apparently in the coop, "especially the one that sounded hungry for fox, ran home, never to return." When Cock-a-doodle-do doesn't deter the fox, Bob simply resorts to trying out all the animal sounds he's learned on the fox, including "yum-yum."

Irony

Bob spends a lot of time tracking down how to crow because "that's what roosters do." But, it was the sounds he had learned other animals make that saved the day when danger threatened the henhouse.

The name Henrietta does not belong to a chicken—it's the cat's name!

Onomatopoeia

As Rooster Bob meets all the animals along the way, he diligently copies their sounds. He woofs, moos, ribbets, meows, and yum-yums until he finally meets "a bird who looked a lot like Bob."

Theme

Having a determined goal and plucky perseverance, plus a dash of originality, overcome a myriad of obstacles.

Tone

A light and gently amused attitude toward Rooster Bob's unique social problem applauds his streak of individualism.

"You need to stop clucking and learn how to crow so you can wake up the girls every morning." First, Bob learns to woof and wag. He learns to moo and tries cud-chewing. Finally, "there in the middle of the road was a bird who looked a lot like Bob." When he finally learns the right sound, "Bob woke up the hens with a loud Cock-a-doodle-do," or, if he felt like it, a "Meow-Woof, Ribbet-Mooo, Yum-Yum-Bugs!"

Wit/Humor

The Cock-a-doodle-do sound doesn't frighten away the fox, but the creature is "terrified and amazed by all the animals in the coop, especially the one that sounded hungry for fox." Bob has not only called out all the animal sounds he knows, he's even combined some of the sounds on the spot—like "YUM-YUM-FOX"!

Every morning, Bob wakes the henhouse with Cock-a-doodle-do! Or any sound "he felt like."

*****

Pelley, Kathleen T. *Inventor McGregor.* Illus. by Michael Chesworth. New York: Farrar, Straus and Giroux, c2006.

> Hector McGregor, inventor, leaves his home workshop to work in a laboratory but finds his inspiration comes from being around his cheery wife, five children, and a hen called Hattie.
>
> > **Curriculum Tie-in:** Science (Inventions), Social Science (Creativity/ Inspiration), Social Science (Love), Social Science (Values)
> >
> > **Art Style:** Humorous watercolor *Cartoons*

DEVICES

Alliteration

"Squeaky skates, squiggly spoons, wobbly wagons"
"Whirled and whooshed and wheeched"
"Rousing reel"
"Loopy lane"
"Torn to tatters"
"Flip this flap"
"Swing and swoop and swish"
"Bunch of bobbing balloons"
"Bounding boots"
"Gadgets and gizmos"
"Bewildered and befuddled"
"Hoot and a holler"

Atmosphere

Hector McGregor is pleased with his "happy, happy home."

"With a blob of glue or a squirt of oil, with a tap of his hammer or a shimmy here and a shimmy there, Hector McGregor fixed whatever needed fixing, and sent everyone on their way with a skip, a hop, and a hum."

Hector McGregor "liked to stroll down the winding lane at the back of his house where the bluebells grew and the smell of wet heather lingered long and sweet."

"He sang a snippet of a song or twirled a whirl of a fling or sometimes he pulled out his palette and his easel to paint a picture. Then back to his work he went with a heart that was both happy and full."

He would "concoct some thingamabob or thingamajig to make their world a little better or brighter."

Connotation

Hector McGregor is a happy man, content with his life. He liked to *stroll* and sing a *snippet* of a song. He feels none of life's pressures to conform to a working schedule and allows his mind to indulge in idle thoughts.

Irony

When he lives in a "higgledy-piggledy" hub-bub, Hector MeGregor has no trouble inventing things; when he's in a sterile laboratory with no distractions and plenty of equipment, there is nothing needing his attention. No ideas come to him. He cannot invent.

Paradox

At home, Hector McGregor invents most anything that needs inventing. Ideas simmer and spark. Diversions enable him to "produce one more incredible invention after another." He still finds time to "stroll down the winding lane ... and smell wet heather long and sweet." In a laboratory with all the time he needs, all the equipment he needs, and no distractions, "no ideas come to him." He can invent "just as long as he could sing and paint, and fiddle and fling, and love all that he had to love."

Simile

"A barking noise as loud as a hundred wolfhounds"
"Popped his head from the pillow like a Jack from his box"

Theme

Creative work and inspiration flow from a contented soul and loving environment. He paints "a picture of a marmalade cat curled up in a patch of sunlight. Then back to his inventing he went with a heart that was happy and full."

*****

Pfister, Marcus. *Holey Moley.* Trans. by J. Alison James. New York: North-South Books, c2006.

  Two mole brothers can't agree; one wants to dig a deep hole, and the other wants to make a high hill.

  Curriculum Tie-in: Social Science (Character Development—Cooperation), Social Science (Family Relationships—Siblings)

  Art Style: Charmingly humorous *Cartoons*

DEVICES

Antithesis

The mole brothers' argument escalates to a physical confrontation, and so "Tim shoved Matt.... Matt pushed Tim."

Counterpoint

"I don't want to play with you anymore!" Tim says.
"Who would want to play with you anyway?" Matt replies.

"... Tim began to dig his own hole."
"... Matt worked just as hard on his hill."

"By digging a hole, Tim had tossed up a pile of dirt, making a small hill."
"By building up a hill, Matt had had to dig up dirt, leaving a small hole."

Matt "decided to go take a peek at Tim's hole and see how he was coming along."
Tim "slipped through the grass to spy on Matt" to see "just how big his hill would be."

Irony

One mole wanted a hole; one wanted a hill. "If we'd worked together, then you would have had a deep hole, and I would have a huge hill."

Paradox

Each mole wanted to do something different. At first they each tried to convince the other to participate in the same activity. When neither would agree to the other's preference, they stormed off to do their separate projects. Eventually, they realize that by digging together Tim got his deep hole to crawl into and Matt got his high hill to climb. Each was able to accomplish his own goal by working together doing exactly what each wanted to do. Tim "curled up happily in his hole." Matt "climbed up his hill."

Parallelism

"Tim longed to lie down in his hole and take a nap, ..."
"Matt longed to be high on his hill, looking out over the world."

"When Tim saw Matt's hill, he shook his head."
"When Matt saw Tim's hole, he couldn't believe his eyes!"

Theme

Separate goals can be more readily achieved through mutual cooperation. "The two little moles put all their energy into the work ... soon the hole was big enough so both of them could stretch out side by side. And the hill was so huge," it was high enough for both to climb to look over the top.

*****

*Raven, Marot Theis.** *Night Boat to Freedom.* Illus. by E. B. Lewis. New York: (Melanie Kroupa Books) Farrar, Straus and Giroux, c2006.
> At the request of fellow slave Granny Judith, Christmas John risks his life to take runaways across a river from Kentucky to Ohio, as based on slave narratives recorded in the 1930s.
>> **Curriculum Tie-in:** History (Slavery), History (Underground Railroad), Social Science (Character Development—Courage)
>> **Art Style:** Full-page painted *Expressionism*

DEVICES

Aphorism

"... what scares the head is best done with the heart."
"... love don't stop at a river, and no river's wide enough to keep us apart."
"Freedom's got no color for me without you."
"In the dark of the moon we are *all* the colors of freedom."

Atmosphere

A sense of the tense, historical import of their activities is conveyed through the timing of these illicit acts.
"Then Granny Judith spoke so low even the dark couldn't hear her."
"Night after night it [old boat] kept me and my secret safe as I'd hurry back in the dark—boat and me making it to shore just as the mornin' star lit the sky."
"Black moon by black moon, I made the river trips, and square by square, Granny Judith's quilt grew."

Colloquialism

"I can see the river, too, that swept by *old master's Big House* in Kentucky keepin' us a boat trip away from Ohio and freedom."
"... boiling and stirring up *hanks* of thread."
"I grew so quiet you could've heard a *sewin' needle fall on feathers.*"
"All the next day, my mind saw the overseer *layin' the rawhide* on my back if I got caught."

Imagery

"And bamboo turning turkey red, the color that stole Granny Judith from Africa and put her in slavery."

"It was black-dark and I couldn't see her, but I felt her eyes."

"I just rowed in the cold, prayin' nobody would hear my oars slap-slapping through the water."

She cried, "holdin' up her arms to the last whisper of night."

"Slowly, pink mornin' cracked the sky."

Inference

Given the opportunity at last, Christmas John tore off to his own freedom, "but near some muddy ground my feet slowed.... How could I leave Granny Judith?" Despite her blessing to go, he can't leave her.

Metaphor

The row boat served as a protective cradle that helped escaping slaves begin life anew. After each time it made a successful trip across the river safely, it would rock empty and peacefully, having done its work for the night.

Paradox

When it's time for the boy to row himself to freedom, Granny Judith hands Christmas John a new turkey-red shirt. This is the color that lured her into slavery; it will be his freedom color.

Granny Judith, at first, refuses to accompany Christmas John to freedom, saying, "I'd just get you caught ... slow you down." But, Christmas John echoes her own advice to him. "What scares the head is best done with the heart. Let me take you across."

She may end up being the reason that patrollers capture them, but "Freedom's got no color for me without you." The swift, agile child will pace himself to the old woman's ability. They will fail together or succeed together.

Parallelism

"No mornin' star yet! No dogs!" Noting these two facts, the boy judges it is still safe enough for him and his grandmother to take their chance on a freedom run, too.

Simile

"I was twelve summers grown and a strong hulk of a boy, but I was *feeble as a baby...*"

"I tore off *faster than a wild horse...*"

"I wrapped the quilt around her *like a big warm hug...*"

"... in that new day risin' I watched it *rock peaceful as a babe's cradle...*"

Symbol

The colors of cloth dyes Granny Judith creates and finds irresistible represent the slave's fate. As a child she was tricked with pieces of red flannel that were used to lure her "till they got her across a river and onto a ship." To her dismay, "the pretty color of red turned the sad color of slavery for me."

She proposes rowing slaves across the river so they "got a chance to learn the color of freedom!" She tells the boy, "I'll be here prayin' and waitin' to know what color Molly wore to freedom." Later when he reports "blue" to Granny Judith, "it made her smile something beautiful."

"'What color is freedom tonight, Christmas John?' Granny Judith'd ask when I'd sneak back into our cabin. I'd tell her yellow, indigo, green—the colors worn by the people in the night, people I could touch but never see."

Granny "had a dream-vision to make a quilt and stretch out the freedom colors in pretty squares like a rainbow bridge from side to side." When only two squares remain, Granny tells the boy, "Dream says we got to get ourselves over the river, 'cause the danger's gonna grow awful."

Finally, after Christmas John rows many others to freedom, Granny Judith hands him the nearly finished quilt. "You take my night colors to the freedom side where they belong."

Theme

When Christmas John asks her, "What color is freedom tonight?" Granny Judith holds her arms up to the "last whisper of night." She tells him, "You and me, child! You and me!" Stitches of love and selflessness can be stronger than any chains that seek to enslave the human spirit.

*****

Recorvits, Helen. *Yoon and the Christmas Mitten.* Illus. by Gabi Swaiatowska. New York: (Frances Foster Books) Farrar, Straus and Giroux, c2006.

> Yoon, a Korean American, is excited to hear about Santa Claus and Christmas at her school, but her family tells her that such things are not part of their Korean tradition.

>> **Curriculum Tie-in:** Geography (Korea), Social Science (Holidays), Social Science (Immigrants)

>> **Art Style:** Dreamy paintings, suggestive of an ethnic Asian *Impressionism*

DEVICES

Ambiguity

So as not to miss receiving a Christmas gift, Yoon places food treats in the bushes to attract thankful birds in hopes they will tell Mr. Santa Claus, "Little

Yoon is here! She is here in America!" However, her parents are alarmed. "Look! Look! There are so many birds! They are attacking our bushes!"

Yoon recalls her school friends saying that "Santa Claus would not come until I fell asleep. I closed my eyes and I wished and waited." Later she awakens, hearing the floor creak. A shadow figure creeps to her bed, carrying a big box, which is laid on the floor next to her bed. "My heart danced. It must be Santa Claus!"

Yoon brings to school to show her class "the piece of the North Pole that Mr. Santa Claus had brought me." She finds in her Christmas mitten a red and white striped candy cane like the school picture book illustration of the North Pole.

Antithesis

"That is not the North Pole."
"That is peppermint candy."

"It is not the Korean way."
"... America is our home now."

Atmosphere

The gap between cultures is expressed in the first sentence of the story: "My name is Yoon, I came here from Korea, a country far away."

Though her father is abruptly dismissive when Yoon tries to show him the story about Santa Claus—"We are Korean. Santa Claus is not our custom"—Her mother lovingly tries to make amends, coming into her room at night: "Here, Little Yoon. I saved some for you. Your favorite." She sets a plate of sliced sweet pears on the table by Yoon's bed. She smoothes her hair and kisses her cheek.

Even Yoon's father stops to think when she asks him if the family is not now both Korean and American. "My father sat quietly for a few moments."

Colloquialism

Yoon helps her father accept the concept of combining American and Korean customs. "You are *full of shining wisdom*, Little Yoon."

Yoon tells students after holiday vacation about the special spicy cabbage called *kimchee* they eat to celebrate New Year's.

Counterpoint

Yoon's mother shows her the lotus flower she is embroidering on the corner of a new tablecloth the family will give to a neighbor as a New Year's Day gift. "Do you think this is pretty?"

"Yes Mother. Pretty."

Then, Yoon quickly adds, "I learned a pretty song in school today. It is about a reindeer with a red nose. This reindeer is Santa Claus's favorite."

"Yoon, I have told you. It is not the Korean way."
"But Father, you have also told me that America is our home now."
The school children urge Yoon to eat her candy cane.
"Eat it? I could never eat it."
"Eat it! Yes!"
". . . maybe I could take a tiny taste."

Foreshadow

Yoon pins a colorful mitten to the bottom corner of her blanket in a persistent effort to attract Mr. Santa Claus on Christmas Eve. Her mother sees it when she tucks Yoon in. "My mother sighed. After she left, I heard my father and mother whispering in the front room." Her father comes in and asks her about the "Christmas mitten." She tells him when Santa comes, "that is where he will leave my surprise." Perhaps, for the sake of their precious child, these parents will force themselves to embrace a foreign custom.

Inference

Despite efforts by her parents to quash Yoon's interest in the Santa Claus tradition, "I went to sleep, dreaming of a village at the North Pole."
The tide turns in Yoon's favor for acknowledging American customs after she reminds her father that the transplanted family is both Korean and American: "My father sat quietly for a few moments." Then he tells her, "You have given me something to think about."

Parallelism

"Look in the box . . . Mr. Santa Claus brought me a new red dress."
"'Well!' my father said, smiling at my mother."

"'And look! . . . Mr. Santa Clause brought me a piece of the North Pole!'"
"'Well!' my mother said, smiling at my father."

"I told my teacher and the boys and girls all about our New Year's celebration."
"I told them about our fine dinner. . . ."
"I told them about the good-luck wishes."

Point-of-View

Yoon is puzzled by her parents' response to her excitement about Christmas customs, since they want her to participate in both her native Korean and her adopted American cultures. "I told my father all about the man in the red suit. I showed him the picture of the red-and-white striped North Pole." Her father pushes the book away. Yoon wonders, "Why did my father not like Mr. Santa Claus? Why did my father not like Christmas?"

Yoon's teacher reads a story about a tall Christmas tree decorated with beautiful colored lights. "How would Mr. Santa Claus even find my dark house without colored lights to show him the way?"

She thinks that by attracting birds with bits of bread and the popcorn ball she received, "they would eat the treats and fly, fly away to the North Pole. They would sing a song for Santa Claus. They would tell him where to find me."

Yoon thinks the candy cane she finds in her Christmas mitten is "a piece of the North Pole" that "Mr. Santa Claus brought me." When she tells her class at school about it, they finally convince her it should be eaten. "I tasted the magic of Christmas and it is sweet."

Theme

Yoon's parents need to be reminded that "America is our home now. Are we not both Korean and American?" It is good to combine customs and thereby doubly benefit from the richness of both.

*****

*Reynolds, Peter H. *So Few of Me.* Cambridge, MA: Candlewick Press, c2006.

>When Leo one day wishes there were two of him and it happens, and happens again and again, he learns more of him is not the answer to his over-scheduling woes.
>
>**Curriculum Tie-in:** Social Science (Time Management), Social Science (Values)
>
>**Art Style:** Deceptively simple pen line, watercolor *Cartoons*

DEVICES

Satire

Perhaps a second Leo would be the answer to take care of the growing "list of things to do." Suddenly the list grows and two Leos aren't enough to finish everything. Even with five Leos the workload is too much. A sixth one "came in to help organize the lot." A lengthy meeting resulted in the hiring of a seventh. But, they discovered "there was seven times as much work!" Eight were needed "just to catch our breath." After ten Leos, "each one busier than the next," there was "no time to stop, no time to rest!"

"Leo himself was exhausted. He slipped away to take a nap." Angrily the other nine demanded to know, "What were you doing?" When he replies that he was dreaming, they retort, "Dreaming was NOT on the list!"

Leo concludes, "What if I did less—but did my BEST?" "Then ONE Leo is all I need." And, he would still have time to dream.

Theme

It's not how much we accomplish that is satisfying, it's the quality of what we do. We must not value an insatiable effort to schedule our lives with unfulfilling activities. A good idea is to concentrate on doing less but doing our best and allowing time to dream.

*****

Sauer, Tammi. *Cowboy Camp.* Illus. by Mike Reed. New York: Sterling, c2005.
> Although Avery cannot eat the right grub, is allergic to horses, and gets rope burns from lassos, he learns at camp that he is uniquely qualified in the most important cowboy quality.
> > **Curriculum Tie-in:** Career Education (Cowboy), Social Science (Individuality)
> > **Art Style:** Humorous full-page *Expressionism* in *Cartoons*

DEVICES

Antihero

Poor Avery is not a good example of a cowboy. Black Bart is fooled into believing that Avery can't be from the Cowboy Camp because he can't do cowboy things like twirl a lasso or eat beans or ride horses. He wants to put a stop to Cowboy Camp, but he leaves in disgust, convinced he "musta made a wrong turn somewhere." This kid is no cowboy.

Aptronym

"Black Bart" is the name of the bad guy. The good guy is named "Cowboy Dan."

The kids who want to become cowboys have the right kind of cowboy names, such as Hank or Jimmy Jean, except "Avery," whose name better suits someone who can't ride a horse or lasso one, or eat a typical cowboy meal of beans and grits.

Archetype

"Out of the shadows stepped the meanest looking cowboy Avery had ever seen." Black Bart intends to "put a stop to Cowboy Camp. Cowboy Dan and his gangs of good cowboys are makin' it too hard to be a bad guy."

Colloquialism

"Rustlin' rattlesnakes!"
"It'll be daybreak soon and time's a wastin'."
"First things first, though, buckaroos. It's chow time."
"... campers turned in for some shut-eye, ..."
"... bravest durn cowboy I ever laid eyes on, ..."

Irony

Avery can't ride a horse, eat beans, or twirl a lasso. Even Black Bart can see he's not a cowboy. Still, "no one but a real cowboy could outsmart the likes of Black Bart."

Paradox

The least capable of the cowboy trainees actually saves the future of the camp. "Avery had to think fast. He couldn't let anything happen to Cowboy Dan and his Cowboy Camp." He demonstrates his ineptness, thereby convincing Black Bart to leave. "Little feller, you're no cowboy." Cowboy Dan pronounces, "No one but a real cowboy could outsmart the likes of Black Bart." Avery can't do cowboy things, but he is the "bravest durn cowboy" anyway.

Parallelism

"Whoever heard of a cowboy who didn't like grits and beans?
Whoever heard of a cowboy named Avery?
Whoever heard of a cowboy who was allergic to horses?
Whoever heard of a cowboy who got rope burns?"

"Avery discovered he couldn't stomach a single bite of cowboy food.
Avery discovered he was allergic to horses.
Avery discovered he had a bad case of rope burn."

When Black Bart tests Avery's "cowboy-ness," he says, "All cowboys eat beans. All cowboys ride horses. All cowboys know how to lasso."

Satire

Avery (whoever heard of a cowboy with that name!) went to Cowboy Camp to learn cowboy skills. But, "he knew he was all wrong." His belt buckle was too big. His hat was too small. His boots were too red. He just wasn't "cowboy material." He sits outside his tent "and tried to think cowboy thoughts." Even Black Bart can see nobody like Avery would be at a Cowboy Camp. Strangely, the only cowboy who doesn't act like a cowboy makes it possible for the camp to continue to train cowboys that do look and act like real cowboys. So, what are the characteristics of a real cowboy?

*****

*Schotter, Roni. *Mama, I'll Give You the World.* Illus. by S. Saelig
Gallagher. New York: (Schwartz & Wade) Random House, c2006.

> At Walter's World of Beauty, Luisa's secret plans are underway to create
> a very special birthday celebration for her hard-working single mother
> who is employed there as a stylist.
>
> > **Curriculum Tie-in:** Career Education (Beautician), Social Science
> > (Character Development—Kindness), Social Science (Family
> > Relationship—Parent/Child)
> >
> > **Art Style:** Lively *Expressionism* in *Cartoons*

DEVICES

Ambiguity

A photograph at her mother's workstation shows Luisa's Mama "long ago—
happy and dancing—in a large room that looks like a palace." Her mother says
the name of the palace is Roseland. Not realizing the place is a ballroom, Luisa
"thinks her mother has made up the name because she loves flowers."

Mama saves her tips for Luisa's college fund. She speaks of giving the
"world" to Luisa. Luisa thinks, "No, tonight I will give the World to you for
your birthday." While Mama plans a fine future for her daughter, Luisa is planning a night reminiscent of Mama's past happy dancing nights right there in
Walter's World of Beauty.

Connotation

Mama's skillful hands can take a woman's *dark tangles* of hair and turn
them into an *ocean of gentle waves.* Women can walk into the salon with
untamed, unattractive hair and walk out looking well groomed and beautiful.

Most of the salon's customers come looking less than their best like the
"*go-everywhere* hair" that must be coaxed into a becoming style.

Foreshadow

On the eve of Mama's birthday, Luisa has "whispered her secret in the ear
of each of Mama's favorite customers" as she plans the evening's special dance
in the salon.

To get Mama back to the shop that evening, Luisa pretends to have left a
book at the salon. They must return to get it. "Mama sighs and puts on her
coat. Luisa tries not to smile."

Imagery

"... there by Walter's Bottles of Beauty, with names that whisper promises—
Raspberry Radiance, Evening Glamour Glow, Sunday Night Soother ..."

"... Mama, like a magician, turns Mrs. Koo's dark hair the color of sunset ..."

"... braid Hazel Mae Dixon's go-everywhere hair till it looks like neat shiny rows of licorice."

"... the giant pink and purple rollers that turn Mrs. Rodriguez's dark tangles into an ocean of gentle waves."

"Outside, the world stretches before them—dark, mysterious, and twinkling with store and street and starlight."

Inference

"When Papa was around, Mama loved to dance, but Mama doesn't dance anymore. Mama hardly ever smiles, but when she does, she is the prettiest flower in the world."

Luisa is the adored pet of the salon: "Everyone greets her—Walter, Rupa, Georges, but especially Mama."

Mama takes seriously her single parenting job: "First things first. Luisa does her school work."

Luisa is sensitively concerned: "She writes a story for English about a girl with a magic brush that brushes people's cares away."

Mama has bittersweet memories of Roseland: "Her eyes look at something far away and once upon a time—something Luisa can only guess at."

Mama saves her tip money for her daughter: "Mama wants Luisa to learn everything."

Metaphor

"Everyone in the world is a flower," her mother always tells Luisa. "Together, they make a bouquet ... [for] each one comes in a special size and shape.... Mama is the prettiest flower in the world." Mama's happiest time was at a place named after a flower, the Roseland ballroom.

Motif

"First things first." Mama's priority is raising a daughter with good career options. She makes "a place for Luisa—on a cushion, under the palm tree," for Luisa to do her homework, and Mama saves all her tip money for Luisa's college education.

To get Mama back to the salon for the surprise party, Luisa fakes leaving a book behind. "It's for my book report. Don't you always tell me 'first things first'?"

Mama blushes when she sees the decorations and guests at her surprise birthday party. She gathers Luisa into her arms. "First things first," she says.

Point-of-View

It is from Luisa's perspective that a dance at the beauty salon after hours will help bring back Mama's smile. Mama last danced at the Roseland "palace," where she was happy and smiling. Luisa will recreate that ballroom in the salon, and her mother will again be happy and will smile.

Simile

Mrs. Fogelman's hair is "fluffy and high as a great, gray cloud."

Mama's wearing the "prettiest dress—the one with the roses and violets and vines that encircle Mama's waist the way Luisa's arms do when they hug."

Luisa's eyes open "wide as Walter's windows."

Hazel Mae's braids look "like neat, shiny rows of licorice."

Symbol

The "world" represents several meanings to Luisa and to her Mama: To Mama, the outside *world* is large with future possibilities for her daughter. She tells Luisa, "The world is big. One day if I can, I will give the *world* to you."

Luisa, too, has special secret plans for her mother right where Mama works, Walter's *World* of Beauty. Luisa thinks, "Tonight, if I can, I will give the *World* to you."

The salon restores confidence and brings happiness to each customer. Mama says everyone in the *world* is a flower. And, though "Mama hardly ever smiles ... when she does, she is the prettiest flower in the *world*."

Outside the shop "the *world* stretches before them.... Luisa and Mama stand together looking at it, feeling oh, so small. Mama's hair sparkles in the light. So do her eyes." As the two walk back into the shop for the surprise party, "music fills the *World*." Luisa tells her mother she "wanted to turn the *World* into Roseland" for her.

With everyone dancing at the surprise birthday party dance, "the *World* seems to sparkle and spin faster and faster around them."

"And the way Mr. Anselmo smiles at Mama and the way she smiles back at him makes Luisa think there is no more beautiful place in the *world* than this *World*—the *world* they are dancing in now."

Tone

Walter's World of Beauty salon becomes a magic shop for bringing joy to the lives of the "flowers" who are Mama's customers, as well as the employees who work in this world of beauty.

Luisa "helps Mrs. Mallory, bent over and sad as she inches into the World on her walker, but smiling and standing nearly straight an hour later, when, feeling beautiful again, she leaves." She "sprays fussy Mrs. Fogelman's hair that refuses to stand up and obey until Mama teases it with a comb so it can't help standing up, just the way Mrs. Fogelman likes it!"

The surprise party does surprise Mama. "She looks at Walter, Rupa, and Georges smiling at her. She looks at Mrs. Mallory's two old feet tapping beside her walker, like two new feet. She looks at Mrs. Fogelman's great, gray cloud of hair turned golden by the lights and changed into a clear-weather cloud." When she looks into Luisa's eyes, "Luisa sees that Mama's eyes are no longer far away. They are near and clear and wet with tears."

*****

Smith, Cynthia Leitich and Greg Smith. *Santa Knows.* Illus. by Steve Bjorkman. New York: (Dutton Children's Books) Penguin, c2006.

> Armed with the facts, young Alfie sets out to prove to the world that Santa Claus does not exist—but no one pays attention, especially his sister Noelle, whose only request of the man in red is a nicer big brother.
>
> **Curriculum Tie-in:** Social Science (Character Development—Self-Improvement), Social Science (Family Relationships—Siblings), Social Science (Holidays)
>
> **Art Style:** *Expressionism* in *Cartoons*

DEVICES

Allusion

Alfie settles down to wait up for Santa to not arrive. "Humbug!" he mutters, alluding to Charles Dickens' Mr. Scrooge.

When Santa enters through the chimney and presents himself to a shocked Alfie Snorkelpuss, Alfie can think of nothing to say. Santa merrily asks him, "What's the matter? Reindeer got your tongue?" (As in the phrase "Cat got your tongue?")

Ambiguity

Alfie suddenly finds he has magically passed through the gateway of Santa's bag onto the toy shop conveyor belt. Santa's elves do not recognize him as a real child but are impressed with his likeness: "The elves in plastics know their stuff."

But, they aren't satisfied with his facial expression:

"Hmm, it has an unpleasant expression."

"Still, Santa must've put in the order for a reason."

Alfie is popped into a box on the belt and whizzed away. The elves go on cocoa break never knowing the truth, though he tries to tell them: "I'm not a toy." They respond: "What a snazzy doll."

Aptronym

The grumpy, disbelieving scientific expert is Alfie *Snorkelpuss,* and his little sister, who does believe in Santa, is *Noelle.*

Foreshadow

The toy shop elves are impressed with the size of Alfie, who they believe is a real-sized boy doll:

"Who gets this one?" asks an elf clerk.

"Check the paperwork," a distribution elf suggests.

"Let's worry about it later," says their boss as they leave on cocoa break.

Where is Alfie destined to go? His little sister did say in her letter to Santa, "All I want for Christmas is a nicer big brother."

Hyperbole

Alfie knows the concept of Santa is not possible. He reasons, "There is no way anyone could deliver kajillions of pounds of gifts to hundreds of millions of kids all in one night."

Irony

Alfie, who doesn't believe in Santa and annoyingly corroborates his nonbelief with scientific facts whether anyone wants to hear them or not, suddenly finds himself thrust into elf technology.

They, now, don't believe in him. "What a snazzy doll." They note his lifelike size. "Grab a big box!" He declares, "I need air-holes!" The elves are impressed. "Just do what it says."

Finally, Alfie is humbled and finds himself the answer to his sister's request of Santa—a nicer big brother. Alfie has not only become a believer in Santa Claus, he believes he "can be a nice boy. A nicer big brother." He promises Santa, "I'll be the nicest big brother in the world."

Motif

"Belief" is the recurring theme pattern in this tale of an overbearing brother and his long-suffering little sister. He yanks off the mantle the Christmas stocking his sister has hung there. "Why bother?" he asks her. "I believe," Noelle whispers.

Alfie researches and offers his proof that Santa is not possible. Noelle says, "Santa Claus believes in people who believe in him."

Only after Alfie is boxed up by mistake as a toy in Santa's workshop does he conclude, "I believe in elf science and technology." And, he believes in Santa. And, he believes he can be a nice boy. Especially important, he believes he can be a nicer big brother, maybe the nicest big brother in the world. He tells this to his sister. She says, "I know. I believe in you!"

Parallelism

"He read books about flying.
He read books about reindeer.
He read books about flying reindeer.
He read every book he could find about Santa Claus, elves, Christmas Eve, and the North Pole."

"Alfie was cold.
Alfie was hungry.
Alfie was lonely.
And, Alfie was just a little scared."

"I believe in you.
I believe in elf science and technology, too.
What's more, I believe I can be a nice boy."

Poetic Justice

Alfie, at first, refuses to believe in Santa. Then Santa's elves won't believe in him. He's just a doll, albeit a "snazzy" one. And, one that can talk: "I need air-holes!"

All little sister Noelle wants for Christmas is a nicer big brother. After his frightening experience in a toy box at the elf factory, Alfie wakes up to find his sister has "tugged the ribbon loose and the box fell open revealing Alfie." He promises her, "From now on I'm going to be a nicer big brother." His sister knew she would get what she asked for. "I know. I believe in you!" Alfie, who did not believe in Santa, certainly does now. He's been transformed into his little sister's Christmas gift.

Tone

Cynical and irreverent Alfie points out precisely why Santa can't exist. "The weight alone would cripple an old fat man," he says about Santa's gift pack. He chastises believers: "Wake up and smell the cookies! At least they're for real."

Wit/Humor

In the toy factory, Alfie is noticed on the toy shop conveyor belt. The elves are impressed with his lifelike size: "The elves in plastics know their stuff!"

Nevertheless, they do find fault with his workmanship: "It has an unpleasant expression."

Alfie is alarmed to find he's being packaged. "Hey, elfin guys?" They stroll away. "Guys? Anybody? Help!" They stubbornly refuse to believe in him, not even when he talks to them. "Just do what it says," and then they calmly walk away on their cocoa break.

*****

Smith, Linda. *Mrs. Crump's Cat.* Illus. by David Roberts. New York: HarperCollins Children's Books, c2006.

Cranky Mrs. Crump has no use for cats, but when she finds a stray shivering on her doorstep, her life is subtly—and pleasantly—transformed.

Curriculum Tie-in: Social Science (Character Development—Kindness)

Art Style: Watercolor *Cartoons*

DEVICES

Antithesis

"I did not find you. . . ."
"You were on my porch step. . . ."

"When the cat is dry, Mrs. Crump thought, I'll send it on its way."
"When the cat was dry, it curled itself around Mrs. Crump's ankles."

"You have bought a collar, soap, livers, tuna, two pints of cream, and a shiny red dish."
"You may as well have a cat to go with them."

Aptronym

Mrs. *Crump* has "no use for a cat." She pronounces them "sneaky by nature, finicky as well." She speaks curtly to the grocer. She declares the cat "a lot of trouble. It's been one thing after another." She sounds like someone who fits such an unpleasant name.

Inference

Despite having no use for a cat, Mrs. Crump's behavior belies her words. She keeps finding ways not to put it out of her life.

". . . somehow the door did not quite shut, and the cat slipped in." Because the cat was wet, "she wrestled a log into place" in the fireplace so it would get dry.

When she shops, she also comes home with a pint of cream and a "shiny red dish." And, the walk home "seemed far shorter than the way there."

The sky is clear, but "I smell rain," so the cat is not put outside.

The next time she shops, her purchases include "a bar of brown soup, a pint of cream, . . . and a dainty yellow collar with a silver bell."

She puts up a found-notice for the cat's owner, but it's pinned "in a dusty corner." She then buys "six fat livers and a can of tuna."

Paradox

Mrs. Crump inquires of the grocer whether anyone has responded to her sign about the cat. "Sorry. No one asked about the cat today." Mrs. Crump "found herself singing on the way home." She doesn't seem irritated that no one has stepped forth to claim the stray cat she is trying to get rid of. By the end of the week, the grocer tells her no one has responded to her sign. "It was the strangest thing, but somehow Mrs. Crump was not the least bit surprised."

*****

Squires, Janet. *The Gingerbread Cowboy.* Illus. by Holly Berry. New York: HarperCollins Children's Books, c2006.

> A freshly baked gingerbread cowboy escapes from the ranch kitchen and eludes his pursuers in this American western version of the Gingerbread Boy.
>
> **Curriculum Tie-in:** Literature (Folktale, Modern)
>
> **Art Style:** Blend of *Cartoon* and *Folk* in a rodeo-romping Wild West theme

DEVICES

Atmosphere

The Gingerbread Cowboy "jumped over a horned lizard gobbling up ants" and "wriggled through the corral fence and raced away as fast as his boots could carry him . . . until he came to a band of javelinas munching on cactus pads."

Colloquialism

"Giddyup, giddyup as fast as you can, . . ."

"Yee-haw!"

"Stampede!"

Imagery

The rancher's wife tires of making biscuits for breakfast so makes a gingerbread cowboy instead. "She took raisins, candies, and nuts and gave him two bright eyes, a laughing mouth, and a cowboy vest with fringe."

The Gingerbread Cowboy "galloped past a big prickly cactus."

Irony

As the Gingerbread Cowboy leaps on the coyote's nose, he is focused on eluding the rancher's wife's lariat. "Ha! Ha! Ha!" he shouts as the lasso falls short. "They missed!"

"But I won't," says the coyote. He proceeds to swallow the Gingerbread Cowboy in one gulp.

Parallelism

The rancher's wife always baked biscuits every morning while the rancher saddled his horses and fed the cattle.

"Biscuits with butter, biscuits with honey, biscuits with jelly...."

The shape of the gingerbread boy was not that of just any boy:
"He had boots on his feet.
He had a hat on his head.
And, he had a big buckle made of spun sugar."

Parody

This gingerbread cookie in this version of the classic tale is a cowboy with a cowboy vest and fringe and a big buckle made of spun sugar. As he races away, he calls, "Giddyup, giddyup as fast as you can." Those who fail to catch this gingerbread cookie include a horned lizard, a roadrunner, a band of javelinas, a herd of long-horned cattle, some hungry cowboys, and the rancher wife's lariat. He wriggles under a corral fence, gallops past a big prickly cactus, ducks between the legs of the cattle, and turns down a canyon. It's a coyote who invites him aboard his back at the edge of the canyon river.

Simile

The rancher's wife's breakfast biscuits were "plump as pillows, soft as clouds, and tasty as a big Texas barbecue."

"... as quick as the flick of a pony's tail ..."

The coyote "tossed the Gingerbread Cowboy into the air like a flapjack on a griddle...."

Tone

After making biscuits every morning, "One day just as the sun was coming up, the rancher's wife decided she was tired of making biscuits." She mixes up gingerbread dough, instead, and "cut out the shape of a boy—but not just any boy."

When the roadrunner sees the Gingerbread Cowboy, he tells him, "I was about to have a lizard for breakfast. But I think I'll eat you instead." The long-horned cattle see the Gingerbread Cowboy and think, "Mmmm. No more grass for us! We want gingerbread!"

The "Gingerbread Cowboy was feeling mighty pleased with himself."

Wit/Humor

Visually, the final illustration shows the rancher's wife and the coyote, with bandana and hat, together in the kitchen. She is directing him how to cut out a gingerbread cowboy from rolled dough. Also interested in the process is the rancher, who watches the culinary lesson over their shoulders.

*****

Stevens, Janet and Susan Stevens Crummel. *Cook-A-Doodle-Doo.* Illus. by Janet Stevens. Orlando, FL: (Voyager Books) Harcourt, c1999.

With the questionable help of his friends, Big Brown Rooster manages to bake a strawberry shortcake that would have pleased his great grandmother, Little Red Hen.

Curriculum Tie-in: Health/Nutrition (Recipes/Cooking), Social Science (Team Cooperation)

Art Style: Full, lushly rendered watercolor and colored pencil *Expressionism* in *Cartoons*

DEVICES

Allusion

Big Brown Rooster finds himself in the position his distant relative, Little Red Hen, was in. When she wanted the taste of bread, she had to make it herself. He wants the taste of strawberry shortcake.

Colloquialism

The barnyard animals are skeptical about the idea of Big Brown Rooster trying to make strawberry shortcake:

"Have you lost your marbles, Rooster?" asks Cat.

"Cooking is in my blood—it's a family tradition," replies Rooster.

Inference

The "family tradition" Big Brown Rooster refers to is his Great Grandmother, Little Red Hen, who preceded him in culinary efforts.

The finished strawberry shortcake, which falls to the floor, is eaten up by Potbelly Pig, who has the audacity to then suggest, "Now we can make something else." The cooking team members are incensed. Iguana glares, "How about a plump juicy roast pig?" Potbelly Pig hurtfully shouts back the taunt. "How about iguana potpie—or—or—turtle soup!"

Motif

In this version of the tale of baking, eager, if inept, teamwork is the prevailing attitude. Instead of "Not I," everyone responds, "I can." Turtle can "read recipes." Iguana can "get stuff!"—or "do that." Pig can "taste."

Parallelism

Regarding the ill-fated shortcake disaster, each short-tempered, frustrated animal is quick to cast blame:
"Pig ate it," whined Turtle.
"Iguana dropped it," pouted Pig.
"Turtle should have caught it," grumbled Iguana.

Pun

Big Brown Rooster says *Cook*-a-doodle-doo.
Strawberry shortcake for Big Brown Rooster. No more *chicken feed* for him.
The first ingredient is *flour*. Helpful Iguana dashes outside and comes back to present the cook with a petunia.
The cooks must *sift* the flour. Pig associates this concept with searching through garbage looking for lunch. He dives into the flour in the bowl, "throwing it everywhere."
The recipe requires *measuring* the flour, so Iguana grabs a ruler and finds the sifted flour is four inches tall.
A *stick* of butter comes in the form of a branch out in the yard as one stick.
The inexperienced cooks find scissors don't work very well to "*cut* the butter" into the flour. And, a baseball bat isn't suitable to *beat* the egg.

Stereotype/Reverse Stereotype

When Little Red Hen wanted help baking bread, the dog, cat, and goose all declared, "Not I." But, Big Brown Rooster has no trouble getting helpers. Even after an accident prevents everyone (except Potbelly Pig) from tasting the finished recipe, everyone is ready to help make strawberry shortcake again. Eagerly, they declare, "I will!"

Theme

A big job can be accomplished through group effort and willing cooperation, even when efforts aren't perfect. "We made this shortcake as a team, and teams work together," said Rooster. The second time "it was a lot easier than the first time!"

*****

Teague, Mark. *Pigsty.* New York: Scholastic, c1994.
>   Wendell's mother told him to clean his room because it was turning into a pigsty, but he didn't mind sharing his space with a couple of pigs until, eventually, the mess and the number of pigs became intolerable.
>   **Curriculum Tie-in:** Social Science (Values)
>   **Art Style:** Pastel *Cartoons* reminiscent of 1950s lifestyle

DEVICES

Ambiguity

When Wendell's mother declares his messy room a "pigsty," she doesn't realize how precise her description is. Pigs have actually moved in and soon usurp more and more space. He tells his mother, "I've had enough." She assumes he's ready to finally clean the room and hands him a broom, telling him, "Your room is your responsibility."

Aphorism

Wendell and the pigs are living in a tenuous relationship. But, when the mess becomes even too much for him, he suddenly remembers an appropriate saying: "Many hooves make light work."

Foreshadow

After enjoying the initial novelty of sharing his room with a couple of pigs, Wendell sees "the mess had grown a bit worse." He reconciles the idea of sharing: "Pigs are all right as long as it's only one or two." But, with all the fun and games going on, "the mess just grew and grew." Will more pigs come, too?

Pun

"Many *hooves* make light work."
The pigs, lying everywhere, "*hogged*" his pillows.

Tone

Amazingly, Wendell seems perfectly tolerant of a most unsuitable situation and is not upset by the abrupt appearance of pigs in his room. "In fact they had a wonderful time. They played Monopoly until late each night … and left the pieces lying all over the floor."

"The pig didn't seem to mind the mess, and Wendell found he didn't mind the pig, either." More pigs came.

The "arrangement deteriorated as the pigs took liberties chewing his baseball cards and sitting on his basketball and leaving hoof prints on his comic books." A cleaning crew was organized. "From a pig's point of view, it was a bit too clean." They left.

"From that day on, Wendell kept his room clean … except for those nights when his friends came by to play Monopoly."

*****

*Tingle, Tim. *Crossing Bok Chitto: A Choctaw Tale of Friendship and Freedom.* Illus. by Jeanne Rorex Bridges. El Paso, TX: Cinco Puntos Press, c2006.

>   In the 1800s a Choctaw girl becomes friends with a slave boy from a plantation across the great river, and when she learns that his family is in trouble, she helps them cross to freedom.

>   **Curriculum Tie-in:** History (Indians of North America), History (Slavery), Social Science (Character Development—Courage), Social Science (Friendship)

>   **Art Style:** Hauntingly evocative acrylic *Folk* art

DEVICES

Allusion

"You know that we call you Little Mo. But you know that is not your real name. Your name is Moses. Now, Moses, get us across that river!" They are "bound for the Promised Land."

"… before the War Between the States, in the days before the Trail of Tears …" (By treaty decree in 1830, the Choctaws were forced from their homes in Mississippi to begin the trek to Indian Territory in Oklahoma. They became the first Native Americans to walk the Trail of Tears.)

Antithesis

"… this night's journey is not about darkness and safety. It is about faith. It is about freedom."

Aphorism

"One day trouble came. It always does, in stories or in life, trouble comes."

Counterpoint

When the Choctaw girl first heard the slave songs, she "had never heard music like this before, but it touched her deeply."

When Little Mo first heard the Choctaw women's stamp dance to the men's chanting, he "had never heard music like this before, but it touched him deeply."

"You move not too fast, not too slow, eyes to the ground, away you go!" Little Mo's father shares this wisdom with him to avoid notice by the plantation owners.

Repeating this same wisdom, Little Mo has occasion to later remind his father that it will also help them escape across the river to freedom.

"It sounded like a fun game to play," Little Mo thinks as he leads the lost girl to the river bank.

She, in turn, offers to lead him across the muddy water, thinking, "This will be a fun game to play."

"The Choctaws talk about the bravery of that little girl, Martha Tom. The black people talk about the faith of that little boy, Moses. But the white people tell it best. They talk about the night their forefathers witnessed seven black spirits, walking on the water—to their freedom!"

Flash-Forward

"And so began a friendship that would last for years."

"The descendants of those people still talk about that night."

Foreshadow

"What happened next would change Martha Tom's life forever." She meets the slaves for the first time and later befriends a particular family.

"We're having a ceremony tonight, the crossing kind!" This urgent call from the Choctaw girl's mother to all the village women prepares them for stealth and drama in an act of enabling an escape to freedom.

Irony

When a young Choctaw girl strays away from her homeland and safety, Little Mo leads her back to the river bank. Later, she pays him back by leading him and his family across the same river to their freedom.

To the slave owners, the vision of the Choctaw women dressed in white and carrying candles as they emerge from the fog "looked to them like a band of angels."

As the young Choctaw girl stepped forth with her hand outstretched toward the runaway slaves, it appeared to them that "she was walking on water." No shots were fired. The watching slave catchers did not realize there were hidden rocks just beneath the water surface. The girl and the slaves appeared to be walking on the water. They were not bothered.

Motif

"We are bound for the Promised Land" is the rallying call to worship, a beacon of hope toward which each one strives, and a morale booster.

"You move not too fast, not too slow, eyes to the ground, away you go!" Little Mo's dad shares this wisdom with him as the secret to avoid plantation house attention. It also becomes useful to get to the river's edge without arousing suspicion.

Paradox

With a steady gait and eyes cast down, plantation slaves walk among plantation owners, "invisible" to them as they determinedly walk away to their freedom. "They walked into the circle of lanterns, but the light shone right through them. They walked so close to the dogs they could have stroked the dogs' fur, but even the dogs did not know they were there."

Parallelism

"On one side of the river lived the Choctows, a nation of Indian people. On the other side lived the plantation owners and their slaves."

"When the river flooded, they built the stones up. When the river sank in times of drought, they built the stones down, always just beneath the muddy surface of the water."

"In the days before the War Between the States, in the days before the Trail of Tears, Bok Chitto was a boundary."

"I want every one of you to find something small and precious, something to give your mother to remember you by, something she can hide, something they can't take away."

"Pack quickly, pack light, and pack for running."

Simile

"Martha Tom knew her mother could cackle like a mad crow on the outside, while inside she would coo like a dove with love for her daughter."

". . . a hundred voices came in reply, like spirit voices, whispering . . ."

Symbol

The rallying song "Promised Land," which called slaves to worship, became reality as they walked across the river the night they crossed to the promised land of freedom from Mississippi slavery.

Theme

The differences that divide cultures are insignificant contrasted to the similarities of our common humanity. Moses and Martha admire and are drawn to each other's differences but find friendship based on mutual characteristics.

*****

Williams, Laura E. *The Best Winds.* Illus. by Eujin Kim Neilan. Honesdale, PA: Boyds Mills Press, c2006.
 A grandfather shows his grandson how to make a kite but the boy would rather play video games or go skateboarding—until he tries to impress his friends by flying the finished kite without his grandfather's guidance.
 Curriculum Tie-in: Geography (Korea), Social Science (Character Development—Respect), Social Science (Ethnic Relations), Social Science (Family Relationships—Grandparent/Grandchild), Social Science (Love)
 Art Style: Exquisite acrylic *Expressionism* in *Folk* art

DEVICES

Aphorism

When the boy apologizes for the kite he repaired that is not as beautiful as the first one, his grandfather says, "It's not beauty that makes a kite good and true. It's the care and love that go into making it."

Atmosphere

In this generational and immigrant family, images hark back to the old country through words like "bamboo," "shield kite," "small village by the sea," "ginkgo tree leaves," and "old rice paper."

Foreshadow

The old man and the boy were to fly the kite together. "Suddenly, he pictured himself flying this magnificent kite with all his friends watching. He couldn't wait until the next morning."
 The kite tangles in a tree. There is "a big ugly tear in it ... [and] with a heavy heart, the boy slowly walked home."
 There is no money to buy a replacement. "He ran his hands along the frame of the kite. It still held strong. In a flash, he knew what he had to do."

Inference

The grandfather realizes that the repaired kite his grandson makes is the result of a lesson well learned. "I have a feeling this kite is far finer than the first one."

They work together to make the repaired kite perform correctly. The grandfather's hand covers the boy's when the kite threatens to crash. "You did it!" said the boy. The grandfather corrects him, "We did it." Then he lets go.

Finally, the boy is receptive: "Then he told the story of long, long ago, and Jinho listened."

Motif

The grandfather's hands serve as a barometer for the story's changing emotional climate. Before the grandson develops appreciation for his grandfather's ways, the old man's hands are stiff and clumsy, wrinkled, pale, and quivery. As the boy warms to him, the hands become strong and warm with the effects of love.

Simile

"fingers as stiff as bamboo"
"hands wrinkled as old rice paper"
"voice chirped on and on like a cricket in the background"
"hands quivered like the leaves on the ginkgo tree"
"hands as pale as fish bellies"
"tails snapping back and forth like angry snakes"
"kite fell to the sidewalk like an injured bird"
"cupped his hand like a seashell to his ear"
"two hands as strong as mountains"
"hand, warm as love"

Theme

Mutual respect for generational differences brings appreciation for what can be brought to a relationship.

A boy of Korean descent has nearly forsaken the ways of his heritage until his grandfather intrudes on his American lifestyle.

*****

Wojciechowski, Susan. *A Fine St. Patrick's Day.* Illus. by Tom Curry. New York: Random House, c2004.

Two towns, Tralee and Tralah, compete in an annual St. Patrick's Day decorating contest that Tralah boastfully always wins, but when the townspeople's hearts are put to the test by a little man with pointed ears, Tralee wins with no effort at all.

Curriculum Tie-in: Literature (Folktale, Original), Social Science (Character Development—Empathy), Social Science (Competition), Social Science (Holidays), Social Science (Team Cooperation), Social Science (Values)

Art Style: Vibrant color acrylic *Folk*

DEVICES

Alliteration

"glimmering glorious green miracle"

Colloquialism

". . . though she's but a wee lass of six . . ."

" 'Tis surely a fine idea. . . .' Twas a fine idea, to be sure."

Shades of paint: "Emerald Isle, Limerick Lime, or Galway Green."

". . . sure and begorra . . ."

Inference

The townspeople from Tralee have not had time to decorate because they were helping the stranger free his cattle from a muddy stream. And, though they know they have lost the contest, yet one more year, they can have a St. Patrick's picnic, anyway. They ride out to invite him to their St. Patrick's party.

"All they found was a single cowbell. It was made of shining gold." Then, "Little Fiona Riley remembered that when the man thanked her at the river, he said, 'You have already won.'" Their town, which is a beautiful bright green, is already changing back. As the "sun began to sink behind the hills, the town slowly faded back to its real colors."

This little man of "red trousers, a brown leather apron, and boots decorated with gold bells" had a "beard down to his stomach. Pointed ears stuck out beneath the brim of his hat. His horse had long satin ribbons braided into its mane." What manner of individual has intervened to make sure the right town has won the decorating competition?

Irony

The town with no time to decorate for the annual St. Patrick's Day competition, because its residents stopped to help an unfortunate stranger, won the decorating contest for the first time ever.

The town that refused to help the beseeching stranger, because its residents were busy decorating, lost the competition for the first time.

Theme

Doing something for fun can be even more rewarding than doing it to win a competition. The "people of Tralee would no longer compete with Tralah to win another trophy. They would decorate their town and share a meal of lamb and boiled potatoes simply for the joy of it."

*****

*Wood, Nancy. *Mr. and Mrs. God in the Creation Kitchen.* Illus. by Timothy Basil Ering. Cambridge, MA: Candlewick Press, c2006.
> Mr. and Mrs. God have frying pans and mixing bowls and an oven big enough to roast a star as the lively duo of married chefs get us all started.
> > **Curriculum Tie-in:** Religion (Creation), Science (Evolution)
> > **Art Style:** Ink and acrylic full-page *Expressionism* in *Cartoons*

DEVICES

Allusion

With a nod to the Jewish-Christian tradition of creation, Mr. and Mrs. God have fun in this version of accomplishing the task, including a few mistakes along the way that need correcting.

"Something very large and round was baking in the oven. When the timer rang, Mr. God opened the oven door and let the giant orb roll itself out into the universe.... 'I'm going to call it the sun.'"

"Oh my! It was bigger than he'd meant it to be.... Mrs. God was quite upset. The enormous, ghastly things had the biggest tails imaginable.... He wished he could take them back.... He grabbed a red-hot coal from the oven and flung it down. KA-BOOM!" No more dinosaurs.

Antithesis

"Mrs. God did not speak to Mr. God for a thousand years."
"Mr. God wondered what he could do to please her."

Foreshadow

Concerning the final set of creatures Mr. and Mrs. God made:
"I wonder how they'll turn out," said Mr. God.

"Who knows?" said Mrs. God.

"We'll just have to wait and see."

Mr. and Mrs. God look down on a male and female bipedal animal combination, holding each other's hands and looking up into the heavens.

Hyperbole

Mrs. God "got a big bowl and filled it with all the colors she loved. Next she mixed it all together and emptied the bowl into the bluest waters on Earth." Mr. God was working on a project of his own. "Look at that beak!" he shouts. "Then the creature spread its wings and flew off. Straight down to the ocean it went. It ate up Mrs. God's pretty swimming creatures in one gulp. 'How could you?' she said to Mr. God. Mrs. God did not speak to Mr. God for a thousand years."

"... an oven big enough to roast a star."

Imagery

"Deep in the heavens, in a space without beginning or end, was the Creation Kitchen."

As Mr. God began making creatures, "He looked through all the boxes in the pantry to find just the right ingredients. Growls and roars. Sharp teeth. Huge feet."

Inference

"'We forgot something,' Mr. God said. He took a leftover piece of clay and rolled it out, giving it arms and legs and a head. At the last minute, he added a neck.

'What are they?' asked Mrs. God, who was working on a second one.

'Who knows?' said Mr. God. He glued on hair and toes. Eyeballs and ears."

Onomatopoeia

After Mr. God looked through all the boxes in the pantry selecting growls and roars, sharp teeth, and huge feet, he began a new very large creature. Mrs. God was not pleased with the results. Mr. God wished he could "take them back, but they had already made some baby monsters.... What can I do?" He grabbed a red-hot coal from the oven and flung it down. "KA-BOOM!" The dinosaurs were gone.

Parallelism

Mr. God chooses to create "something big. Something with a terrible noise."

He searches the pantry for just the right ingredients: "Growls and roars. Sharp teeth. Huge feet."

Pun

When earth cooled down enough to turn blue, "Mr. God stuck his finger in the *crust* to see how it was coming along."

Satire

Mr. and Mrs. God are depicted as having fun in the kitchen in this light-hearted poke at the serious business of Creation.

Mrs. God pronounced the dinosaurs "hideous," and Mr. God decides "maybe they were a mistake," which he corrects by flinging down on them a "red-hot coal from the oven." But, the whale, also an enormous creature so big that "its tail hung out" of the frying pan, was declared by Mrs. God to be "a masterpiece." They work together on the final creatures. "We'll just have to wait and see" how they turn out as they set man and woman on the big blue orb.

Understatement

Mrs. God "heard the splash and went to take a closer look." She pronounces the whale, "a little large, but it has character."

Mr. God agrees the dinosaurs "were rather unattractive" and wonders if, perhaps, "maybe they were a mistake."

Wit/Humor

"Earth was boiling hot. 'You made it,' said Mr. God. 'You cool it off.' Mrs. God whipped together some clouds and poured them over the glowing ball. At last it began to turn blue."

As Mr. God begins creating animals, he knows they should "be something you'd notice." These first attempts didn't please Mrs. God. "They're hideous.... What were you thinking?"

*****

Yolen, Jane. *Harvest Home*. Illus. by Greg Shed. New York: (Silver Whistle) Harcourt, c2002.

> In lively verse that captures the rhythm of the work and the spirit of community, a young farm girl and her family bring in the new harvest and celebrate with prayers, songs, and a festive meal.
>
> > **Curriculum Tie-in:** Agriculture (Farm Life—Harvesting), Fine Arts (Wheat Twist Dolls)
> >
> > **Art Style:** Soft golden harvest hues and daylight blues in smudgy glowing gouache *Realism*

DEVICES

Atmosphere

"... Gramps and Dad, who, boy and man,
Have worked this way their whole lives' span,
Tied to the sun and rain and land, ..."

"We move as one on reaping day.
All time for work and one for play.
It cannot be another way, ..."

"I look around at field and sky,
And at our neighbors so close by,
And think how lucky here am I, ..."

"And then we sing and dance and praise,
To God the Sower prayers we raise, ..."

Imagery

"Above, the sky shines bright and blue; the scythes swing high; our aim is true. The downward swing cuts clean and through ..."
"The sun shines on each golden row, while overhead a lazy crow keeps an eye on us below ..."
"With aching back and blistered palms ... with scythe still singing reapers' psalms ..."
"Beneath the fading harvest sky, a skein of southbound geese flies by ..."

Internal Rhyme

"Ma takes a twist of that last wheat to make a harvest doll so neat, with wheat gold hair and wheat gold feet...."

Metaphor

"The golden crop is gathered in, to store up summer in a bin."
"Jen sets the doll upon a pole, to represent the harvest soul."

Motif

As a running thread through the routines of a satisfying farm year is the single goal: "Bringing the harvest home."

Parallelism

"With wheat gold hair and wheat gold feet, ..."
"Not too quick and not too slow, ..."

"A goodly year. A goodly gain."

Wit/Humor

"Though still young, we both work well
And need not ever rest a spell
(At least that anyone can tell)."

*****

Yolen, Jane. *Raising Yoder's Barn.* Illus. by Bernie Fuchs. New York: Little, Brown and Company, c1998.

> Eight-year-old Matthew tells what happens when fire destroys the barn on his family's farm and all the Amish neighbors come to rebuild it in one day.
>
> > **Curriculum Tie-in:** Geography (Pennsylvania—Amish), History (Barns, United States), Social Science (Neighbor Relationships), Social Science (Team Cooperation)
> >
> > **Art Style:** Full-page detailed *Impressionism* paintings

DEVICES

Aphorism

"Disaster makes even the lamest joke funny."
"... a farm is not a farm without its barn."

Colloquialism

"Grandfather ran from the *Dawdy Haus* to help, ..."

Imagery

"Our sickles swung against the wild mustard that crept in on the growing grain."

"Then one Monday in July turned angry and dark. Black clouds scudded across the sky."

"Soon the palms of my hands were covered with pearly blisters ..."

"... we raked the ashes out the next day and Christian painted his face with them."

"He was a minute of a man, small and dark and wiry, but he could build a big barn."

"... a holiday meal served up by the women: soup with dumplings, ground meat sausages, pickled cabbage, potatoes and applesauce, apple butter slathered on fresh baked bread."

"The barn was finished before dusk with the new moon rising behind it."

"Hay dripped over the barn's low beams."

"... Little sister, her cap slipped back off her head, pulled down the hissing milk into the shiny pails."

Inference

Hoping to physically help with the barn raising, the narrator was satisfied that "My voice would be as good as my hands." He is assigned the job of carrying messages from the architect to the workers.

"We saved the house, but no one could save that barn, though it had stood first before all on our farmland." First comes a barn, then when a farm is successful, a good house follows.

Metaphor

"Papa liked to call that windmill 'God's own right hand.'"

"Fingers of flame grabbed at the barn."

"The sky filled with blue ropes of smoke."

Motif

"Good hands." A worker with good hands is a valuable contributing member of a farm family. Eight-year-old Matthew is proud to be told, "I can see you have good hands." He hoped to be able to put those good hands to work rebuilding the barn. Instead, he is given the assignment of carrying messages. But, when the barn is finished, the scythe is "waiting patiently for the summer, when once again it would fit comfortably into the palms of my good hands."

Parallelism

"... proud to be beside my older brothers,
proud to have such good hands."

"A barn for the cows, for the hay in winter, for the keeping of goats and hens and chickens, for the tools in their proper order."

"I waited to be told, waited for Papa's call. Waited while the first of the frames was ready to be hauled into place."

"Would Papa never notice me?
Would I have no job to do?"

Simile

"... in a field with furrows straight as a good man's life."

"Lightning, like a stooping hawk, ..."

"... hands covered with pearly blisters, like the barley in Mama's soup."
"... attacked his face with a wet cloth till his cheeks were red as flames."
"... so excited he ran back and forth like a dog after hens."
"... that barn grew like a giant flower in the field ..."

Understatement

"... we raked the ashes ... and Christian painted his face with them. Mama was not amused...."

*****

Yorinks, Arthur. *Whitefish Will Rides Again!* Illus. by Mort Drucker. New York: HarperCollins, c1994.
> After cleaning up town, the best sheriff that ever lived was put out to pasture until outlaws returned, requiring his services again.
> **Curriculum Tie-in:** History (Wild West, United States), Literature (Tall Tale), Social Science (Justice)
> **Art Style:** Larger-than-life Wild West pen and watercolor *Expressionism* in *Cartoons*

DEVICES

Alliteration

"... Will wandered. Raised roosters. Rode in the rodeo."
"... a pistol-packing pickpocket, a big bully bank robber."
"... Will was so good at rassling rustlers that soon there were no more rustlers left to rassle."
"... bobcat caught on a cactus."
"... plate of petite peas, ..."
"... you and your weasily weevils ..."
"... happy hyena."

Archetype

These folks are the worst of the worst and the best of the best:
"He was a trouble-making son-of-a-gunmaker.... Bart was so mean rattlesnakes would line up and try to kiss his feet."
"Shoot, just one peep at Will and even the nastiest varmint scrammed. When Jesse James spotted Will's muscles, he shot back to Butte...."

Colloquialism

"best danged sheriff that ever lived"
"dash dang dingle darn it"

"Mighty dog, no"
"you yeller-bellied cowards"
"went plum loco"
"whole tinhorn town"
"This shindig is finito"
"hightailed it out of town"

Hyperbole

"Whitefish Will had the strength of forty mules. Maybe fifty."
"Yup, coyotes learned how to howl just to drown out that stinkweed serenade."
"Bart was so mean rattlesnakes would line up and try to kiss his feet."

Inference

"Meanwhile, back in town, life was plain and peaceful and ripe." This town, which Will had cleaned up, was about to become overrun with bad men. But Will wasn't there to protect them this time because they had sent him to retirement.

Oxymoron

"No more Mr. Nice Bandito."

Satire

"Finally, in his golden years, at his lovely Rio Rancho in the hills, Whitefish Will took up the harmonica." After a life of purpose and importance, there is little appreciation for his having done a job no one else would have wanted to do. Still, he manages to make the community sorry for causing him and the harmonica to come together.

Simile

"faster than a bee-stung billy goat"
"shrieking like a happy hyena"

Solecism

"best danged sheriff"
"... anyways, one day Bart and his gang ..."
"I'm settin' fire"
"No one but Little Frankie could recollect ..."
"had yourself a decent pair of earplugs"

Tone

Folksy conversation:
"Whooee bad!"
"Bart was so mean.... I mean, he was mean."
"What a sheriff! What a man."
"He sure loved playing that thing."
"As for Will, well he got his old job back. And you could bet your britches the West was safe for honest folks once more."

Wit/Humor

"So the townsfolk, grateful as they were—and cheap—put poor Whitefish out to pasture."
"... West was safe for honest folks once more. Especially if you had yourself a decent pair of earplugs."

*****

Young, Amy. *Belinda and the Glass Slipper.* New York: (Viking) Penguin Young Readers Group, c2006.
> Belinda competes with a very ambitious new dancer for the title role in the ballet *Cinderella.*
>> **Curriculum Tie-in:** Fine Arts (Ballet), Social Science (Character Development—Honorable/Dishonorable Conduct)
>> **Art Style:** Expressionistic *Naive* painted drawings

DEVICES

Allusion

Lola feels she has the edge for dancing the lead role in *Cinderella* because, "I have perfect, tiny feet—just right for Cinderella." In the fairy-tale version of the story, Cinderella's small feet enable her to beat out her competitors when the glass slipper is being tried on all the maidens in the kingdom.

Antithesis

Belinda and Lola both want to dance the ballet part of Cinderella. Belinda deserves the role; Lola does not.

Belinda "was nervous" before going into her audition for the Grand Metropolitan Ballet's production of *Cinderella.* Lola also wants the role of Cinderella, "and I *always* get what I want."

Belinda's superior dancing gets her the part. "That's not fair!" Lola mutters.

During rehearsals, when the maestro isn't looking, Lola pushes other dancers and reviles their performances.

On opening night Lola invents a pretext to get Belinda to "help" her by taking advantage of Belinda's good nature. She wants the taller Belinda to reach a "ribbon" for her on a shelf in a closet. Once Belinda is inside, Lola shuts and locks the door on her so she can go on stage and assume Belinda's lead part.

Even when her treachery is exposed, she refuses to step aside in defeat. She rails on. "The prince is mine! I want him!" she snarls. Then she lashes out in a final, fruitless frenzy to retain her brief star status. She tries to "crush Belinda's foot with her heel," and she "sprang after her" when Belinda deftly dances out of her grasp.

Archetype

Lola is a classic spoiled bully. Pridefully, she announces, "I really want this part, and I *always* get what I want."

During rehearsal, "The other dancers didn't like practicing with Lola," who "pushed them out of their pliés and reviled their relevés."

At the after-performance party, when Lola has been exposed, "everyone had a good time except for Lola, who decided she didn't want to be a dancer after all." If she cannot have the lead part, she wants none at all.

Counterpoint

Belinda's gentle, classic professionalism plays sharply against Lola's rough, manipulating tactics.

Lola is not as proficient a dancer as is Belinda. "She knew the steps, but the maestro wished she could jeté a little higher, the way Belinda did. He wished she glissaded more gracefully, like Belinda." She can't leap as high or spin as fast, and she isn't as graceful.

Belinda "did a gorgeous pas de deux." But Lola "swooped in to claim her dance with the prince." He frowns at her.

Belinda "stepped up and curtsied gracefully before the prince. He smiled happily at her."

Lola tries to crush Belinda's foot. Belinda pirouettes out of reach. Lola springs after her. Belinda protects herself with a well-executed battement.

Foreshadow

Belinda, though the better dancer, will not easily obtain the lead part in the *Cinderella* production. "Lola smiled sweetly at Belinda and said, 'I really want this part, and I *always* get what I want.'"

Even after the maestro selects Belinda to dance the part of Cinderella, Belinda will not be able to assume her rightful position easily. "'That's not fair!' Lola muttered."

After failing in her bid to be lead performer in *Cinderella,* Lola "left the ballet to become a hockey player" called "Teensy Toes." Here, she will find success. "She got into lots of fights, but she also won a lot of games."

Inference

Even after losing to Belinda's superior auditioning skills, Lola has not given up on her determination to dance the lead role. On opening night, she makes a desperate bid to unseat the star. "'Can you help me reach my, um, hair ribbon? It's in here, high on a shelf.' Belinda followed Lola into a little closet. When she turned around to help Lola, she heard the door slam and click shut."

Lola lies to get her chance to dance the starring role. "Belinda is sick, and she asked me to dance her part."

What about Belinda's "glass slippers," which will be much too big for Lola? She has a plan. "I'll make them fit," she says.

When she is able, Belinda reclaims her rightful role, thwarting the interloper. Lola tries bluff. "The prince is mine! I want him! And I *always* get what I want!" "Not this time," Belinda calmly tells her. Nothing will prevent the star from performing her role, finally.

Irony

Lola's fierce competitive spirit doesn't suit the ballet atmosphere, but it does lend itself perfectly to hockey. "She got into lots of fights, but she also won a lot of games." The frustrated ballet dancer, an annoyance to fellow dancers, finds happiness and stardom in a venue where her basic nature is welcomed.

Parallelism

"Lola leapt high, but not as high as Belinda."
"Lola spun fast, but not as fast as Belinda."
"Lola was graceful, but not as graceful as Belinda, . . ."

When Lola began to dance, "the maestro wished she could *jeté* a little higher, the way Belinda did."
"He wished she *glissaded* more gracefully, like Belinda."

"Lola tried to crush Belinda's foot with her heel, but Belinda *pirouetted* out of reach."
"Lola sprang after her, but Belinda protected herself with a well-executed *battement*, . . ."

Parody

Just as the fairy tale version of "Cinderella" has a wicked stepmother, who tried to prevent the central character from fulfilling her dreams, a disgruntled dancer locks up the lead performer to prevent her from dancing at the ball with the prince. Belinda is shut in a closet, unable to assume her dancing role. Everyone "was hurrying to get onstage, and no one heard her."

Just as Cinderella's fairy godmother comes to the rescue in the fairy tale, the Fairy Godmother dancer "came by and heard Belinda. She unlocked the [closet] door."

In the fairy tale, Cinderella runs away from the ball, leaving behind a glass slipper at midnight. In the ballet, when the stuffing falls out of the stolen ballet slippers, "Lola ran off the stage on her teeny tiny feet, leaving behind a big glass slipper."

In a reverse of the fairy tale in which all the ladies trying on the glass slipper find it too small to fit them, in this story, the usurper's feet are too small to fit the large slipper belonging to the rightful dancer. "Lola pushed her out of the way. She stuck her foot in the slipper, but of course it was much too big for her, now that the stuffing was gone."

When the ballet prince tried the slipper on Belinda, "It fit perfectly." "Lola sank into a heap. She knew she had lost." "Belinda floated into the prince's arms."

Poetic Justice

Lola has difficulty trying to dance in Belinda's slippers, which are much too large for her. "As Lola leapt and spun, something odd happened to the glass slippers. They wavered and wobbled and began to unravel! Pieces of stuffing fell out, and her feet seemed to shrink." Lola rushed off stage, embarrassed.

Belinda "dazzled the audience, soaring over their heads," whereas Lola "sank into a heap. She knew she had lost."

Simile

Belinda "was as delicate as a snowflake on the wind."
Belinda "dazzled the audience, soaring over their heads like a rainbow."

Surprise/Twist-in-the-Tail

Although Lola's dishonorable bid to dance the lead role in *Cinderella* was soundly quashed, she did not disappear in ignominious defeat. She, too, finds happiness and fulfillment. "She left the ballet to become a hockey player," a career much better suited to her combative personality. "She got into a lot of fights, but she also won a lot of games."

Theme

There is a place for everyone's skills, and matching them to the right endeavor leads to satisfaction.

Understatement

"The ballet was a great success. Everyone said it was one of the best they'd seen. So different! So full of action and emotion!"

In the after-performance party, "everyone had a good time except for Lola, who decided she didn't want to be a dancer after all."

*****

*Young, Ed. *I, Doko: The Tale of a Basket.* New York: Philomel, c2004.

A Nepalese basket tells the story of its use through three generations of a family.

Curriculum Tie-in: Social Science: (Character Development—Respect), Social Science (Family Relationships—Intergenerational)

Art Style: Gouache, pastel, and collage deep-toned *Impressionism* in *Folk*

DEVICES

Aphorism

"What one wishes not upon oneself, one burdens not upon another."

"Even a bird like a crow would feed its feeble father."

The grandson Wangel's love and respect for his grandfather serves to inspire and transform the mindset of a whole village. They learn how elders should be treated.

Foreshadow

"The man and the woman were nervous. How could Yeh-Yeh have let the fire start! Now quarrels often broke out between Yeh-Yeh and the young couple." Old Yeh-Yeh is becoming a burden to the household. His fate is in jeopardy.

Inference

After speaking bluntly to his father about his parents' plans for his grandfather, the boy has awakened his father's humanity:

"After you put Yeh-Yeh on the steps, could you remember to bring Doko back … [so] this way I won't need to buy another Doko when you are old and it is time to leave you on the temple steps. At this, his father's mouth dropped open. He turned slowly back to the cottage without another word."

Personification

The old one, "Yeh-Yeh[,] slipped and broke his hip. From then on, he and I stayed home with the baby."

"Early the next morning, before the mist had risen, Wangel's father left the house with Yeh-Yeh inside me on his back."

Poetic Justice

"It is time to put him on the temple steps.... The priests will take better care of him." Wangel chases after his father. The boy does not want his father to remove his grandfather from the family. He finds a pointed way to change his father's mind. He tells his father to be sure to bring back the basket that has been used to carry his grandfather away. The boy will need it someday when it's time for him to carry his father away. The father's mouth drops open. He immediately and silently changes his mind about leaving the grandfather on the temple steps when he realizes the same thing could happen to him.

Point-of-View

"My name is Doko. It means 'basket' in Nepalese. My master, Yeh-Yeh, picked me from among many baskets. That was many years ago, when his wife, Nei-Nei, and their baby were all young and strong."

Theme

The grandson, Wangel, taught his father mutual respect across the generations, so that all could live out their lives in tolerance and harmony.

Tone

A basket has served an Asian family for many years and has stored up bittersweet memories.

"I still remember the year that the rain didn't come. How brittle I became. Worst of all, an epidemic took Nei-Nei's life. It was I who carried her to her grave. After that, the boy and my master and I were left alone."

"When Wangel turned ten, he, too, helped in the fields, leaving the aging Yeh-Yeh home alone. I was often left, too. I was also growing old."

*****

APPENDIX 1:
RESOURCES LISTED
BY AUTHOR

❖❖❖❖❖❖❖❖❖❖❖

*Adler, David A. *The Babe and I.* Illus. by Terry Widdener. New York: (Gulliver Books) Harcourt Brace & Co., c1999.
Ambiguity. Antithesis. Foreshadow. Inference. Irony. Paradox. Tone.

Allen, Jonathan. *I'm Not Cute!* New York: Hyperion Books for Children, c2005.
Antithesis. Counterpoint. Foreshadow. Motif. Paradox.

Amico, Tom and James Proimos. *Raisin and Grape.* Illus. by Andy Snair. New York: (Dial Books for Young Readers) Penguin Young Readers Group, c2006.
Antithesis. Connotation. Hyperbole. Inference. Pun. Tone. Understatement. Wit/Humor.

Arnosky, Jim. *Grandfather Buffalo.* New York: G. P. Putnam's Sons, c2006.
Atmosphere. Foreshadow. Inference. Motif. Theme.

Asher, Sandy. *Too Many Frogs!* Illus. by Keith Graves. New York: (Philomel Books) Penguin Young Readers Group, c2005.
Allusion. Aphorism. Internal Rhyme. Irony. Parallelism. Theme. Tone.

Ashman, Linda. *Desmond and the Naughtybugs.* Illus. by Anik McGrory. New York: (Dutton Children's Books) Penguin Young Readers Group, c2006.
Foreshadow. Inference. Irony. Parallelism.

Atwood, Margaret. *Up in the Tree.* Toronto, Ontario: Greenwood Books/House of Anansi Press, c1978, 2006.
Antithesis. Hyperbole. Internal Rhyme. Irony. Motif. Parallelism.

Auch, Mary Jane. *Hen Lake.* New York: Holiday House, c1995.
Allusion. Aphorism. Aptronym. Archetype. Colloquialism.

*Connotation. Inference. Motif.
Theme.*

Bang, Molly. *In My Heart.* New York:
Little, Brown and Company,
c2006.
Inference. Motif. Tone.

*Bateman, Teresa. *Keeper of Soles.*
Illus. by Diego Herrera (Yayo).
New York: Holiday House, c2006.
*Ambiguity. Aphorism. Black
Humor. Colloquialism.
Connotation. Imagery. Inference.
Irony. Paradox. Parallelism. Pun.
Understatement.*

Bateman, Teresa. *A Plump and Perky
Turkey.* Illus. by Jeff Shelly. New
York: Marshall Cavendish, c2001.
*Alliteration. Allusion. Ambiguity.
Aptronym. Irony. Parallelism.
Poetic Justice. Surprise/Twist-
of-the-Tail. Theme.
Understatement.*

Bernstein, Dan. *The Tortoise and the
Hare Race Again.* Illus. by
Andrew Glass. New York: Holi-
day House, c2006.
*Alliteration. Allusion. Ambiguity.
Foreshadow. Paradox. Parody.
Pun.*

Borden, Louise. *Across the Blue
Pacific: A World War II Story.*
Illus. by Robert Andrew Parker.
Boston: Houghton Mifflin, c2006.
*Aphorism. Atmosphere.
Connotation. Flashback. Flash-
Forward. Foreshadow. Imagery.
Inference. Motif. Paradox.
Parallelism. Simile. Theme.*

Bowen, Anne. *The Great Match
Tattle Battle.* Illus. by Jaime
Zollars. Morton Grove, IL: Albert
Whitman, c2006.
*Connotation. Paradox.
Parallelism. Poetic Justice.
Theme.*

Bradley, Kimberly Brubaker. *Ballerino
Nate.* Illus. by R. W. Alley. New
York: (Dial Books for Young
Readers) Penguin Young Readers
Group, c2006.
*Ambiguity. Archetype. Inference.
Motif. Parallelism. Stereotype/
Reverse Stereotype.*

Broach, Elise. *Cousin John Is Coming!*
Illus. by Nate Lilly. New York;
(Dial Books for Young Readers)
Penguin Young Readers Group,
c2006.
*Ambiguity. Archetype.
Counterpoint. Inference. Irony.
Paradox.*

Bunge, Daniela. *The Scarves.* Trans.
by Kahryn Bishop. New York:
Penguin Young Readers Group,
c2006.
*Archetype. Counterpoint.
Foreshadow. Inference. Irony.
Symbol.*

Bunting, Eve. *Butterfly House.* Illus. by
Greg Shed. New York: Scholastic
Press, c1999.
*Atmosphere. Connotation. Flash-
Forward. Imagery. Internal
Rhyme. Paradox. Point-of-
View. Simile.*

Bunting, Eve. *One Green Apple.* Illus.
by Ted Lewin. New York:
(Clarion Books) Houghton Mifflin,
c2006.
*Antithesis. Inference. Symbol.
Theme.*

Bunting, Eve. *Pop's Bridge.* Illus. by C.
F. Payne. New York: Harcourt,
c2006.
*Antithesis. Aphorism. Foreshadow.
Inference. Metaphor. Simile.
Symbol. Theme.*

Bynum, Janie. *Nutmeg and Barley: A
Budding Friendship.* Cambridge,
MA: Candlewick Press, c2006.

*Ambiguity. Antithesis. Foreshadow.
Parallelism. Theme.*

Chen, Chih-Yuan. *The Featherless
Chicken.* Alhambra, CA: Heryin
Books, c2006.
*Alliteration. Archetype.
Connotation. Inference.
Internal Rhyme. Irony. Satire.
Serendipity. Simile. Theme.
Tone. Wit/Humor.*

*Coombs, Kate. *The Secret-Keeper.*
Illus. by Heather M. Solomon.
New York: (Atheneum Books for
Young Readers) Simon &
Schuster, c2006.
*Ambiguity. Connotation.
Foreshadow. Imagery.
Inference. Irony. Metaphor.
Motif. Serendipity. Simile.
Symbol. Tone.*

Crummel, Susan Stevens. *Ten Gallon
Bart.* Illus. by Dorothy Donohue.
Tarrytown, NY: Marshall
Cavendish, c2006.
*Allusion. Archetype.
Colloquialism. Connotation.
Inference. Internal Rhyme.
Motif. Parody. Poetic Justice.
Pun. Solecism. Stereotype/
Reverse Stereotype. Tone.
Wit/Humor.*

*Cullen, Lynn. *Moi & Marie
Antoinette.* Illus. by Amy Young.
New York: Bloomsbury Publi-
shing, c2006.
*Archetype. Atmosphere.
Counterpoint. Foreshadow.
Hyperbole. Inference. Motif.
Parallelism. Point-of-View.
Serendipity. Simile. Surprise/
Twist-in-the-Tail. Wit/Humor.*

da Costa, Deborah. *Snow in Jerusalem.*
Illus. by Cornelius Van Wright &
Ying-Hwa Hu. Morton Grove, IL:
Albert Whitman, c2001.

*Connotation. Counterpoint.
Imagery. Simile. Symbol.
Theme.*

Danziger, Paula. *Barfburger Baby, I
Was Here First.* Illus. by G. Brian
Karas. New York: (Penguin Young
Readers Group) G. P. Putnam's
Sons, c2004.
Inference. Irony. Motif.

Edwards, Pamela Duncan. *The Mixed-
Up Rooster.* Illus. by Megan
Lloyd. New York: HarperCollins
Children's Books, c2006.
*Foreshadow. Parallelism. Pun.
Serendipity. Stereotype/
Reverse Stereotype. Theme.
Wit/Humor.*

Eversole, Robyn. *The Gift Stone.* Illus.
by Allen Garns. New York: Alfred
A. Knopf, c1998.
*Antithesis. Aphorism.
Atmosphere. Connotation.
Inference. Irony. Metaphor.
Motif. Parallelism. Simile.
Symbol.*

Fleming, Candace. *Muncha! Muncha!
Muncha!* Illus. by G. Brian Karas.
New York: Atheneum Books for
Young Readers, c2002.
*Allusion. Aptronym. Irony. Motif.
Onomatopoeia. Parallelism.
Surprise/Twist-in-the-Tail.*

*Frank, John. *The Toughest Cowboy,
or How the Wild West Was
Tamed.* Illus. by Zachary Pullen.
New York: Simon & Schuster
Books for Young Readers, c2004.
*Allusion. Ambiguity. Aptronym.
Atmosphere. Colloquialism.
Foreshadow. Hyperbole.
Inference. Irony. Parallelism.
Pun. Simile. Solecism.
Stereotype/Reverse Stereotype.
Tone. Understatement. Wit/
Humor.*

*Franklin, Kristine L. *The Gift*. Illus. by
Barbara Lavallee. San Francisco:
Chronicle Books, c1999.
Ambiguity. Connotation.
Foreshadow. Imagery.
Inference. Irony.
Onomatopoeia. Simile.
Surprise/Twist-in-the-Tail.
Symbol. Theme.

Garland, Sherry. *My Father's Boat*.
Illus. by Ted Rand. New York:
Scholastic Press, c1998.
Antithesis. Aphorism. Connotation.
Counterpoint. Imagery. Metaphor.
Parallelism. Simile. Theme.

Gerstein, Mordicai. *Carolinda Clatter!*
New Milford, CT: (Roaring Brook
Press) Holtzbrinck, c2005.
Allusion. Antithesis. Aptronym.
Counterpoint. Flash-Forward.
Foreshadow. Hyperbole. Internal
Rhyme. Irony. Metaphor. Motif.
Parallelism. Wit/Humor.

Goode, Diane. *The Most Perfect Spot*.
New York: HarperCollins Children's
Books, c2006.
Foreshadow. Irony. Motif. Pun.

Henkes, Kevin. *Kitten's First Full*
Moon. New York: (Greenwillow
Books) HarperCollins, c2004.
Irony. Motif. Tone.

High, Linda Oatman. *Barn Savers*.
Illus. by Ted Lewin. Honesdale,
PA: Boyds Mills Press, c1999.
Atmosphere. Connotation. Imagery.
Metaphor. Parallelism. Simile.

James, Simon. *The Wild Woods*.
Cambridge, MA: Candlewick Press,
c1993.
Inference. Motif. Point-of-View.
Wit/Humor.

Jeffers, Oliver. *Lost and Found*. New
York: (Philomel) Penguin Young
Readers Group, c2005.
Antithesis. Foreshadow. Inference.
Irony.

Jenkins, Emily. *That New Animal*.
Illus. by Pierce Pratt. New York:
(Frances Foster Books) Farrar,
Straus and Giroux, c2005.
Black Humor. Paradox.
Parallelism. Point-of-View.

Johnson, Angela. *Wind Flyers*. Illus.
by Loren Long. New York: Simon
& Schuster Books for Young
Readers, c2007.
Connotation. Imagery. Inference.
Motif. Paradox. Parallelism.

Johnson, Lindan Lee. *Dream Jar*. Illus.
by Serena Curmi. New York:
Houghton Mifflin, c2005.
Allusion. Antithesis. Foreshadow.
Inference. Motif. Parallelism.
Symbol. Understatement.

*Johnston, Tony. *Angel City*. Illus. by
Carole Byard. New York:
(Philomel) Penguin Young
Readers Group, c2006.
Allusion. Ambiguity. Antithesis.
Atmosphere. Colloquialism.
Connotation. Counterpoint.
Foreshadow. Imagery.
Inference. Metaphor. Motif.
Paradox. Parallelism. Simile.
Symbol. Theme. Tone. Wit/
Humor.

Johnston, Tony. *The Barn Owls*. Illus. by
Deborah Kogan Ray. Watertown,
MA: Charlesbridge, c2000.
Antithesis. Atmosphere. Imagery.
Metaphor. Motif. Parallelism.
Simile. Tone.

Karon, Jan. *Violet Comes to Stay*.
Story by Melanie Cecka. Illus. by
Emily Arnold McCully. New
York: (Viking) Penguin Young
Readers Group, c2006.
Alliteration. Aphorism.
Connotation. Foreshadow.
Imagery. Inference. Irony.
Motif. Onomatopoeia. Point-
of-View. Simile. Theme.

Kasza, Keiko. *Grandpa Toad's Secrets.*
New York: G. P. Putnam's Sons,
c1995.
Irony. Motif. Oxymoron.
Serendipity. Stereotype/
Reverse Stereotype. Surprise/
Twist-of-the-Tail. Tone. Wit/
Humor.

Kessler, Christina. *The Best Beekeeper
of Lalibela: A Tale from Africa.*
Illus. by Leonard Jenkins. New
York: Holiday House, c2006.
Antithesis. Aphorism.
Atmosphere. Foreshadow. Pun.
Serendipity. Simile. Stereotype.

Krensky, Stephen. *How Santa Lost His
Job.* Illus. by S. D. Schindler. New
York: (Aladdin) Simon &
Schuster, c2001.
Foreshadow. Inference. Irony.
Paradox. Satire.
Understatement.

*Lamm, C. Drew. *Gauchada.* Illus. by
Fabian Negrin. New York: Alfred
A. Knopf, c2002.
Antithesis. Atmosphere.
Connotation. Flashback.
Imagery. Internal Rhyme.
Irony. Metaphor. Motif.
Parallelism. Surprise/Twist-of-
the-Tail. Theme.

Lasky, Kathryn. *Pirate Bob.* Illus. by
David Clark. Watertown, MA:
Charlesbridge, c2006.
Antihero. Antithesis. Archetype.
Atmosphere. Black Humor.
Colloquialism. Connotation.
Hyperbole. Imagery. Inference.
Motif. Parallelism. Theme.

Lee-Tai, Amy. *A Place Where
Sunflowers Grow.* Illus. by Felicia
Hoshino. San Francisco:
Children's Book Press, c2006.
Aphorism. Atmosphere.
Connotation. Inference. Motif.
Symbol. Theme.

McClintock, Barbara. *Adele & Simon.*
New York: (Frances Foster Books)
Farrar, Straus and Giroux, c2006.
Aptronym. Foreshadow. Inference.
Parallelism. Wit/Humor.

McElligott, Matthew. *Backbeard and
the Birthday Suit.* New York:
Walker & Company, c2006.
Allusion. Ambiguity. Antihero.
Antithesis. Aphorism.
Aptronym. Archetype.
Atmosphere. Colloquialism.
Hyperbole. Irony. Point-of-
View. Solecism. Wit/Humor.

Manushkin, Fran. *The Shivers in the
Fridge.* Illus. by Paul O. Zelinsky.
New York: (Dutton Children's
Books) Penguin Young Readers
Group, c2006.
Inference. Motif. Parallelism.
Point-of-View. Pun.
Understatement. Wit/Humor.

Michelson, Richard. *Across the Alley.*
Illus. by E. B. Lewis. New York:
(Penguin Young Readers Group)
G. P. Putnam's Sons, c2006.
Aphorism. Counterpoint.
Inference. Irony. Metaphor.
Point-of-View. Simile.
Stereotype/Reverse Stereotype.
Theme.

*Montserrat, Pep. *Ms. Rubinstein's
Beauty.* New York: Sterling, c2006.
Antithesis. Atmosphere.
Connotation. Counterpoint.
Inference. Motif. Parallelism.
Surprise/Twist-in-the-Tail.
Theme.

Nelson, Vaunda Micheaux. *Almost to
Freedom.* Illus. by Colin Bootman.
Minneapolis, MN: (Carolrhoda)
Lerner, c2003.
Allusion. Atmosphere.
Colloquialism. Foreshadow.
Hyperbole. Imagery. Inference.
Parallelism. Personification.

*Poetic Justice. Point-of-View.
Simile. Solecism.
Understatement.*

Palatini, Margie. *Bad Boys Get Cookie!* Illus. by Henry Cole. New York: HarperCollins Children's Books, c2006.
Allusion. Foreshadow. Inference. Motif. Parallelism. Poetic Justice. Pun. Tone. Understatement. Wit/Humor.

Pearson, Tracey Campbell. *Bob.* New York: Farrar, Straus and Giroux, c2002.
Ambiguity. Irony. Onomatopoeia. Theme. Tone. Wit/Humor.

Pelley, Kathleen T. *Inventor McGregor.* Illus. by Michael Chesworth. New York: Farrar, Straus and Giroux, c2006.
Alliteration. Atmosphere. Connotation. Irony. Paradox. Simile. Theme.

Pfister, Marcus. *Holey Moley.* Trans. by J. Alison James. New York: North-South Books, c2006.
Antithesis. Counterpoint. Irony. Paradox. Parallelism. Theme.

*Raven, Marot Theis. *Night Boat to Freedom.* Illus. by E. B. Lewis. New York: (Melanie Kroupa Books) Farrar, Straus and Giroux, c2006.
Aphorism. Atmosphere. Colloquialism. Imagery. Inference. Metaphor. Paradox. Parallelism. Simile. Symbol. Theme.

Recorvits, Helen. *Yoon and the Christmas Mitten.* Illus. by Gabi Swaiatowska. New York: (Frances Foster Books) Farrar, Straus and Giroux, c2006.
Ambiguity. Antithesis. Atmosphere. Colloquialism. Counter-point. Foreshadow.

Inference. Parallelism. Point-of-View. Theme.

*Reynolds, Peter H. *So Few of Me.* Cambridge, MA: Candlewick Press, c2006.
Satire. Theme.

Sauer, Tammi. *Cowboy Camp.* Illus. by Mike Reed. New York: Sterling, c2005.
Antihero. Aptronym. Archetype. Colloquialism. Irony. Paradox. Parallelism. Satire.

*Schotter, Roni. *Mama, I'll Give You the World.* Illus. by S. Saelig Gallagher. New York: (Schwartz & Wade) Random House, c2006.
Ambiguity. Connotation. Foreshadow. Imagery. Inference. Metaphor. Motif. Point-of-View. Simile. Symbol. Tone.

Smith, Cynthia Leitich and Greg Smith. *Santa Knows.* Illus. by Steve Bjorkman. New York: (Dutton Children's Books) Penguin, c2006.
Allusion. Ambiguity. Aptronym. Foreshadow. Hyperbole. Irony. Motif. Parallelism. Poetic Justice. Tone. Wit/Humor.

Smith, Linda. *Mrs. Crump's Cat.* Illus. by David Roberts. New York: HarperCollins Children's Books, c2006.
Antithesis. Aptronym. Inference. Paradox.

Squires, Janet. *The Gingerbread Cowboy.* Illus. by Holly Berry. New York: HarperCollins Children's Books, c2006.
Atmosphere. Colloquialism. Imagery. Irony. Parallelism. Parody. Simile. Tone. Wit/Humor.

Stevens, Janet and Susan Stevens Crummel. *Cook-A-Doodle-Doo*. Illus. by Janet Stevens. Orlando, FL: (Voyager Books) Harcourt, c1999.
  Allusion. Colloquialism. Inference. Motif. Parallelism. Pun. Stereotype/Reverse Stereotype. Theme.

Teague, Mark. *Pigsty*. New York: Scholastic, c1994.
  Ambiguity. Aphorism. Foreshadow. Pun. Tone.

*Tingle, Tim. *Crossing Bok Chitto: A Choctaw Tale of Friendship and Freedom*. Illus. by Jeanne Rorex Bridges. El Paso, TX: Cinco Puntos Press, c2006.
  Allusion. Antithesis. Aphorism. Counterpoint. Flash-Forward. Foreshadow. Irony. Motif. Paradox. Parallelism. Simile. Symbol. Theme.

Williams, Laura E. *The Best Winds*. Illus. by Eujin Kim Neilan. Honesdale, PA: Boyds Mills Press, c2006.
  Aphorism. Atmosphere. Foreshadow. Inference. Motif. Simile. Theme.

Wojciechowski, Susan. *A Fine St. Patrick's Day*. Illus. by Tom Curry. New York: Random House, c2004.
  Alliteration. Colloquialism. Inference. Irony. Theme.

*Wood, Nancy. *Mr. and Mrs. God in the Creation Kitchen*. Illus. by Timothy Basil Ering. Cambridge, MA: Candlewick Press, c2006.
  Allusion. Antithesis. Foreshadow. Hyperbole. Imagery. Inference.

Parallelism. Pun. Satire. Understatement. Wit/Humor.

Yolen, Jane. *Harvest Home*. Illus. by Greg Shed. New York: (Silver Whistle) Harcourt, c2002.
  Atmosphere. Imagery. Internal Rhyme. Metaphor. Motif. Parallelism. Wit/Humor.

Yolen, Jane. *Raising Yoder's Barn*. Illus. by Bernie Fuchs. New York: Little,. Brown and Company, c1998.
  Aphorism. Colloquialism. Imagery. Inference. Metaphor. Motif. Parallelism. Simile Understatement.

Yorinks, Arthur. *Whitefish Will Rides Again!* Illus. by Mort Drucker. New York: HarperCollins, c1994.
  Alliteration. Archetype. Colloquialism. Hyperbole. Inference. Oxymoron. Satire. Simile. Solecism. Tone. Wit/Humor.

Young, Amy. *Belinda and the Glass Slipper*. New York: (Viking) Penguin Young Readers Group, c2006.
  Allusion. Antihero. Archetype. Counterpoint. Foreshadow. Inference. Irony. Parallelism. Parody. Poetic Justice. Simile. Surprise/Twist-in-the-Tail. Theme. Understatement.

*Young, Ed. *I, Doko: The Tale of a Basket*. New York: Philomel, c2004.
  Aphorism. Foreshadow. Inference. Personification. Poetic Justice. Point-of-View. Theme. Tone.

APPENDIX 2:
RESOURCES LISTED
BY TITLE

❖❖❖❖❖❖❖❖❖❖❖

Across the Alley. Michelson, Richard. Illus. by E. B. Lewis. New York: (Penguin Young Readers Group) G. P. Putnam's Sons, c2006.
Aphorism. Counterpoint. Inference. Irony. Metaphor. Point-of-View. Simile. Stereotype/Reverse Stereotype. Theme.

Across the Blue Pacific: A World War II Story. Borden, Louise. Illus. by Robert Andrew Parker. Boston: Houghton Mifflin, c2006.
Aphorism. Atmosphere. Connotation. Flashback. Flash-Forward. Foreshadow. Imagery. Inference. Motif. Paradox. Parallelism. Simile. Theme.

Adele & Simon. McClintock, Barbara. New York: (Frances Foster Books) Farrar, Straus and Giroux, c2006.
Aptronym. Foreshadow. Inference. Parallelism. Wit.

Almost to Freedom. Nelson, Vaunda Micheaux. Illus. by Colin Bootman.

Minneapolis, MN: (Carolrhoda) Lerner, c2003.
Allusion. Atmosphere. Colloquialism. Foreshadow. Hyperbole. Imagery. Inference. Parallelism. Personification. Poetic Justice. Point-of-View. Simile. Solecism. Understatement.

*Angel City. Johnston, Tony. Illus. by Carole Byard. New York: (Philomel) Penguin Young Readers Group, c2006.
Allusion. Ambiguity. Antithesis. Atmosphere. Colloquialism. Connotation. Counterpoint. Foreshadow. Imagery. Inference. Metaphor. Motif. Paradox. Parallelism. Simile. Symbol. Theme. Tone. Wit/Humor.

*The Babe and I. Adler, David A. Illus. by Terry Widdener. New York: (Gulliver Books) Harcourt Brace & Co., c1999.

Ambiguity. Antithesis.
Foreshadow. Inference. Irony.
Paradox. Tone.

Backbeard and the Birthday Suit.
McElligott, Matthew. New York:
Walker & Company, c2006.
Allusion. Ambiguity. Antihero.
Antithesis. Aphorism.
Aptronym. Archetype.
Atmosphere. Colloquialism.
Hyperbole. Irony. Point-of-
View. Wit/Humor.

Bad Boys Get Cookie! Palatini,
Margie. Illus. by Henry Cole. New
York: HarperCollins Children's
Books, c2006.
Allusion. Foreshadow. Inference.
Motif. Parallelism. Poetic
Justice. Pun. Tone.
Understatement. Wit/Humor.

Ballerino Nate. Bradley, Kimberly
Brubaker. Illus. by R. W. Alley.
New York: (Dial Books for Young
Readers) Penguin Young Readers
Group, c2006.
Ambiguity. Archetype. Inference.
Motif. Parallelism. Stereotype/
Reverse Stereotype.

Barfburger Baby, I Was Here First.
Danziger, Paula. Illus. by G. Brian
Karas. New York: (Penguin Young
Readers Group) G. P. Putnam's
Sons, c2004.
Inference. Irony. Motif.

The Barn Owls. Johnston, Tony. Illus. by
Deborah Kogan Ray. Watertown,
MA: Charlesbridge, c2000.
Atmosphere. Imagery. Metaphor.
Motif. Parallelism. Simile. Tone.

Barn Savers. High, Linda Oatman.
Illus. by Ted Lewin. Honesdale,
PA: Boyds Mills Press, c1999.
Atmosphere. Connotation.
Imagery. Metaphor.
Parallelism. Simile.

Belinda and the Glass Slipper. Young,
Amy. New York: (Viking) Penguin
Young Readers Group, c2006.
Allusion. Antihero. Archetype.
Counterpoint. Foreshadow.
Inference. Irony. Parallelism.
Parody. Poetic Justice.
Simile. Surprise/Twist-in-
the-Tail. Theme. Under-
statement.

The Best Beekeeper of Lalibela: A
Tale from Africa. Kessler, Christina.
Illus. by Leonard Jenkins. New York:
Holiday House, c2006.
Antithesis. Aphorism.
Atmosphere. Foreshadow. Pun.
Serendipity. Simile.
Stereotype.

The Best Winds. Williams, Laura E. Illus.
by Eujin Kim Neilan. Honesdale,
PA: Boyds Mills Press, c2006.
Aphorism. Atmosphere.
Foreshadow. Inference. Motif.
Simile. Theme.

Bob. Pearson, Tracey Campbell. New
York: Farrar, Straus and Giroux,
c2002.
Ambiguity. Irony. Onomatopoeia.
Theme. Tone. Wit/Humor.

Butterfly House. Bunting, Eve. Illus. by
Greg Shed. New York: Scholastic
Press, c1999.
Atmosphere. Connotation. Flash-
Forward. Imagery. Internal
Rhyme. Paradox. Point-of-
View. Simile.

Carolinda Clatter! Gerstein, Mordicai.
New Milford, CT: (Roaring Brook
Press) Holtzbrinck, c2005.
Allusion. Antithesis. Aptronym.
Counterpoint. Flash-Forward.
Foreshadow. Hyperbole.
Internal Rhyme. Irony.
Metaphor. Motif. Parallelism.
Wit/Humor.

Cook-A-Doodle-Doo. Stevens, Janet and Susan Stevens Crummel. Illus. by Janet Stevens. Orlando, FL: (Voyager Books) Harcourt, c1999.
> *Allusion. Colloquialism. Inference. Motif. Parallelism. Pun. Stereotype/Reverse Stereotype. Theme.*

Cousin John Is Coming! Broach, Elise. Illus. by Nate Lilly. New York: (Dial Books for Young Readers) Penguin Young Readers Group, c2006.
> *Ambiguity. Archetype. Counterpoint. Irony. Paradox.*

Cowboy Camp. Sauer, Tammi. Illus. by Mike Reed. New York: Sterling, c2005.
> *Antihero. Aptronym. Archetype. Colloquialism. Irony. Paradox. Parallelism. Satire.*

*Crossing Bok Chitto: A Choctaw Tale of Friendship and Freedom. Tingle, Tim. Illus. by Jeanne Rorex Bridges. El Paso, TX: Cinco Puntos Press, c2006.
> *Allusion. Antithesis. Aphorism. Counterpoint. Flash-Forward. Foreshadow. Irony. Motif. Paradox. Parallelism. Simile. Symbol. Theme.*

Desmond and the Naughtybugs. Ashman, Linda. Illus. by Anik McGrory. New York: (Dutton Children's Books) Penguin Young Readers Group, c2006.
> *Foreshadow. Inference. Irony. Parallelism.*

Dream Jar. Johnson, Kindan Lee. Illus. by Serena Curmi. New York: Houghton Mifflin, c2005.
> *Allusion. Antithesis. Foreshadow. Inference. Motif. Parallelism. Symbol. Understatement.*

The Featherless Chicken. Chen, Chih-Yuan. Alhambra, CA: Heryin Books, c2006.
> *Alliteration. Archetype. Connotation. Inference. Internal Rhyme. Irony. Satire. Serendipity. Simile. Theme. Tone. Wit/Humor.*

A Fine St. Patrick's Day. Wojciechowski, Susan. Illus. by Tom Curry. New York: Random House, c2004.
> *Alliteration. Colloquialism. Inference. Irony. Theme.*

*Gauchada. Lamm, C. Drew. Illus. by Fabian Negrin. New York: Alfred A. Knopf, c2002.
> *Antithesis. Atmosphere. Connotation. Flashback. Imagery. Internal Rhyme. Irony. Metaphor. Motif. Parallelism. Surprise/Twist-in-the-Tail. Theme.*

*The Gift. Franklin, Kristine L. Illus. by Barbara Lavallee. San Francisco: Chronicle Books, c1999.
> *Ambiguity. Connotation. Foreshadow. Imagery. Inference. Irony. Onomatopoeia. Simile. Surprise/Twist-in-the-Tail. Symbol. Theme.*

The Gift Stone. Eversole, Robyn. Illus. by Allen Garns. New York: Alfred A. Knopf, c1998.
> *Antithesis. Aphorism. Atmosphere. Connotation. Inference. Irony. Metaphor. Motif. Parallelism. Simile. Symbol.*

The Gingerbread Cowboy. Squires, Janet. Illus. by Holly Berry. New York: HarperCollins Children's Books, c2006.

Atmosphere. Colloquialism.
Imagery. Irony. Parallelism.
Parody. Simile. Tone. Wit/
Humor.

Grandfather Buffalo. Arnosky, Jim.
New York: G. P. Putnam's Sons,
c2006.
Atmosphere. Foreshadow.
Inference. Motif. Theme.

Grandpa Toad's Secrets. Kasza, Keiko.
New York: G. P. Putnam's Sons,
c1995.
Irony. Motif. Oxymoron.
Serendipity. Stereotype/Reverse
Stereotype. Surprise/Twist-in-
the-Tail. Tone. Wit/Humor.

The Great Math Tattle Battle. Bowen,
Anne. Illus. by Jaime Zollars.
Morton Grove, IL: Albert
Whitman, c2006.
Connotation. Paradox.
Parallelism. Poetic Justice.
Theme.

Harvest Home. Yolen, Jane. Illus. by
Greg Shed. New York: (Silver
Whistle) Harcourt, c2002.
Atmosphere. Imagery. Internal
Rhyme. Metaphor. Motif.
Parallelism. Wit/Humor.

Hen Lake. Auch, Mary Jane. New
York: Holiday House, c1995.
Allusion. Aphorism. Aptronym.
Archetype. Colloquialism.
Connotation. Inference. Motif.
Theme.

Holey Moley. Pfister, Marcus. Trans.
by J. Alison James. New York:
North-South Books, c2006.
Antithesis. Counterpoint. Irony.
Paradox. Parallelism. Theme.

How Santa Lost His Job. Krensky,
Stephen. Illus. by S. D. Schindler.
New York: (Aladdin) Simon &
Schuster, c2001.

Foreshadow. Inference. Irony.
Paradox. Satire.
Understatement.

*I, Doko: The Tale of a Basket. Young,
Ed. New York: Philomel, c2004
Aphorism. Foreshadow. Inference.
Personification. Poetic Justice.
Point-of-View. Theme. Tone.

I'm Not Cute! Allen, Jonathan. New
York: Hyperion Books for
Children, c2005.
Antithesis. Counterpoint.
Foreshadow. Motif. Paradox.

In My Heart. Bang, Molly. New York:
Little, Brown and Company,
c2006.
Inference. Motif. Tone.

Inventor McGregor. Pelley, Kathleen
T. Illus. by Michael Chesworth.
New York: Farrar, Straus and
Giroux, c2006.
Alliteration. Atmosphere.
Connotation. Irony. Paradox.
Simile. Theme.

*Keeper of Soles. Bateman, Teresa.
Illus. by Diego Herrera (Yayo).
New York: Holiday House, c2006.
Ambiguity. Aphorism. Black
Humor. Colloquialism.
Connotation. Imagery.
Inference. Irony. Paradox.
Parallelism. Pun.
Understatement.

Kitten's First Full Moon. Henkes,
Kevin. New York: (Greenwillow
Books) HarperCollins, c2004.
Irony. Motif. Tone.

Lost and Found. Jeffers, Oliver. New
York: (Philomel) Penguin Young
Readers Group, c2005.
Antithesis. Foreshadow. Inference.
Irony.

*Mama, I'll Give You the World.
Schotter, Roni. Illus. by S. Saelig

Gallagher. New York: (Schwartz & Wade) Random House, c2006.
Ambiguity. Connotation. Foreshadow. Imagery. Inference. Metaphor. Motif. Point-of-View. Simile. Symbol. Tone.

The Mixed-Up Rooster. Edwards, Pamela Duncan. Illus. by Megan Lloyd. New York: HarperCollins Children's Books, c2006.
Foreshadow. Parallelism. Pun. Serendipity. Theme. Wit/Humor.

*Moi & Marie Antoinette. Cullen, Lynn. Illus. by Amy Young. New York: Bloomsbury Publishing, c2006.
Archetype. Atmosphere. Counterpoint. Foreshadow. Hyperbole. Inference. Motif. Parallelism. Point-of-View. Serendipity. Simile. Surprise/Twist-in-the-Tail. Wit/Humor.

The Most Perfect Spot. Goode, Diane. New York: HarperCollins Children's Books, c2006.
Foreshadow. Irony. Motif. Pun.

Mr. and Mrs. God in the Creation Kitchen. Wood, Nancy. Illus. by Timothy Basil Ering. Cambridge, MA: Candlewick Press, c2006.
Allusion. Antithesis. Foreshadow. Hyperbole. Imagery. Inference. Onomatopoeia. Parallelism. Pun. Satire. Understatement. Wit/Humor.

Mrs. Crump's Cat. Smith, Linda. Illus. by David Roberts. New York: HarperCollins Children's Books, c2006.
Antithesis. Aptronym. Inference. Paradox.

*Ms. Rubinstein's Beauty. Montserrat, Pep. New York: Sterling, c2006.
Antithesis. Atmosphere. Connotation. Counterpoint. Inference. Motif. Parallelism. Surprise/Twist-in-the-Tail. Theme.

Muncha! Muncha! Muncha! Fleming, Candace. Illus. by G. Brian Karas. New York: Atheneum Books for Young Readers, c2002.
Allusion. Aptronym. Irony. Onomatopoeia. Parallelism. Surprise/Twist-in-the-Tail.

My Father's Boat. Garland, Sherry. Illus. by Ted Rand. New York: Scholastic Press, c1998.
Antithesis. Aphorism. Connotation. Counterpoint. Imagery. Metaphor. Parallelism. Simile. Theme.

*Night Boat to Freedom. Raven, Marot Theis. Illus. by E. B. Lewis. New York: (Melanie Kroupa Books) Farrar, Straus and Giroux, c2006.
Aphorism. Atmosphere. Colloquialism. Imagery. Inference. Metaphor. Paradox. Parallelism. Simile. Symbol. Theme.

Nutmeg and Barley: A Budding Friendship. Bynum, Janie. Cambridge, MA: Candlewick Press, c2006.
Ambiguity. Antithesis. Foreshadow. Parallelism. Theme.

One Green Apple. Bunting, Eve. Illus. by Ted Lewin. New York: (Clarion Books) Houghton Mifflin, c2006.
Antithesis. Inference. Symbol. Theme.

Pigsty. Teague, Mark. New York: Scholastic, c1994.
Ambiguity. Aphorism. Foreshadow. Pun. Tone.

Pirate Bob. Lasky, Kathryn. Illus. by
David Clark. Watertown, MA:
Charlesbridge, c2006.
  *Antihero. Antithesis. Archetype.
  Atmosphere. Black Humor.
  Colloquialism. Connotation.
  Hyperbole. Imagery. Inference.
  Motif. Parallelism. Theme.*

A Place Where Sunflowers Grow. Lee-
Tai, Amy. Illus. by Felicia
Hoshino. San Francisco:
Children's Book Press, c2006.
  *Aphorism. Atmosphere.
    Connotation. Inference. Motif.
    Symbol. Theme.*

A Plump and Perky Turkey. Bateman,
Teresa. Illus. by Jeff Shelly. New
York: Marshall Cavendish, c2001.
  *Alliteration. Allusion. Ambiguity.
    Aptronym. Irony. Parallelism.
    Poetic Justice. Surprise/Twist-
    of-the-Tail. Theme.
  Understatement.*

Pop's Bridge. Bunting, Eve. Illus. by C. F.
Payne. New York: Harcourt, c2006.
  *Antithesis. Aphorism.
    Foreshadow. Inference.
    Metaphor. Simile. Symbol.
    Theme.*

Raisin and Grape. Amico, Tom and
James Proimos. Illus. by Andy
Snair. New York: (Dial Books for
Young Readers) Penguin Young
Readers Group, c2006.
  *Antithesis. Connotation.
    Hyperbole. Inference. Pun.
    Tone. Understatement. Wit/
    Humor.*

Raising Yoder's Barn. Yolen, Jane. Illus.
by Bernie Fuchs. New York: Little,
Brown and Company, c1998.
  *Aphorism. Colloquialism.
    Imagery. Inference. Metaphor.
    Motif. Parallelism. Simile.
    Understatement.*

Santa Knows. Smith, Cynthia Leitich
and Greg Smith. Illus. by Steve
Bjorkman. New York: (Dutton
Children's   Books)   Penguin,
c2006.
  *Allusion. Ambiguity. Aptronym.
    Foreshadow. Hyperbole. Irony.
    Motif. Parallelism. Poetic
    Justice. Tone. Wit/Humor.*

The Scarves. Bunge, Daniela. Trans.
by Kahryn Bishop. New York:
Penguin Young Readers Group,
c2006.
  *Archetype. Counterpoint.
    Foreshadow. Inference. Irony.
    Symbol.*

*The Secret-Keeper. Coombs, Kate.
Illus. by Heather M. Solomon.
New York: (Atheneum Books for
Young   Readers)   Simon   &
Schuster, c2006.
  *Ambiguity. Connotation.
    Foreshadow. Imagery.
    Inference. Irony. Metaphor.
    Motif. Serendipity. Simile.
    Symbol. Tone.*

The Shivers in the Fridge. Manushkin,
Fran. Illus. by Paul O. Zelinsky.
New York: (Dutton Children's
Books) Penguin Young Readers
Group, c2006.
  *Inference. Motif. Parallelism.
    Point-of-View. Pun.
    Understatement. Wit/Humor.*

Snow in Jerusalem. da Costa, Deborah.
Illus. by Cornelius Van Wright &
Ying-Hwa Hu. Morton Grove, IL:
Albert Whitman, c2001.
  *Connotation. Counterpoint.
    Imagery. Simile. Symbol.
    Theme.*

*So Few of Me. Reynolds, Peter H.
Cambridge,   MA: Candlewick
Press, c2006.
  Satire. Theme.

Ten Gallon Bart. Crummel, Susan Stevens. Illus. by Dorothy Donohue. Tarrytown, NY: Marshall Cavendish, c2006.
Allusion. Archetype.
Colloquialism. Connotation.
Inference. Internal Rhyme.
Motif. Parody. Poetic Justice.
Pun. Stereotype/Reverse
Stereotype. Tone.
Wit/Humor.

That New Animal. Jenkins, Emily. Illus. by Pierce Pratt. New York: (Frances Foster Books) Farrar, Straus and Giroux, c2005.
Black Humor. Paradox.
Parallelism. Point-of-View.

Too Many Frogs! Asher, Sandy. Illus. by Keith Graves. New York: (Philomel Books) Penguin Young Readers Group, c2005.
Allusion. Aphorism. Internal
Rhyme. Irony. Parallelism.
Theme. Tone.

The Tortoise and the Hare Race Again. Bernstein, Dan. Illus. by Andrew Glass. New York: Holiday House, c2006.
Alliteration. Allusion. Ambiguity.
Foreshadow. Paradox. Parody.
Pun.

*The Toughest Cowboy, or How the Wild West Was Tamed. Frank, John. Illus. by Zachary Pullen. New York: Simon & Schuster Books for Young Readers, c2004.
Allusion. Ambiguity. Aptronym.
Atmosphere. Colloquialism.
Foreshadow. Hyperbole.
Inference. Irony. Parallelism.
Pun. Simile. Solecism.
Stereotype/Reverse Stereotype.
Tone. Understatement. Wit/
Humor.

Up in the Tree. Atwood, Margaret. Toronto, Ontario: Greenwood Books/House of Anansi Press, c1978, 2006.
Antithesis. Hyperbole. Internal
Rhyme. Irony. Motif.
Parallelism.

Violet Comes to Stay. Karon, Jan. Story by Melanie Cecka. Illus. by Emily Arnold McCully. New York: (Viking) Penguin Young Readers Group, c2006.
Alliteration. Aphorism.
Connotation. Foreshadow.
Imagery. Inference. Irony.
Motif. Onomatopoeia. Point-
of-View. Simile. Theme.

Whitefish Will Rides Again! Yorinks, Arthur. Illus. by Mort Drucker. New York: HarperCollins, c1994.
Alliteration. Archetype.
Colloquialism. Hyperbole.
Inference. Oxymoron. Satire.
Simile. Tone. Wit/Humor.

The Wild Woods. James, Simon. Cambridge, MA: Candlewick Press, c1993.
Inference. Motif. Point-of-View.
Wit/Humor.

Wind Flyers. Johnson, Angela. Illus. by Loren Long. New York: Simon & Schuster Books for Young Readers, c2007.
Connotation. Imagery. Inference.
Motif. Paradox. Parallelism.

Yoon and the Christmas Mitten. Recorvits, Helen. Illus. by Gabi Swaiatowska. New York: (Frances Foster Books) Farrar, Straus and Giroux, c2006.
Ambiguity. Antithesis.
Atmosphere. Colloquialism.
Counterpoint. Foreshadow.
Inference. Parallelism. Point-
of-View. Theme.

APPENDIX 3:
RESOURCES LISTED
BY DEVICES

❖❖❖❖❖❖❖❖❖❖❖

Alliteration	*Foreshadow*	*Point-of-View*
Allusion	*Hyperbole*	*Pun*
Ambiguity	*Imagery*	*Satire*
Antihero	*Inference*	*Serendipity*
Antithesis	*Internal Rhyme*	*Simile*
Aphorism	*Irony*	*Solecism*
Aptronym	*Metaphor*	*Stereotype/Reverse*
Archetype	*Motif*	*Stereotype*
Atmosphere	*Onomatopoeia*	*Surprise/*
Black Humor	*Oxymoron*	*Twist-in-the-Tail*
Colloquialism	*Paradox*	*Symbol*
Connotation	*Parallelism*	*Theme*
Counterpoint	*Parody*	*Tone*
Flashback	*Personification*	*Understatement*
Flash-Forward	*Poetic Justice*	*Wit/Humor*

ALLITERATION

Repeated consonant sounds occurring at the beginnings of neighboring words.

Bateman, Teresa. *A Plump and Perky Turkey.* Illus. by Jeff Shelly. New York: Marshall Cavendish, c2001.
> **Other Devices:** *Allusion. Ambiguity. Aptronym. Irony. Parallelism. Poetic Justice. Surprise/Twist-in-the-Tail. Theme. Understatement.*

Bernstein, Dan. *The Tortoise and the Hare Race Again.* Illus. by Andrew Glass. New York: Holiday House, c2006.
> **Other Devices:** *Allusion. Ambiguity. Foreshadow. Paradox. Parody. Pun.*

Chen, Chih-Yuan. *The Featherless Chicken.* Alhambra, CA: Heryin Books, c2006.
> **Other Devices:** *Archetype. Connotation. Inference. Internal Rhyme. Irony. Satire. Serendipity. Simile. Theme. Tone. Wit/Humor.*

Karon, Jan. *Violet Comes to Stay.* Story by Melanie Cecka. Illus. by Emily Arnold McCully. New York: (Viking) Penguin Young Readers Group, c2006.
> **Other Devices:** *Aphorism. Connotation. Foreshadow. Imagery. Inference. Irony. Motif. Onomatopoeia. Point-of-View. Simile. Theme.*

Pelley, Kathleen T. *Inventor McGregor.* Illus. by Michael Chesworth. New York: Farrar, Straus and Giroux, c2006.
> **Other Devices:** *Atmosphere. Connotation. Irony. Paradox. Simile. Theme.*

Wojciechowski, Susan. *A Fine St. Patrick's Day.* Illus. by Tom Curry. New York: Random House, c2004.
> **Other Devices:** *Colloquialism. Inference. Irony. Theme.*

Yorinks, Arthur. *Whitefish Will Rides Again!* Illus. by Mort Drucker. New York: HarperCollins, c1994.
> **Other Devices:** *Archetype. Colloquialism. Hyperbole. Inference. Oxymoron. Satire. Simile. Solecism. Tone. Wit/Humor.*

ALLUSION

Brief reference in one literary work to either another literary work or to a presumably familiar person, historical event, place, or object.

Asher, Sandy. *Too Many Frogs!* Illus. by Keith Graves. New York: (Philomel Books) Penguin Young Readers Group, c2005.
> **Other Devices:** *Aphorism. Internal Rhyme. Irony. Parallelism. Theme. Tone.*

Auch, Mary Jane. *Hen Lake.* New York: Holiday House, c1995.
> **Other Devices:** *Aphorism. Aptronym. Archetype. Colloquialism. Connotation. Inference. Motif. Theme.*

Bateman, Teresa. *A Plump and Perky Turkey.* Illus. by Jeff Shelly. New York: Marshall Cavendish, c2001.
> **Other Devices:** *Alliteration. Ambiguity. Aptronym. Irony. Parallelism. Poetic Justice. Surprise/Twist-in-the-Tail. Theme. Understatement.*

Bernstein, Dan. *The Tortoise and the Hare Race Again.* Illus. by Andrew Glass. New York: Holiday House, c2006.
> **Other Devices:** *Alliteration. Ambiguity. Foreshadow. Paradox. Parody. Pun.*

Crummel, Susan Stevens. *Ten Gallon Bart.* Illus. by Dorothy Donohue. Tarrytown, NY: Marshall Cavendish, c2006.
> **Other Devices:** *Colloquialism. Connotation. Inference. Internal Rhyme. Motif. Parody. Poetic Justice. Pun. Solecism. Stereotype/Reverse Stereotype. Tone. Wit/Humor.*

Fleming, Candace. *Muncha! Muncha! Muncha!* Illus. by G. Brian Karas. New York: Atheneum Books for Young Readers, c2002.
> **Other Devices:** *Aptronym. Irony. Motif. Onomatopoeia. Parallelism. Surprise/Twist-in-the-Tail.*

*****Frank, John.** *The Toughest Cowboy, or How the Wild West Was Tamed.* Illus. by Zachary Pullen. New York: Simon & Schuster Books for Young Readers, c2004.
> **Other Devices:** *Ambiguity. Aptronym. Atmosphere. Colloquialism. Hyperbole. Inference. Irony. Parallelism. Pun. Simile. Solecism. Stereotype/Reverse Stereotype. Tone. Understatement. Wit/Humor.*

Gerstein, Mordicai. *Carolinda Clatter!* New Milford, CT: (Roaring Brook Press) Holtzbrinck, c2005.
> **Other Devices:** *Antithesis. Aptronym. Counterpoint. Flash-Forward. Foreshadow. Hyperbole. Internal Rhyme. Irony. Metaphor. Motif. Parallelism. Wit/Humor.*

Johnson, Lindan Lee. *Dream Jar.* Illus. by Serena Curmi. New York: Houghton Mifflin, c2005.
> **Other Devices:** *Antithesis. Foreshadow. Inference. Motif. Parallelism. Symbol. Understatement.*

*****Johnston, Tony.** *Angel City.* Illus. by Carole Byard. New York: (Philomel) Penguin Young Readers Group, c2006.
> **Other Devices:** *Ambiguity. Antithesis. Atmosphere. Colloquialism. Connotation. Counterpoint. Foreshadow. Imagery. Inference. Metaphor. Motif. Paradox. Parallelism. Simile. Symbol. Theme. Tone. Wit/Humor.*

McElligott, Matthew. *Backbeard and the Birthday Suit.* New York: Walker & Company, c2006.
> **Other Devices:** *Ambiguity. Antihero. Antithesis. Aphorism. Aptronym. Archetype. Atmosphere. Colloquialism. Hyperbole. Irony. Point-of-View. Solecism. Wit/Humor.*

Nelson, Vaunda Micheaux. *Almost to Freedom.* Illus. by Colin Bootman. Minneapolis, MN: (Carolrhoda) Learner, c2003.
> **Other Devices:** *Atmosphere. Colloquialism. Foreshadow. Hyperbole. Imagery. Inference. Parallelism. Personification. Poetic Justice. Point-of-View. Simile. Solecism. Understatement.*

Palatini, Margie. *Bad Boys Get Cookie!* Illus. by Henry Cole. New York: HarperCollins Children's Books, c2006.
> **Other Devices:** *Foreshadow. Inference. Motif. Parallelism. Poetic Justice. Pun. Tone. Understatement. Wit/Humor.*

Smith, Cynthia Leitich and Greg Smith. *Santa Knows.* Illus. by Steve Bjorkman. New York: (Dutton Children's Books) Penguin, c2006.
> **Other Devices:** *Ambiguity. Aptronym. Foreshadow. Hyperbole. Irony. Motif. Parallelism. Poetic Justice. Tone. Wit/Humor.*

Stevens, Janet and Susan Stevens Crummel. *Cook-A-Doodle-Doo.* Orlando, FL: (Voyager Books) Harcourt, c1999.
> **Other Devices:** *Colloquialism. Inference. Motif. Parallelism. Pun. Stereotype/Reverse Stereotype. Theme.*

*Tingle, Tim. *Crossing Bok Chitto: A Choctaw Tale of Friendship and Freedom.* Illus. by Jeanne Rorex Bridges. El Paso, TX: Cinco Puntos Press, c2006.
> **Other Devices:** *Antithesis. Aphorism. Counterpoint. Flash-Forward. Foreshadow. Irony. Motif. Paradox. Parallelism. Simile. Symbol. Theme.*

*Wood, Nancy. *Mr. and Mrs. God in the Creation Kitchen.* Illus. by Timothy Basil Ering. Cambridge, MA: Candlewick Press, c2006.
> **Other Devices:** *Antithesis. Foreshadow. Hyperbole. Imagery. Inference. Onomatopoeia. Parallelism. Pun. Satire. Understatement. Wit/Humor.*

Young, Amy. *Belinda and the Glass Slipper.* New York: (Viking) Penguin Young Readers Group, c2006.
> **Other Devices:** *Antihero. Archetype. Counterpoint. Foreshadow. Inference. Irony. Parallelism. Parody. Poetic Justice. Simile. Surprise/Twist-in-the-Tail. Theme. Understatement.*

AMBIGUITY

Richness of alternative meanings from the same language or more than one meaning simultaneously.

*Adler, David A. *The Babe and I.* Illus. by Terry Widdener. New York: (Gulliver Books) Harcourt Brace & Co., c1999.
> **Other Devices:** *Antithesis. Foreshadow. Inference. Irony. Paradox. Tone.*

*Bateman, Teresa. *Keeper of Soles.* Illus. by Diego Herrera (Yayo). New York: Holiday House, c2006.
> **Other Devices:** *Aphorism. Black Humor. Colloquialism. Connotation. Imagery. Inference. Irony. Paradox. Parallelism. Pun. Understatement.*

Bateman, Teresa. *A Plump and Perky Turkey.* Illus. by Jeff Shelly. New York: Marshall Cavendish, c2001.
> **Other Devices:** *Alliteration. Allusion. Aptronym. Irony. Parallelism. Poetic Justice. Surprise/Twist-in-theTail. Theme. Understatement.*

Bernstein, Dan. *The Tortoise and the Hare Race Again.* Illus. by Andrew Glass. New York: Holiday House, c2006.
> **Other Devices:** *Alliteration. Allusion. Foreshadow. Paradox. Parody. Pun.*

Bradley, Kimberly Brubaker. *Ballerino Nate.* Illus. by R. W. Alley. New York: (Dial Books for Young Readers), Penguin Young Readers Group, c2006.

   Other Devices: *Archetype. Inference. Motif. Parallelism. Stereotype/ Reverse Stereotype.*

Broach, Elise. *Cousin John Is Coming!* Illus. by Nate Lilly. New York: (Dial Books for Young Readers) Penguin Young Readers Group, c2006.

   Other Devices: *Archetype. Counterpoint. Inference. Irony. Paradox.*

Bynum, Janie. *Nutmeg and Barley: A Budding Friendship.* Cambridge, MA: Candlewick Press, c2006.

   Other Devices: *Antithesis. Foreshadow. Parallelism. Theme.*

*Coombs, Kate. *The Secret-Keeper.* Illus. by Heather M. Solomon. New York: (Atheneum Books for Young Readers) Simon & Schuster, c2006.

   Other Devices: *Connotation. Foreshadow. Imagery. Inference. Irony. Metaphor. Motif. Serendipity. Simile. Symbol. Tone.*

*Frank, John. *The Toughest Cowboy, or How the Wild West Was Tamed.* Illus. by Zachary Pullen. New York: Simon & Schuster Books for Young Readers, c2004.

   Other Devices: *Allusion. Aptronym. Atmosphere. Colloquialism. Foreshadow. Hyperbole. Inference. Irony. Parallelism. Pun. Simile. Solecism. Stereotype/Reverse Stereotype. Tone. Understatement. Wit/Humor.*

*Franklin, Kristine L. *The Gift.* Illus. by Barbara Lavallee. San Francisco: Chronicle Books, c1999.

   Other Devices: *Connotation. Foreshadow. Imagery. Inference. Irony. Onomatopoeia. Simile. Surprise/Twist-in-the-Tail. Symbol. Theme.*

*Johnston, Tony. *Angel City.* Illus. by Carole Byard. New York: (Philomel) Penguin Young Readers Group, c2006.

   Other Devices: *Allusion. Antithesis. Atmosphere. Colloquialism. Connotation. Counterpoint. Foreshadow. Imagery. Inference. Metaphor. Motif. Paradox. Parallelism. Simile. Symbol. Theme. Tone. Wit/Humor.*

McElligott, Matthew. *Backbeard and the Birthday Suit.* New York: Walker & Company, c2006.

   Other Devices: *Allusion. Antihero. Antithesis. Aphorism. Aptronym. Archetype. Atmosphere. Colloquialism. Hyperbole. Irony. Point-of-View. Solecism. Wit/Humor.*

Pearson, Tracey Campbell. *Bob.* New York: Farrar, Straus and Giroux, c2002.

   Other Devices: *Irony. Onomatopoeia. Theme. Tone. Wit/Humor.*

Recorvits, Helen. *Yoon and the Christmas Mitten.* Illus. by Gabi Swaiatowska. New York: (Frances Foster Books) Farrar, Straus and Giroux, c2006.

   Other Devices: *Antithesis. Atmosphere. Colloquialism. Counterpoint. Foreshadow. Inference. Parallelism. Point-of-View. Theme.*

*Schotter, Roni. *Mama, I'll Give You the World.* Illus. by S. Saelig Gallagher. New York: (Schwartz & Wade) Random House, c2006.

Other Devices: *Connotation. Foreshadow. Imagery. Inference. Metaphor. Motif. Point-of-View. Simile. Symbol. Tone.*

Smith, Cynthia Leitich and Greg Smith. *Santa Knows.* Illus. by Steve Bjorkman. New York: (Dutton Children's Books) Penguin, c2006.
Other Devices: *Allusion. Aptronym. Foreshadow. Hyperbole. Irony. Motif. Parallelism. Poetic Justice. Tone. Wit/Humor.*

Teague, Mark. *Pigsty.* New York: Scholastic, c1994.
Other Devices: *Aphorism. Foreshadow. Pun. Tone.*

ANTIHERO

Protagonist lacking virtues and estimable traits of traditional heroic qualities such as courage or fortitude and, instead, possessing rather pathetic, comic, or even antisocial traits while rejecting conventional value expectations.

Lasky, Kathryn. *Pirate Bob.* Illus. by David Clark. Watertown, MA: Charlesbridge, c2006.
Other Devices: *Antithesis. Archetype. Atmosphere. Black Humor. Colloquialism. Connotation. Hyperbole. Imagery. Inference. Motif. Parallelism. Theme.*

McElligott, Matthew. *Backbeard and the Birthday Suit.* New York: Walker & Company, c2006.
Other Devices: *Allusion. Ambiguity. Antithesis. Aphorism. Aptronym. Archetype. Atmosphere. Colloquialism. Hyperbole. Irony. Point-of-View. Solecism. Wit/Humor.*

Sauer, Tammi. *Cowboy Camp.* Illus. by Mike Reed. New York: Sterling, c2005.
Other Devices: *Aptronym. Archetype. Colloquialism. Irony. Paradox. Parallelism. Satire.*

ANTITHESIS

Balanced grammatical placement of sharply opposing thoughts, usually in two phrases, clauses, or sentences to heighten their effect by contrast: "You are going; I am staying."

*Adler, David A. *The Babe and I.* Illus. by Terry Widdener. New York: (Gulliver Books) Harcourt Brace & Co., c1999.
Other Devices: *Ambiguity. Foreshadow. Inference. Irony. Paradox. Tone.*

Allen, Jonathan. *I'm Not Cute!* New York: Hyperion Books for Children, c2005.
Other Devices: *Counterpoint. Foreshadow. Motif. Paradox.*

Amico, Tom and James Proimos. *Raisin and Grape.* Illus. by Andy Snair. New York: (Dial Books for Young Readers) Penguin Young Readers Group, c2006.

Other Devices: *Connotation. Hyperbole. Inference. Pun. Tone. Understatement. Wit/Humor.*

Atwood, Margaret. *Up in the Tree.* Toronto, Ontario: Greenwood Books/ House of Anansi Press, c1978, 2006.
  Other Devices: *Hyperbole. Internal Rhyme. Irony. Motif. Parallelism.*

Bunting, Eve. *One Green Apple.* Illus. by Ted Lewin. New York: (Clarion Books) Houghton Mifflin, c2006.
  Other Devices: *Inference. Symbol. Theme.*

Bunting, Eve. *Pop's Bridge.* Illus. by C. F. Payne. New York: Harcourt, c2006.
  Other Devices: *Aphorism. Foreshadow. Inference. Metaphor. Simile. Symbol. Theme.*

Bynum, Janie. *Nutmeg and Barley: A Budding Friendship.* Cambridge, MA: Candlewick Press, c2006.
  Other Devices: *Ambiguity. Foreshadow. Parallelism. Theme.*

Eversole, Robyn. *The Gift Stone.* Illus. by Allen Garns. New York: Alfred A. Knopf, c1998.
  Other Devices: *Aphorism. Atmosphere. Connotation. Inference. Irony. Metaphor. Motif. Parallelism. Simile. Symbol.*

Garland, Sherry. *My Father's Boat.* Illus. by Ted Rand. New York: Scholastic Press, c1998.
  Other Devices: *Aphorism. Connotation. Counterpoint. Imagery. Metaphor. Parallelism. Simile. Theme.*

Gerstein, Mordicai. *Carolinda Clatter!* New Milford, CT: (Roaring Brook Press) Holtzbrinck, c2005.
  Other Devices: *Allusion. Aptronym. Counterpoint. Flash-Forward. Foreshadow. Hyperbole. Internal Rhyme. Irony. Metaphor. Motif. Parallelism. Wit/Humor.*

Jeffers, Oliver. *Lost and Found.* New York: (Philomel) Penguin Young Readers Group, c2005.
  Other Devices: *Foreshadow. Inference. Irony.*

Johnson, Lindan Lee. *Dream Jar.* Illus. by Serena Curmi. New York: Houghton Mifflin, c2005.
  Other Devices: *Allusion. Foreshadow. Inference. Motif. Parallelism. Symbol. Understatement.*

*****Johnston, Tony.** *Angel City.* Illus. by Carole Byard. New York: (Philomel) Penguin Young Readers Group, c2006.
  Other Devices: *Allusion. Ambiguity. Atmosphere. Colloquialism. Connotation. Counterpoint. Foreshadow. Imagery. Inference. Metaphor. Motif. Paradox. Parallelism. Simile. Symbol. Theme. Tone. Wit/Humor.*

Kessler, Christina. *The Best Beekeeper of Lalibela: A Tale from Africa.* Illus. by Leonard Jenkins. New York: Holiday House, c2006.
  Other Devices: *Aphorism. Atmosphere. Foreshadow. Pun. Serendipity. Simile.*

***Lamm, C. Drew.** *Gauchada.* Illus. by Fabian Negrin. New York: Alfred A. Knopf, c2002.

> **Other Devices:** *Atmosphere. Connotation. Flashback. Imagery. Internal Rhyme. Irony. Metaphor. Motif. Parallelism. Surprise/Twist-in-the-Tail. Theme.*

Lasky, Kathryn. *Pirate Bob.* Illus. by David Clark. Watertown, MA: Charlesbridge, c2006.

> **Other Devices:** *Antihero. Archetype. Atmosphere. Black Humor. Colloquialism. Connotation. Hyperbole. Imagery. Inference. Motif. Parallelism. Theme.*

McElligott, Matthew. *Backbeard and the Birthday Suit.* New York: Walker & Company, c2006.

> **Other Devices:** *Allusion. Ambiguity. Antihero. Aphorism. Aptronym. Archetype. Atmosphere. Colloquialism. Hyperbole. Irony. Point-of-View. Solecism. Wit/Humor.*

***Montserrat, Pep.** *Ms. Rubinstein's Beauty.* New York: Sterling, c2006.

> **Other Devices:** *Antithesis. Atmosphere. Connotation. Counterpoint. Inference. Motif. Parallelism. Surprise/Twist-in-the-Tail. Theme.*

Pfister, Marcus. *Holey Moley.* Trans. by J. Alison James. New York: North-South Books, c2006.

> **Other Devices:** *Counterpoint. Irony. Paradox. Parallelism. Theme.*

Recorvits, Helen. *Yoon and the Christmas Mitten.* Illus. by Gabi Swaiatowska. New York: (Frances Foster Books) Farrar, Straus and Giroux, c2006.

> **Other Devices:** *Ambiguity. Atmosphere. Colloquialism. Counterpoint. Foreshadow. Inference. Parallelism. Point-of-View. Theme.*

Smith, Linda. *Mrs. Crump's Cat.* Illus. by David Roberts. New York: HarperCollins Children's Books, c2006.

> **Other Devices:** *Aptronym. Inference. Paradox.*

***Tingle, Tim.** *Crossing Bok Chitto: A Choctaw Tale of Friendship and Freedom.* Illus. by Jeanne Rorex Bridges. El Paso, TX: Cinco Puntos Press, c2006.

> **Other Devices:** *Allusion. Aphorism. Counterpoint. Flash-Forward. Foreshadow. Irony. Motif. Paradox. Parallelism. Simile. Symbol. Theme.*

***Wood, Nancy.** *Mr. and Mrs. God in the Creation Kitchen.* Illus. by Timothy Basil Ering. Cambridge, MA: Candlewick Press, c2006.

> **Other Devices:** *Allusion. Foreshadow. Hyperbole. Imagery. Inference. Onomatopoeia. Parallelism. Pun. Satire. Understatement. Wit/Humor.*

APHORISM

Short, pointed statement expressing a wise, clever, general truth—a maxim, proverb, adage, epigram, saying, or truism about life, sometimes with a new twist.

Asher, Sandy. *Too Many Frogs!* Illus. by Keith Graves. New York: (Philomel Books) Penguin Young Readers Group, c2005.
> **Other Devices:** *Allusion. Internal Rhyme. Irony. Parallelism. Theme. Tone.*

Auch, Mary Jane. *Hen Lake.* New York: Holiday House, c1995.
> **Other Devices:** *Allusion. Aptronym. Archetype. Colloquialism. Connotation. Inference. Motif. Theme.*

*Bateman, Teresa. *Keeper of Soles.* Illus. by Diego Herrera (Yayo). New York: Holiday House, c2006.
> **Other Devices:** *Ambiguity. Black Humor. Colloquialism. Connotation. Imagery. Inference. Irony. Paradox. Parallelism. Pun. Understatement.*

Borden, Louise. *Across the Blue Pacific: A World War II Story.* Illus. by Robert Andrew Parker. Boston: Houghton Mifflin, c2006.
> **Other Devices:** *Atmosphere. Connotation. Flashback. Flash-Forward. Foreshadow. Imagery. Inference. Motif. Paradox. Parallelism. Simile. Theme.*

Bunting, Eve. *Pop's Bridge.* Illus. by C. F. Payne. New York: Harcourt, c2006.
> **Other Devices:** *Antithesis. Foreshadow. Inference. Metaphor. Simile. Symbol. Theme.*

Eversole, Robyn. *The Gift Stone.* Illus. by Allen Garns. New York: Alfred A. Knopf, c1998.
> **Other Devices:** *Antithesis. Atmosphere. Connotation. Inference. Irony. Metaphor. Motif. Parallelism. Simile. Symbol.*

Garland, Sherry. *My Father's Boat.* Illus. by Ted Rand. New York: Scholastic Press, c1998.
> **Other Devices:** *Antithesis. Connotation. Counterpoint. Imagery. Metaphor. Parallelism. Simile. Theme.*

Karon, Jan. *Violet Comes to Stay.* Story by Melanie Cecka. Illus. by Emily Arnold McCully. New York: (Viking) Penguin Young Readers Group, c2006.
> **Other Devices:** *Alliteration. Connotation. Foreshadow. Imagery. Inference. Irony. Motif. Onomatopoeia. Point-of-View. Simile. Theme.*

Kessler, Christina. *The Best Beekeeper of Lalibela: A Tale from Africa.* Illus. by Leonard Jenkins. New York: Holiday House, c2006.
> **Other Devices:** *Antithesis. Atmosphere. Foreshadow. Pun. Serendipity. Simile.*

Lee-Tai, Amy. *A Place Where Sunflowers Grow.* Illus. by Felicia Hoshino. San Francisco: Children's Book Press, c2006.
> **Other Devices:** *Atmosphere. Connotation. Inference. Motif. Symbol. Theme.*

McElligott, Matthew. *Backbeard and the Birthday Suit.* New York: Walker & Company, c2006.

Other Devices: *Allusion. Ambiguity. Antihero. Antithesis. Aptronym. Archetype. Atmosphere. Colloquialism. Hyperbole. Irony. Point-of-View. Solecism. Wit/Humor.*

Michelson, Richard. *Across the Alley.* Illus. by E. B. Lewis. New York: (Penguin Young Readers Group) G. P. Putnam's Sons, c2006.
    Other Devices: *Counterpoint. Inference. Irony. Metaphor. Point-of-View. Simile. Stereotype/Reverse Stereotype. Theme.*

*****Raven, Marot Theis.** *Night Boat to Freedom.* Illus. by E. B. Lewis. New York: (Melanie Kroupa Books) Farrar, Straus and Giroux, c2006.
    Other Devices: *Atmosphere. Colloquialism. Imagery. Inference. Metaphor. Paradox. Parallelism. Simile. Symbol. Theme.*

Teague, Mark. *Pigsty.* New York: Scholastic, c1994.
    Other Devices: *Ambiguity. Foreshadow. Pun. Tone.*

*****Tingle, Tim.** *Crossing Bok Chitto: A Choctaw Tale of Friendship and Freedom.* Illus. by Jeanne Rorex Bridges. El Paso, TX: Cinco Puntos Press, c2006.
    Other Devices: *Allusion. Antithesis. Counterpoint. Flash-Forward. Foreshadow. Irony. Motif. Paradox. Parallelism. Simile. Symbol. Theme.*

Williams, Laura E. *The Best Winds.* Illus. by Eujin Kim Neilan. Honesdale, PA: Boyds Mills Press, c2006.
    Other Devices: *Atmosphere. Foreshadow. Inference. Motif. Simile. Theme.*

Yolen, Jane. *Raising Yoder's Barn.* Illus. by Bernie Fuchs. New York: Little, Brown and Company, c1998.
    Other Devices: *Colloquialism. Imagery. Inference. Metaphor. Motif. Parallelism. Simile. Understatement.*

*****Young, Ed.** *I, Doko: The Tale of a Basket.* New York: Philomel, c2004.
    Other Devices: *Foreshadow. Inference. Personification. Poetic Justice. Point-of-View. Theme. Tone.*

APTRONYM

Personal name associated to character or occupation.

Auch, Mary Jane. *Hen Lake.* New York: Holiday House, c1995.
    Other Devices: *Allusion. Aphorism. Archetype. Colloquialism. Connotation. Inference. Motif. Theme.*

Bateman, Teresa. *A Plump and Perky Turkey.* Illus. by Jeff Shelly. New York: Marshall Cavendish, c2001.
    Other Devices: *Alliteration. Allusion. Ambiguity. Irony. Parallelism. Poetic Justice. Surprise/Twist-in-the-Tail. Theme. Understatement.*

Fleming, Candace. *Muncha! Muncha! Muncha!* Illus. by G. Brian Karas. New York: Atheneum Books for Young Readers, c2002.
    Other Devices: *Allusion. Irony. Motif. Onomatopoeia. Parallelism. Surprise/Twist-in-the-Tail.*

*Frank, John. *The Toughest Cowboy, or How the Wild West Was Tamed.*
Illus. by Zachary Pullen. New York: Simon & Schuster Books for Young
Readers, c2004.
> Other Devices: *Allusion. Ambiguity. Atmosphere. Colloquialism. Fore-
> shadow. Hyperbole. Inference. Irony. Parallelism. Pun. Simile. Solecism.
> Stereotype/Reverse Stereotype. Tone. Understatement. Wit/Humor.*

Gerstein, Mordicai. *Carolinda Clatter!* New Milford, CT: (Roaring Brook
Press) Holtzbrinck, c2005.
> Other Devices: *Allusion. Antithesis. Counterpoint. Flash-Forward.
> Foreshadow. Hyperbole. Internal Rhyme. Irony. Metaphor. Motif. Paral-
> lelism. Wit/Humor.*

McClintock, Barbara. *Adele & Simon.* New York: (Frances Foster Books)
Farrar, Straus and Giroux, c2006.
> Other Devices: *Foreshadow. Inference. Parallelism. Wit/Humor.*

McElligott, Matthew. *Backbeard and the Birthday Suit.* New York: Walker
& Company, c2006.
> Other Devices: *Allusion. Ambiguity. Antihero. Antithesis. Aphorism.
> Archetype. Atmosphere. Colloquialism. Hyperbole. Irony. Point-of-
> View. Solecism. Wit/Humor.*

Sauer, Tammi. *Cowboy Camp.* Illus. by Mike Reed. New York: Sterling,
c2005.
> Other Devices: *Antihero. Archetype. Colloquialism. Irony. Paradox.
> Parallelism. Satire.*

Smith, Cynthia Leitich and Greg Smith. *Santa Knows.* Illus. by Steve
Bjorkman. New York: (Dutton Children's Books) Penguin, c2006.
> Other Devices: *Allusion. Ambiguity. Foreshadow. Hyperbole. Irony.
> Motif. Parallelism. Poetic Justice. Tone. Wit/Humor.*

Smith, Linda. *Mrs. Crump's Cat.* Illus. by David Roberts. New York: Harper-
Collins Children's Books, c2006.
> Other Devices: *Antithesis. Inference. Paradox.*

ARCHETYPE

*That which represents the most typical and essential characteristics shared by
the class.*

Auch, Mary Jane. *Hen Lake.* New York: Holiday House, c1995.
> Other Devices: *Allusion. Aphorism. Aptronym. Colloquialism. Conno-
> tation. Inference. Motif. Theme.*

Bradley, Kimberly Brubaker. *Ballerino Nate.* Illus. by R. W. Alley. New
York: (Dial Books for Young Readers) Penguin Young Readers Group,
c2006.
> Other Devices: *Ambiguity. Inference. Motif. Parallelism. Stereotype/
> Reverse Stereotype.*

Broach, Elise. *Cousin John Is Coming!* Illus. by Nate Lilly. New York: (Dial Books for Young Readers) Penguin Young Readers Group, c2006.
   Other Devices: *Ambiguity. Counterpoint. Inference. Irony. Paradox.*
Bunge, Daniela. *The Scarves.* Trans. by Kahryn Bishop. New York: Penguin Young Readers Group, c2006.
   Other Devices: *Counterpoint. Foreshadow. Inference. Irony. Symbol.*
Chen, Chih-Yuan. *The Featherless Chicken.* Alhambra, CA: Heryin Books, c2006.
   Other Devices: *Alliteration. Connotation. Inference. Internal Rhyme. Irony. Satire. Serendipity. Simile. Theme. Tone. Wit/Humor.*
Crummel, Susan Stevens. *Ten Gallon Bart.* Illus. by Dorothy Donohue. Tarrytown, NY: Marshall Cavendish, c2006.
   Other Devices: *Allusion. Colloquialism. Connotation. Inference. Internal Rhyme. Motif. Parody. Poetic Justice. Pun. Solecism. Stereotype/ Reverse Stereotype. Tone. Wit/Humor.*
*****Cullen, Lynn.** *Moi & Marie Antoinette.* Illus. by Amy Young. New York: Bloomsbury Publishing, c2006.
   Other Devices: *Atmosphere. Counterpoint. Foreshadow. Hyperbole. Inference. Motif. Parallelism. Point-of-View. Serendipity. Simile. Surprise/Twist-in-the-Tail. Wit/Humor.*
Lasky, Kathryn. *Pirate Bob.* Illus. by David Clark. Watertown, MA: Charlesbridge, c2006.
   Other Devices: *Antihero. Antithesis. Atmosphere. Black Humor. Colloquialism. Connotation. Hyperbole. Imagery. Inference. Motif. Parallelism. Theme.*
McElligott, Matthew. *Backbeard and the Birthday Suit.* New York: Walker & Company, c2006.
   Other Devices: *Allusion. Ambiguity. Antihero. Antithesis. Aphorism. Aptronym. Atmosphere. Colloquialism. Hyperbole. Irony. Point-of-View. Solecism. Wit/Humor.*
Sauer, Tammi. *Cowboy Camp.* Illus. by Mike Reed. New York: Sterling, c2005.
   Other Devices: *Antihero. Aptronym. Colloquialism. Irony. Paradox. Parallelism. Satire.*
Yorinks, Arthur. *Whitefish Will Rides Again!* Illus. by Mort Drucker. New York: HarperCollins, c1994.
   Other Devices: *Alliteration. Colloquialism. Hyperbole. Inference. Oxymoron. Satire. Simile. Solecism. Tone. Wit/Humor.*
Young, Amy. *Belinda and the Glass Slipper.* New York: (Viking) Penguin Young Readers Group, c2006.
   Other Devices: *Allusion. Antihero. Counterpoint. Foreshadow. Inference. Irony. Parallelism. Parody. Poetic Justice. Simile. Surprise/Twist-in-the-Tail. Theme. Understatement.*

ATMOSPHERE

General emotional or social climate developed through dialogue and descriptions of settings and details about how things look, sound, feel, taste, and smell in order to establish reader expectations and attitudes.

Arnosky, Jim. *Grandfather Buffalo.* New York: G. P. Putnam's Sons, c2006.
   Other Devices: *Foreshadow. Inference. Motif. Theme.*
Borden, Louise. *Across the Blue Pacific: A World War II Story.* Illus. by Robert Andrew Parker. Boston: Houghton Mifflin, c2006.
   Other Devices: *Aphorism. Connotation. Flashback. Flash-Forward. Foreshadow. Imagery. Inference. Motif. Paradox. Parallelism. Simile. Theme.*
Bunting, Eve. *Butterfly House.* Illus. by Greg Shed. New York: Scholastic Press, c1999.
   Other Devices: *Connotation. Flash-Forward. Imagery. Internal Rhyme. Paradox. Point-of-View. Simile.*
*Cullen, Lynn. *Moi & Marie Antoinette.* Illus. by Amy Young. New York: Bloomsbury Publishing, c2006.
   Other Devices: *Archetype. Counterpoint. Foreshadow. Hyperbole. Inference. Motif. Parallelism. Point-of-View. Serendipity. Simile. Surprise/Twist-in-the-Tail. Wit/Humor.*
Eversole, Robyn. *The Gift Stone.* Illus. by Allen Garns. New York: Alfred A. Knopf, c1998.
   Other Devices: *Antithesis. Aphorism. Connotation. Inference. Irony. Metaphor. Motif. Parallelism. Simile. Symbol.*
*Frank, John. *The Toughest Cowboy, or How the Wild West Was Tamed.* Illus. by Zachary Pullen. New York: Simon & Schuster Books for Young Readers, c2004.
   Other Devices: *Allusion. Ambiguity. Aptronym. Colloquialism. Foreshadow. Hyperbole. Inference. Irony. Parallelism. Pun. Simile. Solecism. Stereotype/Reverse Stereotype. Tone. Understatement. Wit/Humor.*
High, Linda Oatman. *Barn Savers.* Illus. by Ted Lewin. Honesdale, PA: Boyds Mills Press, c1999.
   Other Devices: *Connotation. Imagery. Metaphor. Parallelism. Simile.*
*Johnston, Tony. *Angel City.* Illus. by Carole Byard. New York: (Philomel) Penguin Young Readers Group, c2006.
   Other Devices: *Allusion. Ambiguity. Antithesis. Colloquialism. Connotation. Counterpoint. Foreshadow. Imagery. Inference. Metaphor. Motif. Paradox. Parallelism. Simile. Symbol. Theme. Tone. Wit/Humor.*
Johnston, Tony. *The Barn Owls.* Illus. by Deborah Kogan Ray. Watertown, MA: Charlesbridge, c2000.
   Other Devices: *Imagery. Metaphor. Motif. Parallelism. Simile. Tone.*
Kessler, Christina. *The Best Beekeeper of Lalibela: A Tale from Africa.* Illus. by Leonard Jenkins. New York: Holiday House, c2006.

Other Devices: *Antithesis. Aphorism. Foreshadow. Pun. Serendipity. Simile.*

*Lamm, C. Drew. *Gauchada.* Illus. by Fabian Negrin. New York: Alfred A. Knopf, c2002.

Other Devices: *Antithesis. Connotation. Flashback. Imagery. Internal Rhyme. Irony. Metaphor. Motif. Parallelism. Surprise/Twist-in-the-Tail. Theme.*

Lasky, Kathryn. *Pirate Bob.* Illus. by David Clark. Watertown, MA: Charlesbridge, c2006.

Other Devices: *Antihero. Antithesis. Archetype. Black Humor. Colloquialism. Connotation. Hyperbole. Imagery. Inference. Motif. Parallelism. Theme.*

Lee-Tai, Amy. *A Place Where Sunflowers Grow.* Illus. by Felicia Hoshino. San Francisco: Children's Book Press, c2006.

Other Devices: *Aphorism. Connotation. Inference. Motif. Symbol. Theme.*

McElligott, Matthew. *Backbeard and the Birthday Suit.* New York: Walker & Company, c2006.

Other Devices: *Allusion. Ambiguity. Antihero. Antithesis. Aphorism. Aptronym. Archetype. Colloquialism. Hyperbole. Irony. Point-of-View. Solecism. Wit/Humor.*

*Montserrat, Pep. *Ms. Rubinstein's Beauty.* New York: Sterling, c2006.

Other Devices: *Antithesis. Connotation. Counterpoint. Inference. Motif. Parallelism. Surprise/Twist-in-the-Tail. Theme.*

Nelson, Vaunda Micheaux. *Almost to Freedom.* Illus. by Colin Bootman. Minneapolis, MN: (Carolrhoda) Learner, c2003.

Other Devices: *Allusion. Colloquialism. Foreshadow. Hyperbole. Imagery. Inference. Parallelism. Personification. Poetic Justice. Point-of-View. Simile. Solecism. Understatement.*

Pelley, Kathleen T. *Inventor McGregor.* Illus. by Michael Chesworth. New York: Farrar, Straus and Giroux, c2006.

Other Devices: *Alliteration. Irony. Paradox. Simile. Theme.*

*Raven, Marot Theis. *Night Boat to Freedom.* Illus. by E. B. Lewis. New York: (Melanie Kroupa Books) Farrar, Straus and Giroux, c2006.

Other Devices: *Aphorism. Colloquialism. Imagery. Inference. Metaphor. Paradox. Parallelism. Simile. Symbol. Theme.*

Recorvits, Helen. *Yoon and the Christmas Mitten.* Illus. by Gabi Swaiatowska. New York: (Frances Foster Books) Farrar, Straus and Giroux, c2006.

Other Devices: *Ambiguity. Antithesis. Colloquialism. Counterpoint. Foreshadow. Inference. Parallelism. Point-of-View. Theme.*

Squires, Janet. *The Gingerbread Cowboy.* Illus. by Holly Berry. New York: HarperCollins Children's Books, c2006.

Other Devices: *Colloquialism. Imagery. Irony. Parallelism. Parody. Simile. Tone. Wit/Humor.*

Williams, Laura E. *The Best Winds.* Illus. by Eujin Kim Neilan. Honesdale, PA: Boyds Mills Press, c2006.
>   **Other Devices:** *Aphorism. Foreshadow. Inference. Motif. Simile. Theme.*

Yolen, Jane. *Harvest Home.* Illus. by Greg Shed. New York: (Silver Whistle) Harcourt, c2002.
>   **Other Devices:** *Atmosphere. Imagery. Internal Rhyme. Metaphor. Motif. Parallelism. Wit/Humor.*

BLACK HUMOR

Grotesque, grim, gruesome, or horrifying elements juxtaposed humorously for shock value, sometimes called gallows humor when the topic is joking about death.

*Bateman, Teresa. *Keeper of Soles.* Illus. by Diego Herrera (Yayo). New York: Holiday House, c2006.
>   **Other Devices:** *Ambiguity. Aphorism. Colloquialism. Imagery. Inference. Irony. Paradox. Parallelism. Pun. Understatement.*

Jenkins, Emily. *That New Animal.* Illus. by Pierce Pratt. New York: (Frances Foster Books) Farrar, Straus and Giroux, c2005.
>   **Other Devices:** *Paradox. Parallelism. Point-of-View.*

Lasky. Kathryn. *Pirate Bob.* Illus. by David Clark. Watertown, MA: Charlesbridge, c2006.
>   **Other Devices:** *Antihero. Antithesis. Archetype. Atmosphere. Colloquialism. Connotation. Hyperbole. Imagery. Inference. Motif. Parallelism. Theme.*

COLLOQUIALISM

Words identifiable with a specific ethnic, geographical, or social situation or everyday use.

Auch, Mary Jane. *Hen Lake.* New York: Holiday House, c1995.
>   **Other Devices:** *Allusion. Aphorism. Aptronym. Archetype. Connotation. Inference. Motif. Theme.*

*Bateman, Teresa. *Keeper of Soles.* Illus. by Diego Herrera (Yayo). New York: Holiday House, c2006.
>   **Other Devices:** *Ambiguity. Aphorism. Black Humor. Connotation. Imagery. Inference. Irony. Paradox. Parallelism. Pun. Understatement.*

Crummel, Susan Stevens. *Ten Gallon Bart.* Illus. by Dorothy Donohue. Tarrytown, NY: Marshall Cavendish, c2006.
>   **Other Devices:** *Allusion. Archetype. Connotation. Inference. Internal Rhyme. Motif. Parody. Poetic Justice. Pun. Solecism. Stereotype/Reverse Stereotype. Tone. Wit/Humor.*

*Frank, John. *The Toughest Cowboy, or How the Wild West Was Tamed.* Illus. by Zachary Pullen. New York: Simon & Schuster Books for Young Readers, c2004.
> **Other Devices:** *Allusion. Ambiguity. Aptronym. Atmosphere. Foreshadow. Hyperbole. Inference. Irony. Parallelism. Pun. Simile. Solecism. Stereotype/Reverse Stereotype. Tone. Understatement. Wit/Humor.*

*Johnston, Tony. *Angel City.* Illus. by Carole Byard. New York: (Philomel) Penguin Young Readers Group, c2006.
> **Other Devices:** *Allusion. Ambiguity. Antithesis. Atmosphere. Connotation. Counterpoint. Foreshadow. Imagery. Inference. Metaphor. Motif. Paradox. Parallelism. Simile. Symbol. Theme. Tone. Wit/Humor.*

Lasky, Kathryn. *Pirate Bob.* Illus. by David Clark. Watertown, MA: Charlesbridge, c2006.
> **Other Devices:** *Antihero. Antithesis. Archetype. Atmosphere. Black Humor. Connotation. Hyperbole. Imagery. Inference. Motif. Parallelism. Theme.*

McElligott, Matthew. *Backbeard and the Birthday Suit.* New York: Walker & Company, c2006.
> **Other Devices:** *Allusion. Ambiguity. Antihero. Antithesis. Aphorism. Aptronym. Archetype. Atmosphere. Hyperbole. Irony. Point-of-View. Solecism. Wit/Humor.*

Nelson, Vaunda Micheaux. *Almost to Freedom.* Illus. by Colin Bootman. Minneapolis, MN: (Carolrhoda) Learner, c2003.
> **Other Devices:** *Allusion. Atmosphere. Foreshadow. Hyperbole. Imagery. Inference. Parallelism. Personification. Poetic Justice. Point-of-View. Simile. Solecism. Understatement.*

*Raven, Marot Theis. *Night Boat to Freedom.* Illus. by E. B. Lewis. New York: (Melanie Kroupa Books) Farrar, Straus and Giroux, c2006.
> **Other Devices:** *Aphorism. Atmosphere. Imagery. Inference. Metaphor. Paradox. Parallelism. Simile. Symbol. Theme.*

Recorvits, Helen. *Yoon and the Christmas Mitten.* Illus. by Gabi Swaiatowska. New York: (Frances Foster Books) Farrar, Straus and Giroux, c2006.
> **Other Devices:** *Ambiguity. Antithesis. Atmosphere. Counterpoint. Foreshadow. Inference. Parallelism. Point-of-View. Theme.*

Sauer, Tammi. *Cowboy Camp.* Illus. by Mike Reed. New York: Sterling, c2005.
> **Other Devices:** *Antihero. Aptronym. Archetype. Irony. Paradox. Parallelism. Satire.*

Squires, Janet. *The Gingerbread Cowboy.* Illus. by Holly Berry. New York: HarperCollins Children's Books, c2006.
> **Other Devices:** *Atmosphere. Imagery. Irony. Parallelism. Parody. Simile. Tone. Wit/Humor.*

Stevens, Janet and Susan Stevens Crummel. *Cook-A-Doodle-Doo.* Illus. by Janet Stevens. Orlando, FL: (Voyager Books) Harcourt, c1999.

Other Devices: *Allusion. Inference. Motif. Parallelism. Pun. Stereotype/Reverse Stereotype. Theme.*

Wojciechowski, Susan. *A Fine St. Patrick's Day.* Illus. by Tom Curry. New York: Random House, c2004.

Other Devices: *Alliteration. Inference. Irony. Theme.*

Yolen, Jane. *Raising Yoder's Barn.* Illus. by Bernie Fuchs. New York: Little, Brown and Company, c1998.

Other Devices: *Aphorism. Imagery. Inference. Metaphor. Motif. Parallelism. Simile. Understatement.*

Yorinks, Arthur. *Whitefish Will Rides Again!* Illus. by Mort Drucker. New York: HarperCollins, c1994.

Other Devices: *Alliteration. Archetype. Hyperbole. Inference. Oxymoron. Satire. Simile. Solecism. Tone. Wit/Humor.*

CONNOTATION

Implications, emotions, or suggestions evoked by a particular word, as in the difference between "statesman" and "politician."

Amico, Tom and James Proimos. *Raisin and Grape.* Illus. by Andy Snair. New York: (Dial Books for Young Readers) Penguin Young Reader's Group, c2006.

Other Devices: *Antithesis. Hyperbole. Inference. Pun. Tone. Understatement. Wit/Humor.*

Auch, Mary Jane. *Hen Lake.* New York: Holiday House, c1995.

Other Devices: *Allusion. Aphorism. Aptronym. Archetype. Colloquialism. Inference. Motif. Theme.*

*Bateman, Teresa. *Keeper of Soles.* Illus. by Diego Herrera (Yayo). New York: Holiday House, c2006.

Other Devices: *Ambiguity. Aphorism. Black Humor. Colloquialism. Imagery. Inference. Irony. Paradox. Parallelism. Pun. Understatement.*

Borden, Louise. *Across the Blue Pacific: A World War II Story.* Illus. by Robert Andrew Parker. Boston: Houghton Mifflin, c2006.

Other Devices: *Aphorism. Atmosphere. Flashback. Flash-Forward. Foreshadow. Imagery. Inference. Motif. Paradox. Parallelism. Simile. Theme.*

Bowen, Anne. *The Great Math Tattle Battle.* Illus. by Jaime Zollars. Morton Grove, IL: Albert Whitman, c2006.

Other Devices: *Paradox. Parallelism. Poetic Justice. Theme.*

Bunting, Eve. *Butterfly House.* Illus. by Greg Shed. New York: Scholastic Press, c1999.

Other Devices: *Atmosphere. Flash-Forward. Imagery. Internal Rhyme. Paradox. Simile.*

Chen, Chih-Yuan. *The Featherless Chicken.* Alhambra, CA: Heryin Books, c2006.

Other Devices: *Alliteration. Archetype. Inference. Internal Rhyme. Irony. Satire. Serendipity. Simile. Theme. Tone. Wit/Humor.*

*Coombs, Kate. *The Secret-Keeper.* Illus. by Heather M. Solomon. New York: (Atheneum Books for Young Readers) Simon & Schuster, c2006.

Other Devices: *Ambiguity. Foreshadow. Imagery. Inference. Irony. Metaphor. Motif. Serendipity. Simile. Symbol. Tone.*

Crummel, Susan Stevens. *Ten Gallon Bart.* Illus. by Dorothy Donohue. Tarrytown, NY: Marshall Cavendish, c2006.

Other Devices: *Allusion. Archetype. Colloquialism. Inference. Internal Rhyme. Motif. Parody. Poetic Justice. Pun. Solecism. Stereotype/Reverse Stereotype. Tone. Wit/Humor.*

da Costa, Deborah. *Snow in Jerusalem.* Illus. by Cornelius Van Wright & Ying-Hwa Hu. Morton Grove, IL: Albert Whitman, c2001.

Other Devices: *Counterpoint. Imagery. Simile. Symbol. Theme.*

Eversole, Robyn. *The Gift Stone.* Illus. by Allen Garns. New York: Alfred A. Knopf, c1998.

Other Devices: *Antithesis. Aphorism. Atmosphere. Inference. Irony. Metaphor. Motif. Parallelism. Simile. Symbol.*

*Franklin, Kristine L. *The Gift.* Illus. by Barbara Lavallee. San Francisco: Chronicle Books, c1999.

Other Devices: *Ambiguity. Foreshadow. Imagery. Inference. Irony. Onomatopoeia. Simile. Surprise/Twist-in-the-Tail. Symbol. Theme.*

Garland, Sherry. *My Father's Boat.* Illus. by Ted Rand. New York: Scholastic Press, c1998.

Other Devices: *Antithesis. Aphorism. Counterpoint. Imagery. Metaphor. Parallelism. Simile. Theme.*

High, Linda Oatman. *Barn Savers.* Illus. by Ted Lewin. Honesdale, PA: Boyds Mills Press, c1999.

Other Devices: *Atmosphere. Imagery. Metaphor. Parallelism. Simile.*

Johnson, Angela. *Wind Flyers.* Illus. by Loren Long. New York: Simon & Schuster Books for Young Readers, c2007.

Other Devices: *Imagery. Inference. Motif. Paradox. Parallelism.*

*Johnston, Tony. *Angel City.* Illus. by Carole Byard. New York: (Philomel) Penguin Young Readers Group, c2006.

Other Devices: *Allusion. Ambiguity. Antithesis. Atmosphere. Colloquialism. Counterpoint. Foreshadow. Imagery. Inference. Metaphor. Motif. Paradox. Parallelism. Simile. Symbol. Theme. Tone. Wit/Humor.*

Karon, Jan. *Violet Comes to Stay.* Story by Melanie Cecka. Illus. by Emily Arnold McCully. New York: (Viking) Penguin Young Readers Group, c2006.

Other Devices: *Alliteration. Aphorism. Foreshadow. Imagery. Inference. Irony. Motif. Onomatopoeia. Point-of-View. Simile. Theme.*

*Lamm, C. Drew. *Gauchada.* Illus. by Fabian Negrin. New York: Alfred A. Knopf, c2002.

Other Devices: *Antithesis. Atmosphere. Flashback. Imagery. Internal Rhyme. Irony. Metaphor. Motif. Parallelism. Surprise/Twist-in-the-Tail. Theme.*

Lasky, Kathryn. *Pirate Bob.* Illus. by David Clark. Watertown, MA: Charles-bridge, c2006.

Other Devices: *Antihero, Antithesis. Archetype. Atmosphere. Black Humor. Colloquialism. Hyperbole. Imagery. Inference. Motif. Parallel-ism. Theme.*

Lee-Tai, Amy. *A Place Where Sunflowers Grow.* Illus. by Felicia Hoshino. San Francisco: Children's Book Press, c2006.

Other Devices: *Aphorism. Atmosphere. Inference. Motif. Symbol. Theme.*

*****Montserrat, Pep.** *Ms. Rubinstein's Beauty.* New York: Sterling, c2006.

Other Devices: *Antithesis. Atmosphere. Counterpoint. Inference. Motif. Parallelism. Surprise/Twist-in-the-Tail. Theme.*

Pelley, Kathleen T. *Inventor McGregor.* Illus. by Michael Chesworth. New York: Farrar, Straus and Giroux, c2006.

Other Devices: *Alliteration. Atmosphere. Irony. Paradox. Simile. Theme.*

*****Schotter, Roni.** *Mama, I'll Give You the World.* Illus. by S. Saelig Gal-lagher. New York: (Schwartz & Wade) Random House, c2006.

Other Devices: *Ambiguity. Foreshadow. Imagery. Inference. Metaphor. Motif. Point-of-View. Simile. Symbol. Tone.*

COUNTERPOINT

Simultaneous contrast in order to note the varied interaction of one with the other.

Allen, Jonathan. *I'm Not Cute!* New York: Hyperion Books for Children, c2005.

Other Devices: *Antithesis. Foreshadow. Motif. Paradox.*

Broach, Elise. *Cousin John Is Coming!* Illus. by Nate Lilly. New York: (Dial Books for Young Readers) Penguin Young Readers Group, c2006.

Other Devices: *Ambiguity. Archetype. Inference. Irony. Paradox.*

Bunge, Daniela. *The Scarves.* Trans. by Kahryn Bishop. New York: Penguin Young Readers Group, c2006.

Other Devices: *Archetype. Foreshadow. Inference. Irony. Symbol.*

*****Cullen, Lynn.** *Moi & Marie Antoinette.* Illus. by Amy Young. New York: Bloomsbury Publishing, c2006.

Other Devices: *Archetype. Atmosphere. Foreshadow. Hyperbole. Infer-ence. Motif. Parallelism. Point-of-View. Serendipity. Simile. Surprise/ Twist-in-the-Tail. Wit/Humor.*

da Costa, Deborah. *Snow in Jerusalem.* Illus. by Cornelius Van Wright & Ying-Hwa Hu. Morton Grove, IL: Albert Whitman, c2001.

Other Devices: *Connotation. Imagery. Simile. Symbol. Theme.*

Garland, Sherry. *My Father's Boat.* Illus. by Ted Rand. New York: Scholastic Press, c1998.

> **Other Devices:** *Antithesis. Aphorism. Connotation. Imagery. Metaphor. Parallelism. Simile. Theme.*

Gerstein, Mordicai. *Carolinda Clatter!* New Milford, CT: (Roaring Brook Press) Holtzbrinck, c2005.

> **Other Devices:** *Allusion. Antithesis. Aptronym. Flash-Forward. Foreshadow. Hyperbole. Internal Rhyme. Irony. Metaphor. Motif. Parallelism. Wit/Humor.*

*****Johnston, Tony.** *Angel City.* Illus. by Carole Byard. New York: (Philomel) Penguin Young Readers Group, c2006.

> **Other Devices:** *Allusion. Ambiguity. Antithesis. Atmosphere. Colloquialism. Connotation. Foreshadow. Imagery. Inference. Metaphor. Motif. Paradox. Parallelism. Simile. Symbol. Theme. Tone. Wit/Humor.*

Michelson, Richard. *Across the Alley.* Illus. by E. B. Lewis. New York: (Penguin Young Readers Group) G. P. Putnam's Sons, c2006.

> **Other Devices:** *Aphorism. Inference. Irony. Metaphor. Point-of-View. Simile. Stereotype/Reverse Stereotype. Theme.*

*****Montserrat, Pep.** *Ms. Rubinstein's Beauty.* New York: Sterling, c2006.

> **Other Devices:** *Antithesis. Atmosphere. Connotation. Inference. Motif. Parallelism. Surprise/Twist-in-the-Tail. Theme.*

Pfister, Marcus. *Holey Moley.* Trans. by J. Alison James. New York: North-South Books, c2006.

> **Other Devices:** *Antithesis. Irony. Paradox. Parallelism. Theme.*

Recorvits, Helen. *Yoon and the Christmas Mitten.* Illus. by Gabi Swaiatowska. New York: (Frances Foster Books) Farrar, Straus and Giroux, c2006.

> **Other Devices:** *Ambiguity. Antithesis. Atmosphere. Colloquialism. Foreshadow. Inference. Parallelism. Point-of-View. Theme.*

*****Tingle, Tim.** *Crossing Bok Chitto: A Choctaw Tale of Friendship and Freedom.* Illus. by Jeanne Rorex Bridges. El Paso, TX: Cinco Puntos Press, c2006.

> **Other Devices:** *Allusion. Antithesis. Aphorism. Flash-Forward. Foreshadow. Irony. Motif. Paradox. Parallelism. Simile. Symbol. Theme.*

Young, Amy. *Belinda and the Glass Slipper.* New York: (Viking) Penguin Young Readers Group, c2006.

> **Other Devices:** *Allusion. Antihero. Archetype. Foreshadow. Inference. Irony. Parallelism. Parody. Poetic Justice. Simile. Surprise/Twist-in-the-Tail. Theme. Understatement.*

FLASHBACK

Interruption of present action to insert an episode that took place at an earlier time for the purpose of providing information to enlighten the present situation or account for a character's current motivation.

Borden, Louise. *Across the Blue Pacific: A World War II Story.* Illus. by Robert Andrew Parker. Boston: Houghton Mifflin, c2006.
  Other Devices: *Aphorism. Atmosphere. Connotation. Flash-Forward. Foreshadow. Imagery. Inference. Motif. Paradox. Parallelism. Simile. Theme.*
*****Lamm, C. Drew.** *Gauchada.* Illus. by Fabian Negrin. New York: Alfred A. Knopf, c2002.
  Other Devices: *Antithesis. Atmosphere. Connotation. Imagery. Internal Rhyme. Irony. Metaphor. Motif. Parallelism. Surprise/Twist-in-the-Tail. Theme.*

FLASH-FORWARD

Sudden jump forward in time from chronologically narrated events to a later time that shows the conclusion of the present events.

Borden, Louise. *Across the Blue Pacific: A World War II Story.* Illus. by Robert Andrew Parker. Boston: Houghton Mifflin, c2006.
  Other Devices: *Aphorism. Atmosphere. Connotation. Flashback. Foreshadow. Imagery. Inference. Motif. Paradox. Parallelism. Simile. Theme.*
Bunting, Eve. *Butterfly House.* Illus. by Greg Shed. New York: Scholastic Press, c1999.
  Other Devices: *Atmosphere. Connotation. Imagery. Internal Rhyme. Paradox. Point-of-View. Simile.*
Gerstein, Mordicai. *Carolinda Clatter!* New Milford, CT: (Roaring Brook Press) Holtzbrinck, c2005.
  Other Devices: *Allusion. Antithesis. Aptronym. Counterpoint. Foreshadow. Hyperbole. Internal Rhyme. Irony. Metaphor. Motif. Parallelism. Wit/Humor.*
*****Tingle, Tim.** *Crossing Bok Chitto: A Choctaw Tale of Friendship and Freedom.* Illus. by Jeanne Rorex Bridges. El Paso, TX: Cinco Puntos Press, c2006.
  Other Devices: *Allusion. Antithesis. Aphorism. Counterpoint. Foreshadow. Irony. Motif. Paradox. Parallelism. Simile. Symbol. Theme.*

FORESHADOW

Builds expectation for action that will occur and lends plausibility to this action by providing clues ahead of time to events that unfold later in the narrative.

*****Adler, David A.** *The Babe and I.* Illus. by Terry Widdener. New York: (Gulliver Books) Harcourt Brace & Co., c1999.
  Other Devices: *Ambiguity. Antithesis. Inference. Irony. Paradox. Tone.*

Allen, Jonathan. *I'm Not Cute!* New York: Hyperion Books for Children, c2005.
  Other Devices: *Antithesis. Counterpoint. Motif. Paradox.*
Arnosky, Jim. *Grandfather Buffalo.* New York: G. P. Putnam's Sons, c2006.
  Other Devices: *Atmosphere. Inference. Motif. Theme.*
Ashman, Linda. *Desmond and the Naughtybugs.* Illus. by Anik McGrory. New York: (Dutton Children's Books) Penguin Young Readers Group, c2006.
  Other Devices: *Inference. Irony. Parallelism.*
Bernstein, Dan. *The Tortoise and the Hare Race Again.* Illus. by Andrew Glass. New York: Holiday House, c2006.
  Other Devices: *Alliteration. Allusion. Ambiguity. Paradox. Parody. Pun.*
Borden, Louise. *Across the Blue Pacific: A World War II Story.* Illus. by Robert Andrew Parker. Boston: Houghton Mifflin, c2006.
  Other Devices: *Aphorism. Atmosphere. Connotation. Flashback. Flash-Forward. Imagery. Inference. Motif. Paradox. Parallelism. Simile. Theme.*
Bunge, Daniela. *The Scarves.* Trans. by Kahryn Bishop. New York: Penguin Young Readers Group, c2006.
  Other Devices: *Archetype. Counterpoint. Inference. Irony. Symbol.*
Bunting, Eve. *Pop's Bridge.* Illus. by C. F. Payne. New York: Harcourt, c2006.
  Other Devices: *Antithesis. Aphorism. Inference. Metaphor. Simile. Symbol. Theme.*
Bynum, Janie. *Nutmeg and Barley: A Budding Friendship.* Cambridge, MA: Candlewick Press, c2006.
  Other Devices: *Ambiguity. Antithesis. Parallelism. Theme.*
*Coombs, Kate. *The Secret-Keeper.* Illus. by Heather M. Solomon. New York: (Atheneum Books for Young Readers) Simon & Schuster, c2006.
  Other Devices: *Ambiguity. Connotation. Imagery. Inference. Irony. Metaphor. Motif. Serendipity. Simile. Symbol. Tone.*
*Cullen, Lynn. *Moi & Marie Antoinette.* Illus. by Amy Young. New York: Bloomsbury Publishing, c2006.
  Other Devices: *Archetype. Atmosphere. Counterpoint. Hyperbole. Inference. Motif. Parallelism. Point-of-View. Serendipity. Simile. Surprise/Twist-in-the-Tail. Wit/Humor.*
Edwards, Pamela Duncan. *The Mixed-Up Rooster.* Illus. by Megan Lloyd. New York: HarperCollins Children's Books, c2006.
  Other Devices: *Parallelism. Pun. Serendipity. Stereotype/Reverse Stereotype. Theme. Wit/Humor.*
*Frank, John. *The Toughest Cowboy, or How the Wild West Was Tamed.* Illus. by Zachary Pullen. New York: Simon & Schuster Books for Young Readers, c2004.

Other Devices: *Allusion. Ambiguity. Aptronym. Atmosphere. Collo-quialism. Hyperbole. Inference. Irony. Parallelism. Pun. Simile. Sole-cism. Stereotype/Reverse Stereotype. Tone. Understatement. Wit/Humor.*

*Franklin, Kristine L. *The Gift.* Illus. by Barbara Lavallee. San Francisco: Chronicle Books, c1999.

Other Devices: *Ambiguity. Connotation. Imagery. Inference. Irony. Onomatopoeia. Simile. Surprise/Twist-in-the-Tail. Symbol. Theme.*

Gerstein, Mordicai. *Carolinda Clatter!* New Milford, CT: (Roaring Brook Press) Holtzbrinck, c2005.

Other Devices: *Allusion. Antithesis. Aptronym. Counterpoint. Flash-Forward. Hyperbole. Internal Rhyme. Irony. Metaphor. Motif. Parallel-ism. Wit/Humor.*

Goode, Diane. *The Most Perfect Spot.* New York: HarperCollins Children's Books, c2006.

Other Devices: *Irony. Motif. Pun.*

Jeffers, Oliver. *Lost and Found.* New York: (Philomel) Penguin Young Read-ers Group, c2005.

Other Devices: *Antithesis. Inference. Irony.*

Johnson, Lindan Lee. *Dream Jar.* Illus. by Serena Curmi. New York: Houghton Mifflin, c2005.

Other Devices: *Allusion. Antithesis. Inference. Motif. Parallelism. Symbol. Understatement.*

*Johnston, Tony. *Angel City.* Illus. by Carole Byard. New York: (Philomel) Penguin Young Readers Group, c2006.

Other Devices: *Allusion. Ambiguity. Antithesis. Atmosphere. Colloquialism. Connotation. Counterpoint. Imagery. Inference. Meta-phor. Motif. Paradox. Parallelism. Simile. Symbol. Theme. Tone. Wit/Humor.*

Karon, Jan. *Violet Comes to Stay.* Story by Melanie Cecka. Illus. by Emily Arnold McCully. New York: (Viking) Penguin Young Readers Group, c2006.

Other Devices: *Alliteration. Aphorism. Connotation. Imagery. Infer-ence. Irony. Motif. Onomatopoeia. Point-of-View. Simile. Theme.*

Kessler, Christina. *The Best Beekeeper of Lalibela: A Tale from Africa.* Illus. by Leonard Jenkins. New York: Holiday House, c2006.

Other Devices: *Antithesis. Aphorism. Atmosphere. Pun. Serendipity. Simile.*

Krensky, Stephen. *How Santa Lost His Job.* Illus. by S. D. Schindler. New York: (Aladdin) Simon & Schuster, c2001.

Other Devices: *Inference. Irony. Paradox. Satire. Understatement.*

McClintock, Barbara. *Adele & Simon.* New York: (Frances Foster Books) Farrar, Straus and Giroux, c2006.

Other Devices: *Aptronym. Inference. Parallelism. Wit/Humor.*

Nelson, Vaunda Micheaux. *Almost to Freedom.* Illus. by Colin Bootman. Minneapolis, MN: (Carolrhoda) Lerner, c2003.
> **Other Devices:** *Allusion. Atmosphere. Colloquialism. Hyperbole. Imagery. Inference. Parallelism. Personification. Poetic Justice. Point-of-View. Simile. Solecism. Understatement.*

Palatini, Margie. *Bad Boys Get Cookie!* Illus. by Henry Cole. New York: HarperCollins Children's Books, c2006.
> **Other Devices:** *Allusion. Inference. Motif. Parallelism. Poetic Justice. Pun. Tone. Understatement. Wit/Humor.*

Recorvits, Helen. *Yoon and the Christmas Mitten.* Illus. by Gabi Swaiatowska. New York: (Frances Foster Books) Farrar, Straus and Giroux, c2006.
> **Other Devices:** *Ambiguity. Antithesis. Atmosphere. Colloquialism. Counterpoint. Inference. Parallelism. Point-of-View. Theme.*

*Schotter, Roni. *Mama, I'll Give You the World.* Illus. by S. Saelig Gallagher. New York: (Schwartz & Wade) Random House, c2006.
> **Other Devices:** *Ambiguity. Connotation. Imagery. Inference. Metaphor. Motif. Point-of-View. Simile. Symbol. Tone.*

Smith, Cynthia Leitich and Greg Smith. *Santa Knows.* Illus. by Steve Bjorkman. New York: (Dutton Children's Books) Penguin, c2006.
> **Other Devices:** *Allusion. Ambiguity. Aptronym. Hyperbole. Irony. Motif. Parallelism. Poetic Justice. Tone. Wit/Humor.*

Teague, Mark. *Pigsty.* New York: Scholastic, c1994.
> **Other Devices:** *Ambiguity. Aphorism. Pun. Tone.*

*Tingle, Tim. *Crossing Bok Chitto: A Choctaw Tale of Friendship and Freedom.* Illus. by Jeanne Rorex Bridges. El Paso, TX: Cinco Puntos Press, c2006.
> **Other Devices:** *Allusion. Antithesis. Aphorism. Counterpoint. Flash-Forward. Irony. Motif. Paradox. Parallelism. Simile. Symbol. Theme.*

Williams, Laura E. *The Best Winds.* Illus. by Eujin Kim Neilan. Honesdale, PA: Boyds Mills Press, c2006.
> **Other Devices:** *Aphorism. Atmosphere. Inference. Motif. Simile. Theme.*

*Wood, Nancy. *Mr. and Mrs. God in the Creation Kitchen.* Illus. by Timothy Basil Ering. Cambridge, MA: Candlewick Press, c2006.
> **Other Devices:** *Allusion. Antithesis. Hyperbole. Imagery. Inference. Onomatopoeia. Parallelism. Pun. Satire. Understatement. Wit/Humor.*

Young, Amy. *Belinda and the Glass Slipper.* New York: (Viking) Penguin Young Readers Group, c2006.
> **Other Devices:** *Allusion. Antihero. Archetype. Counterpoint. Inference. Irony. Parallelism. Parody. Poetic Justice. Simile. Surprise/Twist-in-the-Tail. Theme. Understatement.*

*Young, Ed. *I, Doko: The Tale of a Basket.* New York: Philomel, c2004.
> **Other Devices:** *Aphorism. Inference. Personification. Poetic Justice. Point-of-View. Theme. Tone.*

HYPERBOLE

Obvious and extravagant exaggeration not meant to be taken literally.

Amico, Tom and James Proimos. *Raisin and Grape.* Illus. by Andy Snair. New York: (Dial Books for Young Readers) Penguin Young Readers Group, c2006.
>   **Other Devices:** *Antithesis. Connotation. Hyperbole. Inference. Pun. Tone. Understatement. Wit/Humor.*

Atwood, Margaret. *Up in the Tree.* Toronto, Ontario: Greenwood Books/ House of Anansi Press, c1978, 2006.
>   **Other Devices:** *Antithesis. Internal Rhyme. Irony. Motif. Parallelism.*

*Cullen, Lynn. *Moi & Marie Antoinette.* Illus. by Amy Young. New York: Bloomsbury Publishing, c2006.
>   **Other Devices:** *Archetype. Atmosphere. Counterpoint. Foreshadow. Inference. Motif. Parallelism. Point-of-View. Serendipity. Simile. Surprise/Twist-in-the-Tail. Wit/Humor.*

*Frank, John. *The Toughest Cowboy, or How the Wild West Was Tamed.* Illus. by Zachary Pullen. New York: Simon & Schuster Books for Young Readers, c2004.
>   **Other Devices:** *Allusion. Ambiguity. Aptronym. Atmosphere. Colloquialism. Foreshadow. Inference. Irony. Parallelism. Pun. Simile. Solecism. Stereotype/Reverse Stereotype. Tone. Understatement. Wit/ Humor.*

Gerstein, Mordicai. *Carolinda Clatter!* New Milford, CT: (Roaring Brook Press) Holtzbrinck, c2005.
>   **Other Devices:** *Allusion. Antithesis. Aptronym. Counterpoint. Flash-Forward. Foreshadow. Internal Rhyme. Irony. Metaphor. Motif. Parallelism. Wit/Humor.*

Lasky, Kathryn. *Pirate Bob.* Illus. by David Clark. Watertown, MA: Charlesbridge, c2006.
>   **Other Devices:** *Antihero. Antithesis. Archetype. Atmosphere. Black Humor. Colloquialism. Connotation. Imagery. Inference. Motif. Parallelism Theme.*

McElligott, Matthew. *Backbeard and the Birthday Suit.* New York: Walker & Company, c2006.
>   **Other Devices:** *Allusion. Ambiguity. Antihero. Antithesis. Aphorism. Aptronym. Archetype. Atmosphere. Colloquialism. Irony. Point-of-View. Solecism. Wit/Humor.*

Nelson, Vaunda Micheaux. *Almost to Freedom.* Illus. by Colin Bootman. Minneapolis, MN: (Carolrhoda) Learner, c2003.
>   **Other Devices:** *Allusion. Atmosphere. Colloquialism. Foreshadow. Imagery. Inference. Parallelism. Personification. Poetic Justice. Point-of-View. Simile. Solecism. Understatement.*

Smith, Cynthia Leitich and Greg Smith. *Santa Knows.* Illus. by Steve Bjorkman. New York: (Dutton Children's Books) Penguin, c2006.

Other Devices: *Allusion. Ambiguity. Aptronym. Foreshadow. Irony. Motif. Parallelism. Poetic Justice. Tone. Wit/Humor.*

*Wood, Nancy.** *Mr. and Mrs. God in the Creaton Kitchen.* Illus. by Timothy Basil Ering. Cambridge, MA: Candlewick Press, c2006.

Other Devices: *Allusion. Antithesis. Foreshadow. Imagery. Inference. Onomatopoeia. Parallelism. Pun. Satire. Understatement. Wit/Humor.*

Yorinks, Arthur. *Whitefish Will Rides Again!* Illus. by Mort Drucker. New York: HarperCollins, c1994.

Other Devices: *Alliteration. Archetype. Colloquialism. Inference. Oxymoron. Satire. Simile. Solecism. Tone. Wit/Humor.*

IMAGERY

Language that mentally summons pictures that appeal to the senses.

*Bateman, Teresa.** *Keeper of Soles.* Illus. by Diego Herrera (Yayo). New York: Holiday House, c2006.

Other Devices: *Ambiguity. Aphorism. Black Humor. Colloquialism. Connotation. Inference. Irony. Paradox. Parallelism. Pun. Understatement.*

Borden, Louise. *Across the Blue Pacific: A World War II Story.* Illus. by Robert Andrew Parker. Boston: Houghton Mifflin, c2006.

Other Devices: *Aphorism. Atmosphere. Connotation. Flashback. Flash-Forward. Foreshadow. Inference. Motif. Paradox. Parallelism. Simile. Theme.*

Bunting, Eve. *Butterfly House.* Illus. by Greg Shed. New York: Scholastic Press, c1999.

Other Devices: *Atmosphere. Connotation. Flash-Forward. Internal Rhyme. Paradox. Point-of-View. Simile.*

*Coombs, Kate.** *The Secret-Keeper.* Illus. by Heather M. Solomon. New York: (Atheneum Books for Young Readers) Simon & Schuster, c2006.

Other Devices: *Ambiguity. Connotation. Foreshadow. Inference. Irony. Metaphor. Motif. Serendipity. Simile. Symbol. Tone.*

da Costa, Deborah. *Snow in Jerusalem.* Illus. by Cornelius Van Wright & Ying-Hwa Hu. Morton Grove, IL: Albert Whitman, c2001.

Other Devices: *Connotation. Counterpoint. Simile. Symbol. Theme.*

*Franklin, Kristine L.** *The Gift.* Illus. by Barbara Lavallee. San Francisco: Chronicle Books, c1999.

Other Devices: *Ambiguity. Connotation. Foreshadow. Inference. Irony. Onomatopoeia. Simile. Surprise/Twist-in-the-Tail Symbol. Theme.*

Garland, Sherry. *My Father's Boat.* Illus. by Ted Rand. New York: Scholastic Press, c1998.

Other Devices: *Antithesis. Aphorism. Connotation. Counterpoint. Metaphor. Parallelism. Simile. Theme.*

High, Linda Oatman. *Barn Savers.* Illus. by Ted Lewin. Honesdale, PA: Boyds Mills Press, c1999.

Other Devices: *Atmosphere. Connotation. Metaphor. Parallelism. Simile.*

Johnson, Angela. *Wind Flyers.* Illus. by Loren Long. New York: Simon & Schuster Books for Young Readers, c2007.

Other Devices: *Connotation. Inference. Motif. Paradox. Parallelism.*

*****Johnston, Tony.** *Angel City.* Illus. by Carole Byard. New York: (Philomel) Penguin Young Readers Group, c2006.

Other Devices: *Allusion. Ambiguity. Antithesis. Atmosphere. Colloquialism. Connotation. Counterpoint. Foreshadow. Inference. Metaphor. Motif. Paradox. Parallelism. Simile. Symbol. Theme. Tone. Wit/Humor.*

Johnston, Tony. *The Barn Owls.* Illus. by Deborah Kogan Ray. Watertown, MA: Charlesbridge, c2000.

Other Devices: *Atmosphere. Metaphor. Motif. Parallelism. Simile. Tone.*

Karon, Jan. *Violet Comes to Stay.* Story by Melanie Cecka. Illus. by Emily Arnold McCully. New York: (Viking) Penguin Young Readers Group, c2006.

Other Devices: *Alliteration. Aphorism. Connotation. Foreshadow. Inference. Irony. Motif. Onomatopoeia. Point-of-View. Simile. Theme.*

*****Lamm, C. Drew.** *Gauchada.* Illus. by Fabian Negrin. New York: Alfred A. Knopf, c2002.

Other Devices: *Antithesis. Atmosphere. Connotation. Flashback. Internal Rhyme. Irony. Metaphor. Motif. Parallelism. Surprise/Twist-in-the-Tail. Theme.*

Lasky, Kathryn. *Pirate Bob.* Illus. by David Clark. Watertown, MA: Charlesbridge, c2006.

Other Devices: *Antihero. Antithesis. Archetype. Atmosphere. Black Humor. Colloquialism. Connotation. Hyperbole. Inference. Motif. Parallelism. Theme.*

Nelson, Vaunda Micheaux. *Almost to Freedom.* Illus. by Colin Bootman. Minneapolis, MN: (Carolrhoda) Lerner, c2003.

Other Devices: *Allusion. Atmosphere. Colloquialism. Foreshadow. Hyperbole. Inference. Parallelism. Personification. Poetic Justice. Point-of-View. Simile. Solecism. Understatement.*

*****Raven, Marot Theis.** *Night Boat to Freedom.* Illus. by E. B. Lewis. New York: (Melanie Kroupa Books) Farrar, Straus and Giroux, c2006.

Other Devices: *Aphorism. Atmosphere. Colloquialism. Inference. Metaphor. Paradox. Parallelism. Simile. Symbol. Theme.*

*****Schotter, Roni.** *Mama, I'll Give You the World.* Illus. by S. Saelig Gallagher. New York: (Schwartz & Wade) Random House, c2006.

Other Devices: *Ambiguity. Connotation. Foreshadow. Inference. Metaphor. Motif. Point-of-View. Simile. Symbol. Tone.*

Squires, Janet. *The Gingerbread Cowboy.* Illus. by Holly Berry. New York: HarperCollins Children's Books, c2006.

    Other Devices: *Atmosphere. Colloquialism. Irony. Parallelism. Parody. Simile. Tone. Wit/Humor.*

*Wood, Nancy. *Mr. and Mrs. God in the Creation Kitchen.* Illus. by Timothy Basil Ering. Cambridge, MA: Candlewick Press, c2006.

    Other Devices: *Allusion. Antithesis. Foreshadow. Hyperbole. Inference. Onomatopoeia. Parallelism. Pun. Satire. Understatement. Wit/ Humor.*

Yolen, Jane. *Harvest Home.* Illus. by Greg Shed. New York: (Silver Whistle) Harcourt, c2002.

    Other Devices: *Atmosphere. Internal Rhyme. Metaphor. Motif. Parallelism. Wit/Humor.*

Yolen, Jane. *Raising Yoder's Barn.* Illus. by Bernie Fuchs. New York: Little, Brown and Company, c1998.

    Other Devices: *Aphorism. Colloquialism. Inference. Metaphor. Motif. Parallelism. Simile. Understatement.*

INFERENCE

Drawing reasonable conclusions based upon limited clues presented.

*Adler, David A. *The Babe and I.* Illus. by Terry Widdener. New York: (Gulliver Books) Harcourt Brace & Co., c1999.

    Other Devices: *Ambiguity. Antithesis. Foreshadow. Irony. Paradox. Tone.*

Amico, Tom and James Proimos. *Raisin and Grape.* Illus. by Andy Snair. New York: (Dial Books for Young Readers) Penguin Young Readers Group, c2006.

    Other Devices: *Antithesis. Connotation. Hyperbole. Pun. Tone. Understatement. Wit/Humor.*

Arnosky, Jim. *Grandfather Buffalo.* New York: G. P. Putnam's Sons, c2006.

    Other Devices: *Atmosphere. Foreshadow. Motif. Theme.*

Ashman, Linda. *Desmond and the Naughtybugs.* Illus. by Anik McGrory. New York: (Dutton Children's Books) Penguin Young Readers Group, c2006.

    Other Devices: *Foreshadow. Irony. Parallelism.*

Auch, Mary Jane. *Hen Lake.* New York: Holiday House, c1995.

    Other Devices: *Allusion. Aphorism. Aptronym. Archetype. Colloquialism. Connotation. Motif. Theme.*

Bang, Molly. *In My Heart.* New York: Little, Brown and Company, c2006.

    Other Devices: *Motif. Tone.*

*Bateman, Teresa. *Keeper of Soles*. Illus. by Diego Herrera (Yayo). New York: Holiday House, c2006.
> **Other Devices:** *Ambiguity. Aphorism. Black Humor. Colloquialism. Connotation. Imagery. Irony. Paradox. Parallelism. Pun. Understatement.*

Borden, Louise. *Across the Blue Pacific: A World War II Story*. Illus. by Robert Andrew Parker. Boston: Houghton Mifflin, c2006.
> **Other Devices:** *Aphorism. Atmosphere. Connotation. Flashback. Flash-Forward. Foreshadow. Imagery. Motif. Paradox. Parallelism. Simile. Theme.*

Bradley, Kimberly Brubaker. *Ballerino Nate*. Illus. by R. W. Alley. New York: (Dial Books for Young Readers), Penguin Young Readers Group, c2006.
> **Other Devices:** *Ambiguity. Archetype. Motif. Parallelism. Stereotype/ Reverse Stereotype.*

Broach, Elise. *Cousin John Is Coming!* Illus. by Nate Lilly. New York: (Dial Books for Young Readers) Penguin Young Readers Group, c2006.
> **Other Devices:** *Ambiguity. Archetype. Counterpoint. Irony. Paradox.*

Bunge, Daniela. *The Scarves*. Trans. by Kahryn Bishop. New York: Penguin Young Readers Group, c2006.
> **Other Devices:** *Archetype. Counterpoint. Foreshadow. Irony. Symbol.*

Bunting, Eve. *One Green Apple*. Illus. by Ted Lewin. New York: (Clarion Books) Houghton Mifflin, c2006.
> **Other Devices:** *Antithesis. Symbol. Theme.*

Bunting, Eve. *Pop's Bridge*. Illus. by C. F. Payne. New York: Harcourt, c2006.
> **Other Devices:** *Antithesis. Aphorism. Foreshadow. Metaphor. Simile. Symbol. Theme.*

Chen, Chih-Yuan. *The Featherless Chicken*. Alhambra, CA: Heryin Books, c2006.
> **Other Devices:** *Alliteration. Archetype. Connotation. Internal Rhyme. Irony. Satire. Serendipity. Simile. Theme. Tone. Wit/Humor.*

*Coombs, Kate. *The Secret-Keeper*. Illus. by Heather M. Solomon. New York: (Atheneum Books for Young Readers) Simon & Schuster, c2006.
> **Other Devices:** *Ambiguity. Connotation. Foreshadow. Imagery. Irony. Metaphor. Motif. Serendipity. Simile. Symbol. Tone.*

Crummel, Susan Stevens. *Ten Gallon Bart*. Illus. by Dorothy Donohue. Tarrytown, NY: Marshall Cavendish, c2006.
> **Other Devices:** *Allusion. Archetype. Colloquialism. Connotation. Internal Rhyme. Motif. Parody. Poetic Justice. Pun. Solecism. Stereotype/Reverse Stereotype. Tone. Wit/Humor.*

*Cullen, Lynn. *Moi & Marie Antoinette*. Illus. by Amy Young. New York: Bloomsbury Publishing, c2006.
> **Other Devices:** *Archetype. Atmosphere. Counterpoint. Foreshadow. Hyperbole. Motif. Parallelism. Point-of-View. Serendipity. Simile. Surprise/Twist-in-the-Tail. Wit/Humor.*

Eversole, Robyn. *The Gift Stone.* Illus. by Allen Garns. New York: Alfred A. Knopf, c1998.

> **Other Devices:** *Antithesis. Aphorism. Atmosphere. Connotation. Irony. Metaphor. Motif. Parallelism. Simile. Symbol.*

***Frank, John.** *The Toughest Cowboy, or How the Wild West Was Tamed.* Illus. by Zachary Pullen. New York: Simon & Schuster Books for Young Readers, c2004.

> **Other Devices:** *Allusion. Ambiguity. Aptronym. Atmosphere. Colloquialism. Foreshadow. Hyperbole. Irony. Parallelism. Pun. Simile. Solecism. Stereotype/Reverse Stereotype. Tone. Understatement. Wit/Humor.*

***Franklin, Kristine L.** *The Gift.* Illus. by Barbara Lavallee. San Francisco: Chronicle Books, c1999.

> **Other Devices:** *Ambiguity. Connotation. Foreshadow. Imagery. Irony. Onomatopoeia. Simile. Surprise/Twist-in-the-Tail. Symbol. Theme.*

James, Simon. *The Wild Woods.* Cambridge, MA: Candlewick Press, c1993.

> **Other Devices:** *Inference. Motif. Point-of-View. Wit/Humor.*

Jeffers, Oliver. *Lost and Found.* New York: (Philomel) Penguin Young Readers Group, c2005.

> **Other Devices:** *Antithesis. Foreshadow. Irony.*

Johnson, Angela. *Wind Flyers.* Illus. by Loren Long. New York: Simon & Schuster Books for Young Readers, c2007

> **Other Devices:** *Connotation. Imagery. Motif. Paradox. Parallelism.*

Johnson, Lindan Lee. *Dream Jar.* Illus. by Serena Curmi. New York: Houghton Mifflin, c2005.

> **Other Devices:** *Allusion. Antithesis. Foreshadow. Motif. Parallelism. Symbol. Understatement.*

***Johnston, Tony.** *Angel City.* Illus. by Carole Byard. New York: (Philomel) Penguin Young Readers Group, c2006.

> **Other Devices:** *Allusion. Ambiguity. Antithesis. Atmosphere. Colloquialism. Connotation. Counterpoint. Foreshadow. Imagery. Metaphor. Motif. Paradox. Parallelism. Simile. Symbol. Theme. Tone. Wit/Humor.*

Karen, Jan. *Violet Comes to Stay.* Story by Melanie Cecka. Illus. by Emily Arnold McCully. New York: (Viking) Penguin Young Readers Group, c2006.

> **Other Devices:** *Alliteration. Aphorism. Connotation. Foreshadow. Imagery. Irony. Motif. Onomatopoeia. Point-of-View. Simile. Theme.*

Krensky, Stephen. *How Santa Lost His Job.* Illus. by S. D. Schindler. New York: (Aladdin) Simon & Schuster, c2001.

> **Other Devices:** *Foreshadow. Irony. Paradox. Satire. Understatement.*

Lasky, Kathryn. *Pirate Bob.* Illus. by David Clark. Watertown, MA: Charlesbridge, c2006.

> **Other Devices:** *Antihero. Antithesis. Archetype. Atmosphere. Black Humor. Colloquialism. Connotation. Hyperbole. Imagery. Motif. Parallelism. Theme.*

Lee-Tai, Amy. *A Place Where Sunflowers Grow.* Illus. by Felicia Hoshino. San Francisco: Children's Book Press, c2006.
> **Other Devices:** *Aphorism. Atmosphere. Connotation. Motif. Symbol. Theme.*

McClintock, Barbara. *Adele & Simon.* New York: (Frances Foster Books) Farrar, Straus and Giroux, c2006.
> **Other Devices:** *Aptronym. Foreshadow. Parallelism. Wit/Humor.*

Manushkin, Fran. *The Shivers in the Fridge.* Illus. by Paul O. Zelinsky. New York: (Dutton Children's Books) Penguin Young Readers Group, c2006.
> **Other Devices:** *Motif. Parallelism. Point-of-View. Pun. Understatement. Wit/Humor.*

Michelson, Richard. *Across the Alley.* Illus. by E. B. Lewis. (Penguin Young Readers Group) G. P. Putnam's Sons, c2006.
> **Other Devices:** *Aphorism. Counterpoint. Irony. Metaphor. Point-of-View. Simile. Stereotype/Reverse Stereotype. Theme.*

*Montserrat, Pep. *Ms. Rubinstein's Beauty.* New York: Sterling, c2006.
> **Other Devices:** *Antithesis. Atmosphere. Connotation. Counterpoint. Motif. Parallelism. Surprise/Twist-in-the-Tail. Theme.*

Nelson, Vaunda Micheaux. *Almost to Freedom.* Illus. by Colin Bootman. Minneapolis, MN: (Carolrhoda) Lerner, c2003.
> **Other Devices:** *Allusion. Atmosphere. Colloquialism. Foreshadow. Hyperbole. Imagery. Parallelism. Personification. Poetic Justice. Point-of-View. Simile. Solecism. Understatement.*

Palatini, Margie. *Bad Boys Get Cookie!* Illus. by Henry Cole. New York: HarperCollins Children's Books, c2006.
> **Other Devices:** *Allusion. Foreshadow. Motif. Parallelism. Poetic Justice. Pun. Tone. Understatement. Wit/Humor.*

*Raven, Marot Theis. *Night Boat to Freedom.* Illus. by E. B. Lewis. New York: (Melanie Kroupa Books) Farrar, Straus and Giroux, c2006.
> **Other Devices:** *Aphorism. Atmosphere. Colloquialism. Imagery. Metaphor. Paradox. Parallelism. Simile. Symbol. Theme.*

Recorvits, Helen. *Yoon and the Christmas Mitten.* Illus. by Gabi Swaiatowska. New York: (Frances Foster Books) Farrar, Straus and Giroux, c2006.
> **Other Devices:** *Ambiguity. Antithesis. Atmosphere. Colloquialism. Counterpoint. Foreshadow. Inference. Parallelism. Point-of-View. Theme.*

*Schotter, Roni. *Mama, I'll Give You the World.* Illus. by S. Saelig Gallagher. New York: (Schwartz & Wade) Random House, c2006.
> **Other Devices:** *Ambiguity. Connotation. Foreshadow. Imagery. Metaphor. Motif. Point-of-View. Simile. Symbol. Tone.*

Smith, Linda. *Mrs. Crump's Cat.* Illus. by David Roberts. New York: HarperCollins Children's Books, c2006.
> **Other Devices:** *Antithesis. Aptronym. Paradox.*

Stevens, Janet and Susan Stevens Crummel. *Cook-A-Doodle-Doo.* Orlando, FL: (Voyager Books) Harcourt, c1999.
   Other Devices: *Allusion. Colloquialism. Motif. Parallelism. Pun. Stereotype/Reverse Stereotype. Theme.*
Williams, Laura E. *The Best Winds.* Illus. by Eujin Kim Neilan. Honesdale, PA: Boyds Mills Press, c2006.
   Other Devices: *Aphorism. Atmosphere. Foreshadow. Motif. Simile. Theme.*
Wojciechowski, Susan. *A Fine St. Patrick's Day.* Illus. by Tom Curry. New York: Random House, c2004.
   Other Devices: *Alliteration. Colloquialism. Irony. Theme.*
*****Wood, Nancy.** *Mr. and Mrs. God in the Creation Kitchen.* Illus. by Timothy Basil Ering. Cambridge, MA: Candlewick Press, c2006.
   Other Devices: *Allusion. Antithesis. Foreshadow. Hyperbole. Imagery. Onomatopoeia. Parallelism. Pun. Satire. Understatement. Wit/Humor.*
Yolen, Jane. *Raising Yoder's Barn.* Illus. by Bernie Fuchs. New York: Little, Brown and Company, c1998.
   Other Devices: *Aphorism. Colloquialism. Imagery. Metaphor. Motif. Parallelism. Simile. Understatement.*
Yorinks, Arthur. *Whitefish Will Rides Again!* Illus. by Mort Drucker. New York: HarperCollins, c1994.
   Other Devices: *Alliteration. Archetype. Colloquialism. Hyperbole. Oxymoron. Satire. Simile. Solecism. Tone. Wit/Humor.*
Young, Amy. *Belinda and the Glass Slipper.* New York: (Viking) Penguin Young Readers Group, c2006.
   Other Devices: *Allusion. Antihero. Archetype. Counterpoint. Foreshadow. Irony. Parallelism. Parody. Poetic Justice. Simile. Surprise/Twist-in-the-Tail. Theme. Understatement.*
*****Young, Ed.** *I, Doko: The Tale of a Basket.* New York: Philomel, c2004.
   Other Devices: *Aphorism. Foreshadow. Personification. Poetic Justice. Point-of-View. Theme. Tone.*

INTERNAL RHYME

Two or more words that rhyme within a single sentence.

Asher, Sandy. *Too Many Frogs!* Illus. by Keith Graves. New York: (Philomel Books) Penguin Young Readers Group, c2005.
   Other Devices: *Allusion. Aphorism. Irony. Parallelism. Theme. Tone.*
Atwood, Margaret. *Up in the Tree.* Toronto, Ontario: Greenwood Books/House of Anansi Press, c1978, 2006.
   Other Devices: *Antithesis. Hyperbole. Irony. Motif. Parallelism.*
Bunting, Eve. *Butterfly House.* Illus. by Greg Shed. New York: Scholastic Press, c1999.

Other Devices: *Atmosphere. Connotation. Flash-Forward. Imagery. Paradox. Point-of-View. Simile.*

Chen, Chih-Yuan. *The Featherless Chicken.* Alhambra, CA: Heryin Books, c2006.
Other Devices: *Alliteration. Archetype. Connotation. Inference. Irony. Satire. Serendipity. Simile. Theme. Tone. Wit/Humor.*

Crummel, Susan Stevens. *Ten Gallon Bart.* Illus. by Dorothy Donohue. Tarrytown, NY: Marshall Cavendish, c2006.
Other Devices: *Allusion. Archetype. Colloquialism. Connotation. Inference. Motif. Parody. Poetic Justice. Pun. Solecism. Stereotype/ Reverse Stereotype. Tone. Wit/Humor.*

Gerstein, Mordicai. *Carolinda Clatter!* New Milford, CT: (Roaring Brook Press) Holtzbrinck, c2005.
Other Devices: *Allusion. Antithesis. Aptronym. Counterpoint. Flash-Forward. Foreshadow. Hyperbole. Irony. Metaphor. Parallelism. Wit/ Humor.*

*Lamm, C. Drew. *Gauchada.* Illus. by Fabian Negrin. New York: Alfred A. Knopf, c2002.
Other Devices: *Antithesis. Atmosphere. Connotation. Flashback. Imagery. Irony. Metaphor. Motif. Parallelism. Surprise/Twist-in-the-Tail. Theme.*

Yolen, Jane. *Harvest Home.* Illus. by Greg Shed. New York: (Silver Whistle) Harcourt, c2002.
Other Devices: *Atmosphere. Imagery. Metaphor. Motif. Parallelism. Wit/Humor.*

IRONY

A more accurate perception through the unfolding of events, which reveals a truth that turns out to be the opposite of what was anticipated.

*Adler, David A. *The Babe and I.* Illus. by Terry Widdener. New York: (Gulliver Books) Harcourt Brace & Co., c1999.
Other Devices: *Ambiguity. Antithesis. Foreshadow. Inference. Paradox. Tone.*

Asher, Sandy. *Too Many Frogs!* Illus. by Keith Graves. New York: (Philomel Books) Penguin Young Readers Group, c2005.
Other Devices: *Allusion. Aphorism. Internal Rhyme. Parallelism. Theme. Tone.*

Ashman, Linda. *Desmond and the Naughtybugs.* Illus. by Anik McGrory. New York: (Dutton Children's Books) Penguin Young Readers Group, c2006.
Other Devices: *Foreshadow. Inference. Parallelism.*

Atwood, Margaret. *Up in the Tree.* Toronto, Ontario: Greenwood Books/ House of Anansi Press, c1978, 2006.

Other Devices: *Antithesis. Hyperbole. Internal Rhyme. Motif. Parallelism.*

*Bateman, Teresa. *Keeper of Soles.* Illus. by Diego Herrera (Yayo). New York: Holiday House, c2006.

Other Devices: *Ambiguity. Aphorism. Black Humor. Colloquialism. Connotation. Imagery. Inference. Paradox. Parallelism. Pun. Understatement.*

Bateman, Teresa. *A Plump and Perky Turkey.* Illus. by Jeff Shelly. New York: Marshall Cavendish, c2001.

Other Devices: *Alliteration. Allusion. Ambiguity. Aptronym. Parallelism. Poetic Justice. Surprise/Twist-in-the-Tail. Theme. Understatement.*

Broach, Elise. *Cousin John Is Coming!* Illus. by Nate Lilly. New York: (Dial Books for Young Readers) Penguin Young Readers Group, c2006.

Other Devices: *Ambiguity. Archetype. Counterpoint. Inference. Paradox.*

Bunge, Daniela. *The Scarves.* Trans. by Kahryn Bishop. New York: Penguin Young Readers Group, c2006.

Other Devices: *Archetype. Counterpoint. Foreshadow. Inference. Symbol.*

Chen, Chih-Yuan. *The Featherless Chicken.* Alhambra, CA: Heryin Books, c2006.

Other Devices: *Alliteration. Archetype. Connotation. Inference. Internal Rhyme. Satire. Serendipity. Simile. Theme. Tone. Wit/Humor.*

*Coombs, Kate. *The Secret-Keeper.* Illus. by Heather M. Solomon. New York: (Atheneum Books for Young Readers) Simon & Schuster, c2006.

Other Devices: *Ambiguity. Connotation. Foreshadow. Imagery. Inference. Metaphor. Motif. Serendipity. Simile. Symbol. Tone.*

Eversole, Robyn. *The Gift Stone.* Illus. by Allen Garns. New York: Alfred A. Knopf, c1998.

Other Devices: *Antithesis. Aphorism. Atmosphere. Connotation. Inference. Metaphor. Motif. Parallelism. Simile. Symbol.*

Fleming, Candace. *Muncha! Muncha! Muncha!* Illus. by G. Brian Karas. New York: Atheneum Books for Young Readers, c2002.

Other Devices: *Allusion. Aptronym. Motif. Onomatopoeia. Parallelism. Surprise/Twist-in-the-Tail.*

*Frank, John. *The Toughest Cowboy, or How the Wild West Was Tamed.* Illus. by Zachary Pullen. New York: Simon & Schuster Books for Young Readers, c2004.

Other Devices: *Allusion. Ambiguity. Aptronym. Atmosphere. Colloquialism. Foreshadow. Hyperbole. Inference. Parallelism. Pun. Simile. Solecism. Stereotype/Reserve Stereotype. Tone. Understatement. Wit/Humor.*

*Franklin, Kristine L. *The Gift.* Illus. by Barbara Lavallee. San Francisco: Chronicle Books, c1999.

Other Devices: *Ambiguity. Connotation. Foreshadow. Imagery. Inference. Onomatopoeia. Surprise/Twist-in-the-Tail. Simile. Symbol. Theme.*

Gerstein, Mordicai. *Carolinda Clatter!* New Milford, CT: (Roaring Brook Press) Holtzbrinck, c2005.

    Other Devices: *Allusion. Antithesis. Aptronym. Counterpoint. Flash-Forward. Foreshadow. Hyperbole. Internal Rhyme. Metaphor. Motif. Parallelism. Wit/Humor.*

Henke, Kevin. *Kitten's First Full Moon.* New York: (Greenwillow Books) HarperCollins, c2004.

    Other Devices: *Motif. Tone.*

Jeffers, Oliver. *Lost and Found.* New York: (Philomel) Penguin Young Readers Group, c2005.

    Other Devices: *Antithesis. Foreshadow. Inference.*

Karon, Jan. *Violet Comes to Stay.* Story by Melanie Cecka. Illus. by Emily Arnold McCully. New York: (Viking) Penguin Young Readers Group, c2006.

    Other Devices: *Alliteration. Aphorism. Connotation Foreshadow. Imagery. Inference. Motif. Onomatopoeia. Point-of-View. Simile. Theme.*

Kasza, Keiko. *Grandpa Toad's Secrets.* New York: G. P. Putnam's Sons, c1995.

    Other Devices: *Motif. Oxymoron. Serendipity. Stereotype/Reverse Stereotype. Surprise/Twist-in-the-Tail. Tone. Wit/Humor.*

Krensky, Stephen. *How Santa Lost His Job.* Illus. by S. D. Schindler. New York: (Aladdin) Simon & Schuster, c2001.

    Other Devices: *Foreshadow. Inference. Paradox. Satire. Understatement.*

*Lamm, C. Drew. *Gauchada.* Illus. by Fabian Negrin. New York: Alfred A. Knopf, c2002.

    Other Devices: *Antithesis. Atmosphere. Connotation. Flashback. Imagery. Internal Rhyme. Metaphor. Motif. Parallelism. Surprise/Twist-in-the-Tail. Theme.*

McElligott, Matthew. *Backbeard and the Birthday Suit.* New York: Walker & Company, c2006.

    Other Devices: *Allusion. Ambiguity. Antihero. Antithesis. Aphorism. Aptronym. Archetype. Atmosphere. Colloquialism. Hyperbole. Point-of-View. Solecism. Wit/Humor.*

Michelson, Richard. *Across the Alley.* Illus. by E. B. Lewis. New York: (Penguin Young Readers Group) G. P. Putnam's Sons, c2006.

    Other Devices: *Aphorism. Counterpoint. Inference. Metaphor. Point-of-View. Simile. Stereotype/Reverse Stereotype. Theme.*

Pearson, Tracey Campbell. *Bob.* New York: Farrar, Straus and Giroux, c2002.

Other Devices: *Ambiguity. Onomatopoeia. Theme. Tone. Wit/Humor.*

Pelley, Kathleen T. *Inventor McGregor.* Illus. by Michael Chesworth. New York: Farrar, Straus and Giroux, c2006.

    Other Devices: *Alliteration. Atmosphere. Connotation. Paradox. Simile. Theme.*

Pfister, Marcus. *Holey Moley.* Trans. by J. Alison James. New York: North-South Books, c2006.

    Other Devices: *Antithesis. Counterpoint. Paradox. Parallelism. Theme.*

Sauer, Tammi. *Cowboy Camp.* Illus. by Mike Reed. New York: Sterling, c2005.

    Other Devices: *Antihero. Aptronym. Archetype. Colloquialism. Paradox. Parallelism. Satire.*

Smith, Cynthia Leitich and Greg Smith. *Santa Knows.* Illus. by Steve Bjorkman. New York: (Dutton Children's Books) Penguin, c2006.

    Other Devices: *Allusion. Ambiguity. Aptronym. Foreshadow. Hyperbole. Motif. Parallelism. Poetic Justice. Tone. Wit/Humor.*

Squires, Janet. *The Gingerbread Cowboy.* Illus. by Holly Berry. New York: HarperCollins Children's Books, c2006.

    Other Devices: *Atmosphere. Colloquialism. Imagery. Parallelism. Parody. Simile. Tone. Wit/Humor.*

*Tingle, Tim. *Crossing Bok Chitto: A Choctaw Tale of Friendship and Freedom.* Illus. by Jeanne Rorex Bridges. El Paso, TX: Cinco Puntos Press, c2006.

    Other Devices: *Allusion. Antithesis. Aphorism. Counterpoint. Flash-Forward. Foreshadow. Motif. Paradox. Parallelism. Simile. Symbol. Theme.*

Wojciechowski, Susan. *A Fine St. Patrick's Day.* Illus. by Tom Curry. New York: Random House, c2004.

    Other Devices: *Alliteration. Colloquialism. Inference. Theme.*

Young, Amy. *Belinda and the Glass Slipper.* New York: (Viking) Penguin Young Readers Group, c2006.

    Other Devices: *Allusion. Antihero. Archetype. Counterpoint. Foreshadow. Inference. Parallelism. Parody. Poetic Justice. Simile. Surprise/ Twist-in-the-Tail. Theme. Understatement.*

METAPHOR

Two unlike objects compared similarly by substituting one for the other as, for example, when a beautiful car is called "eye candy."

Bunting, Eve. *Pop's Bridge.* Illus. by C. F. Payne. New York: Harcourt, c2006.

    Other Devices: *Antithesis. Aphorism. Foreshadow. Inference. Simile. Symbol. Theme.*

*Coombs, Kate. *The Secret-Keeper.* Illus. by Heather M. Solomon. New York: (Atheneum Books for Young Readers) Simon & Schuster, c2006.
> **Other Devices:** *Ambiguity. Connotation. Foreshadow. Imagery. Inference. Irony. Motif. Serendipity. Simile. Symbol. Tone.*

Eversole, Robyn. *The Gift Stone.* Illus. by Allen Garns. New York: Alfred A. Knopf, c1998.
> **Other Devices:** *Antithesis. Aphorism. Atmosphere. Connotation. Inference. Irony. Motif. Parallelism. Simile. Symbol.*

Garland, Sherry. *My Father's Boat.* Illus. by Ted Rand. New York: Scholastic Press, c1998.
> **Other Devices:** *Antithesis. Aphorism. Connotation. Counterpoint. Imagery. Parallelism. Simile. Theme.*

Gerstein, Mordicai. *Carolinda Clatter!* New Milford, CT: (Roaring Brook Press) Holtzbrinck, c2005.
> **Other Devices:** *Allusion. Antithesis. Aptronym. Counterpoint. Flash-Forward. Foreshadow. Hyperbole. Internal Rhyme. Irony. Motif. Parallelism. Wit/Humor.*

Goode, Diane. *The Most Perfect Spot.* New York: HarperCollins Children's Books, c2006.
> **Other Devices:** *Foreshadow. Motif. Pun.*

High, Linda Oatman. *Barn Savers.* Illus. by Ted Lewin. Honesdale, PA: Boyds Mills Press, c1999.
> **Other Devices:** *Atmosphere. Connotation. Imagery. Parallelism. Simile.*

*Johnston, Tony. *Angel City.* Illus. by Carole Byard. New York: (Philomel) Penguin Young Readers Group, c2006.
> **Other Devices:** *Allusion. Ambiguity. Antithesis. Atmosphere. Colloquialism. Connotation. Counterpoint. Foreshadow. Imagery. Inference. Motif. Paradox. Parallelism. Simile. Symbol. Theme. Tone. Wit/Humor.*

Johnston, Tony. *The Barn Owls.* Illus. by Deborah Kogan Ray. Watertown, MA: Charlesbridge, c2000.
> **Other Devices:** *Atmosphere. Imagery. Motif. Parallelism. Simile. Tone.*

*Lamm, C. Drew. *Gauchada.* Illus. by Fabian Negrin. New York: Alfred A. Knopf, c2002.
> **Other Devices:** *Antithesis. Atmosphere. Connotation. Flashback. Imagery. Internal Rhyme. Irony. Motif. Parallelism. Surprise/Twist-of-the-Tail. Theme.*

Michelson, Richard. *Across the Alley.* Illus. by E. B. Lewis. New York: (Penguin Young Readers Group), G. P. Putnam's Sons, c2006.
> **Other Devices:** *Aphorism. Counterpoint. Inference. Irony. Point-of-View. Simile. Stereotype/Reverse Stereotype. Theme.*

*Raven, Marot Theis. *Night Boat to Freedom.* Illus. by E. B. Lewis. New York: (Melanie Kroupa Books) Farrar, Straus and Giroux, c2006.
> **Other Devices:** *Aphorism. Atmosphere. Colloquialism. Imagery. Inference. Paradox. Parallelism. Simile. Symbol. Theme.*

*Schotter, Roni. *Mama, I'll Give You the World.* Illus. by S. Saelig Gallagher. New York: (Schwartz & Wade) Random House, c2006.
>   **Other Devices:** *Ambiguity. Connotation. Foreshadow. Imagery. Inference. Motif. Point-of-View. Simile. Symbol. Tone.*

Yolen, Jane. *Harvest Home.* Illus. by Greg Shed. New York: (Silver Whistle) Harcourt, c2002.
>   **Other Devices:** *Atmosphere. Imagery. Internal Rhyme. Motif. Parallelism. Wit/Humor.*

Yolen, Jane. *Raising Yoder's Barn.* Illus. by Bernie Fuchs. New York: Little, Brown and Company, c1998.
>   **Other Devices:** *Aphorism. Colloquialism. Imagery. Inference. Motif. Parallelism. Simile. Understatement.*

MOTIF

A recurring theme, character, image, element, or verbal pattern that becomes a dominant part of the main theme.

Allen, Jonathan. *I'm Not Cute!* New York: Hyperion Books for Children, c2005.
>   **Other Devices:** *Antithesis. Counterpoint. Foreshadow. Paradox.*

Arnosky, Jim. *Grandfather Buffalo.* New York: G. P. Putnam's Sons, c2006.
>   **Other Devices:** *Atmosphere. Foreshadow. Inference. Theme.*

Atwood, Margaret. *Up in the Tree.* Toronto, Ontario: Greenwood Books/ House of Anansi Press, c1978, 2006.
>   **Other Devices:** *Antithesis. Hyperbole. Internal Rhyme. Irony. Parallelism.*

Auch, Mary Jane. *Hen Lake.* New York: Holiday House, c1995.
>   **Other Devices:** *Allusion. Aphorism. Aptronym. Archetype. Colloquialism. Connotation. Inference. Theme.*

Bang, Molly. *In My Heart.* New York: Little, Brown and Company, c2006.
>   **Other Devices:** *Inference. Tone.*

Borden, Louise. *Across the Blue Pacific: A World War II Story.* Illus. by Robert Andrew Parker. Boston: Houghton Mifflin, c2006.
>   **Other Devices:** *Aphorism. Atmosphere. Connotation. Flashback. Flash-Forward. Foreshadow. Imagery. Inference. Paradox. Parallelism. Simile. Theme.*

Bradley, Kimberly Brubaker. *Ballerino Nate.* Illus. by R. W. Alley. New York: (Dial Books for Young Readers) Penguin Young Readers Group, c2006.
>   **Other Devices:** *Ambiguity. Archetype. Inference. Parallelism. Stereotype/Reverse Stereotype.*

*Coombs, Kate. *The Secret-Keeper.* Illus. by Heather M. Solomon. New York: (Atheneum Books for Young Readers) Simon & Schuster, c2006.

Other Devices: *Ambiguity. Connotation. Foreshadow. Imagery. Inference. Irony. Metaphor. Serendipity. Simile. Symbol. Tone.*

Crummel, Susan Stevens. *Ten Gallon Bart.* Illus. by Dorothy Donohue. Tarrytown, NY: Marshall Cavendish, c2006.
> **Other Devices:** *Allusion. Archetype. Colloquialism. Connotation. Inference. Internal Rhyme. Parody. Poetic Justice. Pun. Solecism. Stereotype/Reverse Stereotype. Tone. Wit/Humor.*

*Cullen, Lynn. *Moi & Marie Antoinette.* Illus. by Amy Young. New York: Bloomsbury Publishing, c2006.
> **Other Devices:** *Archetype. Atmosphere. Counterpoint. Foreshadow. Hyperbole. Inference. Parallelism. Point-of-View. Serendipity. Simile. Surprise/Twist-in-the-Tail. Wit/Humor.*

Eversole, Robyn. *The Gift Stone.* Illus. by Allen Garns. New York: Alfred A. Knopf, c1998.
> **Other Devices:** *Antithesis. Aphorism. Atmosphere. Connotation. Inference. Irony. Metaphor. Parallelism. Simile. Symbol.*

Fleming, Candace. *Muncha! Muncha! Muncha!* Illus. by G. Brian Karas. New York: Atheneum Books for Young Readers, c2002.
> **Other Devices:** *Allusion. Aptronym. Irony. Onomatopoeia. Parallelism. Surprise/Twist-in-the-Tail.*

Gerstein, Mordicai. *Carolinda Clatter!* New Milford, CT: (Roaring Brook Press) Holtzbrinck, c2005.
> **Other Devices:** *Allusion. Antithesis. Aptronym. Counterpoint. Flash-Forward. Foreshadow. Hyperbole. Internal Rhyme. Irony. Metaphor. Parallelism. Wit/Humor.*

Goode, Diane. *The Most Perfect Spot.* New York: HarperCollins Children's Books, c2006.
> **Other Devices:** *Foreshadow. Irony. Pun.*

Henkes, Kevin. *Kitten's First Full Moon.* New York: (Greenwillow Books) HarperCollins, c2004.
> **Other Devices:** *Irony. Tone.*

James, Simon. *The Wild Woods.* Cambridge, MA: Candlewick Press, c1993.
> **Other Devices:** *Inference. Point-of-View. Wit/Humor.*

Johnson, Angela. *Wind Flyers.* Illus. by Loren Long. New York: Simon & Schuster Books for Young Readers, c2007.
> **Other Devices:** *Connotation. Imagery. Inference. Paradox. Parallelism.*

Johnson, Lindan Lee. *Dream Jar.* Illus. by Serena Curmi. New York: Houghton Mifflin, c2005.
> **Other Devices:** *Allusion. Antithesis. Foreshadow. Inference. Parallelism. Symbol. Understatement.*

*Johnston, Tony. *Angel City.* Illus. by Carole Byard. New York: (Philomel) Penguin Young Readers Group, c2006.
> **Other Devices:** *Allusion. Ambiguity. Antithesis. Atmosphere. Colloquialism. Connotation. Counterpoint. Foreshadow. Imagery. Inference.*

Metaphor. Paradox. Parallelism. Simile. Symbol. Theme. Tone. Wit/ Humor.

Johnston, Tony. *The Barn Owls.* Illus. by Deborah Kogan Ray. Watertown, MA: Charlesbridge, c2000.

    Other Devices: *Atmosphere. Imagery. Metaphor. Parallelism. Simile. Tone.*

Karon, Jan. *Violet Comes to Stay.* Story by Melanie Cecka. Illus. by Emily Arnold McCully. New York: (Viking) Penguin Young Readers Group, c2006.

    Other Devices: *Alliteration. Aphorism. Connotation. Foreshadow. Irony. Onomatopoeia. Point-of-View. Simile. Theme.*

Kasza, Keiko. *Grandpa Toad's Secrets.* New York: G. P. Putnam's Sons, c1995.

    Other Devices: *Irony. Oxymoron. Serendipity. Stereotype/Reverse Stereotype. Surprise/Twist-in-the-Tail. Tone. Wit/Humor.*

*****Lamm, C. Drew.** *Gauchada.* Illus. by Fabian Negrin. New York: Alfred A. Knopf, c2002.

    Other Devices: *Antithesis. Atmosphere. Connotation. Flashback. Imagery. Internal Rhyme. Irony. Metaphor. Parallelism. Surprise/Twist-in-the-Tail. Theme.*

Lasky, Kathryn. *Pirate Bob.* Illus. by David Clark. Watertown, MA: Charlesbridge, c2006.

    Other Devices: *Antihero. Antithesis. Archetype. Atmosphere. Black Humor. Colloquialism. Connotation. Hyperbole. Imagery. Inference. Parallelism. Theme.*

Lee-Tai, Amy. *A Place Where Sunflowers Grow.* Illus. by Felicia Hoshino. San Francisco: Children's Book Press, c2006.

    Other Devices: *Aphorism. Atmosphere. Connotation. Inference. Symbol. Theme.*

Manushkin, Fran. *The Shivers in the Fridge.* Illus. by Paul O. Zelinsky. New York: (Dutton Children's Books) Penguin Young Readers Group, c2006.

    Other Devices: *Inference. Parallelism. Point-of-View. Pun. Understatement. Wit/Humor.*

*****Montserrat, Pep.** *Ms. Rubinstein's Beauty.* New York: Sterling, c2006.

    Other Devices: *Antithesis. Atmosphere. Connotation. Counterpoint. Inference. Parallelism. Surprise/Twist-in-the-Tail. Theme.*

Palatini, Margie. *Bad Boys Get Cookie!* Illus. by Henry Cole. New York; HarperCollins Children's Books, c2006.

    Other Devices: *Allusion. Foreshadow. Inference. Parallelism. Poetic Justice. Pun. Tone. Understatement. Wit/Humor.*

*****Schotter, Roni.** *Mama, I'll Give You the World.* Illus. by S. Saelig Gallagher. New York: (Schwartz & Wade) Random House, c2006.

    Other Devices: *Ambiguity. Connotation. Foreshadow. Imagery. Inference. Metaphor. Point-of-View. Simile. Symbol. Tone.*

Smith, Cynthia Leitich and Greg Smith. *Santa Knows.* Illus. by Steve Bjorkman. New York: (Dutton Children's Books) Penguin, c2006.
> **Other Devices:** *Allusion. Ambiguity. Aptronym. Foreshadow. Hyperbole. Irony. Parallelism. Poetic Justice. Tone. Wit/Humor.*

Stevens, Janet and Susan Stevens Crummel. *Cook-A-Doodle-Doo.* Illus. by Janet Stevens. Orlando, FL: (Voyager Books) Harcourt, c1999.
> **Other Devices:** *Allusion. Colloquialism. Inference. Parallelism. Pun. Stereotype/Reverse Stereotype. Theme.*

*****Tingle, Tim.** *Crossing Bok Chitto: A Choctaw Tale of Friendship and Freedom.* Illus. by Jeanne Rorex Bridges. El Paso, TX: Cinco Puntos Press, c2006.
> **Other Devices:** *Allusion. Antithesis. Aphorism. Counterpoint. Flash-Forward. Foreshadow. Irony. Paradox. Parallelism. Simile. Symbol. Theme.*

Williams, Laura E. *The Best Winds.* Illus. by Eujin Kim Neilan. Honesdale, PA: Boyds Mills Press, c2006.
> **Other Devices:** *Aphorism. Atmosphere. Foreshadow. Inference. Simile. Theme.*

Yolen, Jane. *Harvest Home.* Illus. by Greg Shed. New York: (Silver Whistle) Harcourt, c2002.
> **Other Devices:** *Atmosphere. Imagery. Internal Rhyme. Metaphor. Parallelism. Wit/Humor.*

Yolen, Jane. *Raising Yoder's Barn.* Illus. by Bernie Fuchs. New York: Little, Brown and Company, c1998.
> **Other Devices:** *Aphorism. Colloquialism. Imagery. Inference. Metaphor. Parallelism. Simile. Understatement.*

ONOMATOPOEIA

Sound words that reflect meaning by imitating the sound—"hiss," "whoosh," or "dong."

Fleming, Candace. *Muncha! Muncha! Muncha!* Illus. by G. Brian Karas. New York: Atheneum Books for Young Readers, c2002.
> **Other Devices:** *Allusion. Aptronym. Irony. Motif. Parallelism. Surprise/Twist-in-the-Tail.*

*****Franklin, Kristine.** *The Gift.* Illus. by Barbara Lavallee. San Francisco: Chronicle Books, c1999.
> **Other Devices:** *Ambiguity. Foreshadow. Imagery. Inference. Irony. Simile. Surprise/Twist-in-the-Tail. Symbol. Theme.*

Karen, Jan. *Violet Comes to Stay.* Story by Melanie Cecka. Illus. by Emily Arnold McCully. New York: (Viking) Penguin Young Readers Group, c2006.
> **Other Devices:** *Alliteration. Aphorism. Connotation. Foreshadow. Imagery. Inference. Irony. Motif. Point-of-View. Simile. Theme.*

Pearson, Tracey Campbell. *Bob.* New York: Farrar, Straus and Giroux, c2002.

    Other Devices: *Ambiguity. Irony. Theme. Tone. Wit/Humor.*

*Wood, Nancy. *Mr. and Mrs. God in the Creation Kitchen.* Illus. by Timothy Basil Ering. Cambridge, MA: Candlewick Press, c2006.

    Other Devices: *Allusion. Antithesis. Foreshadow. Hyperbole. Imagery. Inference. Parallelism. Pun. Satire. Understatement. Wit/Humor.*

OXYMORON

Startling contradictory word combinations—"thunderous silence," "bold conservatism."

Kasza, Keiko. *Grandpa Toad's Secrets.* New York: G. P. Putnam's Sons, c.1995.

    Other Devices: *Irony. Motif. Serendipity. Stereotype/Reverse Stereotype. Surprise/Twist-in-the-Tail. Tone. Wit/Humor.*

Yorinks, Arthur. *Whitefish Will Rides Again!* Illus. by Mort Drucker. New York: HarperCollins, c1994.

    Other Devices: *Alliteration. Archetype. Colloquialism. Hyperbole. Inference. Satire. Simile. Solecism. Tone. Wit/Humor.*

PARADOX

Truth that reconciles seeming contradictions—"cruel only to be kind."

*Adler, David A. *The Babe and I.* Illus. by Terry Widdener. New York: (Gulliver Books) Harcourt Brace & Co., c1999.

    Other Devices: *Ambiguity. Antithesis. Foreshadow. Inference. Irony. Tone.*

Allen, Jonathan. *I'm Not Cute!* New York: Hyperion Books for Children, c2005.

    Other Devices: *Antithesis. Counterpoint. Foreshadow. Motif.*

*Bateman, Teresa. *Keeper of Soles.* Illus. by Diego Herrera (Yayo). New York: Holiday House, c2006.

    Other Devices: *Ambiguity. Aphorism. Black Humor. Colloquialism. Connotation. Imagery. Inference. Irony. Parallelism. Pun. Understatement.*

Bernstein, Dan. *The Tortoise and the Hare Race Again.* Illus. by Andrew Glass. New York: Holiday House, c2006.

    Other Devices: *Alliteration. Allusion. Ambiguity. Foreshadow. Parody. Pun.*

Borden, Louise. *Across the Blue Pacific: A World War II Story.* Illus. by Robert Andrew Parker. Boston: Houghton Mifflin, c2006.

Other Devices: *Aphorism. Atmosphere. Connotation. Flashback. Flash-Forward. Foreshadow. Imagery. Inference. Motif. Parallelism. Simile. Theme.*

Bowen, Anne. *The Great Math Tattle Battle.* Illus. by Jaime Zollars. Morton Grove, IL: Albert Whitman, c2006.

Other Devices: *Connotation. Parallelism. Poetic Justice. Theme.*

Broach, Elise. *Cousin John Is Coming!* Illus. by Nate Lilly. New York: (Dial Books for Young Readers) Penguin Young Readers Group, c2006.

Other Devices: *Ambiguity. Archetype. Counterpoint. Inference. Irony.*

Bunting, Eve. *Butterfly House.* Illus. by Greg Shed. New York: Scholastic Press, c1999.

Other Devices: *Atmosphere. Connotation. Flashback. Imagery. Internal Rhyme. Point-of-View. Simile.*

Jenkins, Emily. *That New Animal.* Illus. by Pierce Pratt. New York: (Frances Foster Books) Farrar, Straus and Giroux, c2005.

Other Devices: *Black Humor. Parallelism. Point-of-View.*

Johnson, Angela. *Wind Flyers.* Illus. by Loren Long. New York: Simon & Schuster Books for Young Readers, c2007.

Other Devices: *Connotation. Imagery. Inference. Motif. Parallelism.*

*Johnston, Tony. *Angel City.* Illus. by Carole Byard. New York: (Philomel) Penguin Young Readers Group, c2006.

Other Devices: *Allusion. Ambiguity. Antithesis. Atmosphere. Colloquialism. Connotation. Counterpoint. Foreshadow. Imagery. Inference. Metaphor. Motif. Parallelism. Simile. Symbol. Theme. Tone. Wit/Humor.*

Krensky, Stephen. *How Santa Lost His Job.* Illus. by S. D. Schindler. New York: (Aladdin) Simon & Schuster, c2001.

Other Devices: *Foreshadow. Inference. Irony. Satire. Understatement.*

Pelley, Kathleen T. *Inventor McGregor.* Illus. by Michael Chesworth. New York: Farrar, Straus and Giroux, c2006.

Other Devices: *Alliteration. Atmosphere. Connotation. Irony. Simile. Theme.*

Pfister, Marcus. *Holey Moley.* Trans. by J. Alison James. New York: North-South Books, c2006.

Other Devices: *Antithesis. Counterpoint. Irony. Parallelism. Theme.*

*Raven, Marot Theis. *Night Boat to Freedom.* Illus. by E. B. Lewis. New York: (Melanie Kroupa Books) Farrar, Straus and Giroux, c2006.

Other Devices: *Aphorism. Atmosphere. Colloquialism. Imagery. Inference. Metaphor. Parallelism. Simile. Symbol. Theme.*

Sauer, Tammi. *Cowboy Camp.* Illus. by Mike Reed. New York: Sterling, c2005.

Other Devices: *Antihero. Aptronym. Archetype. Colloquialism. Irony. Parallelism. Satire.*

Smith, Linda. *Mrs. Crump's Cat.* Illus. by David Roberts. New York: HarperCollins Children's Books, c2006.

Other Devices: *Antithesis. Aptronym. Inference.*

*Tingle, Tim. *Crossing Bok Chitto: A Choctaw Tale of Friendship and Freedom.* Illus. by Jeanne Rorex Bridges. El Paso, TX: Cinco Puntos Press, c2006.

Other Devices: *Allusion. Antithesis. Aphorism. Counterpoint. Flash-Forward. Foreshadow. Irony. Motif. Parallelism. Simile. Symbol. Theme.*

PARALLELISM

Repetition of phrases or sentences of similar construction for purposes of emphasis—"Where is my hat? Where is my coat? Where are my boots?"

Asher, Sandy. *Too Many Frogs!* Illus. by Keith Graves. New York: (Philomel Books) Penguin Young Readers Group, c2005.

Other Devices: *Allusion. Aphorism. Internal Rhyme. Irony. Theme. Tone.*

Ashman, Linda. *Desmond and the Naughtybugs.* Illus. by Anik McGrory. New York: (Dutton Children's Books) Penguin Young Readers Group, c2006.

Other Devices: *Foreshadow. Inference. Irony.*

Atwood, Margaret. *Up in the Tree.* Toronto, Ontario: Greenwood Books/House of Anansi Press, c1978, 2006.

Other Devices: *Antithesis. Hyperbole. Internal Rhyme. Irony. Motif.*

Bateman, Teresa. *A Plump and Perky Turkey.* Illus. by Jeff Shelly. New York: Marshall Cavendish, c2001.

Other Devices: *Alliteration. Allusion. Ambiguity. Aptronym. Irony. Poetic Justice. Surprise/Twist-in-the-Tail. Theme. Understatement.*

*Bateman, Teresa. *Keeper of Soles.* Illus. by Diego Herrera (Yayo). New York: Holiday House, c2006.

Other Devices: *Ambiguity. Aphorism. Black Humor. Colloquialism. Connotation. Imagery. Inference. Irony. Paradox. Pun. Understatement.*

Borden, Louise. *Across the Blue Pacific: A World War II Story.* Illus. by Robert Andrew Parker. Boston: Houghton Mifflin, c2006.

Other Devices: *Aphorism. Atmosphere. Connotation. Flashback. Flash-Forward. Foreshadow. Imagery. Inference. Motif. Paradox. Simile. Theme.*

Bowen, Anne. *The Great Math Tattle Battle.* Illus. by Jaime Zollars. Morton Grove, IL: Albert Whitman, c2006.

Other Devices: *Connotation. Paradox. Poetic Justice. Theme.*

Bradley, Kimberly Brubaker. *Ballerino Nate.* Illus. by R. W. Alley. New York: (Dial Books for Young Readers) Penguin Young Readers Group, c2006.

Other Devices: *Ambiguity. Archetype. Inference. Motif. Stereotype/Reverse Stereotype.*

Bynum, Janie. *Nutmeg and Barley: A Budding Friendship.* Cambridge, MA: Candlewick Press, c2006.
   Other Devices: *Ambiguity. Antithesis. Foreshadow. Theme.*

*****Cullen, Lynn.** *Moi & Marie Antoinette.* Illus. by Amy Young. New York: Bloomsbury Publishing, c2006.
   Other Devices: *Archetype. Atmosphere. Counterpoint. Foreshadow. Hyperbole. Inference. Point-of-View. Serendipity. Simile. Surprise/ Twist-in-the-Tail. Wit/Humor.*

Edwards, Pamela Duncan. *The Mixed-Up Rooster.* Illus. by Megan Lloyd. New York: HarperCollins Children's Books, c2006.
   Other Devices: *Foreshadow. Pun. Serendipity. Stereotype/Reverse Stereotype. Theme. Wit/Humor.*

Eversole, Robyn. *The Gift Stone.* Illus. by Allen Garns. New York: Alfred A. Knopf, c1998.
   Other Devices: *Antithesis. Aphorism. Atmosphere. Connotation. Inference. Irony. Metaphor. Motif. Simile. Symbol.*

Fleming, Candace. *Muncha! Muncha! Muncha!* Illus. by G. Brian Karas. New York: Atheneum Books for Young Readers, c2002.
   Other Devices: *Allusion. Aptronym. Irony. Motif. Onomatopoeia. Surprise/Twist-in-the-Tail.*

*****Frank, John.** *The Toughest Cowboy, or How the Wild West Was Tamed.* Illus. by Zachary Pullen. New York: Simon & Schuster Books for Young Readers, c2004.
   Other Devices: *Allusion. Ambiguity. Aptronym. Atmosphere. Colloquialism. Foreshadow. Hyperbole. Inference. Irony. Pun. Simile. Solecism. Stereotype/Reverse. Stereotype. Tone. Understatement. Wit/ Humor.*

Garland, Sherry. *My Father's Boat.* Illus. by Ted Rand. New York: Scholastic Press, c1998.
   Other Devices: *Antithesis. Aphorism. Connotation. Counterpoint. Imagery. Metaphor. Simile. Theme.*

Gerstein, Mordicai. *Carolinda Clatter!* New Milford, CT: (Roaring Brook Press) Holtzbrinck, c2005.
   Other Devices: *Allusion. Antithesis. Aptronym. Counterpoint. Flash-Forward. Foreshadow. Hyperbole. Internal Rhyme. Irony. Metaphor. Motif. Wit/Humor.*

High, Linda Oatman. *Barn Savers.* Illus. by Ted Lewin. Honesdale, PA: Boyds Mills Press, c1999.
   Other Devices: *Atmosphere. Connotation. Imagery. Metaphor. Simile.*

Jenkins, Emily. *That New Animal.* Illus. by Pierce Pratt. New York: (Frances Foster Books) Farrar, Straus and Giroux, c2005.
   Other Devices: *Black Humor. Paradox. Point-of-View.*

Johnson, Angela. *Wind Flyers.* Illus. by Loren Long. New York: Simon & Schuster Books for Young Readers, c2007.

Other Devices: *Connotation. Imagery. Inference. Motif. Paradox.*

Johnston, Lindan Lee. *Dream Jar.* Illus. by Serena Curmi. New York: Houghton Mifflin, c2005.

Other Devices: *Allusion. Antithesis. Foreshadow. Inference. Motif. Symbol. Understatement.*

*Johnston, Tony. *Angel City.* Illus. by Carole Byard. New York: (Philomel) Penguin Young Readers Group, c2006.

Other Devices: *Allusion. Ambiguity. Antithesis. Atmosphere. Colloquialism. Connotation. Counterpoint. Foreshadow. Imagery. Inference. Metaphor. Motif. Paradox. Simile. Symbol. Theme. Tone. Wit/Humor.*

Johnston, Tony. *The Barn Owls.* Illus. by Deborah Kogan Ray. Watertown, MA: Charlesbridge, c2000.

Other Devices: *Atmosphere. Imagery. Metaphor. Motif. Simile. Tone.*

*Lamm, C. Drew. *Gauchada.* Illus. by Fabian Negrin. New York: Alfred A. Knopf, c2002.

Other Devices: *Antithesis. Atmosphere. Connotation. Flashback. Imagery. Internal Rhyme. Irony. Metaphor. Motif. Surprise/Twist-of-the-Tail. Theme.*

Lasky, Kathryn. *Pirate Bob.* Illus. by David Clark. Watertown, MA: Charlesbridge, c2006.

Other Devices: *Antihero. Antithesis. Archetype. Atmosphere. Black Humor. Colloquialism. Connotation. Hyperbole. Imagery. Inference. Motif. Theme.*

McClintock, Barbara. *Adele & Simon.* New York: (Frances Foster Books) Farrar, Straus and Giroux, c2006.

Other Devices: *Aptronym. Foreshadow. Inference. Wit.*

Manushkin, Fran. *The Shivers in the Fridge.* Illus. by Paul O. Zelinsky. New York: (Dutton Children's Books) Penguin Young Readers Group, c2006.

Other Devices: *Inference. Motif. Point-of-View. Pun. Understatement. Wit/Humor.*

*Montserrat, Pep. *Ms. Rubinstein's Beauty.* New York: Sterling, c2006.

Other Devices: *Antithesis. Atmosphere. Connotation. Counterpoint. Inference. Motif. Surprise/Twist-in-the-Tail. Theme.*

Nelson, Vaunda Micheaux. *Almost to Freedom.* Illus. by Colin Bootman. Minneapolis, MN: (Carolrhoda) Lerner, c2003.

Other Devices: *Allusion. Atmosphere. Colloquialism. Foreshadow. Hyperbole. Imagery. Inference. Personification. Poetic Justice. Point-of-View. Simile. Solecism. Understatement.*

Palatini, Margie. *Bad Boys Get Cookie!* Illus. by Henry Cole. New York: HarperCollins Children's Books, c2006.

Other Devices: *Allusion. Foreshadow. Inference. Motif. Poetic Justice. Pun. Tone. Understatement. Wit/Humor.*

Pfister, Marcus. *Holey Moley.* Trans. by J. Alison James. New York: North-South Books, c2006.

Other Devices: *Antithesis. Counterpoint. Irony. Paradox. Theme.*

*Raven, Marot Theis. *Night Boat to Freedom.* Illus. by E. B. Lewis. New York: (Melanie Kroupa Books) Farrar, Straus and Giroux, c2006.

Other Devices: *Aphorism. Atmosphere. Colloquialism. Imagery. Inference. Metaphor. Paradox. Simile. Symbol. Theme.*

Recorvits, Helen. *Yoon and the Christmas Mitten.* Illus. by Gabi Swaiatowska. New York: (Frances Foster Books) Farrar, Straus and Giroux, c2006.

Other Devices: *Ambiguity. Antithesis. Atmosphere. Colloquialism. Counterpoint. Foreshadow. Inference. Point-of-View. Theme.*

Sauer, Tammi. *Cowboy Camp.* Illus. by Mike Reed. New York: Sterling, c2005.

Other Devices: *Antihero. Aptronym. Archetype. Colloquialism. Irony. Paradox. Satire.*

Smith, Cynthia Leitich and Greg Smith. *Santa Knows.* Illus. by Steve Bjorkman. New York: (Dutton Children's Books) Penguin, c2006.

Other Devices: *Allusion. Ambiguity. Aptronym. Foreshadow. Hyperbole. Irony. Motif. Poetic Justice. Tone. Wit/Humor.*

Squires, Janet. *The Gingerbread Cowboy.* Illus. by Holly Berry. New York: HarperCollins Children's Books, c2006.

Other Devices: *Atmosphere. Colloquialism. Imagery. Irony. Parody. Simile. Tone. Wit/Humor.*

Stevens, Janet and Susan Stevens Crummel. *Cook-A-Doodle-Doo.* Orlando, FL: (Voyager Books) Harcourt, c1999.

Other Devices: *Allusion. Colloquialism. Inference. Motif. Pun. Stereotype/Reverse Stereotype. Theme.*

*Tingle, Tim. *Crossing Bok Chitto: A Choctaw Tale of Friendship and Freedom.* Illus. by Jeanne Rorex Bridges. El Paso, TX: Cinco Puntos Press, c2006.

Other Devices: *Allusion. Antithesis. Aphorism. Counterpoint. Flash-Forward. Foreshadow. Irony. Motif. Paradox. Simile. Symbol. Theme.*

*Wood, Nancy. *Mr. and Mrs. God in the Creation Kitchen.* Illus. by Timothy Basil Ering. Cambridge, MA: Candlewick Press, c2006.

Other Devices: *Allusion. Antithesis. Foreshadow. Hyperbole. Imagery. Inference. Onomatopoeia. Pun. Satire. Understatement. Wit/Humor.*

Yolen, Jane. *Harvest Home.* Illus. by Greg Shed. New York: (Silver Whistle) Harcourt, c2002.

Other Devices: *Atmosphere. Imagery. Internal Rhyme. Metaphor. Motif. Wit/Humor.*

Yolen, Jane. *Raising Yoder's Barn.* Illus. by Bernie Fuchs. New York: Little, Brown and Company, c1998.

Other Devices: *Aphorism. Colloquialism. Imagery. Inference. Metaphor. Motif. Simile. Understatement.*

Young, Amy. *Belinda and the Glass Slipper.* New York: (Viking) Penguin Young Readers Group, c2006.

Other Devices: *Allusion. Antihero. Archetype. Counterpoint. Fore-shadow. Inference. Irony. Parody. Poetic Justice. Simile. Surprise/Twist-in-the-Tail. Theme. Understatement.*

PARODY

Humorous but recognizable imitation of another literary work in style, charac-ter, plot, language, or theme.

Bernstein, Dan. *The Tortoise and the Hare Race Again.* Illus. by Andrew Glass. New York: Holiday House, c2006.
> Other Devices: *Alliteration. Allusion. Ambiguity. Foreshadow. Para-dox. Pun.*

Crummel, Susan Stevens. *Ten Gallon Bart.* Illus. by Dorothy Donohue. Tarrytown, NY: Marshall Cavendish, c2006.
> Other Devices: *Allusion. Archetype. Colloquialism. Connotation. Inference. Internal Rhyme. Motif. Poetic Justice. Pun. Solecism. Stereo-type/Reverse Stereotype. Tone. Wit/Humor.*

Squires, Janet. *The Gingerbread Cowboy.* Illus. by Holly Berry. New York: HarperCollins Children's Books, c2006.
> Other Devices: *Atmosphere. Colloquialism. Imagery. Irony. Parallel-ism. Simile. Tone. Wit/Humor.*

Young, Amy. *Belinda and the Glass Slipper.* New York: (Viking) Penguin Young Readers Group, c2006.
> Other Devices: *Allusion. Antihero. Archetype. Counterpoint. Fore-shadow. Inference. Irony. Parallelism. Poetic Justice. Simile. Surprise/ Twist-in-the-Tail. Theme. Understatement.*

PERSONIFICATION

Inanimate objects or abstract ideas endowed with human qualities or actions.

Nelson, Vaunda Micheaux. *Almost to Freedom.* Illus. by Colin Bootman. Minneapolis, MN: (Carolrhoda) Lerner, c2003.
> Other Devices: *Allusion. Atmosphere. Colloquialism. Foreshadow. Hyperbole. Imagery. Inference. Parallelism. Poetic Justice. Point-of-View. Simile. Solecism. Understatement.*

*Young, Ed. *I, Doko: The Tale of a Basket.* New York: Philomel, c2004.
> Other Devices: *Aphorism. Foreshadow. Inference. Poetic Justice. Point-of-View. Theme. Tone.*

POETIC JUSTICE

An outcome in which vice is punished and virtue rewarded in a manner appropriate to the situation.

Bateman, Teresa. *A Plump and Perky Turkey.* Illus. by Jeff Shelly. New York: Marshall Cavendish, c2001.
> **Other Devices:** *Alliteration. Allusion. Ambiguity. Aptronym. Irony. Parallelism. Surprise/Twist-in-the-Tail. Theme. Understatement.*

Bowen, Anne. *The Great Math Tattle Battle.* Illus. by Jaime Zollars. Morton Grove, IL: Albert Whitman, c2006.
> **Other Devices:** *Connotation. Paradox. Parallelism. Theme.*

Crummel, Susan Stevens. *Ten Gallon Bart.* Illus. by Dorothy Donohue. Tarrytown, NY: Marshall Cavendish, c2006.
> **Other Devices:** *Allusion. Archetype. Colloquialism. Connotation. Inference. Internal Rhyme. Motif. Parody. Poetic Justice. Pun. Solecism. Stereotype/Reverse Stereotype. Tone. Wit/Humor.*

Nelson, Vaunda Micheaux. *Almost to Freedom.* Illus. by Colin Bootman. Minneapolis, MN: (Carolrhoda) Lerner, c2003.
> **Other Devices:** *Allusion. Atmosphere. Colloquialism. Foreshadow. Hyperbole. Imagery. Inference. Parallelism. Personification. Point-of-View. Simile. Solecism. Understatement.*

Palatini, Margie. *Bad Boys Get Cookie!* Illus. by Henry Cole. New York: HarperCollins Children's Books, c2006.
> **Other Devices:** *Allusion. Foreshadow. Inference. Motif. Parallelism. Pun. Tone. Understatement. Wit/Humor.*

Smith, Cynthia Leitich and Greg Smith. *Santa Knows.* Illus. by Steve Bjorkman. New York: (Dutton Children's Books) Penguin, c2006.
> **Other Devices:** *Allusion. Ambiguity. Aptronym. Foreshadow. Hyperbole. Irony. Motif. Parallelism. Tone. Wit/Humor.*

*Young, Ed. *I, Doko: The Tale of a Basket.* New York: Philomel, c2004.
> **Other Devices:** *Aphorism. Foreshadow. Inference. Personification. Point-of-View. Surprise/Twist-in-the-Tail. Theme. Tone.*

POINT-OF-VIEW

Perspective from which the story is seen and told.

Bunting, Eve. *Butterfly House.* Illus. by Greg Shed. New York: Scholastic Press, c1999.
> **Other Devices:** *Atmosphere. Connotation. Flash-Forward. Imagery. Internal Rhyme. Paradox. Simile.*

*Cullen, Lynn. *Moi & Marie Antoinette.* Illus. by Amy Young. New York: Bloomsbury Publishing, c2006.
> **Other Devices:** *Archetype. Atmosphere. Counterpoint. Foreshadow. Hyperbole. Inference. Motif. Parallelism. Serendipity. Simile. Surprise/ Twist-in-the-Tail. Wit/Humor.*

James, Simon. *The Wild Woods.* Cambridge, MA: Candlewick Press, c1993.
> **Other Devices:** *Inference. Motif. Wit/Humor.*

Jenkins, Emily. *That New Animal.* Illus. by Pierce Pratt. New York: (Frances Foster Books) Farrar, Straus and Giroux, c2005.

> **Other Devices:** *Black Humor. Paradox. Parallelism.*

Karon, Jan. *Violet Comes to Stay.* Story by Melanie Cecka. Illus. by Emily Arnold McCully. New York: (Viking) Penguin Young Readers Group, c2006.

> **Other Devices:** *Alliteration. Aphorism. Connotation. Foreshadow. Imagery. Inference. Irony. Motif. Onomatopoeia. Simile. Theme.*

McElligott, Matthew. *Backbeard and the Birthday Suit.* New York: Walker & Company, c2006.

> **Other Devices:** *Allusion. Ambiguity. Antihero. Antithesis. Aphorism. Aptronym. Archetype. Atmosphere. Colloquialism. Hyperbole. Irony. Solecism. Wit/Humor.*

Manushkin, Fran. *The Shivers in the Fridge.* Illus. by Paul O. Zelinsky. New York: (Dutton Children's Books) Penguin Young Readers Group, c2006.

> **Other Devices:** *Inference. Motif. Parallelism. Pun. Understatement. Wit/Humor.*

Michelson, Richard. *Across the Alley.* Illus. by E. B. Lewis. New York: (Penguin Young Readers Group) G. P. Putnam's Sons, c2006.

> **Other Devices:** *Aphorism. Counterpoint. Inference. Irony. Metaphor. Simile. Stereotype/Reverse Stereotype. Theme.*

Nelson, Vaunda Micheaux. *Almost to Freedom.* Illus. by Colin Bootman. Minneapolis, MN: (Carolrhoda) Learner, c2003.

> **Other Devices:** *Allusion. Atmosphere. Colloquialism. Foreshadow. Hyperbole. Imagery. Inference. Parallelism. Personification. Poetic Justice. Simile. Solecism. Understatement.*

Recorvits, Helen. *Yoon and the Christmas Mitten.* Illus. by Gabi Swaiatowska. New York: (Frances Foster Books) Farrar, Straus and Giroux, c2006.

> **Other Devices:** *Ambiguity. Antithesis. Atmosphere. Colloquialism. Counterpoint. Foreshadow. Inference. Parallelism. Theme.*

*Schotter, Roni. *Mama, I'll Give You the World.* Illus. by S. Saelig Gallagher. New York: (Schwartz & Wade) Random House, c2006.

> **Other Devices:** *Ambiguity. Connotation. Foreshadow. Imagery. Inference. Metaphor. Motif. Simile. Symbol. Tone.*

*Young, Ed. *I, Doko: The Tale of a Basket.* New York: Philomel, c2004.

> **Other Devices:** *Aphorism. Foreshadow. Inference. Personification. Poetic Justice. Surprise/Twist-in-the-Tail. Theme. Tone.*

PUN

Two or more possible applications of a word in a humorous way:

> *Two separate meanings in one word of identical pronunciation and spelling: homonyms—"Rest after eating the rest of the pie."*

Two separate meanings and pronunciations in two words of identical spelling: homographs—"She had a tear in her eye when she discovered the tear in her coat."

Two separate meanings in two words of identical pronunciation but different spelling: homophones—"That fowl has a foul odor."

Amico, Tom and James Proimos. *Raisin and Grape.* Illus. by Andy Snair. New York: (Dial Books for Young Readers) Penguin Young Readers Group, c2006.

> **Other Devices:** *Antithesis. Connotation. Hyperbole. Inference. Pun. Tone. Understatement. Wit/Humor.*

*Bateman, Teresa. *Keeper of Soles.* Illus. by Diego Herrera (Yayo). New York: Holiday House, c2006.

> **Other Devices:** *Ambiguity. Aphorism. Black Humor. Colloquialism. Connotation. Imagery. Inference. Irony. Paradox. Parallelism. Understatement.*

Bernstein, Dan. *The Tortoise and the Hare Race Again.* Illus. by Andrew Glass. New York: Holiday House, c2006.

> **Other Devices:** *Alliteration. Allusion. Ambiguity. Foreshadow. Paradox. Parody.*

Crummel, Susan Stevens. *Ten Gallon Bart.* Illus. by Dorothy Donohue. Tarrytown, New York: Marshall Cavendish, c2006.

> **Other Devices:** *Allusion. Archetype. Colloquialism. Connotation. Inference. Internal Rhyme. Motif. Parody. Poetic Justice. Solecism. Stereotype/Reverse Stereotype. Tone. Wit/Humor.*

Edwards, Pamela Duncan. *The Mixed-Up Rooster.* Illus. by Megan Lloyd. New York: HarperCollins Children's Books, c2006.

> **Other Devices:** *Foreshadow. Parallelism. Serendipity. Stereotype/ Reverse Stereotype. Theme. Wit/Humor.*

*Frank, John. *The Toughest Cowboy, or How the Wild West Was Tamed.* Illus. by Zachary Pullen. New York: Simon & Schuster Books for Young Readers, c2004.

> **Other Devices:** *Allusion. Ambiguity. Aptronym. Atmosphere. Colloquialism. Hyperbole. Inference. Irony. Parallelism. Simile. Solecism. Stereotype/Reverse Stereotype. Tone. Understatement. Wit/Humor.*

Goode, Diane. *The Most Perfect Spot.* New York: HarperCollins Children's Books, c2006.

> **Other Devices:** *Foreshadow. Irony. Motif.*

Kessler, Christina. *The Best Beekeeper of Lalibela: A Tale from Africa.* Illus. by Leonard Jenkins. New York: Holiday House, c2006.

> **Other Devices:** *Antithesis. Aphorism. Atmosphere. Foreshadow. Serendipity. Simile.*

Manushkin, Fran. *The Shivers in the Fridge.* Illus. by Paul O. Zelinsky. New York: (Dutton Children's Books) Penguin Young Readers Group, c2006.

Other Devices: *Inference. Motif. Parallelism. Point-of-View. Understatement. Wit/Humor.*

Palatini, Margie. *Bad Boys Get Cookie!* Illus. by Henry Cole. New York: HarperCollins Children's Books, c2006.

Other Devices: *Allusion. Foreshadow. Inference. Motif. Parallelism. Poetic Justice. Tone. Understatement. Wit/Humor.*

Stevens, Janet and Susan Stevens Crummel. *Cook-A-Doodle-Doo.* Illus. by Janet Stevens. Orlando, FL: (Voyager Books) Harcourt, c1999.

Other Devices: *Allusion. Colloquialism. Inference. Motif. Parallelism. Stereotype/Reverse Stereotype. Theme.*

Teague, Mark. *Pigsty.* New York: Scholastic, c1994.

Other Devices: *Ambiguity. Aphorism. Foreshadow. Tone.*

*Wood, Nancy. *Mr. and Mrs. God in the Creation Kitchen.* Illus. by Timothy Basil Ering. Cambridge, MA: Candlewick Press, c2006.

Other Devices: *Allusion. Antithesis. Foreshadow. Hyperbole. Imagery. Inference. Onomatopoeia. Parallelism. Satire. Understatement. Wit/Humor.*

SATIRE

Pointing out human absurdities through exaggeration and ridicule in a mocking tone that is either sharp and contemptuous or gentle and amusing.

Chen, Chih-Yuan. *The Featherless Chicken.* Alhambra, CA: Heryin Books, c2006.

Other Devices: *Alliteration. Archetype. Connotation. Inference. Internal Rhyme. Irony. Serendipity. Simile. Theme. Tone. Wit/Humor.*

Krensky, Stephen. *How Santa Lost His Job.* Illus. by S. D. Schindler. New York: (Aladdin) Simon & Schuster, c2001.

Other Devices: *Foreshadow. Inference. Irony. Paradox. Understatement.*

*Reynolds, Peter H. *So Few of Me.* Cambridge, MA: Candlewick Press, c2006.

Other Devices: *Theme.*

Sauer, Tammi. *Cowboy Camp.* Illus. by Mike Reed. New York: Sterling, c2005.

Other Devices: *Antihero. Aptronym. Archetype. Colloquialism. Irony. Paradox. Parallelism.*

*Wood, Nancy. *Mr. and Mrs. God in the Creation Kitchen.* Illus. by Timothy Basil Ering. Cambridge, MA: Candlewick Press, c2006.

Other Devices: *Allusion. Antithesis. Foreshadow. Hyperbole. Imagery. Inference. Onomatopoeia. Parallelism. Pun. Understatement. Wit/Humor.*

Yorinks, Arthur. *Whitefish Will Rides Again!* Illus. by Mort Drucker. New York: HarperCollins, c1994.

Other Devices: *Alliteration. Archetype. Colloquialism. Hyperbole. Inference. Oxymoron. Simile. Solecism. Tone. Wit/Humor.*

SERENDIPITY

Accidental good fortune occurring just when it's needed.

Chen, Chih-Yuan. *The Featherless Chicken.* Alhambra, CA: Heryin Books, c2006.
> **Other Devices:** *Alliteration. Archetype. Connotation. Inference. Internal Rhyme. Irony. Satire. Simile. Theme. Tone. Wit/Humor.*

*Coombs, Kate. *The Secret-Keeper.* Illus. by Heather M. Solomon. New York: (Atheneum Books for Young Readers) Simon & Schuster, c2006.
> **Other Devices:** *Ambiguity. Connotation. Foreshadow. Imagery. Inference. Irony. Metaphor. Motif. Simile. Symbol. Tone.*

*Cullen, Lynn. *Moi & Marie Antoinette.* Illus. by Amy Young. New York: Bloomsbury Publishing, c2006.
> **Other Devices:** *Archetype. Atmosphere. Counterpoint. Foreshadow. Hyperbole. Inference. Motif. Parallelism. Point-of-View. Simile. Surprise/Twist-in-the-Tail. Wit/Humor.*

Edwards, Pamela Duncan. *The Mixed-Up Rooster.* Illus. by Megan Lloyd. New York: HarperCollins Children's Books, c2006.
> **Other Devices:** *Foreshadow. Parallelism. Pun. Stereotype/Reverse Stereotype. Theme. Wit/Humor.*

Kasza, Keiko. *Grandpa Toad's Secrets.* New York: G. P. Putnam's Sons, c1995.
> **Other Devices:** *Irony. Motif. Oxymoron. Stereotype/Reverse Stereotype. Surprise/Twist-in-the-Tail. Tone. Wit/Humor.*

Kessler, Christina. *The Best Beekeeper of Lalibela: A Tale from Africa.* Illus. by Leonard Jenkins. New York: Holiday House, c2006.
> **Other Devices:** *Antithesis. Aphorism. Atmosphere. Foreshadow. Pun. Simile.*

SIMILE

Explicit comparison using "like" or "as" or "than" to show how two unlike things have a common recognizable similarity—"She is sweet as pie."

Borden, Louise. *Across the Blue Pacific: A World War II Story.* Illus. by Robert Andrew Parker. Boston: Houghton Mifflin, c2006.
> **Other Devices:** *Aphorism. Atmosphere. Connotation. Flashback. Flash-Forward. Foreshadow. Imagery. Inference. Motif. Paradox. Parallelism. Theme.*

Bunting, Eve. *Butterfly House.* Illus. by Greg Shed. New York: Scholastic Press, c1999.
> **Other Devices:** *Atmosphere. Connotation. Flash-Forward. Imagery. Internal Rhyme. Paradox. Point-of-View.*

Bunting, Eve. *Pop's Bridge.* Illus. by C. F. Payne. New York: Harcourt, c2006.
> **Other Devices:** *Antithesis. Aphorism. Foreshadow. Metaphor. Symbol. Theme.*

Chen, Chih-Yuan. *The Featherless Chicken.* Alhambra, CA: Heryin Books, c2006.
> **Other Devices:** *Alliteration. Archetype. Connotation. Inference. Internal Rhyme. Irony. Satire. Serendipity. Theme. Tone. Wit/Humor.*

*****Coombs, Kate.** *The Secret-Keeper.* Illus. by Heather M. Solomon. New York: (Atheneum Books for Young Readers) Simon & Schuster, c2006.
> **Other Devices:** *Ambiguity. Connotation. Foreshadow. Imagery. Inference. Irony. Metaphor. Motif. Serendipity. Simile. Symbol. Tone.*

*****Cullen, Lynn.** *Moi & Marie Antoinette.* Illus. by Amy Young. New York: Bloomsbury Publishing, c2006.
> **Other Devices:** *Archetype. Atmosphere. Counterpoint. Foreshadow. Hyperbole. Inference. Motif. Parallelism. Point-of-View. Serendipity. Surprise/Twist-in-the-Tail. Wit/Humor.*

da Costa, Deborah. *Snow in Jerusalem.* Illus. by Cornelius Van Wright & Ying-Hwa Hu. Morton Grove, IL: Albert Whitman, c2001.
> **Other Devices:** *Connotation. Counterpoint. Imagery. Symbol. Theme.*

Eversole, Robyn. *The Gift Stone.* Illus. by Allen Garns. New York: Alfred A. Knopf, c1998.
> **Other Devices:** *Antithesis. Aphorism. Atmosphere. Connotation. Inference. Irony. Metaphor. Motif. Parallelism. Symbol.*

*****Frank, John.** *The Toughest Cowboy, or How the Wild West Was Tamed.* Illus. by Zachary Pullen. New York: Simon & Schuster Books for Young Readers, c2004.
> **Other Devices:** *Allusion. Ambiguity. Aptronym. Atmosphere. Colloquialism. Hyperbole. Inference. Irony. Parallelism. Pun. Solecism. Stereotype/Reverse Stereotype. Tone. Understatement. Wit/Humor.*

*****Franklin, Kristine L.** *The Gift.* Illus. by Barbara Lavallee. San Francisco: Chronicle Books, c1999.
> **Other Devices:** *Ambiguity. Connotation. Foreshadow. Imagery. Inference. Irony. Onomatopoeia. Surprise/Twist-in-The-Tail. Symbol. Theme.*

Garland, Sherry. *My Father's Boat.* Illus. by Ted Rand. New York: Scholastic Press, c1998.
> **Other Devices:** *Antithesis. Aphorism. Connotation. Counterpoint. Imagery. Metaphor. Parallelism. Theme.*

High, Linda Oatman. *Barn Savers.* Illus. by Ted Lewin. Honesdale, PA: Boyds Mills Press, c1999.
> **Other Devices:** *Atmosphere. Connotation. Imagery. Metaphor. Parallelism.*

*****Johnston, Tony.** *Angel City.* Illus. by Carole Byard. New York: (Philomel) Penguin Young Readers Group, c2006.

Other Devices: *Allusion. Ambiguity. Antithesis. Atmosphere. Collo-
quialism. Connotation. Counterpoint. Foreshadow. Imagery. Inference.
Metaphor. Motif. Paradox. Parallelism. Symbol. Theme. Tone. Wit/
Humor.*

Johnston, Tony. *The Barn Owls.* Illus. by Deborah Kogan Ray. Watertown,
MA: Charlesbridge, c2000.

Other Devices: *Atmosphere. Imagery. Metaphor. Motif. Parallelism.
Tone.*

Karon, Jan. *Violet Comes to Stay.* Story by Melanie Cecka. Illus. by Emily
Arnold McCully. New York: (Viking) Penguin Young Readers Group, c2006.

Other Devices: *Alliteration. Aphorism. Connotation. Foreshadow.
Imagery. Inference. Irony. Motif. Onomatopoeia. Point-in-View. Theme.*

Kessler, Christina. *The Best Beekeeper of Lalibela: A Tale from Africa.* Illus.
by Leonard Jenkins. New York: Holiday House, c2006.

Other Devices: *Antithesis. Aphorism. Atmosphere. Foresahdow. Pun.
Serendipity.*

Michelson, Richard. *Across the Alley.* Illus. by E. B. Lewis. New York:
(Penguin Young Readers Group) G. P. Putnam's Sons, c2006.

Other Devices: *Aphorism. Counterpoint. Inference. Irony. Metaphor.
Point-of-View. Stereotype/Reverse Stereotype. Theme.*

Nelson, Vaunda Micheaux. *Almost to Freedom.* Illus. by Colin Bootman.
Minneapolis, MN: (Carolrhoda) Lerner, c2003.

Other Devices: *Allusion. Atmosphere. Colloquialism. Foreshadow.
Hyperbole. Imagery. Inference. Parallelism. Personification. Poetic
Justice. Point-of-View. Understatement.*

Pelley, Kathleen T. *Inventor McGregor.* Illus. by Michael Chesworth. New
York: Farrar, Straus and Giroux, c2006.

Other Devices: *Alliteration. Atmosphere. Connotation. Irony. Paradox. Theme.*

*Raven, Marot Theis. *Night Boat to Freedom.* Illus. by E. B. Lewis. New
York: (Melanie Kroupa Books) Farrar, Straus and Giroux, c2006.

Other Devices: *Aphorism. Atmosphere. Colloquialism. Imagery. Inference. Metaphor. Paradox. Parallelism. Symbol. Theme.*

*Schotter, Roni. *Mama, I'll Give You the World.* Illus. by S. Saelig Gallagher. New York: (Schwartz & Wade) Random House, c2006.

Other Devices: *Ambiguity. Connotation. Foreshadow. Imagery. Inference. Metaphor. Motif. Point-in-View. Symbol. Tone.*

Squires, Janet. *The Gingerbread Cowboy.* Illus. by Holly Berry. New York:
HarperCollins Children's Books, c2006.

Other Devices: *Atmosphere. Colloquialism. Imagery. Irony. Parallelism. Parody. Tone. Wit/Humor.*

*Tingle, Tim. *Crossing Bok Chitto: A Choctaw Tale of Friendship and
Freedom.* Illus. by Jeanne Rorex Bridges. El Paso, TX: Cinco Puntos Press,
c2006.

Other Devices: *Allusion. Antithesis. Aphorism. Counterpoint. Flash-Forward. Foreshadow. Irony. Motif. Paradox. Parallelism. Symbol. Theme.*

Williams, Laura E. *The Best Winds.* Illus. by Eujin Kim Neilan. Honesdale, PA: Boyds Mills Press, c2006.

Other Devices: *Aphorism. Atmosphere. Foreshadow. Inference. Motif. Theme.*

Yolen, Jane. *Raising Yoder's Barn.* Illus. by Bernie Fuchs. New York: Little, Brown and Company, c1998.

Other Devices: *Aphorism. Colloquialism. Imagery. Inference. Metaphor. Motif. Parallelism. Understatement.*

Yorinks, Arthur. *Whitefish Will Rides Again!* Illus. by Mort Drucker. New York: HarperCollins, c1994.

Other Devices: *Alliteration. Archetype. Colloquialism. Hyperbole. Inference. Oxymoron. Satire. Solecism. Tone. Wit/Humor.*

Young, Amy. *Belinda and the Glass Slipper.* New York: (Viking) Penguin Young Readers Group, c2006.

Other Devices: *Allusion. Antihero. Archetype. Counterpoint. Foreshadow. Inference. Irony. Parallelism. Parody. Poetic Justice. Surprise/Twist-in-the-Tail. Theme. Understatement.*

SOLECISM

Deviation from conventional usage in grammar, syntax, or pronunciation.

Crummel, Susan Steven. *Ten Gallon Bart.* Illus. by Dorothy Donohue. Tarrytown, NY: Marshall Cavendish, c2006.

Other Devices: *Allusion. Archetype. Colloquialism. Connotation. Inference. Internal Rhyme. Motif. Parody. Poetic Justice. Pun. Stereotype/Reverse Stereotype. Tone. Wit/Humor.*

*Frank, John. *The Toughest Cowboy, or How the Wild West Was Tamed.* Illus. by Zachary Pullen. New York: Simon & Schuster Books for Young Readers, c2004.

Other Devices: *Allusion. Ambiguity. Aptronym. Atmosphere. Colloquialism. Hyperbole. Inference. Irony. Parallelism. Pun. Simile. Stereotype/Reverse Stereotype. Tone. Understatement. Wit/Humor.*

McElligott, Matthew. *Backbeard and the Birthday Suit.* New York: Walker & Company, c2006.

Other Devices: *Allusion. Ambiguity. Antihero. Antithesis. Archetype. Aphorism. Aprtonym. Atmosphere. Colloquialism. Hyperbole. Irony. Point-of-View. Wit/Humor.*

Nelson, Vaunda Micheaux. *Almost to Freedom.* Illus. by Colin Bootman. Minneapolis, MN: (Carolrhoda) Lerner, c2003.

Other Devices: *Allusion. Atmosphere. Colloquialism. Foreshadow. Hyperbole. Imagery. Inference. Parallelism. Personification. Poetic Justice. Point-of-View. Simile. Understatement.*

Yorinks, Arthur. *Whitefish Will Rides Again!* Illus. by Mort Drucker. New York: HarperCollins, c1994.

> **Other Devices:** *Alliteration. Archetype. Colloquialism. Hyperbole. Inference. Oxymoron. Satire. Simile. Tone. Wit/Humor.*

STEREOTYPE/REVERSE STEREOTYPE

Fixed generalized perceptions or the opposite of the expected.

Bradley, Kimberly Brubaker. *Ballerino Nate.* Illus. by R. W. Alley. New York: (Dial Books for Young Readers) Penguin Young Readers Group, c2006.

> **Other Devices:** *Ambiguity. Archetype. Inference. Motif. Parallelism.*

Crummel, Susan Stevens. *Ten Gallon Bart.* Illus. by Dorothy Donohue. Tarrytown, NY: Marshall Cavendish, c2006.

> **Other Devices:** *Allusion, Archetype. Colloquialism. Connotation. Inference. Internal Rhyme. Motif. Parody. Poetic Justice. Pun. Solecism. Tone. Wit/Humor.*

Edwards, Pamela Duncan. *The Mixed-Up Rooster.* Illus. by Megan Lloyd. New York: HarperCollins Children's Books, c2006.

> **Other Devices:** *Foreshadow. Parallelism. Pun. Serendipity. Theme. Wit/Humor.*

Fleming, Candace. *Muncha! Muncha! Muncha!* Illus. by G. Brian Karas. New York: Atheneum Books for Young Readers, c2002.

> **Other Devices:** *Allusion. Aptronym. Irony. Onomatopoeia. Parallelism.*

*Frank, John. *The Toughest Cowboy, or How the Wild West Was Tamed.* Illus. by Zachary Pullen. New York: Simon & Schuster Books for Young Readers, c2004.

> **Other Devices:** *Allusion. Ambiguity. Aptronym. Atmosphere. Colloquialism. Foreshadow. Hyperbole. Inference. Irony. Parallelism. Pun. Simile. Solecism. Tone. Understatement. Wit/Humor.*

Kasza, Keiko. *Grandpa Toad's Secrets.* New York: G. P. Putnam's Sons, c1995.

> **Other Devices:** *Irony. Motif. Oxymoron. Serendipity. Surprise/Twist-in-the-Tail. Tone. Wit/Humor.*

Kessler, Christina. *The Best Beekeeper of Lalibela: A Tale from Africa.* Illus. by Leonard Jenkins. New York: Holiday House, c2006.

> **Other Devices:** *Antithesis. Aphorism. Atmosphere. Foreshadow. Pun. Serendipity. Simile. Stereotype.*

Michelson, Richard. *Across the Alley.* Illus. by E. B. Lewis. New York: (Penguin Young Readers Group) G. P. Putnam's Sons, c2006.

Other Devices: *Aphorism. Counterpoint. Inference. Irony. Metaphor. Point-of-View. Simile. Theme.*

Stevens, Janet and Susan Stevens Crummel. *Cook-A-Doodle-Doo.* Illus. by Janet Stevens. Orlando, FL: (Voyager Books) Harcourt, c1999.

Other Devices: *Allusion. Colloquialism. Inference. Motif. Parallelism. Pun. Theme.*

SURPRISE/TWIST-IN-THE-TAIL

Sudden unexpected turn of fortune or action.

Bateman, Teresa. *A Plump and Perky Turkey.* Illus. by Jeff Shelly. New York: Marshall Cavendish, c2001.

Other Devices: *Alliteration. Allusion. Ambiguity. Aptronym. Irony. Parallelism. Poetic Justice. Theme. Understatement.*

*****Cullen, Lynn.** *Moi & Marie Antoinette.* Illus. by Amy Young. New York: Bloomsbury Publishing, c2006.

Other Devices: *Archetype. Atmosphere. Counterpoint. Foreshadow. Hyperbole. Inference. Motif. Parallelism. Point-of-View. Serendipity. Simile. Wit/Humor.*

Fleming, Candace. *Muncha! Muncha! Muncha!* Illus. by G. Brian Karas. New York: Atheneum Books for Young Readers, c2002.

Other Devices: *Allusion. Aptronym. Irony. Motif. Onomatopoeia. Parallelism.*

*****Franklin, Kristine L.** *The Gift.* Illus. by Barbara Lavallee. San Francisco: Chronicle Books, c1999.

Other Devices: *Ambiguity. Connotation. Foreshadow. Imagery. Inference. Irony. Onomatopoeia. Simile. Symbol. Theme.*

Kasza, Keiko. *Grandpa Toad's Secrets.* New York: G. P. Putnam's Sons, c1995.

Other Devices: *Irony. Motif. Oxymoron. Serendipity. Stereotype/ Reverse Stereotype. Tone. Wit/Humor.*

*****Lamm, C. Drew.** *Gauchada.* Illus. by Fabian Negrin. New York: Alfred A. Knopf, c2002.

Other Devices: *Antithesis. Atmosphere. Connotation. Flashback. Imagery. Internal Rhyme. Irony. Metaphor. Motif. Parallelism. Theme.*

*****Montserrat, Pep.** *Ms. Rubinstein's Beauty.* New York: Sterling, c2006.

Other Devices: *Antithesis. Atmosphere. Connotation. Counterpoint. Inference. Motif. Parallelism. Theme.*

Young, Amy. *Belinda and the Glass Slipper.* New York: (Viking) Penguin Young Readers Group, c2006.

Other Devices: *Allusion. Antihero. Archetype. Counterpoint. Foreshadow. Inference. Irony. Parallelism. Parody. Poetic Justice. Simile. Theme. Understatement.*

SYMBOL

Additional meaning (of a word or item) beyond itself to represent or stand for a more abstract concept or emotion—a nation's flag is a symbol for its country.

Bunge, Daniela. *The Scarves.* Trans. by Kahryn Bishop. New York: Penguin Young Readers Group, c2006.
> **Other Devices:** *Archetype. Counterpoint. Foreshadow. Inference. Irony.*

Bunting, Eve. *One Green Apple.* Illus. by Ted Lewin. New York: (Clarion Books) Houghton Mifflin, c2006.
> **Other Devices:** *Antithesis. Inference. Theme.*

Bunting, Eve. *Pop's Bridge.* Illus. by C. F. Payne. New York: Harcourt, c2006.
> **Other Devices:** *Antithesis. Aphorism. Foreshadow. Inference. Metaphor. Simile. Theme.*

*Coombs, Kate. *The Secret-Keeper.* Illus. by Heather M. Solomon. New York: (Atheneum Books for Young Readers) Simon & Schuster, c2006.
> **Other Devices:** *Ambiguity. Connotation. Foreshadow. Imagery. Inference. Irony. Metaphor. Motif. Serendipity. Simile. Symbol. Tone.*

da Costa, Deborah. *Snow in Jerusalem.* Illus. by Cornelius Van Wright & Ying-Hwa Hu. Morton Grove, IL: Albert Whitman, c2001.
> **Other Devices:** *Connotation. Counterpoint. Imagery. Simile. Theme.*

Eversole, Robyn. *The Gift Stone.* Illus. by Allen Garns. New York: Alfred A. Knopf, c1998.
> **Other Devices:** *Antithesis. Aphorism. Atmosphere. Connotation. Inference. Irony. Metaphor. Motif. Parallelism. Simile.*

*Franklin, Kristine L. *The Gift.* Illus. by Barbara Lavallee. San Francisco: Chronicle Books, c1999.
> **Other Devices:** *Ambiguity. Connotation. Foreshadow. Imagery. Inference. Irony. Onomatopoeia. Simile. Surprise/Twist-in-the-Tail. Theme.*

Johnson, Lindan Lee. *Dream Jar.* Illus. by Serena Curmi. New York: Houghton Mifflin, c2005.
> **Other Devices:** *Allusion. Antithesis. Foreshadow. Inference. Motif. Parallelism. Understatement.*

*Johnston, Tony. *Angel City.* Illus. by Carole Byard. New York: (Philomel) Penguin Young Readers Group, c2006.
> **Other Devices:** *Allusion. Ambiguity. Antithesis. Atmosphere. Colloquialism. Connotation. Counterpoint. Foreshadow. Imagery. Inference. Metaphor. Motif. Paradox. Parallelism. Simile. Theme. Tone. Wit/Humor.*

Lee-Tai, Amy. *A Place Where Sunflowers Grow.* Illus. by Felicia Hoshino. San Francisco: Children's Book Press, c2006.
> **Other Devices:** *Aphorism. Atmosphere. Connotation. Inference. Motif. Theme.*

*Raven, Marot Theis. *Night Boat to Freedom*. Illus. by E. B. Lewis. New York: (Melanie Kroupa Books) Farrar, Straus and Giroux, c2006.
> Other Devices: *Aphorism. Atmosphere. Colloquialism. Imagery. Inference. Metaphor. Paradox. Parallelism. Simile. Theme.*

*Schotter, Roni. *Mama, I'll Give You the World*. Illus. by S. Saelig Gallagher. New York: (Schwartz & Wade) Random House, c2006.
> Other Devices: *Ambiguity. Connotation. Foreshadow. Imagery. Inference. Metaphor. Motif. Point-of-View. Simile. Tone.*

*Tingle, Tim. *Crossing Bok Chitto: A Choctaw Tale of Friendship and Freedom*. Illus. by Jeanne Rorex Bridges. El Paso, TX: Cinco Puntos Press, c2006.
> Other Devices: *Allusion. Antithesis. Aphorism. Counterpoint. Flash-Forward. Foreshadow. Irony. Motif. Paradox. Parallelism. Simile. Theme.*

THEME

Underlying truth or meaning that emerges from the text.

Arnosky, Jim. *Grandfather Buffalo*. New York: G. P. Putnam's Sons, c2006.
> Other Devices: *Atmosphere. Foreshadow. Inference. Motif.*

Asher, Sandy. *Too Many Frogs!* Illus. by Keith Graves. New York: (Philomel Books) Penguin Young Readers Group, c2005.
> Other Devices: *Allusion. Aphorism. Internal Rhyme. Irony. Parallelism. Tone.*

Auch, Mary Jane. *Hen Lake*. New York: Holiday House, c1995.
> Other Devices: *Allusion. Aphorism. Aptronym. Archetype. Colloquialism. Connotation. Inference. Motif.*

Bateman, Teresa. *A Plump and Perky Turkey*. Illus. by Jeff Shelly. New York: Marshall Cavendish, c2001.
> Other Devices: *Alliteration. Allusion. Ambiguity. Aptronym. Irony. Parallelism. Poetic Justice. Surprise/Twist-in-the-Tail. Understatement.*

Borden, Louise. *Across the Blue Pacific: A World War II Story*. Illus. by Robert Andrew Parker. Boston: Houghton Mifflin, c2006.
> Other Devices: *Aphorism. Atmosphere. Connotation. Flashback. Flash-Forward. Foreshadow. Imagery. Inference. Motif. Paradox. Parallelism. Simile.*

Bowen, Anne. *The Great Math Tattle Battle*. Illus. by Jaime Zollars. Morton Grove, IL: Albert Whitman, c2006.
> Other Devices: *Connotation. Paradox, Parallelism. Poetic Justice.*

Bunting, Eve. *One Green Apple*. Illus. by Ted Lewin. New York: (Clarion Books) Houghton Mifflin, c2006.
> Other Devices: *Antithesis. Inference. Symbol.*

Bunting, Eve. *Pop's Bridge*. Illus. by C. F. Payne. New York: Harcourt, c2006.

Other Devices: *Antithesis. Aphorism. Foreshadow. Inference. Metaphor. Simile. Symbol.*

Bynum, Janie. *Nutmeg and Barley: A Budding Friendship.* Cambridge, MA: Candlewick Press, c2006.

   Other Devices: *Ambiguity. Antithesis. Foreshadow. Parallelism.*

Chen, Chih-Yuan. *The Featherless Chicken.* Alhambra, CA: Heryin Books, c2006.

   Other Devices: *Alliteration. Archetype. Connotation. Inference. Internal Rhyme. Irony. Satire. Serendipity. Simile. Tone. Wit/Humor.*

da Costa, Deborah. *Snow in Jerusalem.* Illus. by Cornelius Van Wright & Ying-Hwa Hu. Morton Grove, IL: Albert Whitman, c2001.

   Other Devices: *Connotation. Counterpoint. Imagery. Simile. Symbol.*

Edwards, Pamela Duncan. *The Mixed-Up Rooster.* Illus. by Megan Lloyd. New York: HarperCollins Children's Books, c2006.

   Other Devices: *Foreshadow. Parallelism. Pun. Serendipity. Stereotype/ Reverse Stereotype. Wit/Humor.*

*Franklin, Kristine L. *The Gift.* Illus. by Barbara Lavallee. San Francisco: Chronicle Books, c1999.

   Other Devices: *Ambiguity. Connotation. Foreshadow. Imagery. Inference. Irony. Onomatopoeia. Simile. Surprise/Twist-in-the-Tail. Symbol.*

Garland, Sherry. *My Father's Boat.* Illus. by Ted Rand. New York: Scholastic Press, c1998.

   Other Devices: *Antithesis. Aphorism. Connotation. Counterpoint. Imagery. Metaphor. Parallelism. Simile.*

Henkes, Kevin. *Kitten's First Full Moon.* New York: (Greenwillow Books) HarperCollins, c2004.

   Other Devices: *Irony. Motif.*

*Johnston, Tony. *Angel City.* Illus. by Carole Byard. New York: (Philomel) Penguin Young Readers Group, c2006.

   Other Devices: *Allusion. Ambiguity. Antithesis. Atmosphere. Colloquialism. Connotation. Counterpoint. Foreshadow. Imagery. Inference. Metaphor. Motif. Paradox. Parallelism. Simile. Symbol. Tone. Wit/ Humor.*

Karon, Jan. *Violet Comes to Stay.* Story by Melanie Cecka. Illus. by Emily Arnold McCully. New York: (Viking) Penguin Young Readers Group, c2006.

   Other Devices: *Alliteration. Aphorism. Connotation. Foreshadow. Imagery. Inference. Irony. Motif. Onomatopoeia. Point-of-View. Simile.*

*Lamm, C. Drew. *Gauchada.* Illus. by Fabian Negrin. New York: Alfred A. Knopf, c2002.

   Other Devices: *Antithesis. Atmosphere. Connotation. Flashback. Imagery. Internal Rhyme. Irony. Metaphor. Motif. Parallelism. Surprise/ Twist-in-the-Tail.*

Lasky, Kathryn. *Pirate Bob.* Illus. by David Clark. Watertown, MA: Charles-bridge, c2006.

> **Other Devices:** *Antihero. Antithesis. Archetype. Atmosphere. Black Humor. Colloquialism. Connotation. Hyperbole. Imagery. Inference. Motif. Parallelism.*

Lee-Tai, Amy. *A Place Where Sunflowers Grow.* Illus. by Felicia Hoshino. San Francisco: Children's Book Press, c2006.

> **Other Devices:** *Aphorism. Atmosphere. Connotation. Inference. Motif. Symbol.*

Michelson, Richard. *Across the Alley.* Illus. by E. B. Lewis. New York: (Penguin Young Readers Group) G. P. Putnam's Sons, c2006.

> **Other Devices:** *Aphorism. Counterpoint. Inference. Irony. Metaphor. Point-of-View. Simile. Stereotype/Reverse Stereotype.*

*****Montserrat, Pep.** *Ms. Rubinstein's Beauty.* New York: Sterling, c2006.

> **Other Devices:** *Antithesis. Atmosphere. Connotation. Counterpoint. Inference. Motif. Parallelism. Surprise/Twist-in-the-Tail.*

Pearson, Tracey Campbell. *Bob.* New York: Farrar, Straus and Giroux, c2002.

> **Other Devices:** *Ambiguity. Irony. Onomatopoeia. Tone. Wit/Humor.*

Pelley, Kathleen T. *Inventor McGregor.* Illus. by Michael Chesworth. New York: Farrar, Straus and Giroux, c2006.

> **Other Devices:** *Alliteration. Atmosphere. Connotation. Irony. Paradox. Simile.*

Pfister, Marcus. *Holey Moley.* Trans. by J. Alison James. New York: North-South Books, c2006.

> **Other Devices:** *Antithesis. Counterpoint. Irony. Paradox. Parallelism.*

*****Raven, Marot Theis.** *Night Boat to Freedom.* Illus. by E. B. Lewis. New York: (Melanie Kroupa Books) Farrar, Straus and Giroux, c2006.

> **Other Devices:** *Aphorism. Atmosphere. Colloquialism. Imagery. Inference. Metaphor. Paradox. Parallelism. Simile.*

Recorvits, Helen. *Yoon and the Christmas Mitten.* Illus. by Gabi Swaiatow-ska. New York: (Frances Foster Books) Farrar, Straus and Giroux, c2006.

> **Other Devices:** *Ambiguity. Antithesis. Atmosphere. Colloquialism. Counterpoint. Foreshadow. Inference. Parallelism. Point-of-View.*

*****Reynolds, Peter H.** *So Few of Me.* Cambridge, MA: Candlewick Press, c2006.

> **Other Devices:** *Satire.*

Stevens, Janet and Susan Stevens Crummel. *Cook-A-Doodle-Doo.* Illus. by Janet Stevens. Orlando, FL: (Voyager Books) Harcourt, c1999.

> **Other Devices:** *Allusion. Colloquialism. Inference. Motif. Parallelism. Pun. Stereotype/Reverse Stereotype.*

*****Tingle, Tim.** *Crossing Bok Chitto: A Choctaw Tale of Friendship and Freedom.* Illus. by Jeanne Rorex Bridges. El Paso, TX: Cinco Puntos Press, c2006.

Other Devices: *Allusion. Antithesis. Aphorism. Counterpoint. Flash-Forward. Foreshadow. Irony. Motif. Paradox. Parallelism. Simile. Symbol.*

Williams, Laura E. *The Best Winds.* Illus. by Eujin Kim Neilan. Honesdale, PA: Boyds Mills Press, c2006.

Other Devices: *Aphorism. Atmosphere. Foreshadow. Inference. Motif. Simile.*

Wojciechowski, Susan. *A Fine St. Patrick's Day.* Illus. by Tom Curry. New York: Random House, c2004.

Other Devices: *Alliteration. Colloquialism. Inference. Irony.*

Young, Amy. *Belinda and the Glass Slipper.* New York: (Viking) Penguin Young Readers Group, c2006.

Other Devices: *Allusion. Antihero. Archetype. Counterpoint. Foreshadow. Inference. Irony. Parallelism. Parody. Poetic Justice. Simile. Surprise/Twist-in-the-Tail. Understatement.*

*****Young, Ed.** *I, Doko: The Tale of a Basket.* New York: Philomel, c2004.

Other Devices: *Aphorism. Foreshadow. Inference. Personification. Poetic Justice. Point-of-View. Tone.*

TONE

Writer's pervasive attitude toward his or her subject and/or audience by attitude or words that convey banter, sarcasm, sensitivity, passion, gentleness, contempt, and so on.

*****Adler, David A.** *The Babe and I.* Illus. by Terry Widdener. New York: (Gulliver Books) Harcourt Brace & Co., c1999.

Other Devices: *Ambiguity. Antithesis. Foreshadow. Inference. Irony. Paradox.*

Amico, Tom and James Proimos. *Raisin and Grape.* Illus. by Andy Snair. New York: (Dial Books for Young Readers) Penguin Young Readers Group, c2006.

Other Devices: *Antithesis. Connotation. Hyperbole. Inference. Pun. Understatement. Wit/Humor.*

Asher, Sandy. Too Many Frogs! Illus. by Keith Graves. New York: (Philomel Books) Penguin Young Readers Group, c2005.

Other Devices: *Allusion. Aphorism. Internal Rhyme. Irony. Parallelism. Theme.*

Bang, Molly. *In My Heart.* New York: Little, Brown and Company, c2006.

Other Devices: *Inference. Motif.*

Chen, Chih-Yuan. *The Featherless Chicken.* Alhambra, CA: Heryin Books, c2006.

Other Devices: *Alliteration. Archetype. Connotation. Inference. Internal Rhyme. Irony. Satire. Serendipity. Simile. Theme. Wit/Humor.*

*Coombs, Kate. *The Secret-Keeper.* Illus. by Heather M. Solomon. New York: (Atheneum Books for Young Readers) Simon & Schuster, c2006.
> **Other Devices:** *Ambiguity. Connotation. Foreshadow. Imagery. Inference. Irony. Metaphor. Motif. Serendipity. Simile. Symbol.*

Crummel, Susan Stevens. *Ten Gallon Bart.* Illus. by Dorothy Donohue. Tarrytown, NY: Marshall Cavendish, c2006.
> **Other Devices:** *Allusion. Archetype. Colloquialism. Connotation. Inference. Internal Rhyme. Motif. Parody. Poetic Justice. Pun. Solecism. Stereotype/Reverse Stereotype. Wit/Humor.*

*Frank, John. *The Toughest Cowboy, or How the Wild West Was Tamed.* Illus. by Zachary Pullen. New York: Simon & Schuster Books for Young Readers, c2004.
> **Other Devices:** *Allusion. Ambiguity. Aptronym. Atmosphere. Colloquialism. Foreshadow. Hyperbole. Inference. Irony. Parallelism. Pun. Simile. Solecism. Stereotype/Reverse Stereotype. Understatement. Wit/Humor.*

*Johnston, Tony. *Angel City.* Illus. by Carole Byard. New York: (Philomel) Penguin Young Readers Group, c2006.
> **Other Devices:** *Allusion. Ambiguity. Antithesis. Atmosphere. Colloquialism. Connotation. Counterpoint. Foreshadow. Imagery. Inference. Metaphor. Motif. Paradox. Parallelism. Simile. Symbol. Theme. Wit/Humor.*

Johnston, Tony. *The Barn Owls.* Illus. by Deborah Kogan Ray. Watertown, MA: Charlesbridge, c2000.
> **Other Devices:** *Atmosphere. Imagery. Metaphor. Motif. Parallelism. Simile.*

Kasza, Keiko. *Grandpa Toad's Secrets.* New York: G. P. Putnam's Sons, c1995.
> **Other Devices:** *Irony. Motif. Oxymoron. Serendipity. Stereotype/Reverse Stereotype. Surprise/Twist-in-the-Tail. Tone.*

Palatini, Margie. *Bad Boys Get Cookie!* Illus. by Henry Cole. New York: HarperCollins Children's Books, c2006.
> **Other Devices:** *Allusion. Foreshadow. Inference. Motif. Parallelism. Poetic Justice. Pun. Understatement. Wit/Humor.*

Pearson, Tracey Campbell. *Bob.* New York: Farrar, Straus and Giroux, c2002.
> **Other Devices:** *Ambiguity. Irony. Onomatopoeia. Theme. Wit/Humor.*

*Schotter, Roni. *Mama, I'll Give You the World.* Illus. by S. Saelig Gallagher. New York: (Schwartz & Wade) Random House, c2006.
> **Other Devices:** *Ambiguity. Connotation. Foreshadow. Imagery. Inference. Metaphor. Motif. Point-of-View. Simile. Symbol.*

Smith, Cynthia Leitich and Greg Smith. *Santa Knows.* Illus. by Steve Bjorkman. New York: (Dutton Children's Books) Penguin, c2006.
> **Other Devices:** *Allusion. Ambiguity. Aptronym. Foreshadow. Hyperbole. Irony. Motif. Parallelism. Poetic Justice. Wit/Humor.*

Squires, Janet. *The Gingerbread Cowboy*. Illus. by Holly Berry. New York: HarperCollins Children's Books, c2006.
   Other Devices: *Atmosphere. Colloquialism. Imagery. Irony. Parallelism. Parody. Simile. Wit/Humor.*
Teague, Mark. *Pigsty*. New York: Scholastic, c1994.
   Other Devices: *Ambiguity. Aphorism. Foreshadow. Pun.*
Yorinks, Arthur. *Whitefish Will Rides Again!* Illus. by Mort Drucker. New York: HarperCollins, c1994.
   Other Devices: *Alliteration. Archetype. Colloquialism. Hyperbole. Inference. Oxymoron. Satire. Simile. Solecism. Wit/Humor.*
*Young, Ed. *I, Doko: The Tale of a Basket*. New York: Philomel, c2004.
   Other Devices: *Aphorism. Foreshadow. Inference. Personification. Poetic Justice. Point-of-View. Theme.*

UNDERSTATEMENT

Under-expressing something as less than it really is—"The sinking boat put a damper on their outing."

Amico, Tom and James Proimos. *Raisin and Grape*. Illus. by Andy Snair. New York: (Dial Books for Young Readers) Penguin Young Readers Group, c2006.
   Other Devices: *Antithesis. Connotation. Hyperbole. Inference. Pun. Tone. Wit/Humor.*
*Bateman, Teresa. *Keeper of Soles*. Illus. by Diego Herrera (Yayo). New York: Holiday House, c2006.
   Other Devices: *Ambiguity. Aphorism. Black Humor. Colloquialism. Connotation. Imagery. Inference. Irony. Paradox. Parallelism. Pun.*
Bateman, Teresa. *A Plump and Perky Turkey*. Illus. by Jeff Shelly. New York: Marshall Cavendish, c2001.
   Other Devices: *Alliteration. Allusion. Ambiguity. Aptronym. Irony. Parallelism. Poetic Justice. Surprise/Twist-in-the-Tail. Theme.*
*Frank, John. *The Toughest Cowboy, or How the Wild West Was Tamed*. Illus. by Zachary Pullen. New York: Simon & Schuster Books for Young Readers, c2004.
   Other Devices: *Allusion. Ambiguity. Aptronym. Atmosphere. Colloquialism. Foreshadow. Hyperbole. Inference. Irony. Parallelism. Pun. Simile. Solecism. Stereotype/Reverse Stereotype. Tone. Wit/Humor.*
Johnson, Lindan Lee. *Dream Jar*. Illus. by Serena Curmi. New York: Houghton Mifflin, c2005.
   Other Devices: *Allusion. Antithesis. Foreshadow. Inference. Motif. Parallelism. Symbol.*
Krensky, Stephen. *How Santa Lost His Job*. Illus. by S. D. Schindler. New York: (Aladdin) Simon & Schuster, c2001.

Other Devices: *Foreshadow. Inference. Irony. Paradox. Satire.*

Manushkin, Fran. *The Shivers in the Fridge.* Illus. by Paul O. Zelinsky. New York: (Dutton Children's Books) Penguin Young Readers Group, c2006.

>**Other Devices:** *Inference. Motif. Parallelism. Point-of-View. Pun. Wit/ Humor.*

Nelson, Vaunda Micheaux. *Almost to Freedom.* Illus. by Colin Bootman. Minneapolis, MN: (Carolrhoda) Lerner, c2003.

>**Other Devices:** *Allusion. Atmosphere. Colloquialism. Foreshadow. Hyperbole. Imagery. Inference. Parallelism. Personification. Poetic Justice. Point-of-View. Simile. Solecism.*

Palatini, Margie. *Bad Boys Get Cookie!* Illus. by Henry Cole. New York: HarperCollins Children's Books, c2006.

>**Other Devices:** *Allusion. Foreshadow. Inference. Motif. Parallelism. Poetic Justice. Pun. Tone. Wit/Humor.*

*Wood, Nancy. *Mr. and Mrs. God in the Creation Kitchen.* Illus. by Timothy Basil Ering. Cambridge, MA: Candlewick Press, c2006.

>**Other Devices:** *Allusion. Antithesis. Foreshadow. Hyperbole. Imagery. Inference. Onomatopoeia. Parallelism. Pun. Satire. Wit/Humor.*

Yolen, Jane. *Raising Yoder's Barn.* Illus. by Bernie Fuchs. New York: Little, Brown and Company, c1998.

>**Other Devices:** *Aphorism. Colloquialism. Imagery. Inference. Metaphor. Motif. Parallelism. Simile.*

Young, Amy. *Belinda and the Glass Slipper.* New York: (Viking) Penguin Young Readers Group, c2006.

>**Other Devices:** *Allusion. Antihero. Archetype. Counterpoint. Foreshadow. Inference. Irony. Parallelism. Parody. Poetic Justice. Simile. Surprise/Twist-in-the-Tail. Theme.*

WIT/HUMOR

Perceiving incongruous relationships and expressing them amusingly for purposes of delight and surprise.

Amico, Tom and James Proimos. *Raisin and Grape.* Illus. by Andy Snair. New York: (Dial Books for Young Readers) Penguin Young Readers Group, c2006.

>**Other Devices:** *Antithesis. Connotation. Hyperbole. Inference. Pun. Tone. Understatement.*

Chen, Chih-Yuan. *The Featherless Chicken.* Alhambra, CA: Heryin Books, c2006.

>**Other Devices:** *Alliteration. Archetype. Connotation. Inference. Internal Rhyme. Irony. Satire. Serendipity. Simile. Theme. Tone.*

Crummel, Susan Stevens. *Ten Gallon Bart.* Illus. by Dorothy Donohue. Tarrytown, NY: Marshall Cavendish, c2006.

Other Devices: *Allusion. Archetype. Colloquialism. Connotation. Inference. Internal Rhyme. Motif. Parody. Poetic Justice. Pun. Solecism. Stereotype/Reverse Stereotype. Tone.*

*Cullen, Lynn. *Moi & Marie Antoinette*. Illus. by Amy Young. New York: Bloomsbury Publishing, c2006.

Other Devices: *Archetype. Atmosphere. Counterpoint. Foreshadow. Hyperbole. Inference. Motif. Parallelism. Point-of-View. Serendipity. Simile. Surprise/Twist-in-the-Tail.*

Edwards, Pamela Duncan. *The Mixed-Up Rooster.* Illus. by Megan Lloyd. New York: HarperCollins Children's Books, c2006.

Other Devices: *Foreshadow. Parallelism. Pun. Serendipity. Stereotype/ Reverse Stereotype. Theme.*

*Frank, John. *The Toughest Cowboy, or How the Wild West Was Tamed.* Illus. by Zachary Pullen. New York: Simon & Schuster Books for Young Readers, c2004.

Other Devices: *Allusion. Ambiguity. Aptronym. Atmosphere. Colloquialism. Foreshadow. Hyperbole. Inference. Irony. Parallelism. Pun. Simile. Solecism. Stereotype/Reverse Stereotype. Tone. Understatement.*

Gerstein, Mordicai. *Carolinda Clatter!* New Milford, CT: (Roaring Brook Press) Holtzbrinck, c2005.

Other Devices: *Allusion. Antithesis. Aptronym. Counterpoint. Flash-Forward. Foreshadow. Hyperbole. Internal Rhyme. Irony. Metaphor. Motif. Parallelism.*

James, Simon. *The Wild Woods.* Cambridge, MA: Candlewick Press, c1993.

Other Devices: *Inference. Motif. Point-of-View.*

*Johnston, Tony. *Angel City.* Illus. by Carole Byard. New York: (Philomel) Penguin Young Readers Group, c2006.

Other Devices: *Allusion. Ambiguity. Antithesis. Atmosphere. Colloquialism. Connotation. Counterpoint. Foreshadow. Imagery. Inference. Metaphor. Motif. Paradox. Parallelism. Simile. Symbol. Theme.*

Kasza, Keiko. *Grandpa Toad's Secrets.* New York: G. P. Putnam's Sons, c1995.

Other Devices: *Irony. Motif. Oxymoron. Serendipity. Stereotype/ Reverse Stereotype. Surprise/Twist-in-the-Tail. Tone.*

McClintock, Barbara. *Adele & Simon.* New York: (Frances Foster Books) Farrar, Straus and Giroux, c2006.

Other Devices: *Aptronym. Foreshadow. Inference. Parallelism.*

McElligott, Matthew. *Backbeard and the Birthday Suit.* New York: Walker & Company, c2006.

Other Devices: *Allusion. Ambiguity. Antihero. Antithesis. Aphorism. Aptronym. Archetype. Atmosphere. Colloquialism. Hyperbole. Irony. Point-of-View. Solecism.*

Manushkin, Fran. *The Shivers in the Fridge.* Illus. by Paul O. Zelinsky. New York: (Dutton Children's Books) Penguin Young Readers Group, c2006.

  Other Devices: *Inference. Motif. Parallelism. Point-of-View. Pun. Understatement.*

Palatini, Margie. *Bad Boys Get Cookie!* Illus. by Henry Cole. New York: HarperCollins Children's Books, c2006.

  Other Devices: *Allusion. Foreshadow. Inference. Motif. Parallelism. Poetic Justice. Pun. Tone. Understatement.*

Pearson, Tracey Campbell. *Bob.* New York: Farrar, Straus and Giroux, c2002.

  Other Devices: *Ambiguity. Irony. Onomatopoeia. Theme. Tone.*

Smith, Cynthia Leitich and Greg Smith. *Santa Knows.* Illus. by Steve Bjorkman. New York: (Dutton Children's Books) Penguin, c2006.

  Other Devices: *Allusion. Ambiguity. Aptronym. Foreshadow. Hyperbole. Irony. Motif. Parallelism. Poetic Justice. Tone.*

Squires, Janet. *The Gingerbread Cowboy.* Illus. by Holly Berry. New York: HarperCollins Children's Books, c2006.

  Other Devices: *Atmosphere. Colloquialism. Imagery. Irony. Parallelism. Parody. Simile. Tone.*

*Wood, Nancy. *Mr. and Mrs. God in the Creation Kitchen.* Illus. by Timothy Basil Ering. Cambridge, MA: Candlewick Press, c2006.

  Other Devices: *Allusion. Antithesis. Foreshadow. Hyperbole. Imagery. Inference. Onomatopoeia. Parallelism. Pun. Satire. Understatement.*

Yolen, Jane. *Harvest Home.* Illus. by Greg Shed. New York: (Silver Whistle) Harcourt, c2002.

  Other Devices: *Atmosphere. Imagery. Internal Rhyme. Metaphor. Motif. Parallelism.*

Yorinks, Arthur. *Whitefish Will Rides Again!* Illus. by Mort Drucker. New York: HarperCollins, c1994.

  Other Devices: *Alliteration. Archetype. Colloquialism. Hyperbole. Inference. Oxymoron. Satire. Simile. Solecism. Tone.*

APPENDIX 4:
RESOURCES GROUPED BY ART STYLE

❖❖❖❖❖❖❖❖❖❖❖

Cartoon
Expressionism
Folk

Impressionism
Naive

Realism
Surrealism

CARTOON

Simple or detailed lively line drawings with imaginative, possibly exaggerated features, colored or not.

Allen, Jonathan. *I'm Not Cute!* New York: Hyperion Books for Children, c2005. [Also: *Expressionism*]

Amico, Tom and James Proimos. *Raisin and Grape.* Illus. by Andy Snair. New York: (Dial Books for Young Readers) Penguin Young Readers Group, c2006. [Also: *Expressionism*]

Ashman, Linda. *Desmond and the Naughtybugs.* Illus. by Anik McGrory. New York: (Dutton Children's Books) Penguin Young Readers Group, c2006.

Atwood, Margaret. *Up in the Tree.* Toronto, Ontario: Greenwood Books/House of Anansi Press, c1978, 2006.

Auch, Mary Jane. *Hen Lake.* New York: Holiday House, c1995. [Also: *Expressionism*]

Bang, Molly. *In My Heart.* New York: Little, Brown and Company, c2006. [Also: *Expressionism, Surrealism*]

*Bateman, Teresa. *Keeper of Soles.* Illus. by Diego Herrera (Yayo). New York: Holiday House, c2006. [Also: *Surrealism*]

Bateman, Teresa. *A Plump and Perky Turkey.* Illus. by Jeff Shelly. New York: Marshall Cavendish, c2001. [Also: *Expressionism*]

Bowen, Anne. *The Great Math Tattle Battle*. Illus. by Jaime Zollars. Morton Grove, IL: Albert Whitman, c2006. [Also: *Expressionism, Naive*]

Bradley, Kimberly Brubaker. *Ballerino Nate*. Illus. by R. W. Alley. New York: (Dial Books for Young Readers) Penguin Young Readers Group, c2006.

Broach, Elise. *Cousin John Is Coming!* Illus. by Nate Lilly. New York: (Dial Books for Young Readers) Penguin Young Readers Group, c2006.

Chen, Chih-Yuan. *The Featherless Chicken*. Alhambra, CA: Heryin Books, c2006. [Also: *Expressionism, Folk*]

Danziger, Paula. *Barfburger Baby, I Was Here First*. Illus. by G. Brian Karas. New York: (Penguin Young Readers Group) G. P. Putnam's Sons, c2004.

Edwards, Pamela Duncan. *The Mixed-Up Rooster*. Illus. by Megan Lloyd. New York: HarperCollins Children's Books, c2006. [Also: *Expressionism*]

Fleming, Candace. *Muncha! Muncha! Muncha!* Illus. by G. Brian Karas. New York: Atheneum Books for Young Readers, c2002.

Gerstein, Mordicai. *Carolinda Clatter!* New Milford, CT: (Roaring Brook Press) Holtzbrinck, c2005. [Also: *Expressionism*]

Goode, Diane. *The Most Perfect Spot*. New York: HarperCollins Children's Books, c2006.

Henkes, Kevin. *Kitten's First Full Moon*. New York: (Greenwillow Books) HarperCollins, c2004.

James, Simon. *The Wild Woods*. Cambridge, MA: Candlewick Press, c1993.

Jeffers, Oliver. *Lost and Found*. New York: (Philomel) Penguin Young Readers Group, c2005.

Jenkins, Emily. *That New Animal*. Illus. by Pierce Pratt. New York: (Frances Foster Books) Farrar, Straus and Giroux, c2005. [Also: *Expressionism*]

Johnson, Lindan Lee. *Dream Jar*. Illus. by Serena Curmi. New York: Houghton Mifflin, c2005. [Also: *Expressionism*]

Karon, Jan. *Violet Comes to Stay*. Story by Melanie Cecka. Illus. by Emily Arnold McCully. New York: (Viking) Penguin Young Readers Group, c2006.

Kasza, Keiko. *Grandpa Toad's Secrets*. New York: G. P. Putnam's Sons, c1995.

Krensky, Stephen. *How Santa Lost His Job*. Illus. by S. D. Schindler. New York: (Aladdin) Simon & Schuster, c2001.

Lasky, Kathryn. *Pirate Bob*. Illus. by David Clark. Watertown, MA: Charlesbridge, c2006. [Also: *Expressionism*]

Lee-Tai, Amy. *A Place Where Sunflowers Grow*. Illus. by Felicia Hoshino. San Francisco: Children's Book Press, c2006. [Also: *Folk*]

Manushkin, Fran. *The Shivers in the Fridge*. Illus. by Paul O. Zelinsky. New York: (Dutton Children's Books) Penguin Young Readers Group, c2006. [Also: *Expressionism*]

McClintock, Barbara. *Adele & Simon*. New York: (Frances Foster Books) Farrar, Straus and Giroux, c2006.

McElligott, Matthew. *Backbeard and the Birthday Suit*. New York: Walker & Company, c2006.

Palatini, Margie. *Bad Boys Get Cookie!* Illus. by Henry Cole. New York: HarperCollins Children's Books, c2006.

Pearson, Tracey Campbell. *Bob.* New York: Farrar, Straus and Giroux, c2002.

Pelley, Kathleen T. *Inventor McGregor.* Illus. by Michael Chesworth. New York: Farrar, Straus and Giroux, c2006.

Pfister, Marcus. *Holey Moley.* Trans. by J. Alison James. New York: North-South Books, c2006.

*Reynolds, Peter H. *So Few of Me.* Cambridge, MA: Candlewick Press, c2006.

Sauer, Tammi. *Cowboy Camp.* Illus. by Mike Reed. New York: Sterling, c2005. [Also: *Expressionism*]

*Schotter, Roni. *Mama, I'll Give You the World.* Illus. by S. Saelig Gallagher. New York: (Schwartz & Wade) Random House, c2006. [Also: *Expressionism*]

Smith, Cynthia Leitich and Greg Smith. *Santa Knows.* Illus. by Steve Bjorkman. New York: (Dutton Children's Books) Penguin, c2006. [Also: *Expressionism*]

Smith, Linda. *Mrs. Crump's Cat.* Illus. by David Roberts. New York: HarperCollins Children's Books, c2006.

Squires, Janet. *The Gingerbread Cowboy.* Illus. by Holly Berry. New York: HarperCollins Children's Books, c2006. [Also: *Folk*]

Stevens, Janet and Susan Stevens Crummel. *Cook-A-Doodle-Doo.* Illus. by Janet Stevens. Orlando, FL: (Voyager Books) Harcourt, c1999. [Also: *Expressionism*]

Teague, Mark. *Pigsty.* New York: Scholastic, c1994.

*Wood, Nancy. *Mr. and Mrs. God in the Creation Kitchen.* Illus. by Timothy Basil Ering. Cambridge, MA: Candlewick Press, c2006. [Also: *Expressionism*]

Yorinks, Arthur. *Whitefish Will Rides Again!* Illus. by Mort Drucker. New York: HarperCollins, c1994. [Also: *Expressionism*]

EXPRESSIONISM

Exaggerated or distorted proportions, perspectives, and color, to produce emotional impact and special effect.

*Adler, David A. *The Babe and I.* Illus. by Terry Widdener. New York: (Gulliver Books) Harcourt Brace & Co., c1999.

Allen, Jonathan. *I'm Not Cute!* New York: Hyperion Books for Children, c2005. [Also: *Cartoon*]

Amico, Tom and James Proimos. *Raisin and Grape.* Illus. by Andy Snair. New York: (Dial Books for Young Readers) Penguin Young Readers Group, c2006. [Also: *Cartoon*]

Asher, Sandy. *Too Many Frogs!* Illus. by Keith Graves. New York: (Philomel Books) Penguin Young Readers Group, c2005.

Ashman, Linda. *Desmond and the Naughtybugs.* Illus. by Anik McGrory. New York: (Dutton Children's Books) Penguin Young Readers Group, c2006.

Auch, Mary Jane. *Hen Lake.* New York: Holiday House, c1995. [Also: *Cartoon*]

Bang, Molly. *In My Heart.* New York: Little, Brown and Company, c2006. [Also: *Cartoon, Surrealism*]

Bateman, Teresa. *A Plump and Perky Turkey.* Illus. by Jeff Shelly. New

York: Marshall Cavendish, c2001. [Also: *Cartoon*]

Bernstein, Dan. *The Tortoise and the Hare Race Again.* Illus. by Andrew Glass. New York: Holiday House, c2006.

Bowen, Anne. *The Great Math Tattle Battle.* Illus. by Jaime Zollars. Morton Grove, IL: Albert Whitman, c2006. [Also: *Cartoon, Naive*]

Bunting, Eve. *Pop's Bridge.* Illus. by C. F. Payne. New York: Harcourt, c2006. [Also: *Realism*]

Bynum, Janie. *Nutmeg and Barley: A Budding Friendship.* Cambridge, MA: Candlewick Press, c2006.

Chen, Chih-Yuan. *The Featherless Chicken.* Alhambra, CA: Heryin Books, c2006. [Also: *Cartoon, Folk*]

*Coombs, Kate. *The Secret-Keeper.* Illus. by Heather M. Solomon. New York: (Atheneum Books for Young Readers) Simon & Schuster, c2006. [Also: *Folk*]

Crummel, Susan Stevens. *Ten Gallon Bart.* Illus. by Dorothy Donohue. Tarrytown, NY: Marshall Cavendish, c2006.

*Cullen, Lynn. *Moi & Marie Antoinette.* Illus. by Amy Young. New York: Bloomsbury Publishing, c2006. [Also: *Naive*]

Edwards, Pamela Duncan. *The Mixed-Up Rooster.* Illus. by Megan Lloyd. New York: HarperCollins Children's Books, c2006. [Also: *Cartoon*]

*Frank, John. *The Toughest Cowboy, or How the Wild West Was Tamed.* Illus. by Zachary Pullen. New York: Simon & Schuster Books for Young Readers, c2004.

Gerstein, Mordicai. *Carolinda Clatter!* New Milford, CT: (Roaring Brook Press) Holtzbrinck, c2005. [Also: *Cartoon*]

Jenkins, Emily. *That New Animal.* Illus. by Pierce Pratt. New York: (Frances Foster Books) Farrar, Straus and Giroux, c2005. [Also: *Cartoon*]

Johnson, Angela. *Wind Flyers.* Illus. by Loren Long. New York: Simon & Schuster Books for Young Readers, c2007.

Johnson, Lindan Lee. *Dream Jar.* Illus. by Serena Curmi. New York: Houghton Mifflin, c2005. [Also: *Cartoon*]

Kessler, Christina. *The Best Beekeeper of Lalibela: A Tale from Africa.* Illus. by Leonard Jenkins. New York: Holiday House, c2006.

Lasky, Kathryn. *Pirate Bob.* Illus. by David Clark. Watertown, MA: Charlesbridge, c2006. [Also: *Cartoon*]

Manushkin, Fran. *The Shivers in the Fridge.* Illus. by Paul O. Zelinsky. New York: (Dutton Children's Books) Penguin Young Readers Group, c2006. [Also: *Cartoon*]

Nelson, Vaunda Micheaux. *Almost to Freedom.* Illus. by Colin Bootman. Minneapolis, MN: (Carolrhoda) Lerner, c2003.

*Raven, Marot Theis. *Night Boat to Freedom.* Illus. by E. B. Lewis. New York: (Melanie Kroupa Books) Farrar, Straus and Giroux, c2006.

Sauer, Tammi. *Cowboy Camp.* Illus. by Mike Reed. New York: Sterling, c2005. [Also: *Cartoon*]

*Schotter, Roni. *Mama, I'll Give You the World.* Illus. by S. Saelig Gallagher. New York: (Schwartz & Wade) Random House, c2006. [Also: *Cartoon*]

Smith, Cynthia Leitich and Greg Smith. *Santa Knows.* Illus. by Steve Bjorkman. New York: (Dutton Children's Books) Penguin, c2006. [Also: *Cartoon*]

Stevens, Janet and Susan Stevens Crummel. *Cook-A-Doodle-Doo.* Illus. by Janet Stevens. Orlando, FL: (Voyager Books) Harcourt, c1999. [Also: *Cartoon*]

Williams, Laura E. *The Best Winds.* Illus. by Eujin Kim Neilan. Honesdale, PA: Boyds Mills Press, c2006. [Also: *Folk*]

*Wood, Nancy. *Mr. and Mrs. God in the Creation Kitchen.* Illus. by Timothy Basil Ering. Cambridge, MA: Candlewick Press, c2006.

Yorinks, Arthur. *Whitefish Will Rides Again!* Illus. by Mort Drucker. New York: HarperCollins, c1994. [Also: *Cartoon*]

Young, Amy. *Belinda and the Glass Slipper.* New York: (Viking) Penguin Young Readers Group, c2006. [Also: *Naive*]

FOLK

Perpetuation of design elements and media associated with a generally recognized ethnic or cultural tradition.

Chen, Chih-Yuan. *The Featherless Chicken.* Alhambra, CA: Heryin Books, c2006. [Also: *Cartoon, Expressionism*]

*Coombs, Kate. *The Secret-Keeper.* Illus. by Heather M. Solomon. New York: (Atheneum Books for Young Readers) Simon & Schuster, c2006. [Also: *Expressionism*]

*Franklin, Kristine L. *The Gift.* Illus. by Barbara Lavallee. San Francisco:

Chronicle Books, c1999. [Also: *Naive*]

*Lamm, C. Drew. *Gauchada.* Illus. by Fabian Negrin. New York: Alfred A. Knopf, c2002.

Lee-Tai, Amy. *A Place Where Sunflowers Grow.* Illus. by Felicia Hoshino. San Francisco: Children's Book Press, c2006. [Also: *Cartoon*]

Squires, Janet. *The Gingerbread Cowboy.* Illus. by Holly Berry. New York: HarperCollins Children's Books, c2006. [Also: *Cartoon*]

*Tingle, Tim. *Crossing Bok Chitto: A Choctaw Tale of Friendship and Freedom.* Illus. by Jeanne Rorex Bridges. El Paso, TX: Cinco Puntos Press, c2006.

Williams, Laura E. *The Best Winds.* Illus. by Eujin Kim Neilan. Honesdale, PA: Boyds Mills Press, c2006. [Also: *Expressionism*]

Wojciechowski, Susan. *A Fine St. Patrick's Day.* Illus. by Tom Curry. New York: Random House, c2004.

*Young, Ed. *I, Doko: The Tale of a Basket.* New York: Philomel, c2004. [Also: *Impressionism*]

IMPRESSIONISM

Stippling of paint that results in artistic play with light and color and produces fuzzy outlines rather than precise detail.

Borden, Louise. *Across the Blue Pacific: A World War II Story.* Illus. by Robert Andrew Parker. Boston: Houghton Mifflin, c2006.

Bunting, Eve. *Butterfly House.* Illus. by Greg Shed. New York: Scholastic Press, c1999.

Bunting, Eve. *One Green Apple.* Illus. by Ted Lewin. New York: (Clarion Books) Houghton Mifflin, c2006.

da Costa, Deborah. *Snow in Jerusalem.* Illus. by Cornelius Van Wright & Ying-Hwa Hu. Morton Grove, IL: Albert Whitman, c2001.

Garland, Sherry. *My Father's Boat.* Illus. by Ted Rand. New York: Scholastic Press, c1998.

High, Linda Oatman. *Barn Savers.* Illus. by Ted Lewin. Honesdale, PA: Boyds Mills Press, c1999. [Also: *Realism*]

*Johnston, Tony. *Angel City.* Illus. by Carole Byard. New York: (Philomel) Penguin Young Readers Group, c2006.

Michelson, Richard. *Across the Alley.* Illus. by E. B. Lewis. New York: (Penguin Young Readers Group) G. P. Putnam's Sons, c2006.

Recorvits, Helen. *Yoon and the Christmas Mitten.* Illus. by Gabi Swaiatowska. New York: (Frances Foster Books) Farrar, Straus and Giroux, c2006.

Yolen, Jane. *Raising Yoder's Barn.* Illus. by Bernie Fuchs. New York: Little, Brown and Company, c1998.

*Young, Ed. *I, Doko: The Tale of a Basket.* New York: Philomel, c2004. [Also: *Folk*]

NAIVE

Unsophisticated, childlike, bright, unshaded colors and clear outlines that often disregard perspective.

Bowen, Anne. *The Great Math Tattle Battle.* Illus. by Jaime Zollars.

Morton Grove, IL: Albert Whitman, c2006. [Also: *Cartoon, Expressionism*]

Bunge, Daniela. *The Scarves.* Trans. by Kahryn Bishop. New York: Penguin Young Readers Group, c2006.

*Cullen, Lynn. *Moi & Marie Antoinette.* Illus. by Amy Young. New York: Bloomsbury Publishing, c2006. [Also: *Expressionism*]

*Franklin, Kristine L. *The Gift.* Illus. by Barbara Lavallee. San Francisco: Chronicle Books, c1999. [Also: *Folk*]

*Montserrat, Pep. *Ms. Rubinstein's Beauty.* New York: Sterling, c2006.

Young, Amy. *Belinda and the Glass Slipper.* New York: (Viking) Penguin Young Readers Group, c2006. [Also: *Expressionism*]

REALISM

Lifelike color, texture, proportions, and arrangements as perceived in the visible world, though not adhering to photographic exactitude.

Arnosky, Jim. *Grandfather Buffalo.* New York: G. P. Putnam's Sons, c2006.

Bunting, Eve. *Pop's Bridge.* Illus. by C. F. Payne. New York: Harcourt, c2006. [Also: *Expressionism*]

Eversole, Robyn. *The Gift Stone.* Illus. by Allen Garns. New York: Alfred A. Knopf, c1998.

High, Linda Oatman. *Barn Savers.* Illus. by Ted Lewin. Honesdale, PA: Boyds Mills Press, c1999. [Also: *Impressionism*]

Johnston, Tony. *The Barn Owls.* Illus. by Deborah Kogan Ray. Watertown, MA: Charlesbridge, c2000.

Yolen, Jane. *Harvest Home*. Illus. by Greg Shed. New York: (Silver Whistle) Harcourt, c2002.

SURREALISM

Deliberate and incongruous combinations of lifelike objects that defy everyday logic assembled in an improbable setting for shock effect.

Bang, Molly. *In My Heart*. New York: Little, Brown and Company, c2006. [Also: *Cartoon, Expressionism*]

*Bateman, Teresa. *Keeper of Soles*. Illus. by Diego Herrera (Yayo). New York: Holiday House, c2006. [Also: *Cartoon*]

APPENDIX 5: RESOURCES GROUPED BY CURRICULUM TIE-IN

❖❖❖❖❖❖❖❖❖❖❖

Agriculture
Bee Culture
Farm Life—Harvesting
Food Production—Apples
Food Production—Gardens

Architecture
Bridge Engineering

Art
Expressive Painting

Athletics
Baseball

Career Education
Baseball Player
Beautician
Circus Performer
Cowboy
Fisherman
Violin Musician

Environmental Studies
Barn Recycling
Exploring Nature
Fishing

Fine Arts
Ballet
Western Movies
Wheat Twist Dolls

Geography
Africa
Argentina
Australia—Opal Mining
Jerusalem Living Quarters—
    Muslim, Christian, Jewish,
    Armenian
Korea
Los Angeles
Pennsylvania—Amish
Vietnam

Health/Nutrition
Recipes/Cooking

History
Barns, United States
Early-Twentieth-Century Paris
Golden Gate Bridge, San Francisco,
    California
Great Depression

Indians of North America
Japanese Americans—Internment
    (1942–1945)
Jerusalem—Jews, Muslims
Marie Antoinette, Queen (1755–
    1793), France
Middle Ages—Death
Pirates
Slavery
Tuskegee Airmen, United States
Underground Railroad
Vietnam War (1967–1974)
Wild West, United States
World War II (1939–1945), U.S.
    Army Air Force—Black Pilots
World War II (1939–1945), U.S.
    Navy

Literature
Aesop's Fables
Fairy Tales
Fantasy—Mystery
Folktale, Modern
Folktale, Original
Tall Tale

Mathematics
Adding and Subtracting

Music
Lullabies
Violin

Religion
Creation
Trust and Faith

Science
Bison
Butterflies—Metamorphosis
Cats
Evolution
Inventions
Opal Gemstone
Owls
Penguins
Squirrels

Social Science
Bullying
Character Development—
    Cooperation
Character Development—Courage
Character Development—Empathy
Character Development—Etiquette
Character Development—
    Generosity
Character Development—
    Honorable/Dishonorable
    Behavior
Character Development—Kindness
Character Development—
    Perseverance
Character Development—Respect
Character Development—
    Responsibility
Character Development—
    Self-Confidence
Character Development—
    Self-Esteem
Character Development—
    Self-Improvement
Character Development—
    Self-Reliance
Character Development—
    Tolerance
Character Development—
    Trustworthiness
Competition
Creativity/Inspiration
Elderly
Ethnic Relations
Family Relationships—Cousins
Family Relationships—
    Grandparents/Grandchildren
Family Relationships—
    Intergenerational
Family Relationships—Parent/Child
Family Relationships—Pets
Family Relationships—Siblings
Feminism
Friendship
Greed

Grief
Holidays
Immigrants
Individuality
International Peace Relations
Jealousy
Justice
Love
Neighbor Relationships
Prejudice
Problem Solving—Ingenuity
Psychology—Dreams
Racism
Tale-Bearing
Team Cooperation
Time Management
Values

AGRICULTURE
Bee Culture

Kessler, Christina. *The Best Beekeeper of Lalibela: A Tale from Africa.* Illus. by Leonard Jenkins. New York: Holiday House, c2006.

Farm Life—Harvesting

Yolen, Jane. *Harvest Home.* Illus. by Greg Shed. New York: (Silver Whistle) Harcourt, c2002.

Food Production—Apples

Bunting, Eve. *One Green Apple.* Illus. by Ted Lewin. New York: (Clarion Books) Houghton Mifflin, c2006.

Food Production—Gardens

Fleming, Candace. *Muncha! Muncha! Muncha!* Illus. by G. Brian Karas. New York: Atheneum Books for Young Readers, c2002.

ARCHITECTURE
Bridge Engineering

Bunting, Eve. *Pop's Bridge.* Illus. by C. F. Payne. New York: Harcourt, c2006.

ART
Expressive Painting

Bang, Molly. *In My Heart.* New York: Little, Brown and Company, c2006.

ATHLETICS
Baseball

*Adler, David A. *The Babe and I.* Illus. by Terry Widdener. New York: (Gulliver Books) Harcourt Brace & Co., c1999.

Michelson, Richard. *Across the Alley.* Illus. by E. B. Lewis. New York: (Penguin Young Readers Group) G. P. Putnam's Sons, c2006.

CAREER EDUCATION
Baseball Player

Michelson, Richard. *Across the Alley.* Illus. by E. B. Lewis. New York: (Penguin Young Readers Group) G. P. Putnam's Sons, c2006.

Beautician

*Schotter, Roni. *Mama, I'll Give You the World.* Illus. by S. Saelig Gallagher. New York: (Schwartz & Wade) Random House, c2006.

Circus Performer

*Montserrat, Pep. *Ms. Rubinstein's Beauty.* New York: Sterling, c2006.

Cowboy

Sauer, Tammi. *Cowboy Camp*. Illus. by Mike Reed. New York: Sterling, c2005.

Fisherman

Garland, Sherry. *My Father's Boat.* Illus. by Ted Rand. New York: Scholastic Press, c1998.

Violin Musician

Michelson, Richard. *Across the Alley.* Illus. by E. B. Lewis. New York: (Penguin Young Readers Group) G. P. Putnam's Sons, c2006.

ENVIRONMENTAL STUDIES

Barn Recycling

High, Linda Oatman. *Barn Savers.* Illus. by Ted Lewin. Honesdale, PA: Boyds Mills Press, c1999.

Exploring Nature

James, Simon. *The Wild Woods.* Cambridge, MA: Candlewick Press, c1993.

Fishing

*Franklin, Kristine L. *The Gift*. Illus. by Barbara Lavallee. San Francisco: Chronicle Books, c1999.

FINE ARTS

Ballet

Bradley, Kimberly Brubaker. *Ballerino Nate*. Illus. by R. W. Alley. New York: (Dial Books for Young Readers) Penguin Young Readers Group, c2006.

Auch, Mary Jane. *Hen Lake*. New York: Holiday House, c1995.

Young, Amy. *Belinda and the Glass Slipper*. New York: (Viking) Penguin Young Readers Group, c2006.

Western Movies

Crummel, Susan Stevens. *Ten Gallon Bart*. Illus. by Dorothy Donohue. Tarrytown, NY: Marshall Cavendish, c2006.

Wheat Twist Dolls

Yolen, Jane. *Harvest Home*. Illus. by Greg Shed. New York: (Silver Whistle) Harcourt, c2002.

GEOGRAPHY

Africa

Kessler, Christina. *The Best Beekeeper of Lalibela: A Tale from Africa.* Illus. by Leonard Jenkins. New York: Holiday House, c2006.

Argentina

*Lamm, C. Drew. *Gauchada*. Illus. by Fabian Negrin. New York: Alfred A. Knopf, c2002.

Australia—Opal Mining

Eversole, Robyn. *The Gift Stone*. Illus. by Allen Garns. New York: Alfred A. Knopf, c1998.

Jerusalem Living Quarters— Muslim, Christian, Jewish, Armenian

da Costa, Deborah. *Snow in Jerusalem.* Illus. by Cornelius Van Wright & Ying-Hwa Hu. Morton Grove, IL: Albert Whitman, c2001.

Korea

Recorvits, Helen. *Yoon and the Christmas Mitten.* Illus. by Gabi Swaiatowska. New York: (Frances Foster Books) Farrar, Straus and Giroux, c2006.

Williams, Laura E. *The Best Winds.* Illus. by Eujin Kim Neilan. Honesdale, PA: Boyds Mills Press, c2006.

Los Angeles

*Johnston, Tony. *Angel City.* Illus. by Carole Byard. New York: (Philomel) Penguin Young Readers Group, c2006.

Pennsylvania—Amish

Yolen, Jane. *Raising Yoder's Barn.* Illus. by Bernie Fuchs. New York: Little, Brown and Company, c1998.

Vietnam

Garland, Sherry. *My Father's Boat.* Illus. by Ted Rand. New York: Scholastic Press, c1998.

HEALTH/NUTRITION

Recipes/Cooking

Stevens, Janet and Susan Stevens Crummel. *Cook-A-Doodle-Doo.* Illus. by Janet Stevens. Orlando, FL: (Voyager Books) Harcourt, c1999.

HISTORY

Barns, United States

High, Linda Oatman. *Barn Savers.* Illus. by Ted Lewin. Honesdale, PA: Boyds Mills Press, c1999.

Johnston, Tony. *The Barn Owls.* Illus. by Deborah Kogan Ray. Watertown, MA: Charlesbridge, c2000.

Yolen, Jane. *Raising Yoder's Barn.* Illus. by Bernie Fuchs. New York: Little, Brown and Company, c1998.

Early-Twentieth-Century Paris

McClintock, Barbara. *Adele & Simon.* New York: (Frances Foster Books) Farrar, Straus and Giroux, c2006.

Golden Gate Bridge, San Francisco, California

Bunting, Eve. *Pop's Bridge.* Illus. by C. F. Payne. New York; Harcourt, c2006.

Great Depression

*Adler, David A. *The Babe and I.* Illus. by Terry Widdener. New York: (Gulliver Books) Harcourt Brace & Co., c1999.

Indians of North America

*Tingle, Tim. *Crossing Bok Chitto: A Choctaw Tale of Friendship and Freedom.* Illus. by Jeanne Rorex Bridges. El Paso, TX: Cinco Puntos Press, c2006.

Japanese Americans— Internment (1942–1945)

Lee-Tai, Amy. *A Place Where Sunflowers Grow.* Illus. by Felicia Hoshino. San Francisco: Children's Book Press, c2006.

Jerusalem—Jews, Muslims

da Costa, Deborah. *Snow in Jerusalem.* Illus. by Cornelius Van Wright & Ying-Hwa Hu. Morton Grove, IL: Albert Whitman, c2001.

Marie Antoinette, Queen (1755–1793), France

*Cullen, Lynn. *Moi & Marie Antoinette*. Illus. by Amy Young. New York: Bloomsury Publishing, c2006.

Middle Ages—Death

*Bateman, Teresa. *Keeper of Soles*. Illus. by Diego Herrera (Yayo). New York: Holiday House, c2006.

Pirates

Lasky, Kathryn. *Pirate Bob*. Illus. by David Clark. Watertown, MA: Charlesbridge, c2006.

McElligott, Matthew. *Backbeard and the Birthday Suit*. New York: Walker & Company, c2006.

Slavery

Nelson, Vaunda Micheaux. *Almost to Freedom*. Illus. by Colin Bootman. Minneapolis, MN: (Carolrhoda) Lerner, c2003.

*Raven, Marot Theis. *Night Boat to Freedom*. Illus. by E. B. Lewis. New York: (Melanie Kroupa Books) Farrar, Straus and Giroux, c2006.

*Tingle, Tim. *Crossing Bok Chitto: A Choctaw Tale of Friendship and Freedom*. Illus. by Jeanne Rorex Bridges. El Paso, TX: Cinco Puntos Press, c2006.

Tuskegee Airmen, United States

Johnson, Angela. *Wind Flyers*. Illus. by Loren Long. New York: Simon & Schuster Books for Young Readers, c2007.

Underground Railroad

Nelson, Vaunda Micheaux. *Almost to Freedom*. Illus. by Colin Bootman. Minneapolis, MN: (Carolrhoda) Lerner, c2003.

*Raven, Marot Theis. *Night Boat to Freedom*. Illus. by E. B. Lewis. New York: (Melanie Kroupa Books) Farrar, Straus and Giroux, c2006.

Vietnam War (1967–1974)

Garland, Sherry. *My Father's Boat*. Illus. by Ted Rand. New York: Scholastic Press, c1998.

Wild West, United States

*Frank, John. *The Toughest Cowboy, or How the Wild West Was Tamed*. Illus. by Zachary Pullen. New York: Simon & Schuster Books for Young Readers, c2004.

Yorinks, Arthur. *Whitefish Will Rides Again!* Illus. by Mort Drucker. New York: HarperCollins, c1994.

World War II (1939–1945), U.S. Army Air Force—Black Pilots

Johnson, Angela. *Wind Flyers*. Illus. by Loren Long. New York: Simon & Schuster Books for Young Readers, c2007.

World War II (1939–1945), U.S. Navy

Borden, Louise. *Across the Blue Pacific: A World War II Story*. Illus. by Robert Andrew Parker. Boston: Houghton Mifflin, c2006.

LITERATURE

Aesop's Fables

Bernstein, Dan. *The Tortoise and the Hare Race Again.* Illus. by Andrew Glass. New York: Holiday House, c2006.

Fairy Tales

*Coombs, Kate. *The Secret-Keeper.* Illus. by Heather M. Solomon. New York: (Atheneum Books for Young Readers) Simon & Schuster, c2006.

Gerstein, Mordicai. *Carolinda Clatter!* New Milford, CT: (Roaring Brook Press) Holtzbrinck, c2005.

Palatini, Margie. *Bad Boys Get Cookie!* Illus. by Henry Cole. New York; HarperCollins Children's Books, c2006.

Fantasy—Mystery

Manushkin, Fran. *The Shivers in the Fridge.* New York: (Dutton Children's Books) Penguin Young Readers Group, c2006.

Folktale, Modern

Kasza, Keiko. *Grandpa Toad's Secrets.* New York: G. P. Putnam's Sons, c1995.

Pearson, Tracey Campbell. *Bob.* New York: Farrar, Straus and Giroux, c2002.

Squires, Janet. *The Gingerbread Cowboy.* Illus. by Holly Berry. New York: HarperCollins Children's Books, c2006.

Folktale, Original

Wojciechowski, Susan. *A Fine St. Patrick's Day.* Illus. by Tom Curry. New York: Random House, c2004.

Tall Tale

*Frank, John. *The Toughest Cowboy, or How the Wild West Was Tamed.* Illus. by Zachary Pullen. New York: Simon & Schuster Books for Young Readers, c2004.

Yorinks, Arthur. *Whitefish Will Rides Again!* Illus. by Mort Drucker. New York: HarperCollins, c1994.

MATHEMATICS

Adding and Subtracting

Bowen, Anne. *The Great Math Tattle Battle.* Illus. by Jaime Zollars. Morton Grove, IL: Albert Whitman, c2006.

MUSIC

Lullabies

Gerstein, Mordicai. *Carolinda Clatter!* New Milford, CN: (Roaring Brook Press) Holtzbrinck, c2005.

Violin

Michelson, Richard. *Across the Alley.* Illus. by E. B. Lewis. New York: (Penguin Young Readers Group) G. P. Putnam's Sons, c2006.

RELIGION

Creation

*Wood, Nancy. *Mr. and Mrs. God in the Creation Kitchen.* Illus. by Timothy Basil Ering. Cambridge, MA: Candlewick Press, c2006.

Trust and Faith

Karon, Jan. *Violet Comes to Stay.* Story by Melanie Cecka. Illus. by

Emily Arnold McCully. New York: (Viking) Penguin Young Readers Group, c2006.

SCIENCE

Bison

Arnosky, Jim. *Grandfather Buffalo*. New York: G. P. Putnam's Sons, c2006.

Butterflies—Metamorphosis

Bunting, Eve. *Butterfly House*. Illus. by Greg Shed. New York: Scholastic Press, c1999.

Cats

Henkes, Kevin. *Kitten's First Full Moon*. New York: (Greenwillow Books) HarperCollins, c2004.

Evolution

*Wood, Nancy. *Mr. and Mrs. God in the Creation Kitchen*. Illus. by Timothy Basil Ering. Cambridge, MA: Candlewick Press, c2006.

Inventions

Krensky, Stephen. *How Santa Lost His Job*. Illus. by S. D. Schindler. New York: (Aladdin) Simon & Schuster, c2001.

Pelley, Kathleen T. *Inventor McGregor*. Illus. by Michael Chesworth. New York: Farrar, Straus and Giroux, c2006.

Opal Gemstone

Eversole, Robyn. *The Gift Stone*. Illus. by Allen Garns. New York: Alfred A. Knopf, c1998.

Owls

Johnston, Tony. *The Barn Owls*. Illus. by Deborah Kogan Ray. Watertown, MA: Charlesbridge, c2000.

Penguins

Jeffers, Oliver. *Lost and Found*. New York: (Philomel) Penguin Young Readers Group, c2005.

Squirrels

James, Simon. *The Wild Woods*. Cambridge, MA: Candlewick Press, c1993.

SOCIAL SCIENCE

Bullying

Broach, Elise. *Cousin John Is Coming!* Illus. by Nate Lilly. New York: (Dial Books for Young Readers) Penguin Young Readers Group, c2006.

Character Development—Cooperation

Pfister, Marcus. *Holey Moley*. Trans. by J. Alison James. New York: North-South Books, c2006.

Character Development—Courage

Edwards, Pamela Duncan. *The Mixed-Up Rooster*. Illus. by Megan Lloyd. New York: HarperCollins Children's Books, c2006.

Henkes, Kevin. *Kitten's First Full Moon*. New York: (Greenwillow Books) HarperCollins, c2004.

*Raven, Marot Theis. *Night Boat to Freedom*. Illus. by E. B. Lewis. New York: (Melanie Kroupa Books) Farrar, Straus and Giroux, c2006.

Character Development—Empathy

Asher, Sandy. *Too Many Frogs!* Illus. by Keith Graves. New York: (Philomel Books) Penguin Young Readers Group, c2005.

Bunge, Daniela. *The Scarves.* Trans. by Kahryn Bishop. New York: Penguin Young Readers Group, c2006.

Bunting, Eve. *Pop's Bridge.* Illus. by C. F. Payne. New York: Harcourt, c2006.

da Costa, Deborah. *Snow in Jerusalem.* Illus. by Cornelius Van Wright & Ying-Hwa Hu. Morton Grove, IL: Albert Whitman, c2001.

Danziger, Paula. *Barfburger Baby, I Was Here First.* Illus. by G. Brian Karas. New York: (Penguin Young Readers Group) G. P. Putnam's Sons, c2004.

*Franklin, Kristine L. *The Gift.* Illus. by Barbara Lavallee. San Francisco: Chronicle Books, c1999.

Wojciechowski, Susan. *A Fine St. Patrick's Day.* Illus. by Tom Curry. New York: Random House, c2004.

Character Development—Etiquette

McElligott, Matthew. *Backbeard and the Birthday Suit.* New York: Walker & Company, c2006.

Character Development—Generosity

Eversole, Robyn. *The Gift Stone.* Illus. by Allen Garns. New York: Alfred A. Knopf, c1998.

*Franklin, Kristine L. *The Gift.* Illus. by Barbara Lavallee. San Francisco: Chronicle Books, c1999.

Character Development—Honorable/Dishonorable Behavior

Ashman, Linda. *Desmond and the Naughtybugs.* Illus. by Anik McGrory. New York: (Dutton Children's Books) Penguin Young Readers Group, c2006.

Lasky, Kathryn. *Pirate Bob.* Illus. by David Clark. Watertown, MA: Charlesbridge, c2006.

Palatini, Margie. *Bad Boys Get Cookie!* Illus. by Henry Cole. New York: HarperCollins Children's Books, c2006.

Young, Amy. *Belinda and the Glass Slipper.* New York: (Viking) Penguin Young Readers Group, c2006.

Character Development—Kindness

Asher, Sandy. *Too Many Frogs!* Illus. by Keith Graves. New York: (Philomel Books) Penguin Young Readers Group, c2005.

Atwood, Margaret. *Up in the Tree.* Toronto, Ontario: Greenwood Books/House of Anansi Press, c1978, 2006.

Bynum, Janie. *Nutmeg and Barley: A Budding Friendship.* Cambridge, MA: Candlewick Press, c2006.

*Coombs, Kate. *The Secret-Keeper.* Illus. by Heather M. Solomon. New York: (Atheneum Books for Young Readers) Simon & Schuster, c2006.

*Lamm, C. Drew. *Gauchada*. Illus. by Fabian Negrin. New York: Alfred A. Knopf, c2002.

Lee-Tai, Amy. *A Place Where Sunflowers Grow*. Illus. by Felicia Hoshino. San Francisco: Children's Book Press, c2006.

*Schotter, Roni. *Mama, I'll Give You the World*. Illus. by S. Saelig Gallagher. New York: (Schwartz & Wade) Random House, c2006.

Smith, Linda. *Mrs. Crump's Cat*. Illus. by David Roberts. New York: HarperCollins Children's Books, c2006.

Character Development— Perseverance

Bradley, Kimberly Brubaker. *Ballerino Nate*. Illus. by R. W. Alley. New York: (Dial Books for Young Readers), Penguin Young Readers Group, c2006.

Fleming, Candace. *Muncha! Muncha! Muncha!* Illus. by G. Brian Karas. New York: Atheneum Books for Young Readers, c2002.

Henkes, Kevin. *Kitten's First Full Moon*. New York: (Greenwillow) HarperCollins, c2004.

Kessler, Christina. *The Best Beekeeper of Lalibela: A Tale from Africa*. Illus. by Leonard Jenkins. New York: Holiday House, c2006.

Pearson, Tracey Campbell. *Bob*. New York: Farrar, Straus and Giroux, c2002.

Character Development— Respect

Edwards, Pamela Duncan. *The Mixed-Up Rooster*. Illus. by Megan Lloyd. New York: HarperCollins Children's Books, c2006.

McElligott, Matthew. *Backbeard and the Birthday Suit*. New York: Walker & Company, c2006.

Williams, Laura E. *The Best Winds*. Illus. by Eujin Kim Neilan. Honesdale, PA: Boyds Mills Press, c2006.

*Young, Ed. *I, Doko: The Tale of a Basket*. New York: Philomel, c2004.

Character Development— Responsibility

Crummel, Susan Stevens. *Ten Gallon Bart*. Illus. by Dorothy Donohue. Tarrytown, NY: Marshall Cavendish, c2006.

McClintock, Barbara. *Adele & Simon*. New York: (Frances Foster Books) Farrar, Straus and Giroux, c2006.

Character Development— Self-Confidence

Bunting, Eve. *One Green Apple*. Illus. by Ted Lewin. New York: (Clarion Books) Houghton Mifflin, c2006.

Character Development— Self-Esteem

Allen, Jonathan. *I'm Not Cute!* New York: Hyperion Books for Children, c2005.

Bowen, Anne. *The Great Math Tattle Battle*. Illus. by Jaime Zollars. Morton Grove, IL: Albert Whitman, c2006.

Chen, Chih-Yuan. *The Featherless Chicken*. Alhambra, CA: Heryin Books, c2006.

Danziger, Paula. *Barfburger Baby, I Was Here First*. Illus. by G. Brian

Karas. New York: (Penguin Young Readers Group) G. P. Putnam's Sons, c2004.

Character Development— Self-Improvement

*Frank, John. *The Toughest Cowboy, or How the Wild West Was Tamed.* Illus. by Zachary Pullen. New York: Simon & Schuster Books for Young Readers, c2004.

Smith, Cynthia Leitich and Greg Smith. *Santa Knows.* Illus. by Steve Bjorkman. New York: (Dutton Children's Books) Penguin, c2006.

Character Development— Self-Reliance

Atwood, Margaret. *Up in the Tree.* Toronto, Ontario: Greenwood Books/House of Anansi Press, c1978, 2006.

Broach, Elise. *Cousin John Is Coming!* Illus. by Nate Lilly. New York: (Dial Books for Young Readers) Penguin Young Readers Group, c2006.

Johnson, Lindan Lee. *Dream Jar.* Illus. by Serena Curmi. New York: Houghton Mifflin, c2005.

Kasza, Keiko. *Grandpa Toad's Secrets.* New York: G. P. Putnam's Sons, c1995.

Pearson, Tracey Campbell. *Bob.* New York: Farrar, Straus and Giroux, c2002.

Character Development— Tolerance

McElligott, Matthew. *Backbeard and the Birthday Suit.* New York: Walker & Company, c2006.

Character Development— Trustworthiness

Lasky, Kathryn. *Pirate Bob.* Illus. by David Clark. Watertown, MA: Charlesbridge, c2006.

Competition

Wojciechowski, Susan. *A Fine St. Patrick's Day.* Illus. by Tom Curry. New York: Random House, c2004.

Creativity/Inspiration

Pelley, Kathleen T. *Inventor McGregor.* Illus. by Michael Chesworth. New York: Farrar, Straus and Giroux, c2006.

Elderly

Arnosky, Jim. *Grandfather Buffalo.* New York: G. P. Putnam's Sons, c2006.

Ethnic Relations

Bunting, Eve. *Pop's Bridge.* Illus. by C. F. Payne. New York: Harcourt, c2006.

*Johnston, Tony. *Angel City.* Illus. by Carole Byard. New York: (Philomel) Penguin Young Readers Group, c2006.

Michelson, Richard. *Across the Alley.* Illus. by E. B. Lewis. New York: (Penguin Young Readers Group) G. P. Putnam's Sons, c2006.

Williams, Laura E. *The Best Winds.* Illus. by Eujin Kim Neilan. Honesdale, PA: Boyds Mills Press, c2006.

Family Relationships— Cousins

Broach, Elise. *Cousin John Is Coming!* Illus. by Nate Lilly. New York:

(Dial Books for Young Readers) Penguin Young Readers Group, c2006.

Danziger, Paula. *Barfburger Baby, I Was Here First.* Illus. by G. Brian Karas. New York: (Penguin Young Readers Group) G. P. Putnam's Sons, c2004.

Family Relationships— Grandparents/ Grandchildren

Amico, Tom and James Proimos. *Raisin and Grape.* Illus. by Andy Snair. New York: (Dial Books for Young Readers) Penguin Young Readers Group, c2006.

Arnosky, Jim. *Grandfather Buffalo.* New York: G. P. Putnam's Sons, c2006.

Bunge, Daniela. *The Scarves.* Trans. by Kahryn Bishop. New York: Penguin Young Readers Group, c2006.

Bunting, Eve. *Butterfly House.* Illus. by Greg Shed. New York: Scholastic Press, c1999.

James, Simon. *The Wild Woods.* Cambridge, MA: Candlewick Press, c1993.

Kasza, Keiko. *Grandpa Toad's Secrets.* New York: G. P. Putnam's Sons, c1995.

Williams, Laura E. *The Best Winds.* Illus. by Eujin Kim Neilan. Honesdale, PA: Boyds Mills Press, c2006.

Family Relationships— Intergenerational

*Young, Ed. *I, Doko: The Tale of a Basket.* New York: Philomel, c2004.

Family Relationships— Parent/Child

*Adler, David A. *The Babe and I.* Illus. by Terry Widdener. New York: (Gulliver Books) Harcourt Brace & Co., c1999.

Bang, Molly. *In My Heart.* New York: Little, Brown and Company, c2006.

Garland, Sherry. *My Father's Boat.* Illus. by Ted Rand. New York: Scholastic Press, c1998.

Goode, Diane. *The Most Perfect Spot.* New York: HarperCollins Children's Books, c2006.

High, Linda Oatman. *Barn Savers.* Illus. by Ted Lewin. Honesdale, PA: Boyds Mills Press, c1999.

*Johnston, Tony. *Angel City.* Illus. by Carole Byard. New York: (Philomel) Penguin Young Readers Group, c2006.

Lee-Tai, Amy. *A Place Where Sunflowers Grow.* Illus. by Felicia Hoshino. San Francisco: Children's Book Press, c2006.

*Schotter, Roni. *Mama, I'll Give You the World.* Illus. by S. Saelig Gallagher. New York: (Schwartz & Wade) Random House, c2006.

Family Relationships—Pets

Jenkins, Emily. *That New Animal.* Illus. by Pierce Pratt. New York: (Frances Foster Books) Farrar, Straus and Giroux, c2005.

Family Relationships— Siblings

Bradley, Kimberly Brubaker. *Ballerino Nate.* Illus. by R. W. Alley. New York: (Dial Books for Young

Readers) Penguin Young Readers Group, c2006.

Danziger, Paula. *Barfburger Baby, I Was Here First.* Illus. by G. Brian Karas. New York: (Penguin Young Readers Group) G. P. Putnam's Sons, c2004.

Johnson, Lindan Lee. *Dream Jar.* Illus. by Serena Curmi. New York: Houghton Mifflin, c2005.

McClintock, Barbara. *Adele & Simon.* New York: (Frances Foster Books) Farrar, Straus and Giroux, c2006.

Pfister, Marcus. *Holey Moley.* Trans. by J. Alison James. New York: North-South Books, c2006.

Feminism

Kessler, Christina. *The Best Beekeeper of Lalibela: A Tale from Africa.* Illus. by Leonard Jenkins. New York: Holiday House, c2006.

Friendship

*Adler, David A. *The Babe and I.* Illus. by Terry Widdener. New York: (Gulliver Books) Harcourt Brace & Co., c1999.

Asher, Sandy. *Too Many Frogs!* Illus. by Keith Graves. New York: (Philomel Books) Penguin Young Readers Group, c2005.

Bunting, Eve. *One Green Apple.* Illus. by Ted Lewin. New York: (Clarion Books) Houghton Mifflin, c2006.

Bunting, Eve. *Pop's Bridge.* Illus. by C. F. Payne. New York: Harcourt, c2006.

Bynum, Janie. *Nutmeg and Barley: A Budding Friendship.* Cambridge, MA: Candlewick Press, c2006.

da Costa, Deborah. *Snow in Jerusalem.* Illus. by Cornelius Van Wright &

Yong-Hwa Hu. Morton Grove, IL: Albert Whitman, c2001.

Jeffers, Oliver. *Lost and Found.* New York: (Philomel) Penguin Young Readers Group, c2005.

Lasky, Kathryn. *Pirate Bob.* Illus. by David Clark. Watertown, MA: Charlesbridge, c2006.

Lee-Tai, Amy. *A Place Where Sunflowers Grow.* Illus. by Felicia Hoshino. San Francisco: Children's Book Press, c2006.

Michelson, Richard. *Across the Alley.* Illus. by E. B. Lewis. New York: (Penguin Young Readers Group) G. P. Putnam's Sons, c2006.

*Tingle, Tim. *Crossing Bok Chitto: A Choctaw Tale of Friendship and Freedom.* Illus. by Jeanne Rorex Bridges. El Paso, TX: Cinco Puntos Press, c2006.

Greed

Bateman, Teresa. *A Plump and Perky Turkey.* Illus. by Jeff Shelly. New York: Marshall Cavendish, c2001.

Lasky, Kathryn. *Pirate Bob.* Illus. by David Clark. Watertown, MA: Charlesbridge, c2006.

Palatini, Margie. *Bad Boys Get Cookie!* Illus. by Henry Cole. New York: HarperCollins Children's Books, c2006.

Grief

Borden, Louise. *Across the Blue Pacific: A World War II Story.* Illus. by Robert Andrew Parker. Boston: Houghton Mifflin, c2006.

*Johnston, Tony. *Angel City.* Illus. by Carole Byard. New York: (Philomel) Penguin Young Readers Group, c2006.

Holidays

Krensky, Stephen. *How Santa Lost His Job*. Illus. by S. D. Schindler. New York: (Aladdin) Simon & Schuster, c2001.

Recorvits, Helen. *Yoon and the Christmas Mitten*. Illus. by Gabi Swaiatowska. New York: (Frances Foster Books) Farrar, Straus and Giroux, c2006.

Smith, Cynthia Leitich and Greg Smith. *Santa Knows*. Illus. by Steve Bjorkman. New York: (Dutton Children's Books) Penguin, c2006.

Wojciechowski, Susan. *A Fine St. Patrick's Day*. Illus. by Tom Curry. New York: Random House, c2004.

Immigrants

Bunting, Eve. *One Green Apple*. Illus. by Ted Lewin. New York: (Clarion Books) Houghton Mifflin, c2006.

Recorvits, Helen. *Yoon and the Christmas Mitten*. Illus. by Gabi Swaiatowska. New York: (Frances Foster Books) Farrar, Straus and Giroux, c2006.

Individuality

Chen, Chih-Yuan. *The Featherless Chicken*. Alhambra, CA: Heryin Books, c2006.

Edwards, Pamela Duncan. *The Mixed-Up Rooster*. Illus. by Megan Lloyd. New York: HarperCollins Children's Books, c2006.

*Montserrat, Pep. *Ms. Rubinstein's Beauty*. New York: Sterling, c2006.

Pearson, Tracey Campbell. *Bob*. New York: Farrar, Straus and Giroux, c2002.

Sauer, Tammi. *Cowboy Camp*. Illus. by Mike Reed. New York: Sterling, c2005.

International Peace Relations

da Costa, Deborah. *Snow in Jerusalem*. Illus. by Cornelius Van Wright & Ying-Hwa Hu. Morton Grove, IL: Albert Whitman, c2001.

Jealousy

Danziger, Paula. *Barfburger Baby, I Was Here First*. Illus. by G. Brian Karas. New York: (Penguin Young Readers Group) G. P. Putnam's Sons, c2004.

Jenkins, Emily. *That New Animal*. Illus. by Pierce Pratt. New York: (Frances Foster Books) Farrar, Straus and Giroux, c2005.

Justice

Yorinks, Arthur. *Whitefish Will Rides Again!* Illus. by Mort Drucker. New York: HarperCollins, c1994.

Love

*Lamm, C. Drew. *Gauchada*. Illus. by Fabian Negrin. New York: Alfred A. Knopf, c2002.

*Montserrat, Pep. *Ms. Rubinstein's Beauty*. New York: Sterling, c2006.

Pelley, Kathleen T. *Inventor McGregor*. Illus. by Michael Chesworth. New York: Farrar, Straus and Giroux, c2006.

Williams, Laura E. *The Best Winds*. Illus. by Eujin Kim Neilan. Honesdale, PA: Boyds Mills Press, c2006.

Neighbor Relationships

*Coombs, Kate. *The Secret-Keeper.* Illus. by Heather M. Solomon. New York: (Atheneum Books for Young Readers) Simon & Schuster, c2006.

Yolen, Jane. *Raising Yoder's Barn.* Illus. by Bernie Fuchs. New York: Little, Brown and Company, c1998.

Prejudice

Michelson, Richard. *Across the Alley.* Illus. by E. B. Lewis. New York: (Penguin Young Readers Group) G. P. Putnam's Sons, c2006.

Problem Solving—Ingenuity

Bernstein, Dan. *The Tortoise and the Hare Race Again.* Illus. by Andrew Glass. New York: Holiday House, c2006.

Johnson, Lindan Lee. *Dream Jar.* Illus. by Serena Curmi. New York: Houghton Mifflin, c2005.

Krensky, Stephen. *How Santa Lost His Job.* Illus. by S. D. Schindler. New York: (Aladdin) Simon & Schuster, c2001.

Psychology—Dreams

Johnson, Lindan Lee. *Dream Jar.* Illus. by Serena Curmi. New York: Houghton Mifflin, c2005.

Racism

Johnson, Angela. *Wind Flyers.* Illus. by Loren Long. New York: Simon & Schuster Books for Young Readers, c2007.

Tale-Bearing

Bowen, Anne. *The Great Math Tattle Battle.* Illus. by Jaime Zollars. Morton Grove, IL: Albert Whitman, c2006.

Team Cooperation

Bowen, Anne. *The Great Match Tattle Battle.* Illus. by Jaime Zollars. Morton Grove, IL: Albert Whitman, c2006.

Stevens, Janet and Susan Stevens Crummel. *Cook-A-Doodle-Doo.* Illus. by Janet Stevens. Orlando, FL: (Voyager Books) Harcourt, c1999.

Wojciechowski, Susan. *A Fine St. Patrick's Day.* Illus. by Tom Curry. New York: Random House, c2004.

Yolen, Jane. *Raising Yoder's Barn.* Illus. by Bernie Fuchs. New York: Little, Brown and Company, c1998.

Time Management

*Reynolds, Peter H. *So Few of Me.* Cambridge, MA: Candlewick Press, c2006.

Values

Krensky, Stephen. *How Santa Lost His Job.* Illus. by S. D. Schindler. New York: (Aladdin) Simon & Schuster, c2001.

Pelley, Kathleen T. *Inventor McGregor.* Illus. by Michael Chesworth. New York: Farrar, Straus and Giroux, c2006.

*Reynolds, Peter H. *So Few of Me.* Cambridge, MA: Candlewick Press, c2006.

Teague, Mark. *Pigsty.* New York: Scholastic, c1994.

Wojciechowski, Susan. *A Fine St. Patrick's Day.* Illus. by Tom Curry. New York: Random House, c2004.

APPENDIX 6:
ALL-AGES RESOURCES

❖❖❖❖❖❖❖❖❖❖

*Adler, David A. *The Babe and I.*
Illus. by Terry Widdener. New
York: (Gulliver Books) Harcourt
Brace & Co., c1999.
*Ambiguity. Antithesis.
Foreshadow. Inference. Irony.
Paradox. Tone.*

*Bateman, Teresa. *Keeper of Soles.*
Illus. by Diego Herrera (Yayo).
New York: Holiday House, c2006.
*Ambiguity. Aphorism. Black
Humor. Colloquialism.
Connotation. Imagery.
Inference. Irony. Paradox.
Parallelism. Pun.
Understatement.*

*Coombs, Kate. *The Secret-Keeper.*
Illus. by Heather M. Solomon.
New York: (Atheneum Books for
Young Readers) Simon &
Schuster, c2006.
*Ambiguity. Connotation.
Foreshadow. Imagery.
Inference. Irony. Metaphor.
Motif. Serendipity. Simile.
Symbol. Tone.*

*Cullen, Lynn. *Moi & Marie
Antoinette.* Illus. by Amy Young.
New York: Bloomsbury
Publishing, c2006.
*Archetype. Atmosphere.
Counterpoint. Foreshadow.
Hyperbole. Inference. Motif.
Parallelism. Point-of-View.
Serendipity. Simile. Surprise/
Twist-in-the-Tail. Wit/Humor.*

*Frank, John. *The Toughest Cowboy,
or How the Wild West Was
Tamed.* Illus. by Zachary Pullen.
New York: Simon & Schuster
Books for Young Readers, c2004.
*Allusion. Ambiguity. Aptronym.
Atmosphere. Colloquialism.
Foreshadow. Hyperbole.
Inference. Irony. Parallelism.
Pun. Simile. Solecism.
Stereotype/Reverse Stereotype.
Tone. Understatement. Wit/
Humor.*

*Franklin, Kristine L. *The Gift.* Illus.
by Barbara Lavallee. San
Francisco: Chronicle Books, c1999.

*Ambiguity. Connotation.
   Foreshadow. Imagery.
   Inference. Irony.
   Onomatopoeia. Surprise/Twist-
   in-the-Tail. Simile. Symbol.
   Theme.*

*Johnston, Tony. *Angel City*. Illus. by
   Carole Byard. New York:
   (Philomel) Penguin Young
   Readers Group, c2006.
   *Allusion. Ambiguity. Antithesis.
      Atmosphere. Colloquialism.
      Connotation. Counterpoint.
      Foreshadow. Imagery.
      Inference. Metaphor. Motif.
      Paradox. Parallelism. Simile.
      Symbol. Theme. Tone. Wit/
      Humor.*

*Lamm, C. Drew. *Gauchada*. Illus. by
   Fabian Negrin. New York: Alfred
   A. Knopf, c2002.
   *Antithesis. Atmosphere.
      Connotation. Flashback.
      Imagery. Internal Rhyme.
      Irony. Metaphor. Motif.
      Parallelism. Surprise/Twist-in-
      the-Tail. Theme.*

*Montserrat, Pep. *Ms. Rubinstein's
   Beauty*. New York: Sterling,
   c2006.
   *Antithesis. Atmosphere.
      Connotation. Counterpoint.
      Inference. Motif. Parallelism.
      Surprise/Twist-in-the-Tail.
      Theme.*

*Raven, Marot Theis. *Night Boat to
   Freedom*. Illus. by E. B. Lewis.
   New York: (Melanie Kroupa
   Books) Farrar, Straus and Giroux,
   c2006.
   *Aphorism. Atmosphere.
      Colloquialism. Imagery.*

*Inference. Metaphor. Paradox.
   Parallelism. Simile. Symbol.
   Theme.*

*Reynolds, Peter H. *So Few of Me*.
   Cambridge, MA: Candlewick
   Press, c2006.
   Satire. Theme.

*Schotter, Roni. *Mama, I'll Give You
   the World*. Illus. by S. Saelig
   Gallagher. New York:
   (Schwartz & Wade) Random
   House, c2006.
   *Ambiguity. Connotation.
      Foreshadow. Imagery.
      Inference. Metaphor. Motif.
      Point-of-View. Simile. Symbol.
      Tone.*

*Tingle, Tim. *Crossing Bok Chitto: A
   Choctaw Tale of Friendship and
   Freedom*. Illus. by Jeanne Rorex
   Bridges. El Paso, TX: Cinco
   Puntos Press, c2006.
   *Allusion. Antithesis. Aphorism.
      Counterpoint. Flash-Forward.
      Foreshadow. Irony. Motif.
      Paradox. Parallelism. Simile.
      Symbol. Theme.*

*Wood, Nancy. *Mr. and Mrs. God in
   the Creation Kitchen*. Illus. by
   Timothy Basil Ering. Cambridge,
   MA: Candlewick Press, c2006.
   *Allusion. Antithesis. Foreshadow.
      Hyperbole. Imagery. Inference.
      Parallelism. Pun. Satire.
      Understatement. Wit/Humor.*

*Young, Ed. *I, Doko: The Tale of a
   Basket*. New York: Philomel,
   c2004.
   *Aphorism. Foreshadow. Inference.
      Personification. Poetic
      Justice. Point-of-View. Theme.
      Tone.*

INDEX

❖❖❖❖❖❖❖❖❖❖

About the Author

SUSAN HALL is a journalist and government reporter living in Tipton, Iowa. She is the author of three previous volumes of this work. She is a former public and school librarian.